Eurasian Studies in Business and Economics 6

Series editors
Mehmet Huseyin Bilgin, Istanbul, Turkey
Hakan Danis, San Francisco, CA, USA

Representing
Eurasia Business and Economics Society

More information about this series at http://www.springer.com/series/13544

Mehmet Huseyin Bilgin • Hakan Danis •
Ender Demir • Ugur Can
Editors

Empirical Studies on Economics of Innovation, Public Economics and Management

Proceedings of the 18th Eurasia Business and Economics Society Conference

Springer

Editors
Mehmet Huseyin Bilgin
Faculty of Political Sciences
Istanbul Medeniyet University
Istanbul, Turkey

Hakan Danis
MUFG Union Bank
San Francisco, CA
USA

Ender Demir
Faculty of Tourism
Istanbul Medeniyet University
Istanbul, Turkey

Ugur Can
Eurasia Business and Economic Society
Fatih, Istanbul, Turkey

The authors of individual papers are responsible for technical, content, and linguistic correctness.

ISSN 2364-5067 ISSN 2364-5075 (electronic)
Eurasian Studies in Business and Economics
ISBN 978-3-319-50163-5 ISBN 978-3-319-50164-2 (eBook)
DOI 10.1007/978-3-319-50164-2

Library of Congress Control Number: 2016962703

Printed on acid-free paper

This Springer imprint is published by Springer Nature
The registered company is Springer International Publishing AG
The registered company address is: Gewerbestrasse 11, 6330 Cham, Switzerland

Preface

This is the sixth issue of the Springer's series *Eurasian Studies in Business and Economics*, which is the official book series of the Eurasia Business and Economics Society (EBES, www.ebesweb.org). This issue includes selected papers presented at the 18th EBES Conference that was held on January, 2016, in the School of Business Administration of American University of Sharjah (AUS) in Dubai, U.A.E. All accepted papers for the issue went through peer-review process and benefited from the comments made during the conference as well.

During the conference, participants had many productive discussions and exchanges that contributed to the success of the conference where 118 papers by 221 colleagues from 43 countries were presented. In addition to publication opportunities in EBES journals (*Eurasian Business Review* and *Eurasian Economic Review*, which are also published by Springer), conference participants were given opportunity to submit their full papers to this Issue. We regret that we could accept only a small portion of those papers.

Theoretical and empirical papers in the series cover diverse areas of business, economics, and finance from many different countries, providing a valuable opportunity to researchers, professionals, and students to catch up with the most recent studies in a diverse set of fields across many countries and regions.

The aim of the EBES conferences is to bring together scientists from business, finance, and economics fields, attract original research papers, and provide them publication opportunities. Each issue of the *Eurasian Studies in Business and Economics* covers a wide variety of topics from business and economics and provides empirical results from many different countries and regions that are less investigated in the existing literature. The current issue covers fields such as:

i. MANAGEMENT & MARKETING
ii. ACCOUNTING & FINANCE
iii. ECONOMICS OF INNOVATION
iv. GROWTH & DEVELOPMENT
v. PUBLIC ECONOMICS

Although the papers in this issue may provide empirical results for a specific county or regions, we believe that the readers would have an opportunity to catch up with the most recent studies in a diverse set of fields across many countries and regions and empirical support for the existing literature. In addition, the findings from these papers could be valid for similar economies or regions.

On behalf of the Volume Editors and EBES officers, I would like to thank to all presenters, participants, board members, and keynote speakers, and we are looking forward to seeing you at the upcoming EBES conferences.

Istanbul, Turkey Ender Demir

Eurasia Business and Economics Society

EBES is a scholarly association for scholars involved in the practice and study of economics, finance, and business worldwide. EBES was founded in 2008 with the purpose of not only promoting academic research in the field of business and economics but also encouraging the intellectual development of scholars. In spite of the term "Eurasia," the scope should be understood in its broadest term as having a global emphasis.

EBES aims to bring worldwide researchers and professionals together through organizing conferences and publishing academic journals and increase economics, finance, and business knowledge through academic discussions. To reach its goal, EBES benefits from its executive and advisory boards which consist of well-known academicians from all around the world. Every year, with the inclusion of new members, our executive and advisory boards became more diverse and influential. I would like to thank them for their support.

EBES conferences and journals are open to all economics, finance, and business scholars and professionals around the world. Any scholar or professional interested in economics, finance, and business is welcome to attend EBES conferences. Since 2012, EBES has been organizing three conferences every year: one in Istanbul (usually in late May or early June) and two in Europe or Asia (usually in January and October). Since our first conference, around 6824 colleagues from 91 different countries have joined our conferences and 3904 academic papers have been presented. Also, in a very short period of time, *EBES has reached 1394 members from 76 countries*.

Since 2011, EBES has been publishing two academic journals. One of those journals, *Eurasian Business Review—EBR*, is in the fields of industry and business, and the other one, *Eurasian Economic Review—EER*, is in the fields of economics and finance. Both journals are published biannually, and we are committed to having both journals included in SSCI as soon as possible. Both journals have been published by *Springer* since 2014 and are currently indexed in the Emerging Sources Citation Index, *EconLit*, *Google Scholar*, *EBSCO*, *ProQuest*, *ABI/ INFORM*, *Business Source*, *International Bibliography of the Social Sciences*

(IBSS), *OCLC*, *Research Papers in Economics (RePEc)*, *Summon by ProQuest*, and *TOC Premier*.

Furthermore, since 2014 Springer has started to publish a new conference proceedings series (*Eurasian Studies in Business and Economics*) which includes selected papers from the EBES conferences. The 10th, 11th, 12th, and 13th EBES Conference Proceedings have already been accepted for inclusion in the Thompson Reuters' *Conference Proceedings Citation Index*, and subsequent conference proceedings are in progress.

On behalf of the EBES officers, I sincerely thank you for your participation and look forward to seeing you at our future conferences. In order to improve our future conferences, we welcome your comments and suggestions. Our success is only possible with your valuable feedback and support.

I hope you enjoy the conference and U.A.E.!

With my very best wishes,

Jonathan Batten, PhD
President

Contents

List of Contributors

Jehan A. Abo Sultan MIS Department, Al Ain University of Science and Technology, Abu Dhabi, UAE

Danutė Adomavičiūtė Faculty of Economics and Finance Management, Institute of Economics and Business, Mykolas Romeris University, Vilnius, Lithuania

Mehmet Fatih Aysan Department of Sociology, Istanbul Sehir University, Istanbul, Turkey

Ummugulsum Aysan Department of Social Services, Istanbul University, Istanbul, Turkey

Arkadiusz Babczuk Department of Finance and Accounting, Wroclaw University of Economics, Wroclaw, Poland

Giorgio Carlo Brugnoni Department of Management, Sapienza University of Rome, Rome, Italy

Antanas Buracas Faculty of Social Education, Lithuanian University of Educational Sciences, Vilnius, Lithuania

Nidhi Choudhary FMS-WISDOM, State Bank of India School of Commerce and Banking, Banasthali University, Vanasthali, Rajasthan, India

Wojciech Cieśliński Department of Communication and Management in Sport, University School of Physical Education in Wrocław, Wrocław, Poland

Concetta Colasimone Department of Management, Sapienza University of Rome, Rome, Italy

Dalia Daujotaitė Faculty of Economics and Finance Management, Department of Finance and Taxes, Mykolas Romeris University, Vilnius, Lithuania

Camelia Delcea Department of Informatics and Cybernetics, Bucharest University of Economic Studies, Bucharest, Romania

Paolo Gaspare Conforti Di Lorenzo Studio Legale Delfino e Associati Willkie Farr & Gallagher LLP, Milan, Italy

Raffaele Didonato University of Bari, Bari, Italy

Renata Beata Dylkiewicz Faculty of Economic Sciences, Koszalin University of Technology, Koszalin, Poland

Paulina Katarzyna Dylkiewicz Faculty of Economic Sciences, Koszalin University of Technology, Koszalin, Poland

Dziawgo Ewa Department of Econometrics and Statistics, Nicolaus Copernicus University, Toruń, Poland

Floros Flouros Department of Political Science and International Relations, University of Peloponnese, Corinth, Greece

Ahmet Gulmez Department of Economics, Sakarya University, Sakarya, Turkey

Enrico Giustiniani Italian Association of Financial Analysts and Advisors, Milan, Italy

Elsabeta Ioanas Department of Marketing, Bucharest University of Economic Studies, Bucharest, Romania

Ali Kabasakal Department of Economics, Sakarya University, Sakarya, Turkey

Marian Kachniarz Department of Spatial Economy, Wroclaw University of Economics, Wroclaw, Poland

Faten F. Kharbat MIS and Management Department, Al Ain University of Science and Technology, Abu Dhabi, UAE

Aziz Kutlar Department of Economics, Sakarya University, Sakarya, Turkey

Sonja Lahtinen School of Management, University of Tampere, Tampere, Finland

Lorenzo Lentini Commissione Nazionale per le Società e la Borsa, Milan, Italy

Jason Levy Department of Public Administration, University of Hawaii – West Oahu, Kapolei, HI, USA

Massimo Mariani University of Bari, Bari, Italy

LUM Jean Monnet University, Bari, Italy

Plamena Markova Department of Social and Legal Sciences, Technical University, Varna, Bulgaria

Wasseem Mina Department of Economics and Finance, United Arab Emirates University, Al Ain, UAE

Girish K. Nair International Hospitality Management, Stenden University, Doha, Qatar

Vytas Navickas Faculty of Social Education, Lithuanian University of Educational Sciences, Vilnius, Lithuania

Claudio Palandra Islamic Finance Working Group, Italian Association of Financial Analysts and Advisors, Milan, Italy

Ramona Paun Department of Business and Technology, Webster University, Bangkok, Thailand

Toshko Petrov Department of Social and Legal Sciences, Technical University, Varna, Bulgaria

Fabrizio Petrucci Studio Legale Delfino e Associati Willkie Farr & Gallagher LLP, Milan, Italy

Zbigniew Piepiora Department of Spatial Economy, Wroclaw University of Environmental and Life Sciences, Wroclaw, Poland

Paweł Piepiora Department of Sport Teaching, University School of Physical Education in Wrocław, Wrocław, Poland

Luca Riccetti Department of Management, Sapienza University of Rome, Rome, Italy

Spyros Roukanas Department of International and European Studies, University of Piraeus, Piraeus, Greece

Antonio Salvi LUM Jean Monnet University, Bari, Italy

Pantelis Sklias Department of Political Science and International Relations, University of Peloponnese, Corinth, Greece

Alessandra Tami University of Milan Bicocca, Milan, Italy

Pekka Tuominen School of Management, University of Tampere, Tampere, Finland

Franco Tutino Department of Management, Sapienza University of Rome, Rome, Italy

Joey Valenti Department of Architecture, University of Hawaii at Manoa, Honolulu, HI, USA

Kazimierz Witkowski Department of Sport Teaching, University School of Physical Education in Wrocław, Wrocław, Poland

Peiyong Yu Department of Economics, University of Hawaii – West Oahu, Kapolei, HI, USA

Part I
Accounting & Finance

Islamic Bonds and Real Estate Securitizations: The Italian Perspective for Issuing a Sukuk

Giorgio Carlo Brugnoni, Paolo Gaspare Conforti Di Lorenzo, Raffaele Didonato, Enrico Giustiniani, Lorenzo Lentini, Massimo Mariani, Claudio Palandra, Fabrizio Petrucci, Antonio Salvi, and Alessandra Tami

Abstract The research looks at the possible advantages of which Italian companies and public entities could benefit looking at Islamic finance as a viable alternative to conventional finance, in a context characterized by a growing presence of Islamic citizens throughout Europe and Italy and by increasing interest in investing in Italy by Islamic investors. The research investigates the possibility for an Italian entity (corporate or sovereign) to issue a sukuk with a national real-estate underlying, under the current legal, fiscal and technical framework. The aim is to concretely contribute to the awareness about the opportunities that Islamic finance could bring with it and to promote fiscal, normative and regulatory obstacles removal, in order to create a level playing field—as the United Kingdom did—that would allow Islamic finance to develop also in Italy.

Keywords Islamic finance • Sukuk • Real estate • Securitization

G.C. Brugnoni (✉)
Department of Management, Sapienza University of Rome, Rome, Italy
e-mail: giorgiocarlo.brugnoni@uniroma1.it

P.G.C. Di Lorenzo • F. Petrucci
Studio Legale Delfino e Associati Willkie Farr & Gallagher LLP, Milan, Italy
e-mail: pconforti@delfinowillkie.com; fpetrucci@delfinowillkie.com

R. Didonato
University of Bari, Bari, Italy
e-mail: raffaele_didonato@outlook.com

E. Giustiniani
Italian Association of Financial Analysts and Advisors, Milan, Italy
e-mail: e.giustiniani@finnat.it

L. Lentini
Commissione Nazionale per le Società e la Borsa, Milan, Italy
e-mail: l.lentini@consob.it

M.H. Bilgin et al. (eds.), *Empirical Studies on Economics of Innovation, Public Economics and Management*, Eurasian Studies in Business and Economics 6,
DOI 10.1007/978-3-319-50164-2_1

1 Introduction

In the recent years, Islamic finance progressively developed in Europe, especially in the United Kingdom, in France, in Germany and in Luxembourg. In Italy, although increasing conferences and studies contributed to stimulate the debate, no concrete steps have been taken yet to develop Islamic finance or to effectively make aware Italian institutions and companies about the opportunities that the recourse to Islamic finance could bring with it.

This paper: (a) looks at the Islamic finance development, worldwide and in Europe; (b) analyses some of the possible benefits that the Islamic finance development in Italy could bring with it (both for sovereign and corporate), looking at the main challenges which could contribute to slow down its development; (c) investigates the effective possibility for an Italian entity (corporate or sovereign) to issue a sukuk with a national real-estate underline, under the current legal, fiscal and technical framework; (d) identifies—among the Italian listed companies—the ones which could represent a possible investment target for Islamic finance investors—taking care of their Shariah compliance—and tracks their performance over time.

The aim is to concretely contribute to the awareness about the opportunities that Islamic finance could bring with it and to promote fiscal, normative and regulatory obstacles removal, in order to create a level playing field—as the United Kingdom did—that would allow Islamic finance to develop also in Italy. From our point of view, indeed, a country like Italy—geographically, historically and culturally close to the Middle East and North African Islamic countries—should not lose the opportunity to become a Shariah-compliant financial and economic hub as one of the possible strategic drivers to attract foreign investment from Islamic countries and to support business internationalization towards the Middle East and North African Islamic countries.

M. Mariani
University of Bari, Bari, Italy

LUM Jean Monnet University, Bari, Italy
e-mail: mariani@simmsrl.it

C. Palandra
Islamic Finance Working Group, Italian Association of Financial Analysts and Advisors, Milan, Italy
e-mail: claudio.palandra@postevita.it

A. Salvi
LUM Jean Monnet University, Bari, Italy
e-mail: salvi@lum.it

A. Tami
University of Milan Bicocca, Milan, Italy
e-mail: alessandra.tami@unimib.it

The paper is structured as follows. Section "Islamic Finance: Global Trends and Development in Europe" gives a synthetic overview on the Islamic finance development, worldwide and with a specific focus on Europe. Section "Islamic Finance in Italy: Possible Benefits and Main Challenges Towards Companies Internationalization and Foreign Capital Investments" thinks over the possible benefits that Islamic finance in Italy could bring with it. Section "Engineering of Sukuks for Public and Private Italian Entities" investigates the possibilities and the main obstacles for an Italian public entity to structure an Islamic financial operation under the current Italian normative and fiscal framework. Section "Islamic Real Estate Funds and Investments" carries out an analysis of the industry of Islamic Real-Estate funds—in particular focusing on what appears to be the most innovative form of real estate vehicle, namely the Real-Estate Investment Trust (REIT)—and provides some insight on how a *Shariah*-compliant real estate investment could be realized in Italy through viable long-term vehicles managed by professional operators. Section "Islamic Italian Stock-Index: A New Methodology to Build an Italian Listed Company Sharia-Compliant Portfolio" proposes a Sharia-compliant stock index on the Italian stock market and compares its performance with the market index of the Italian Stock Exchange in terms of risk and return, in order to evaluate the ability to develop efficient investment despite the limitations imposed by the Sharia. Section "Financing Italian SMEs: May Be *Sukuks* Considered as a Viable Alternative?" thinks over sukuks as a possible viable alternative for Italian SMEs to raise funds. Section "Italian Tax System and Sukuks: Fiscal Challenges Towards a More Level Playing Filed" concludes the paper with some closing remarks underlining the main fiscal challenges regarding Islamic finance products among the current Italian fiscal framework.[1]

2 Islamic Finance: Global Trends and Development in Europe

In the recent years, Islamic finance has developed significantly. Although it still represents a marginal share of the global financial system, an increasing interest has spread worldwide. Islamic finance assets, which in the mid-1990s amounted at

[1]Sections "Islamic Finance: Global Trends and Development in Europe" and "Islamic Finance in Italy: Possible Benefits and Main Challenges Towards Companies Internationalization and Foreign Capital Investments" are by Giorgio Carlo Brugnoni. Section "Engineering of Sukuks for Public and Private Italian Entities" is by Antonio Salvi, Fabrizio Petrucci and Paolo Gaspare Conforti di Lorenzo. Section "Islamic Real Estate Funds and Investments" is by Massimo Mariani, Lorenzo Lentini and Raffaele Didonato. Section "Islamic Italian Stock-Index: A New Methodology to Build an Italian Listed Company Sharia-Compliant Portfolio" is by Claudio Palandra. Section "Financing Italian SMEs: May Be *Sukuks* Considered as a Viable Alternative?" is by Alessandra Tami. Section "Italian Tax System and Sukuks: Fiscal Challenges Towards a More Level Playing Filed" is by Enrico Giustiniani.

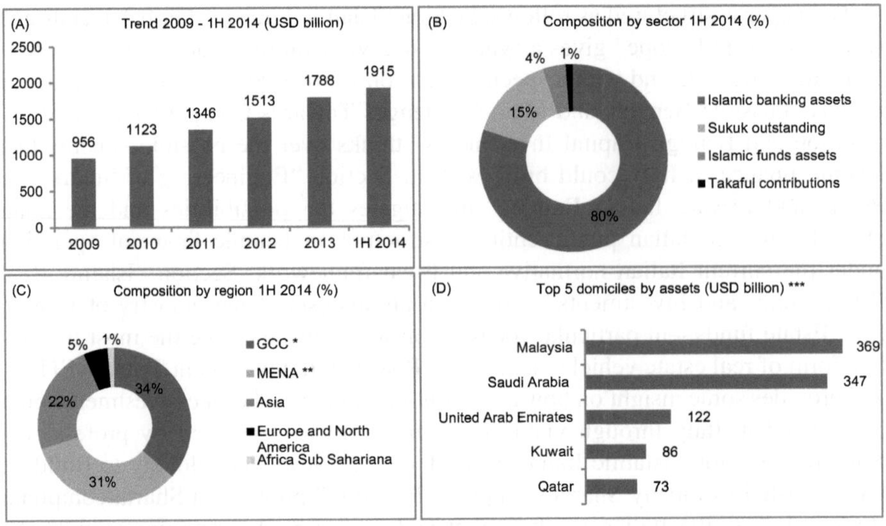

Fig. 1 Islamic finance assets. Source: own elaboration on data from KFH Research Limited (2014). *Single asterisk Gulf Cooperation Council* (GCC). *Double asterisk Middle East and North Africa* (MENA). *Triple asterisk* Iran excluded; 2013 for Islamic banking and takaful; 3Q 2014 for sukuk and Islamic funds; for Malaysia including also the Islamic banking assets of the *Development Finance Institutions*

around 150 billion/USD, in 2009 grew to 956 billion/USD, reaching 1.788 billion/USD in 2013 and 1.915 billion/USD in the first half of 2014 (Fig. 1a). Overall, between 2009 and 2013, Islamic finance grew at a compound annual growth rate (CAGR) of around 17% (KFH Research Limited 2014). Together with the more traditional cultural, economic and financial determinant factors, in the last years, Islamic finance development has been influenced also by the increasing interest by western economies, which have identified Islamic finance not only as a viable funding source alternative to the conventional ones, but also as a factor able to positively affect the economic and financial relationships worldwide and as an instrument to support integration and financial inclusion policies, especially in the countries more traditionally characterized by a relevant and increasing share of Muslim population.

Although originally focused among Islamic economies—as in the Gulf Cooperation Council (GCC), in particular in Saudi Arabia and in the United Arab Emirates (UAE), and in Asia, in particular in Malaysia—Islamic finance is today taking increasing relevance also outside the more traditional regions of reference. The Gulf Cooperation Council (GCC), the Middle East and North Africa (MENA) and Asia represent respectively around 34%, 31% and 22% of the Islamic finance industry as a whole (Fig. 1c), with Malaysia and Saudi Arabia leading the market (Fig. 1d), respectively for the sukuk sector and the banking sector.

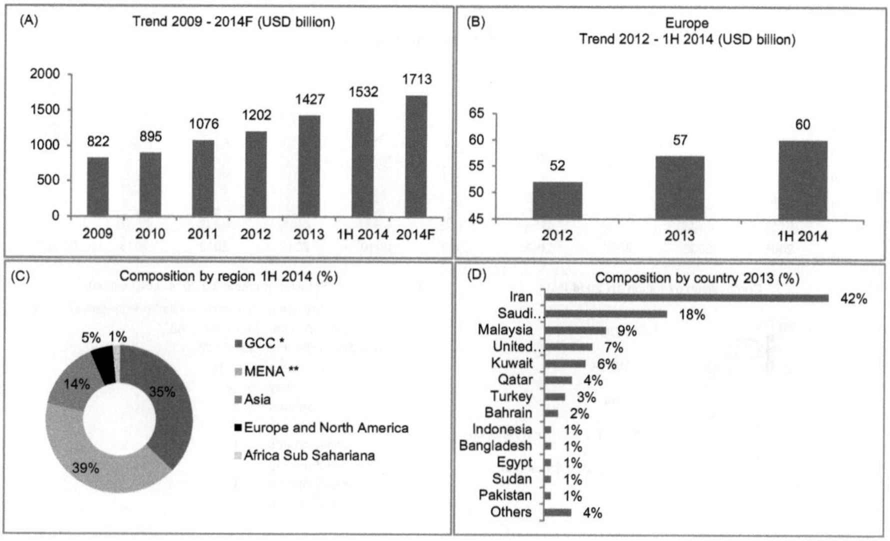

Fig. 2 Islamic banking. Source: own elaboration on data from KFH Research Limited (2014). *Single asterisk Gulf Cooperation Council* (GCC). *Double asterisk Middle East and North Africa* (MENA)

Born providing basic banking services, Islamic finance evolved over time, expanding to capital markets—with the development of Shariah-compliant market indexes, of the sukuk market and of Islamic investment funds—and to insurance services (*takaful*). Overall, the Islamic finance industry is dominated by the banking sector (80%), followed by the sukuk market (15%) and by Islamic investment funds (4%), while the takaful contribution remains still marginal (1%) (Fig. 1b).

The Islamic banking sector, which represents almost 80% of the Islamic finance industry as whole (Fig. 1b), has developed significantly in the last years, reaching 1.713 billion/USD of total assets from 822 billion/USD in 2009 (Fig. 2a). Overall, between 2008 and 2013 Islamic banking grew at a compound annual growth rate (CAGR) of around 17% (KFH Research Limited 2014). The Gulf Cooperation Council (GCC) and the Middle East and North Africa (MENA) cover respectively around 35% and 39% of the sector (Fig. 2c), with Iran and Saudi Arabia leading the market (Fig. 2d).

In Europe the Islamic banking development looks still marginal—although in progressively growing (Fig. 2b)—and mainly focused in the United Kingdom—where 6 Islamic banks operate[2] and 13 conventional banks offer Shariah-compliant

[2]Al Rayan Bank, Bank of London and Middle East, European Islamic Investment Bank, Gatehouse Bank, Qatar Islamic Bank UK, Abu Dhabi Islamic Bank UK (KFH Research Limited 2014).

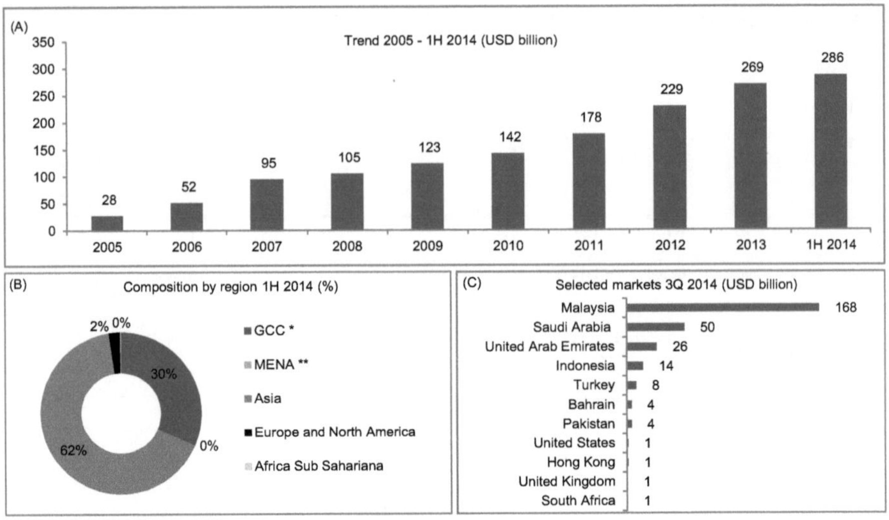

Fig. 3 Sukuk outstanding. Source: own elaboration on data from KFH Research Limited (2014). *Single asterisk Gulf Cooperation Council* (GCC). *Double asterisk Middle East and North Africa* (MENA)

products and services through Islamic finance windows[3]—in France and in Germany—where Shariah-compliant banking services are offered by conventional banks through Islamic windows. Moreover, on July 2015 the Turkish bank Kuveyt Turk launched in Germany KT Bank AG, the first Islamic bank in the Euro area. Of course, the first player role that these countries have played in terms of Islamic banking development could be explained by the potential increasing demand for Islamic finance products and services coming from the relevant and increasing share of Muslim population which characterizes these countries.

The sukuk market, which represents around 15% of the Islamic finance industry (Fig. 1b), shows a significant development in terms of outstanding. At the end of 2013 it doubled its size (269 billion/USD) in comparison to 2009 (123 billion/USD). At mid-2014 it reached 286 billion/USD, an amount 10 times higher the 28 billion/USD in 2005(Fig. 3a). Data on sukuk issuances between 2005 and 2008 (Fig. 4a) show a progressive growing dynamic, interrupted only in 2008—when the sukuk market was conditioned by the global financial crisis effects on the real economy (Gomel et al. 2010)—and in 2013—when the sukuk market was affected by the effects on the global financial markets of the decision by the United Sates Federal Reserve to gradually reduce is quantitative easing program (Standard & Poor's 2014; Thomson Reuters 2014) and by the decrease in the issuances in Malaysia (Fig. 4b), facing a relevant slowdown of public investments, which in

[3]Ahli United Bank, ABC International Bank, Barclays, BNP Paribas, Bristol & West, Citibank, Deutsche Bank, United National Bank, Europe Arab Bank, HSBC Amanah, Lloyds Bank, Royal Bank of Scotland, Standard Chartered (KFH Research Limited 2014).

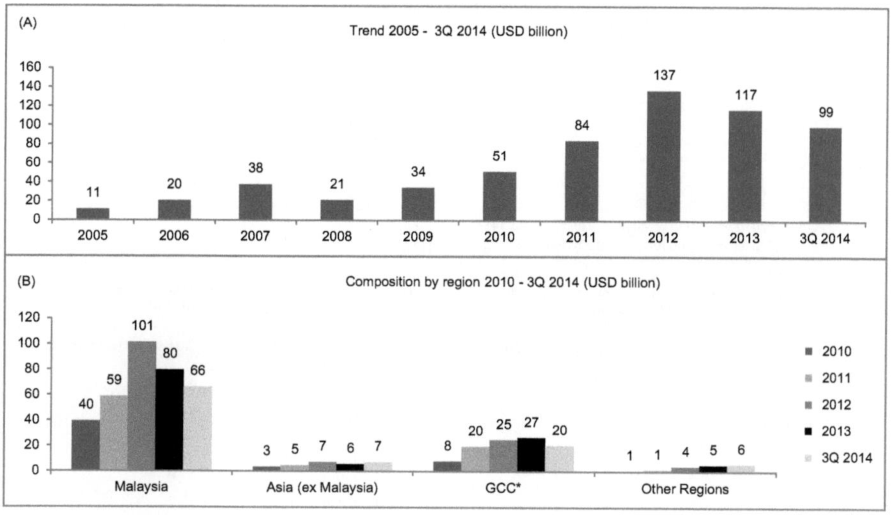

Fig. 4 Sukuk issuances. Source: own elaboration on data from Thomson Reuters (2014). *Single asterisk Gulf Cooperation Council* (GCC)

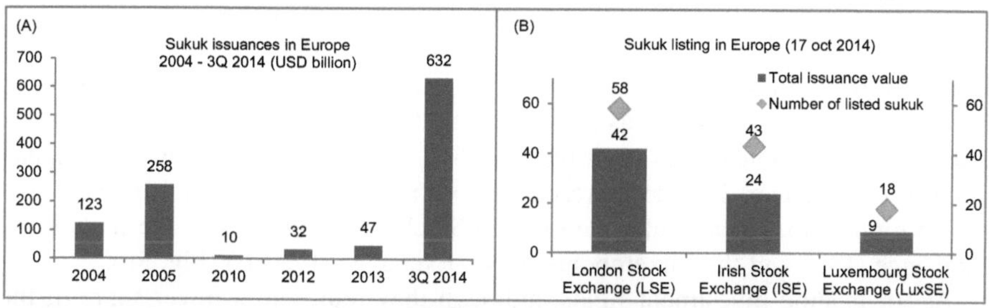

Fig. 5 Sukuk in Europe. Source: own elaboration on data from KFH Research Limited (2014)

the past contributed to support the increasing development of the sukuk market in the country (Standard & Poor's 2014). Malaysia leads the market, both in terms of outstanding (Fig. 3c) and issuances (Fig. 4b), followed by Saudi Arabia and United Arab Emirates (Fig. 3c). Overall, the sukuk sector is concentrated in Asia (62%) and in the Gulf Cooperation Council (GCC) (30%) (Fig. 3b).

Outside the more traditional countries, in Europe the sukuk market looks quite significant (Fig. 5a). The first European sukuk was issued in 2004 in Germany by the Federal State of Saxony-Anhalt (100 million/€, 5 years). In 2005, the first corporate sukuk in Europe was issued in the United Kingdom (143 million/£, 9 years). In 2010, 2012 and 2013 other sukuk issuances followed in the United Kingdom, in France, in Germany and in Luxembourg. Moreover, in 2014 the United Kingdom issued the first European sovereign sukuk (200 million/£, 5 years) followed by Luxembourg (200 million/€, 5 years). According to Thomson

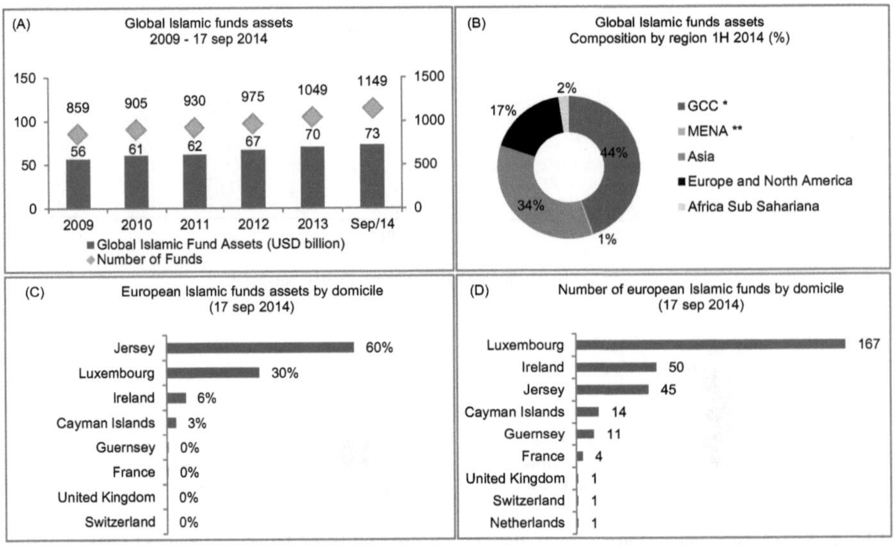

Fig. 6 Islamic investment funds. Source: own elaboration on data from KFH Research Limited (2014). *Single asterisk Gulf Cooperation Council* (GCC). *Double asterisk Middle East and North Africa* (MENA)

Reuters (2014), these issuances could represent a stimulus to the development of the sukuk market in Europe, as they could be followed by other corporate sukuk issuances in the same countries or by sovereign sukuk issuances in other European countries. Moreover, Europe represents also a relevant international listing destination for sukuks, in particular the London Stock Exchange (LSE), the Irish Stock Exchange (ISE) and the Luxembourg Stock Exchange (LuxSE) (Fig. 5b).

As for Islamic investment funds, although they represent a lower share of the Islamic finance industry as a whole, in the last years they have registered a relevant development, both in terms of asset under management and number of funds (Fig. 6a). The Gulf Cooperation Council (GCC) and Asia represents the most relevant markets in terms of asset under management (respectively 44% and 34%) (Fig. 6b), with Saudi Arabia and Malaysia representing more than 67% of the market by domicile (KFH Research Limited 2014). Europe, with 294 Islamic funds an around 12 billion/USD of assets under management at 17th September 2014, cover 16% of the sector worldwide (Fig. 6b and c) (17% together with North America) (Fig. 6b). The most significant countries are Jersey, whose 45 funds manage around the 60% of the assets under management in Europe, Luxembourg, which with 167 funds represent around the 30% of the market, and Ireland, whose 50 funds cover the 6% of the market. The appeal of Europe as a domicile for Islamic funds—in particular Luxembourg and Jersey—comes from the combination of fiscal benefits, sophisticated regulation and efficiency, which allow Islamic funds outsourcing a number of operational activities to take advantages of the expertise of the local service providers (KFH Research Limited 2014). Moreover, in countries as Ireland, France and Malta, the regulatory authorities have progressively introduced some guidelines in order to facilitate the registration of Islamic investment funds.

For further information on Islamic finance and on its development worldwide and in Europe refer to: Kammer et al. (2015), Di Mauro et al. (2013), Gomel et al. (2010), KFH Research Limited (2014), Standard & Poor's (2014) and Thomson Reuters (2014).

3 Islamic Finance in Italy: Possible Benefits and Main Challenges Towards Companies Internationalization and Foreign Capital Investments

As shown in the previous section (Section "Islamic Finance: Global Trends and Development in Europe"), in the recent years Islamic finance progressively developed in Europe, especially in the United Kingdom, in France, in Germany and in Luxembourg. In Italy, although increasing conferences and studies contributed to stimulate the debate, no concrete steps have been taken yet to develop Islamic finance or to effectively make aware the Italian institutions and companies about the opportunities that the recourse to Islamic finance could bring with it.

Italian companies and public entities could benefit looking at Islamic finance as a viable alternative to conventional finance, in a contest characterized by a growing presence of Islamic citizens throughout Europe and Italy and by an increasing interest in investing in Italy as a viable investment alternative for Islamic investors. For public entities, Islamic finance could be a viable financing alternative to support project finance operations, public–private partnerships initiatives and securitization of real estate, in order to promote impact investments (as for urban regeneration, transports and infrastructure improving, smart energy solutions) or just to diversify financing sources. For Italian companies Islamic finance, more than representing a viable alternative to raise funds among funding diversification strategies, could be a key factor to support internationalization plans and business opportunities, especially for those companies typically oriented towards Islamic markets, as the Gulf Cooperation Council (GCC) and the Middle East and North Africa (MENA). Moreover, Islamic finance could represent a strategic driver to attract foreign investment in Italy from Islamic countries, in order to financially support the growth and the consolidation of the Italian productive sector and the improvement of its international competitiveness.

As known, the Italian productive sector is typically characterized by some structural gaps—as the small size of the companies on average, the weak productivity, the low capitalization and the relevant dependence on the banking system to satisfy the financial needs—which could contribute to limit the international competitiveness of Italian companies (Ciferri et al. 2015; D'Aurizio and Cristadoro

2015). In particular, the relevant dependence of Italian companies on banking financial debt in spite of capital resources represents a weakening factor because it makes their ordinary activity and their investment plans strictly influenced by the credit market conditions and it reduces their financial flexibility in taking initiatives to catch business development opportunities, both on national and international markets. Therefore, the strengthening of Italian companies' capitalization and the consolidation of their size represent relevant priorities in order to support their capacity to compete on international markets and to foster long-term growth strategies (Ciferri et al. 2015; Reviglio et al. 2013).

From this point of view, the development of Islamic finance, together with the increasing investment diversification strategies being adopted by investors of the Gulf Cooperation Council (GCC), could represent a relevant strategic opportunity for the Italian system in order to intercept liquidity and capital inflows from Islamic countries to financially support the growth and the development of the Italian productive system, in particular for those companies characterized by activities and financial structures in line with the Shariah requisites in order to be financed. The analysis conducted in section "Islamic Italian Stock-Index: A New Methodology to Build an Italian Listed Company Sharia-Compliant Portfolio" shows that some of the Italian listed companies already satisfy the Shariah-compliant requirements and could be, therefore, viable investment opportunities for the Islamic investors. Moreover, if we consider the widespread appeal of the *Made in Italy* around the world, in particular in the richest countries among the Middle East and North Africa (MENA) as the Gulf Cooperation Council (GCC) ones, the potentialities of Italian companies, financially supported by the resources that could inflow from these countries, could represent a relevant element of stimulus for the development of the Italian productive system in order to achieve a higher international competitiveness. Therefore, although normative and regulatory obstacles, added to some cultural prejudices still persisting in Italy, make illusory to imagine that in the short term the Italian financial system could effectively open to Islamic finance institutions and to the diffusion and commercialization of Shariah-compliant financial products and services and that an Italian Islamic banking sector could effectively develop in Italy—as in other European countries, as in the United Kingdom, in Germany and in France, it has been happening—it could be anyway important that Italian companies—in particular the ones whose businesses are characterized by relevant potentiality and natural orientation to internationalization—understand the strategic value to deal with Shariah requisites in order to represent a viable and interesting investment opportunity also for Islamic investors. Moreover, as highlighted also by the Bank of Italy (Gomel et al. 2010), more than representing a channel to attract new and foreign capitals, Islamic finance could really represent relevant factor able to contribute to the internationalization of Italian companies towards Middle East and North African economies. From this point of view, Italian companies could look at Islamic finance institutions not only as financing sources but also as strategic partners among the internationalization process.

Anyway, Italian public and financial institutions could play a relevant role in promoting internationalization initiatives, not only through the financial support of exports operations and of direct investments, but also fostering the attraction of foreign investments when they could be strategic and functional in order to significantly support initiatives and projects aimed to strengthen the Italian productive system and to improve Italian companies' competitiveness on international markets. From this point of view, a relevant role in attracting foreign capital inflows to support the strengthening of the Italian productive system is played by the *Italian Strategic Fund* (FSI), owned by the Italian National Promotional Bank *Cassa Depositi e Prestiti* (CDP) (80%) and by the *Bank of Italy* (20%). In particular, for the purpose of this paper, the joint venture with the Qatar Holding LLC (QH) and the investment agreement with the Kuwait Investment Authority (KIA) look quite significant. In March 2013, the *Italian Strategic Fund* (FSI) and the *Qatar Holding LLC* (QH) (investment vehicle by the Qatar Investment Authority), following an investment agreement signed in November 2012, established a 50/50 joint venture named *IQ Made in Italy Investment Company*, with an initial capital of 300 million/€ (although the *Italian Strategic Fund* and the *Qatar Holding* might increase the capital up to 2 billion/€) and with an investment perimeter which includes Italian companies operating in selected *Made in Italy* sectors, such as food and food distribution, fashion and luxury goods, furnishing and design, tourism, leisure and lifestyle. The aim is to support the *Made in Italy* sector, investing in Italian companies with significant potentiality of growth and international expansion, in order to increase their value also through aggregation in order to consolidate Italian brands, their transformation and their growth, both inside Italy and abroad. Moreover, in June 2014, the *Italian Strategic Fund* (FSI) and the *Kuwait Investment Authority* (KIA) created *FSI Investments* as a common investment company with 2.185 billion/€ of assets and commitments, owned by the *Italian Strategic Fund* (FSI) (77%)—which contributed with around 1.2 billion/€, conferring its investment portfolio and other—and by the *Kuwait Investment Authority* (KIA) (23%). In the future, the capital of FSI Investments could be increased through commitments of new co-investors. FSI Investments has the same investment perimeter of FSI, excluding gaming and alcohol, sectors in which KIA cannot invest.

4 Engineering of Sukuks for Public and Private Italian Entities

Sukuks are an important way of financing open to many types of economic operators (companies, governments and supranational institutions), not only Muslim operators. The western multinationals are in fact increasingly (including, for example, General Electric, Nomura, Standard Chartered) complementing the traditional instruments with sukuks in order to raise capital, both within the conventional bonds markets, and the Islamic financial markets. In Europe, between June 25 and October 7, 2014, countries like the United Kingdom and Luxembourg issued sukuks for a total of approximately 480 million/€ and experienced a backlog of approximately 3.3 billion/€ by different types of institutional subjects. The Luxembourg operation was the first issue in the world in Euro.

In Italy there already are schemes and financial instruments which, by their nature, are suited to the dictates of the Sharia, among these there are: the securitization of public real estate, project financing, public–private partnership (PPP) and the financial public leasing; while the securitization of real assets, mini-bonds and participation bonds, better suit the corporate sector. The Italian legislation on financial instruments (such as the new rules on mini-bonds and equity instruments) is in line with the highest international standards. In particular, the recent legislation on participation bonds facilitates the issuance of project bonds. The sukuk instrument aligns to project bonds, of our own legislation, because they are both characterized by the need to be supported by the cash flow generated by activities of real estate management, then identifying them as asset-based tools.

A case history allows us to compare the profitability, also in order to highlight how the widespread view that sukuks tend to be more expensive than conventional bond is not necessarily true. This is the case of the UAE company TDIC based in Abu Dhabi, which owns some of the most important real estate development transactions of the Arab public field, which, in 2009, issued two separate securities, a conventional bond and a sukuk, with identical issue currency (USD), expiration (2014), issue value ($1 billion), placement and trading platform (London Stock Exchange). An important difference between these two bonds was the different issue coupon, in fact, for the conventional bond it was set at 6.5% while for the sukuk it was set at 4.95%. One reason lies in the characteristics of the market of the two products: the sukuk is generally less liquid than conventional bonds, as the trend of investors is to hold to maturity. Obviously, if the sukuk market should expand and become deeper, it would then be reasonable to expect a downward trend in yield spreads.

Under current Italian law, in a hypothetical case of realization of a public work in Italy, provided that the process can be adopted through a PPP procedure, the source of financing could be a lease-back of public assets, with the establishment of a special purpose vehicle that would issue the bonds through which financing the work (Fig. 7).

In structuring a Shariah-compliant PPP, to make sure that such an operation can be sustainable in terms of tax burden imposed by the current Italian legislation, the role of the lender should not be limited to that of a mere lender but, in accordance with the well-known principle of profit and loss-sharing inspiring Shariah-compliant finance, the lender should take an active role in the project, for instance as a shareholder (Musharaka financing) or owner (Ijara financing). We should also consider that the Islamic finance PPPs have so far been structured so that lenders could use a direct guarantee on the real estate to be asset-based or asset-backed issued. Obviously, this significantly reduces any risk for the lender and makes this solution particularly attractive for investors rather than others. Assuming the use of PPP for the realization in Italy of a transaction valued approximate at 100 million/€, with a maximum duration of 5.7 years, the cost of financing would probably not differ much from that of a conventional financing. Assuming that the possible rating

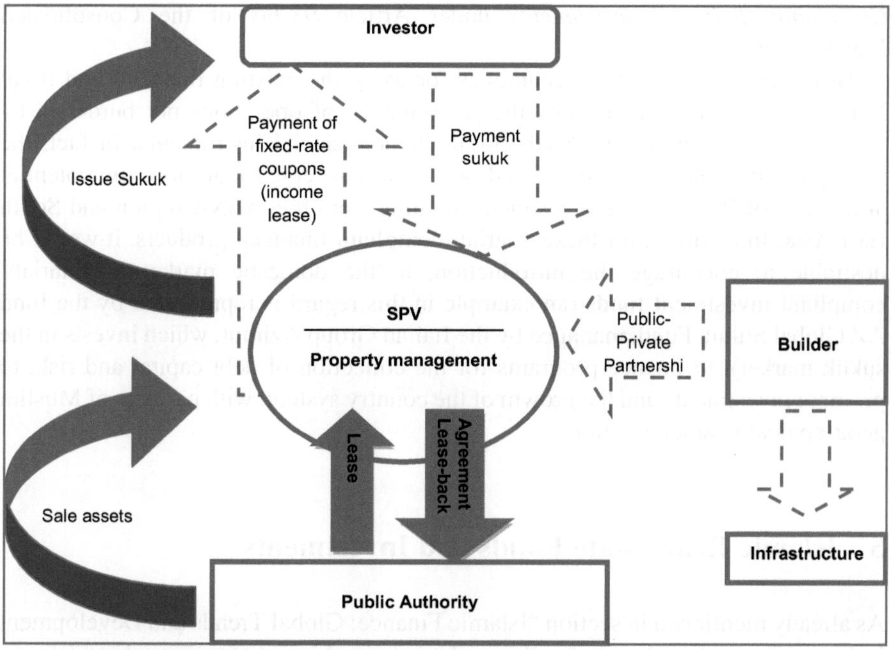

Fig. 7 Hypothesis of Italian public sukuk issue: financial scheme

given to the issue will be BBB (current Italian rating), we could conceive as follows:

- A *pro-tempore* fixed rate equal to a 6-month Euribor (or 5/7 years IRS) increased by 70–80 basis points,
- A cost of the up-front oscillating between 0.1 and 0.2% of the nominal amount placed.

In fact, there is a strong international practice which shows how the PPP technique, with lease-back assets, has been taken in various public Shariah-compliant transactions.

Islamic finance in Italy is nowadays impractical because the tax law weighs heavily on transactions such as that related to the issuance of sukuks. The nature of asset-based tools, in fact, means that indirect taxes on the transfer of real estate are paid twice in favor of the Italian Financial Administration. Therefore, we need a rule that changes the tax structure of this type of transactions and equalizes them to the ordinary banking and financial transactions that have the necessary exemptions. The main Shariah-compliant financial products, in fact, can be easily equated—without debasing their peculiarities—to the typical characteristics of similar products of conventional finance and to the *securities* cases referred to under Article 1, paragraph 1-*bis* of the Consolidated Finance Act and, therefore, also to that of

Community financial instruments under Article 93-*bis* of the Consolidated Finance Act.

However, there are other techniques for using the existing financial and fiscal Italian regulations, which allow the performance of operations not burdened by double taxation, supporting Shariah-compliant financial instruments. In fact, the tools presented should be considered only as a first representation of the potential attractions of Italy, for the investments coming from the MENA region and South East Asia. In addition, for these Shariah-compliant financial products, it would be desirable to encourage the introduction, in the domestic market of Shariah-compliant investment funds (an example in this regard is represented by the fund AZ Global Sukuk Fund, managed by the Italian Group Azimut, which invests in the sukuk market), to finance programs for the collection of debt capital and risk, to promote investments and the growth of the country system, with partners of Muslim geographical characterization.

5 Islamic Real Estate Funds and Investments

As already mentioned in section "Islamic Finance: Global Trends and Development in Europe", the last decade has been characterized by a steep growth of Islamic Finance, which has led the Western countries to pay a greater attention to this sector, promoting the development of products, services and institutions dedicated to it. This section carries out an analysis of the industry of Islamic Real-Estate funds, and in particular focuses on what appears to be the most innovative form of real estate vehicle, namely the Real-Estate Investment Trust (REIT). Indeed, the real estate asset management industry constitutes an ideal platform where the level of integration of Islamic finance in Europe can be primarily tested. The prèsence of tangible underlying assets facilitates the creation of *Riba*-free structures. Moreover, the provision by the asset manager of professional services based on fiduciary duties and peculiar incentive fee mechanisms may lead to a balanced set of rights and obligations consistent with the *Shariah* principles of social justice, mutual cooperation and risk-sharing among the parties (Shawamreh 2012).

This section, in particular, aims at providing some insight on how a *Shariah*-compliant real estate investment could be realized in Italy through viable long-term vehicles managed by professional operators. In doing so, a couple of solutions are presented, which certainly differs in form and, to a certain degree, also in substance: firstly, we consider the structuring of a real estate fund together with the appointment of a specialized asset manager; secondly, we illustrate the experience of Real-Estate Investment Trusts (REITs) as flexible investment vehicles which, once listed, may give prompt access to the retail market. In both cases evidence shows that although a number of regulatory barriers still discourages the diffusion of *Shariah*-compliant initiatives, some additional efforts in designing the basic structure of the transactions could allow to overcome such obstacles with a sufficient level of confidence, especially where a *Shariah* supervisory board is timely involved not only in the day-to-day monitoring of the investments, but also in drafting the constitution documents and arranging an effective governance tailored for the needs of the participating entities.

With respect to real estate funds, Islamic finance practitioners have traditionally adopted either *muḏāraba*-based or *wakālah*-based schemes in order to govern the contractual relationship between the asset manager and the investors. This exercise relies on the use of the *muḏāraba* agreements for structuring an Italian closed-end fund, in which Islamic investors *(rabb-ul-maal)* provide cash contributions to be invested in several real estate businesses, while the independent asset manager *(mudārib)* only performs professional services and maintains exclusive responsibility over the management activity.

In order to preserve the corporate nature of the vehicle, which makes *rabb-ul-maal* and *mudārib* authentic partners in the initiative, we suggest the formation of a fixed-capital investment company (so-called *Sicaf*) recently introduced into Italian law, following the last changes in the European legislation (Directive 2011/61/UE) which have secured a remarkable level of harmonization in this subject matter. The extreme flexibility of Sicaf facilitates a quite faithful replication of the functioning (perhaps of the spirit too) of *muḏāraba-based* real estate funds. Also, the faculty to obtain a *manager passport* valid throughout Member States allows the creation of multiple local vehicles sharing a single asset manager based in the European headquarter. Further advantages associated with this corporate solution are represented by the potential issuance of limited-voting shares or financial instruments with participating rights and the admissibility of in-kind contributions as well as drawdown demandable upon actual investment opportunities.

The above structure is consistent with the *muḏāraba* principle according to which the asset manager cannot bear the risk of capital loss, unless a breach of contract or other misconduct is assessed (therefore *ad hoc* guarantees provided by the manager and covering such events are admissible). In light of the asset manager's duty to comply with a predetermined investment policy the agreement with investors would qualify as *restricted muḏāraba,* where the restrictions upon the manager derive from the operational limits set forth in the constitution documents and justify the correspondent supervisory powers granted to *rabb-ul-maal* by means of special investor rights clauses (IFSB 2009) (veto power, appointment of candidates within consultative committee and other governance rights). Of course the investment activity carried out by the asset manager shall adhere to the specific restrictions imposed by *Shariah*, which influence not only the type of asset, but also the investment technique, prohibiting the use of financial leverage and the trading of instruments incorporating a guaranteed return on investment (e.g. *preferred stock)* (McMillen 2000). In terms of risk-reward exposure, while *rabb-ul-maal* only bears the risk of losses, the remuneration of *mudārib* is directly dependent on the outcome of the business venture. In the context of Islamic real estate funds, the fee structure takes into account the prohibition of *gharar* elements: therefore, the profit of the asset manager shall be calculated in accordance with criteria clearly defined *ex ante*, in order to prevent any excessive uncertainty or unpredictable amount. Also, the need for maintaining a constant correlation between business

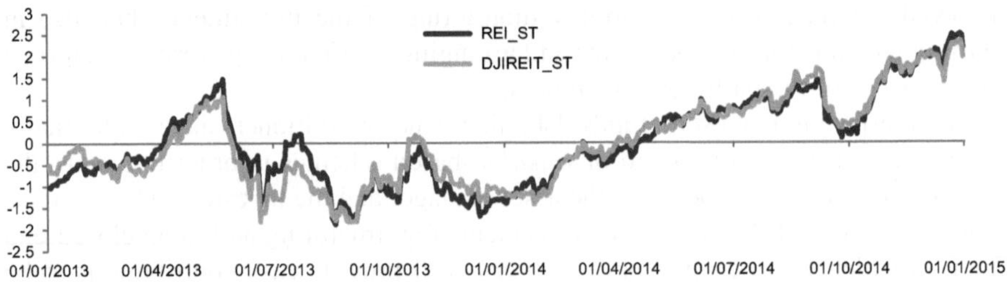

Fig. 8 Standardized variables trend

results and remuneration of the *mudārib* inhibits the provision in the agreement of any fixed compensation (*lump sum*) unrelated to the actual amount of profits available for investors.

However, advance payments charged on the account of future profits may be tolerated where construed as provisional, and subject to final adjustment, provided that a periodic asset valuation is conducted (*constructive tandheedh*) and profit equalization reserves are in place to stabilize the cash flows in adverse market conditions (McMillen 2008). Finally an empirical analysis is performed, with the aim of investigating the effectiveness of the Islamic model for REITs where compared to classic REITs. The analysis is based on the observation of the *Dow Jones Islamic Real Estate Investment Trust index (DJIREIT),* which measures the global performance of Shariah-compliant REITs, using the *Dow Jones Equity All REIT Index (REI)* as a benchmark (Fig. 8).

This analysis highlights how the performance of the REITs and the Islamic REITs is dictated mainly by external factors, with reference to the strong correlation between the two indices, and thus their trends over the period considered. Nevertheless, the analysis of daily percent changes of the two indices shows a greater stability of the Islamic REITs index, although this finding is partly due to factors of scale (the average value for the *Dow Jones Equity All REIT Index* is in fact about six times greater than the other).

Therefore, based on data taken into account, it seems that the Islamic REITs, despite the limitations imposed by the Shariah-compliant structure, performed in line with classic REITs, and then the improvement and diffusion of this vehicle could be important in order to enable Islamic investors to inject new liquidity into western economies, without them being penalized by different returns due to the different structure of the REIT.

6 Islamic Italian Stock-Index: A New Methodology to Build an Italian Listed Company Sharia-Compliant Portfolio

The strong economic growth of Southeast Asian emerging markets together with the hegemony on oil production by middle-east countries is contributing to the creation of well-being, offering new opportunities in service sectors. These nations, strongly linked to the Islamic religion, are developing their own vision of financial investments that reflect the guidelines of their faith. This process led to the creation of the expression *Islamic finance* by which we mean the set of all the principles and rules governing the matter of investments suitable to the investor ensure respect for the pillars of Islam. The increasing need for funding along with a vision more ethical finance is offering an opportunity to bring out the Islamic finance from its main markets. Before analyzing in detail the analytical aspects related to Islamic investments is interesting to understand the principles that characterize the nature of those investments.

The Islamic law of Shariah gives an exhaustive list of principles that separate what is allowed from what is not allowed: only investments in eligible companies/ business are considered acceptable. The principles of Shariah are attributable to four prohibitions: Riba, Maisir, Gharar and Haram. The first principle, the Riba, is the belief that money alone cannot generate more money and that therefore the interest on the debts are not allowed: this excludes virtually all banks and financial companies from non-Islamic countries. The prohibition of Maisir preclude investment in business related to excessive risk such as lotteries, games; the insurance companies are not allowed for being financial institutions perceived as sophisticated gamblers. The principle of Gharar precludes investment in excessively uncertain activities such as derivatives, where it is assumed that there may be asymmetry in information between the counterparties. Finally, the principle Haram prohibits investment in not considered dignified activities such as pornography, alcohol and the military industry.

Shariah laws strongly influence the investment process, both from the investable universe, leading to the exclusion of certain business, and because of the need to comply with capital ratios consistent with these principles. A stock index Sharia-compliant on Italian stock market has been build and the results are compared with the market index of the Italian Stock Exchange in terms of risk and return. Therefore, in order to evaluate the ability to develop efficient investment despite the limitations imposed by the Sharia, the analysis is made on the Italian stock market from December 2002 to December 2014, to fit over an economic cycle. The construction of the Sharia-compliant equity portfolio has been divided into three levels. At first, we translated the principles of Shariah into budget ratios, to see which companies conduct business with methods in line with Islamic laws. Then, we built the short list composed of all compliant companies, year by year. Finally, we developed a methodology to define the weight of investments in individual companies, in order to limit the concentration in big-cap stocks.

6.1 Islamic Financial Ratios and Stock Selection

We considered three indicators related to the prohibition of Riba and Gharar; their aim is to highlight if there is a high exposure to financial interest, both active and passive. The first (1) shows if a company has a huge financial debt (Riba). The other two ratios (2, 3) are explanatory of operational and commercial policies: the holding of stock of high liquidity and short-term investments implies the collection of interest (Riba), while a high value of receivables due from customers shows that the companies exposed to the high uncertainty of their customers' ability to pay back (Gharar).

$$\frac{D}{C} = \frac{Total\ Debt}{12m\ average\ market\ capitalization} \tag{1}$$

$$\frac{Cash}{C} = \frac{Cash + interest\ bearing\ asset}{12m\ average\ market\ capitalization} \tag{2}$$

$$\frac{R}{C} = \frac{Account\ receivable}{12m\ average\ market\ capitalization} \tag{3}$$

For each financial ratio, we set an acceptability threshold equal to 0.33; we considered a company of *Ftse-Mib All Share* eligible, for year X, only if all three ratios, for the year X − 1, were not violated. On average, each year, only 13% was consistent with the Islamic ratio (Fig. 9).

6.2 Short-Lists Analysis

In order to highlight the preference of Islamic ratios to certain business, we considered the historical evolution of sector allocation using the classification *ICB supersector* provided by Standard & Poor's. The construction process has shown a bias towards the companies of industrial sector and personal goods where every year, on average, is invested about respectively 23% and 15%. The less interesting for Islamic ratios are the automobiles, construction, utilities and, obviously, the financial sector (Fig. 10).

We highlighted a bias per sector; it is interesting to assess the composition of the lists in terms of market capitalization. We identified three sets: the Big Caps, with

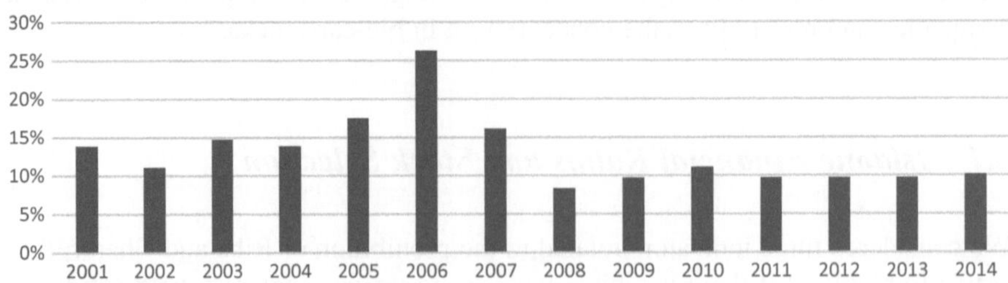

Fig. 9 Ftse-Mib All Share historical rate of Sharia-compliant companies

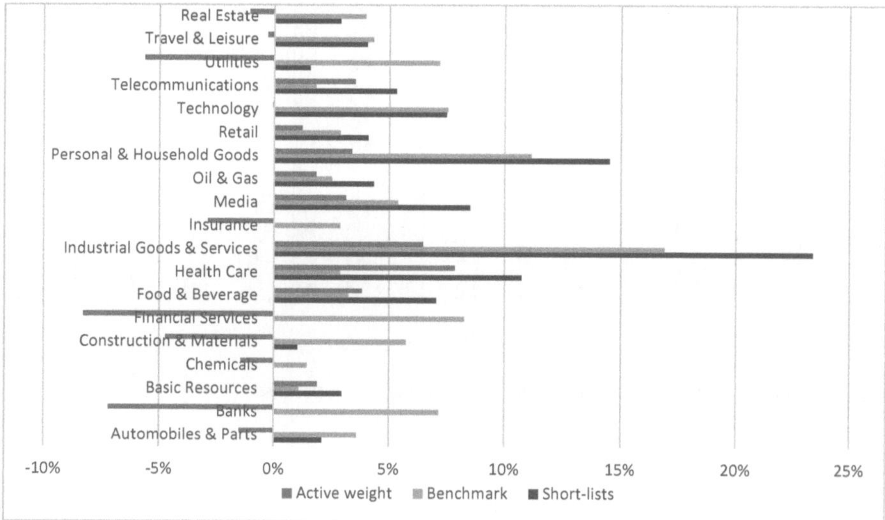

Fig. 10 Sector exposure: short-lists versus Ftse All-Share

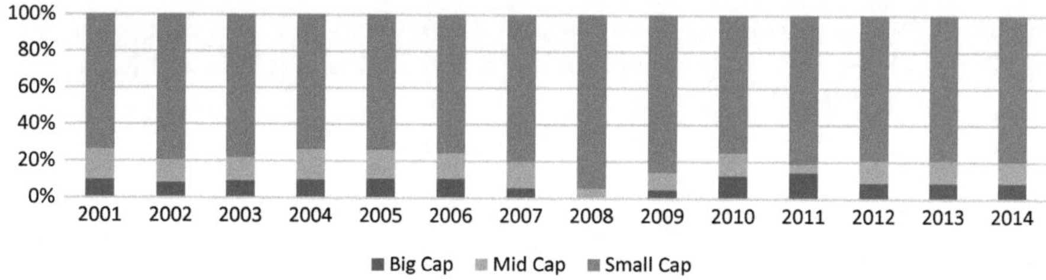

Fig. 11 Allocation per market capitalization

average annual capitalization higher than 10 billion/€, the Mid Caps with average annual capitalization between 2 and 10 billion/€ and the Small Caps with capitalization <2 billion/€. It is clear that the subgroup of Small Caps is favorite from the selection process, weighing on average about 79% of the portfolio compared with 12% of Mid Caps and about 9% of the Big Caps (Fig. 11).

6.3 *Weighting Companies Process*

We created a methodology to define the individual stocks weights. We used a recursive process, with upper and lower bounds in concentration in order to limit the concentration in Small Caps. We chose an admission limit of 0.35% to exclude all securities with lower relative capitalization, and a concentration limit on individual security equal to 15%; then, the portfolio's weight was rebalanced to 100%,

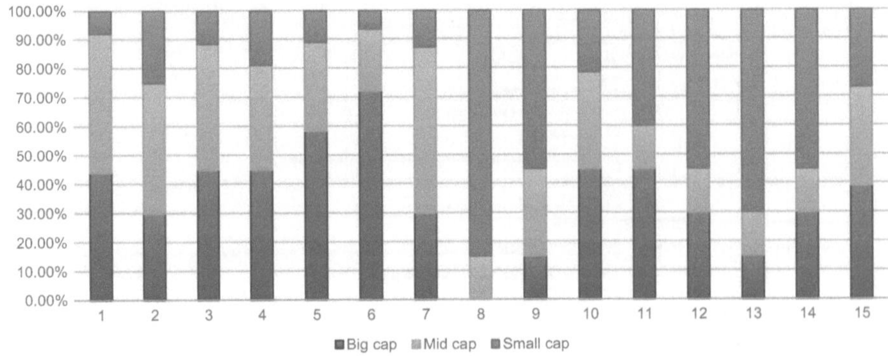

Fig. 12 Allocation per market capitalization after weighting process

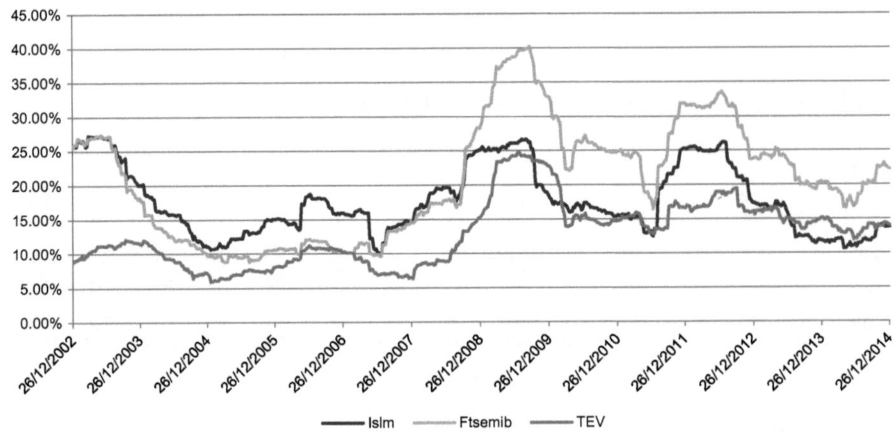

Fig. 13 Historical total-return: Islamic Index versus Benchmark

by distributing investments of over 15% and Small Caps excluded on the rest of the portfolio. The process is carried out recursively until the investments in individual stocks was <15% (Fig. 12).

After having built the portfolios, we evaluated the performance and the ex-post risk of portfolios, also identifying the possible presence of predominant styles (Fig. 13). We considered the total-return time series, i.e. including dividends, in order to compare the performance of both the portfolio securities and the benchmark, rebalancing the portfolios at the beginning of the year.

Comparing the ex-post risk of the portfolio and the benchmark (Fig. 14), we obtained rather different results: since 2008 onwards, the volatility of the portfolios is significantly lower because of the exclusion of banking and insurance companies from the lists.

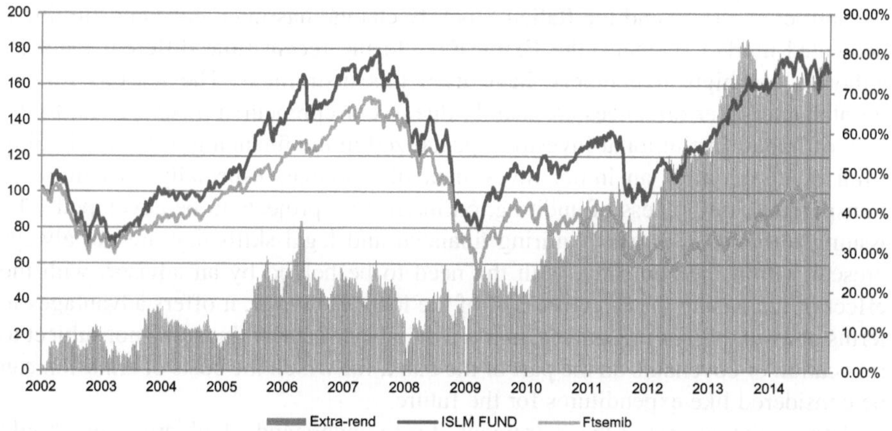

Fig. 14 Historical ex-post risk: Islamic Index versus Benchmark

To sum up, a Sharia-compliant index has shown a risk-return profile particularly interesting between 2002 and 2014. From 2008 onwards, the index showed strong growth and a significant reduction in volatility. The method of weighting of the securities has greatly influenced the results obtained by the Islamic Index because it has greatly mitigated the presence of Small-Caps. However, this was necessary to decrease the dependence on risk factors unrelated to the ability of selection of Shariah-compliant ratios. The cumulative return obtained by the Shariah-compliant index was greater portfolio of roughly 80%, while delivering a rather different behavior and a significant underperformance in 2004 and 2007. The Islamic Index compared to the benchmark was more volatile in the first phase, until 2007, and then more limited.

7 Financing Italian SMEs: May Be *Sukuks* Considered as a Viable Alternative?

The Italian Small Companies are characterized by a greater reliance on bank debt compared to other European countries. Consob (*Commissione Nazionale per le Società e la Borsa*, that is the Italian public authority responsible for regulating the Italian financial markets) points out that in late 2013 in the United States bank loans to non-financial companies weighed only 4% of GDP, while in the Eurozone reached 45% and in Italy 52% (Vegas 2015). Faced with the difficulties of banks to provide new credit, the challenge is to turn to other sources of funding, to have access to the financial market. The use of the market has been facilitated by recent measures that have made accessible to small entities the issue of bonds (called *mini bonds*) which can be placed on the market. A new legislation to companies and financial Intermediaries has favored the issuance of these financial instruments

(Meiani et al. 2015) and the Italian Stock Exchange has intervened constituting a dedicated market segment, the ExtraMOT. In the recent time different realities, although not high in numbers, have used this instrument. The reasons for the unsatisfactory performances are mainly due to entrepreneurship culture and to the lack of Italian Institutional Investors specialized in the financing of SMEs. Issuing Mini bonds requires an initial investment of resources especially on culture of transparency, on process of auditing, on interesting projects to be developed. The issuing of bonds is a task requiring financial and legal skills that are not always present within the company, with the need to be helped by an advisor, with the effect of increasing the effective cost of the loan. However, it offers advantages in terms of availability of resources, market visibility, security financing not subject to revocation or covenants on the part of the bank, for which the costs of emission can be considered like expenditures for the future.

Against the interest of the instrument, it is to understand which processes should be implemented instead of SME to enter the *sukuk* market and the feasibility of the project.

The alternative of issuing *sukuk* actually has to deal with the characteristics of the instrument and with the expectations of investors who value the instrument as an investment choice of saving. In fact, the instrument should take the dictates of sharia and therefore should be an instrument that gives the right to participate in a deal to share the profits (and losses), for which the *sukuk* get involved as a source of financial resources. The transaction is structured so that the *sukuks*, as observed by the AAOIFI (Accounting and Auditing Organization for Islamic Financial Institutions), are "certificates of equal value representing undivided shares in the ownership of the tangible assets, usufructs and services or (in the ownership of) the assets of particular projects or special investment activity" (AAOIFI 2008, p. 307). Therefore, *sukuks* cannot be issued in connection with the indistinct financing of company, like a mini bond, choice that instead become feasible by issuing shares, if the issuing company meets the requirements established by the standard of Sharia. However, the issue of shares involves reflections on governance, often not appreciated by SMEs. It is necessary to have a special purpose vehicle for a specific project that would be financed by issuing *sukuk*, distinguish this investment from all the other corporate investments. The choice therefore requires the establishment of a legal vehicle for the project, which results will be shared between owners of the sukuks.

The fulfillment of the various statutory and fiscal aspects of the operation is therefore a process not always easily approachable by SMEs. However, the problem may have different solutions, especially for those organizations that are attractive for the investor.

Another thing to point out is about which activities can be financed: the choice must be about real assets and no financial investments. Financing the construction of the factory in which to manage a business, or the construction of buildings is therefore an area where the *sukuk* can be usefully used. The leasing contract is, however, compliant with sharia, because it is structured like payment of periodic fees related to the use of an asset, so, with some specifications, it will be consistent with the expectations of an Islamic investor.

An interesting case of study could be the one of a construction cooperative company. The problem of construction of houses to be made available to people on terms consistent with the characteristics of buyers' remains a challenge for Italy, where over the years, investments were made especially for the housing market. The house in cooperative society is an alternative for quality housing at affordable prices. However, the problem is the financing of the construction in situations where banks have reduced the availability of funding for these alternatives. To answer the need to ensure the continuing of business, the cooperative firm has decided to finance their activity issuing mini bonds to offer to shareholders the opportunity to access the house by signing a lease agreement. The issue in 2013 was successful, giving the opportunity to the Cooperative societies to continue the business. The investment, through a structured loan securitization of leasing, with the guarantee by the properties below, could be feasible even with an issuance of properly structured sukuk. Especially fiscal aspects, however, make the process expensive, and thus its feasibility, the process requiring an adjustment of the same tax laws to make them compatible with the expected return of the under writers of sukuk. The different disposals of real estate have in fact a significant burden on the economy of this project, reducing the margin of the project. However, given the importance of funding for projects to the construction and to the redevelopment of the Italian housing, issuing sukuk by structured transactions may be an attractive alternative. There remains the problem of the size of the investment, that clearly, given the fixed costs of process, the structured operation is feasible only for emissions that can justify the whole project.

8 Italian Tax System and Sukuks: Fiscal Challenges Towards a More Level Playing Filed

In Europe, some countries have adapted their tax legislation to provide an adequate framework for the development of Islamic finance products, generally choosing to frame these kind of unconventional financial instruments—for the purposes of the deductibility by the issuer side and for the purposes of taxation by the investor side—in comparable categories of interest-bearing financial instruments, as to achieve an equivalence between products that perform similar economic goals. In Italy, although increasing conferences and studies contributed to stimulate the debate, no concrete steps have been taken.

Following Italian tax doctrine, financial instruments could be defined as *shares* based on the criterion of remuneration, or as *bonds* based on the criterion of the right to refund the capital. As sukuk is an extremely flexible instrument, it is never quite easy to standardize them on one of the three cases referred by the Italian fiscal system: *bonds*, *shares* or *atypical securities*. Moreover, to each type of financial instrument different tax implications follow, such as to make the instrument, even if financially alternative and/or competitive, totally undesirable from a fiscal point of view for a company or equal to a bond. The Italian Civil Code (Art. 2411) provides that the repayment of bond capital, may be affected, in some way, by the economic performance of the company, and therefore have a certain randomness to risk more pronounced than a traditional bonds, approaching the risk concept of sukuk given by the Sharia. Moreover, according to the Italian Revenue Agency, "the bonds themselves are identified according to the right to refund the capital" (Italian Revenue Agency 2013, p. 8). Therefore, it would seem very difficult to identify sukuk in bonds discipline without a new fiscal interpretation. The solution adopted in the UK in order to protect investors in Shariah-compliant products from the risk of capital losses looks quite interesting and, if adopted also in Italy, it would make the tax treatment of a sukuk equal to that of a traditional bond. A sukuk subscriber may require the *Financial Services Compensation Scheme*, in order to have the amount lost refunded if the sukuk does not pay back the nominal capital. Subscribers can accept or reject this possibility. If they accept, the bank will repay the sukuk subscriber and, in this case, he will not be considered as fully compliant with Islamic principles, but with this mechanism, it is respected both the Shariah principle of *profit-loss sharing* and the deposits protection principle in conventional finance. Any interpretation of the sukuk as a *participation bond* would be focused on the spirit of Article 109, paragraph 9 of TUIR (The Italian Income Tax Act), designed to prevent that the company distribute *occult dividends* in the form of interest or similar. The return of a sukuk, although not predetermined and uncertain, effectively looks as a return aligned to similar parameters as those of traditional bonds (Euribor, IRS, etc.). Adopting some conditions in defining sukuks' offerings, it could be possible to support the interpretation that the remuneration of such instruments, although variable, strictly linked to profits and not predetermined in order to be Sharia-compliant—does not necessary constitute preconditions to achieve the distribution of *occult dividends* in other forms. Anyway, the mechanism of sukuks' returns could meet the interest of the Italian Revenue Agency as it is aligned with a maximum interest expense, it costs the same to which the issuer would certainly encounter with a traditional bond completely similar, which could yield, in fact, even down or vanish in times of downward performance of the business. These characters of remuneration could, through interpretation, allow to exclude the sukuk from the discipline of *non-deductibility* sub article 109 of TUIR (The Income Tax Act) and, therefore, to exclude them also from the fiscal system similar to the shares in relation to the taxation of the investor.

In the absence of a specific case regarding sukuks and of a clear interpretation by the Italian Revenue Agency about Islamic financial instruments, if sukuks could not be identified as *participation bonds* [Art. 44, paragraph 2, letter. C of TUIR (the Italian Income Tax Act)] because it does not guarantee the total capital refund or in the *shares* because their payments that are not fully parameterized to earnings, they could be considered among the *atypical securities*, whose tax scheme is still governed by art. 5 of Decree n. 512/1983, which provides for the application of a punitive tax regime, as part of the remuneration related to the financial performance of the company is not tax deductible for the issuer. For the Italian investors, taxation will necessarily be a direct result of the fiscal classification of the instrument by the issuer side (shares, bonds or atypical security), analyzing each issue, from time to time, according to the official documentation available by the intermediary. Anyway, for the investor (both Italian and foreign) the taxation would be currently almost the same (currently at 26%) in the case the sukuk is considered as a *participatory bond*, as a *bond*, as a *share* or as an *atypical security*.

To conclude, we believe that any legislative interpretation about Islamic instruments would be desirable, in order to ensure an adequate degree of flexibility to the financial system or, possibly, to reduce the relevant asymmetries still existing in tax treatment between different countries among the European Union, so that the same financial instrument may be classified differently in the country of the issuer from that of the investor. A clear and unique qualification of these securities is also important because the same instrument can have a different nature in different contexts. It happens that a security is considered equity for banking supervisory purposes and debt for tax purposes. The evolution of the financial instruments is helping to thin the line between risk capital and debt capita. It will be necessary, therefore, to reflect on the traditional definitions of the Italian tax system, inadequate to grasp today the characteristics of the new shares and similar financial instruments, as well as those of bonds and other securities such as sukuk.

Acknowledgements This research is by the *Islamic Finance Working Group* of the *Italian Association of Financial Analysts and Advisors*. We thank *Studio Legale Delfino e Associati Willkie Farr & Gallagher LLP*, in particular Fabrizio Petrucci and Paolo Gaspare Conforti di Lorenzo, for their precious support.

References

AAOIFI (Accounting and Auditing Organization for Islamic Financial Institutions). (2008). *Shariah standards for financial institutions*. Bahrain: AAOIFI.

Ciferri, D., Antellini Russo, F., & Palazzo, A. 2015. *Crescere per competere. Il caso del Fondo Strategico Italiano [Growing up to compete. The case of the Italian Strategic Fund]* (Cassa Depositi e Prestiti, Paper, 1/2015).

D'Aurizio, L., & Cristadoro, R. (2015). *Le caratteristiche principali dell'internazionalizzazione delle imprese italiane [The Italian firms' international activity]* (Occasional Papers, 261/March 2015). Bank of Italy.

Di Mauro, F., Caristi, P., Couderc, S., Di Maria, A., Ho, L., Kaur Grewal, B., Masciantonio, S., Ongena, S., & Zaher, S. (2013). *Islamic finance in Europe* (Occasional Paper Series, 146/June 2013). European Central Bank.

Directive 2011/61/EU of the European Parliament and of the Council. (2011, June 8). *Alternative investment fund managers and amending Directives 2003/41/EC and 2009/65/EC and regulations (EC) No 1060/2009 and (EU) No 1095/2010* [online]. Accessed June 6, 2016, from http://eur-lex.europa.eu/LexUriServ/LexUriServ.do?uri=OJ:L:2011:174:0001:0073:EN:PDF

Gomel, G., Cicogna, A., De Falco, D., Della Penna, M. V., Di Bona De Sarzana, L., Di Maria, A., Di Natale, P., Freni, A., Masciantonio, S., Oddo, G., & Vadalà, E. (2010). *Finanza islamica e sistemi finanziari convenzionali. Tendenze di mercato, profili di supervisione e implicazioniper le attività di banca centrale* [*Islamic finance and conventional financial systems*] (Occasional Papers, 73/October 2010). Bank of Italy.

IFSB (Islamic Financial Services Board). (2009). *Guiding principles on governance for Islamic collective investment schemes* [online]. Accessed June 6, 2016, from http://www.ifsb.org/standard/ifsb6.pdf

Italian Revenue Agency. (2013, March 6). *Circular 4/E*. Italy.

Kammer, A., Norat, M., Pinon, M., Prasad, A., Towe, C., Zeidane, Z., & IMF Staff Team. (2015). *Islamic finance: opportunities, challenges and policy options* (Staff Discussion Note, 15/05, April). International Monetary Fund.

KFH Research Limited. (2014). *Global Islamic Finance: Propositions to Europe*. Kuala Lumpur: KFH Research Limited.

McMillen, M. J. T. 2000. Islamic Shariah-compliant project finance: Collateral security and financing structure case studies. *Fordham International Law Journal*, *24*(2), Article 6, 1184–1263.

McMillen, M. J. T. (2008). Asset securitization sukuk and Islamic capital markets: structural issues in these formative years. *Wisconsin International Law Journal, 25*(4), 703–772.

Meiani, A., Rizzi, L., & Sabatini, D. (2015). *Guida ai mini bond [Guideto minibonds]*. Milan: Bancaria Editrice.

Reviglio, E., Del Bufalo, G., Ciferri, D., & Palazzo, A. 2013. *Capitale per lo sviluppo. Strumenti finanziari europei a sostegno delle imprese e degli investimenti* [*Capital for growth. European financial instruments to support firms and investments*] (Monografic Report, 2/2013). Cassa Depositi e Prestiti.

Shawamreh, C. (2012). Islamic legal theory and the context of Islamist movements. *Notre Dame Journal of International and Comparative Law, 2*(2), 197–223.

Standard & Poor's. (2014). *Islamic finance outlook 2015* [online]. Accessed June 10, 2016, from https://ribh.files.wordpress.com/2014/09/islamicfinanceoutlook2015.pdf

Thomson Reuters. (2014). *Sukuk Perceptions & Forecast 2015. Beyond traditional markets*. Thomson Reuters.

Vegas, G. (2015, May 11). *Annual meeting with the financial market. President Speach*. Milan: Consob (Commissione Nazionale per le Società e la Borsa) [online]. Accessed June 6, 2016, from http://www.consob.it/documents/11973/232763/dsc2015.pdf/13006036-d566-44d7-9719-52b206db8cdb

The Role and Impact of Performance Audit in Public Governance

Dalia Daujotaitė and Danutė Adomavičiūtė

Abstract The paper analyses the impact of an important external control tool—performance audit in the area of public governance. This survey is based on the data on performance audits of the National Audit Office of Lithuania (NAOL). It is stated that the implementation of accepted recommendations consequently led to the improvement performance. The correction allows saving funds, decreasing expenses, improving performance quality, and strengthening management, administration, and organizational processes and improving legislation, introducing financial discipline. It is the performance audit recommendations that can significantly affect the organization and the functioning of the political and administrative apparatus. There is also presented the performance audit model, which novelty stems from its ability to demonstrate the correlation links between the principal concepts of the performance audit, levels of management and external environment. The basis for the model is represented by production processes of public activities that consume resources and/or production factors in order to produce products or services. The cost effect is created through the outcomes of the three elements—economy, effectiveness, and efficiency.

Keywords Performance audit • Public governance • Accountability • Performance audit model • Impact

D. Daujotaitė (✉)
Faculty of Economics and Finance Management, Department of Finance and Taxes, Mykolas Romeris University, Vilnius, Lithuania
e-mail: daujotaite@mruni.eu

D. Adomavičiūtė
Faculty of Economics and Finance Management, Institute of Economics and Business, Mykolas Romeris University, Vilnius, Lithuania
e-mail: adomaviciute.d@gmail.com

M.H. Bilgin et al. (eds.), *Empirical Studies on Economics of Innovation, Public Economics and Management*, Eurasian Studies in Business and Economics 6,
DOI 10.1007/978-3-319-50164-2_2

1 Introduction

In the rapidly changing, complex world with limited resources and numerous uncertainties, performance audit significantly affects not only the effective public sector governance but also the strengthening of the State economy and the improvement of public welfare. The essence of performance audit is the objective assessment of the functionality of the activity, programs and/or systems of public sector organizations from the point of view of their economy of performance, effectiveness and efficiency, and the promotion of the progress in performance and management. By providing unbiased, objective assessments of whether public resources are managed responsibly and effectively with the aim to achieve the intended results, auditors help public sector organizations to achieve accountability and integrity, improve operations and instill confidence among citizens and stakeholders. The public sector auditor's role supports the governance responsibilities of oversight, insight, and foresight. Performance audit must focus both on the failures and promote the conditions for success.

The study of performance audit can be related to doctrines belonging to New Public Management (NPM) ideas. When applying the NPM doctrines, more attention was payed to performance and accountability in the public sector. Economy, efficiency and effectiveness (the three E's) became dominant themes in the restructuring. According to Mulgan (2001), public managers had to pay more attention to accountability for performance. In Lithuania, performance audit is carried out by the Auditor General under the mandate granted by the State Control Act (2001), which defines the National Audit Office (NAO) as the supreme government audit institution, accountable to the Seimas. The law came into force 1 March 2002. The legal framework for the public sector was revised and new mandates introduced. A number of performance and accountability mechanisms were introduced within this framework. Lithuania embracing NPM and performance audit is a part of an international movement which includes Organization for Economic Co-operation and Development (OECD) member countries.

Thus, the NPM principles promoted the necessity to use the audit and control mechanisms. Audits and evaluations have become important tools in providing information about how public money is spent (Power 1997; Pollitt et al. 1999; Hood et al. 1999; Reichborn-Kjennerud 2015). To ensure successful, fair and transparent management and allocation of public resources and to increase accountability of the public sector, some essential changes were introduced in the assessment of performance. Any assessment of performance in terms of changes in financial performance turned out to be no longer adequate. The classical supervisory and control systems focusing on evaluating financial statements and compliance with respective standards only failed to comply with the new requirements. Thus there is an increasing and tangible need for performance audit whose functions have become multi-dimensional and more complex covering the assessment of the public sector performance, programs and/or systems from the point of view their economy, efficiency and effectiveness.

In accordance with ISSAI 3000 (INTOSAI 2004) and good management practices, performance audit reports play a crucial role. It is important for citizens, public institutions, legislators, the media and etc. to control and to obtain information about the outcomes of different government activities. Moreover, performance audit visualizes performance and events of the public sector that are most important for both politicians and the public, and making it possible to distinguish legitimate activity from any illegal actions. Audit reports that are made public significantly contribute to the enforcement of accountability and transparency as the fundamental democratic values of each State that are indispensable in ensuring the proper management of public funds on behalf of citizens and tax payers. Performance audit also provides answers to a range of questions, such as 'do we get value for the money, or is it possible to spend the money better or more wisely'? A criterion of good governance is that all public services (or all government programs) are subjected to audit. Legitimacy and trust are essential values in all government undertakings, and performance audit may contribute to strengthening these values by producing public and reliable information on the economy, efficiency and effectiveness of government programs.

An important aspect in this context is the public accountability, which means that the heads of government programs are held responsible for efficient and effective management of such activities. Accountability presupposes public insight into the activities of the program or the ministry. The auditor's independence is another important point in conducting the audit of different government organizations. Researches on impact of performance audit have attracted considerable attention of Lithuanian and foreign researchers and practitioners. The impact of performance audit on public sector organizations has been investigated by a number of foreign (Tremblay and Malsch 2015; Raudla et al. 2015; Waring and Morgan 2007; Funkhouser 2011; Pollitt et al. 1999; Pollitt 2003; Power 1997; Leeuw 1996; Barzelay 2000; Hood et al. 1999) and Lithuanian authors (Mackevičius 2001; Puškorius 2004; Lakis 2007, etc.). Numerous research efforts conducted in the period yielded abundant and highly valuable results. The research activities covered several areas; therefore the findings obtained as a result were complex and versatile in nature. The positive impact of the development of performance auditing has been widely recognized by a number of foreign and national researchers (Waring and Morgan 2007; Funkhouser 2011; Pollitt et al. 1999; Power 1997; Mackevičius 2001; Puškorius 2004; Lakis 2007) both in relation to the assessment of the general economic growth of the State, and of attainments of individual economic entities.

The study about recommendations in ensuring the results of performance audit in the Lithuanian public sector was highlighted by Lakis and Nemanytė (2014), who claimed that the implementation of audit recommendations shows the effectiveness of audit institutions. The present article focuses on the public sector performance audit of the relevant programs and activities, performed by NAOL (the Supreme Audit Institution (SAI) of Lithuania). According to Lonsdale and Bechberger (2011), the main function of a SAI is to exercise control over the auditees, however, its secondary goal is to contribute to improvement of their performance. In accordance with Reichborn-Kjennerud and Johnsen (2011), performance audit is one method that the SAI uses to assure efficiency and effectiveness of public funds.

With this paper, we seek to identify the most important impact of the implemented recommendations for the society, parliamentarians and for the management of public institutions. In order to achieve this aim, the following tasks were defined: to provide argumentative framework about role and impact of performance audit; to present a model of performance audit in the public governance; to identify the performance audits' impact in the Lithuanian public sector. The present paper specifically focused on the logical analysis of scientific researchers of Lithuania and foreign authors and legal acts, data analysis and comparison, classification, specification and generalization. The study involved an examination of total 79 performance audit reports submitted in 2011–2014. An important task was to identify and examine the principal mistakes and shortcomings in the performance of the auditees, and the nature of the recommendations. The process of the implementation of the recommendations was discussed with the auditors of the National Audit Office of Lithuania responsible for the monitoring of the implementation of the recommendations.

2 Concept of Performance Audit

A review of the literature showed some differences in how researchers define the concept of performance audit. From political perspectives performance audit appears as a socially constructed and changeable object of knowledge. Furthermore, the analysis on the impact of performance audit has provided contradicting findings. Some researchers see performance audit as inherently complicit in protecting political structures, while others highlight the critical role of performance auditing in modernizing and transforming public sector's efficiency. The review of the literature shows that research on performance audit remains fragmented and is not a robust and coherent body of knowledge.

From managerial perspective performance audit appears as a structured evaluation process that is realized at different levels and stages, see Fig. 1. According to Tremblay and Malsch (2015), defining the auditors' activity is a hard task, as it is always subject to changes and interpretations. On the other hand, without a robust and legitimate definition of their activities and their mission, professionals could hardly represent themselves as relevant experts and get the social and commercial benefits from the recognition of their specific competencies.

Scientific literature sources define performance auditing in a number of different ways. For example, Waring and Morgan (2007, p. 323) defined performance audit "a systematic, objective assessment of the accomplishments or processes of a government program or activity for the purpose of determining its effectiveness, economy, or efficiency". According to INTOSAI's Auditing Standards (AS 1.0.38 and 1.0.40) performance auditing is defined as follows: Performance auditing is concerned with the audit of economy, efficiency and effectiveness and embraces:

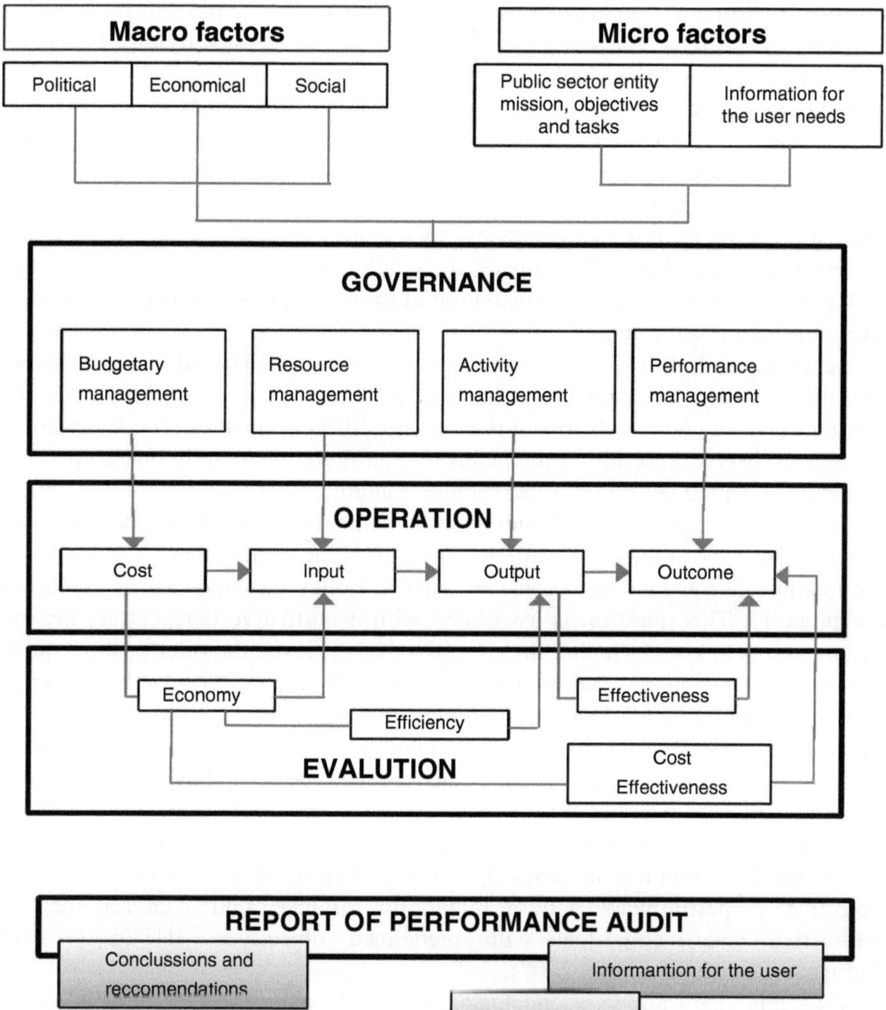

Fig. 1 Model of the performance audit. Source: Daujotaitė (2010)

(a) Audit of the economy of administrative activities in accordance with sound administrative principles and practices, and management policies;
(b) Audit of the efficiency of utilization of human, financial and other resources, including examination of information systems, performance measures and monitoring arrangements, and procedures followed by audited entities for remedying identified deficiencies; and
(c) Audit of the effectiveness of performance in relation to achievement of the objectiveness of the audited entity, and audit of the actual impact of activities compared with the intended impact (INTOSAI 1992).

Thus, performance audits can be broadly described as audits that focus on the efficiency, the effectiveness and the economy of public sector activities. Efficiency means to ensure whether goods and services are produced in stimulated time without reducing quality and quantity with optimum utilization of scarce resources or not. It is output oriented and focuses on maximization of output by minimizing input or resources. Economy means the acquisition of the appropriate quality and quantity of financial, physical, information and human resources at the appropriate time and minimum cost. Effectiveness means achievement of the objectives or targets of an organization. It evaluates the relationship between expected or target and actual result from the implementation of program, project, function and activities. It is also result oriented.

According to Pollitt (2003), earlier research on a transnational level has shown that different SAI interpret the concept of performance audit in different ways, consequently conducting such audits in a very different manner. The summary of the above observations allows a conclusion that there is no really one correct and generally accepted definition of performance audit.

The essence of performance audit is to find answers to two basic questions: Are things being done in the right way? Are the right things being done? The answer to the first question would be to consider whether policy decisions are being carried out properly. This question is associated with a normative perspective, i.e., the auditor wants to know whether the executive has observed the rules or the requirements. The question may be extended to whether the activities carried out are also considered appropriate and the right things are being done. The scope for analysis becomes considerably wider when the second question—whether the right things are being done—is asked, whether the adopted policies have been suitably implemented,—or whether adequate means have been employed. The question refers to effectiveness or the impact on the society. The question might even imply that a government undertaking—or a chosen measure to achieve a certain objective. A performance auditor might, for instance, find a chosen measure ineffective and inconsistent with predefined objectives (INTOSAI 2004; European Court of Auditors 2007).

Thus this study allows a conclusion that up to date, there has not been any unanimous opinion as to a comprehensive and accurate definition of the concept. Different authors have analyzed and defined public sector performance audit by reference to different viewpoints and from different perspectives. The theoretical analysis leads to the conclusion that public sector performance audit should be perceived as a measure stimulating an entity audited to further improve its operating and management processes with a view to enhancing its performance results.

The theoretical analysis of the issue under consideration concluded that the ongoing public sector reforms presupposed a new paradigm for the audit policy enforced by the Supreme Audit Institution that facilitated evaluation of performance based on performance audit methodologies with a clear focus upon the evaluation of performance results. Performance audit is a type of state audit. In many countries Supreme Audit Institutions have been increasingly gaining importance, they have occupied a clearly defined constitutional position in the State, have ensured their independence and the required level of professionalism to carry out performance audits.

Supreme Audit Institutions have a task to balance and integrate the targets of two types of accountability: compliance accountability and performance accountability. Compliance accountability based on financial audit contributes to ensuring the proper management of public finance and assets. Performance accountability is based upon performance audit, facilitates and stimulates the accountability of the public sector, result-driven management respecting the needs of population, and the progress of financial management and control systems.

3 The Model of Performance Audit in Public Governance

Various management models are presented in the scientific literature. It is noted that the same logical model is used both for common tools for public managers and public performance auditors. The public sector performance audit model is based on a number of key principles, such as integrity, systemic approach, innovativeness etc., but the principles of financial management are the essential public finance management principles providing the grounds for linking of financial management process with managerial objectives. Usually are identified seven principles for financial management (see Table 1): target setting, planning, budgeting,

Table 1 Performance audit based on the evaluation of management processes

No	Financial management processes	Performance management task	Activity management task	Resource management task	Budgetary management task
1	Target setting	Performance targets			
2	Planning		Activity plans, prodution planning	Investment plans, staff frame, etc.	
3	Budgeting		Activity budget	Resource budgeting	Organisation budget
4	Implementing and manage-ment control		Activities, processes	Use of resources	Accounting and internal control
5	Presentation of accounts		Activity statistics	Revenue and expenditure accounts	Presentation of accounts
6	Follow up and		Key figures for efficiency	Key figures for the use of resources	
7	Evaluation	Measuring effective-ness (restating of performance targets)			

implementing and management control, presentation of accounts, follow-up and reporting, evaluation, which are closely related to basic principal objectives of management such as performance management, activity management, recourse management, budgetary management. They have relevant interrelationships and the impact of the results upon any subsequent processes (see Table 1).

As shown in the Table 1, the constituent parts are interrelated thus allowing an assumption that a certain selection of such constituents has a greater impact in a certain stage. It is evident that each part distinguished is relevant and plays an important role in conducting public sector performance audit. The proposed public sector performance audit model integrates the principal performance audit elements with the different types of management—governance, operation and evaluation, see Fig. 1.

The analysis of the relationship between the 3 E's points is to one more issue. In the relationship objectives—resources—cost of resources (inputs), the key importance lies with the resources (inputs). They are acquired and accumulated (in the course of the annual receipt of budgetary funds, through purchasing the necessary buildings, materials and equipment, through recruiting and employing qualified staff, through its training and qualification into a human capital, etc.). The point is that for any set period of time when they are made available to the respective public sector organization for the purpose of meeting its objectives, the resources are relatively scarce, i.e., they are always limited in quantity and quality. It is their quantity and quality that is of the utmost importance for the successful achievement of the results. The bottom line is that the resources determine the achievement of the targeted results, and not vice versa. In other words, the objectives do not yield resources although they require certain amount of resources in order to be achieved.

4 The Impact of Performance Audit: Theoretical Aspect

According to Tremblay and Malsch (2015), they reveal two different perspectives to performance audit: positive impact and critical evaluation. According to Morin (2004), positive impact, when auditors formulated relevant recommendations, lead to improving performance and that audit had a preventive effect on public sector managers. Morin (2001) who argued that initially demonstrated that many auditor recommendations appeared to be taken lightly by the audited organizations and parliamentarians considering the delay within which the audited organizations enacted prescribed yet non-binding recommendations. In the other hand, according to Morin (2008) the audit impacts were perceived as more significant when auditors are subtle, and when individuals within the audited organization are favorably disposed. Parliamentarians appear to have a decisive influence on the impact auditors will or will not have on the management of organizations audited; however, press coverage may surprisingly have a negative effect on long-term improvements.

In accordance with Tremblay and Malsch (2015), Van Loocke and Put (2011), it is three significant factors that contribute to an increased impact of performance auditing; media pressure, pressure from interest groups, pressure from parliament; relationship auditor/auditee during the audit, the audit report, follow-up of recommendations; willingness from the audited organization, ongoing reform in the audited entity. The authors consider that SAIs can use this knowledge to optimize factors that are within their control such as the auditor/auditee relation, develop influencing strategies for the factors outside of their range of influence, invest sufficient resources in the audit selection and planning, increase their efforts to disseminate their audit results and confer with all relevant stakeholders. We in the same way as Raudla et al. (2015) confirm too that when Parliamentarians pay attention to performance audit and when media attention leads to political debate, the adoption of recommendations given the performance audit reports is implemented more successfully.

Some scientists discuss of performance audit as a 'political' technology rather than a neutral expertise. Their criticisms are related to the new public management that has been sustaining the explosion of audit practices in the public sector. This has already been discussed. Another issue of performance audit is the managerial aspect based on logical business model and it has already been discussed when we presented performance audit model. According to Tremblay and Malsch (2015), Bourn (2007) who argued that whether auditors make a positive or a negative impact essentially depends on the perception that the different parties involved and concerned have on the performance audit. One of the most important objectives of performance audit is to legitimate a government, and the success of performance auditing should be discussed and measured in this respect. The performance audit is a rather complex process where perceptions are often more important that reality and outcomes are often unpredictable.

Pollitt et al. (1999) the impact of the performance audit work undertaken by five European SAIs (the Dutch Algemene Rekenkamer, the French Cour des Comptes, the UK National Audit Office, the Swedish Riksrevisionsverket and the Finnish Valtiontalouden tarkastusvirasto). They considered amongst other things what SAIs themselves stated with regard to the impact of their performance audit work, whether and how SAIs measure their impacts, which efforts SAIs make to enhance the impact of their work, if there any negative (side) effects to performance audit work, etc. In seeking answers to their questions, the authors were able to bring a number of interesting findings to the fore. Altogether their evidence suggested that performance audits do have an impact. After all, in each of the countries they examined performance audits did lead to changes to government activities. In many cases the reactions to auditors' recommendations also led to substantial savings in public funds. In addition, the authors drew attention to the possibility that performance audits also produce a deterrent effect arising simply from the fact that they exist, as well as a more general educational impact.

5 Performance Audit Impact in The Lithuania Public Sector

The analysis of the public sector management functions allows a conclusion that the periodic assessment of the processes based on stringent performance audit standards serves as a stimulus to managers and employees of an entity to continuously improve the processes and seek further progress. The analysis also shows that any management may be identified and justified only provided it is expressed in terms of performance. The results of a survey of 79 performance audit reports published by NAOL show that there is growing recognition of the importance that the state audit institution of Lithuania plays in ensuring accountability and good governance. The positive impact of the mandatory requirements implemented by the state audit institution of Lithuania was noted by President Adamkus (2012), "This office ensures that the nation's wealth is used legitimately and effectively, and monitors how the nation's budget is executed. It also successfully fulfills the functions of an audit authority, with which it was entrusted by the European Council and Commission's regulations".

NAOL performance audit recommendations has a huge impact in seeking to improve organizations activities, reduce costs, improve service quality, strengthen management, administrative, organizational processes, and achieve the predefined objectives; furthermore, the recommendations are instrumental in identifying any current and any potential problems that may adversely affect the institution's or organization's performance. The scope of performance audit are shown in Table 2, that present the number of completed performance audits and the number of audited entities in each year.

The performance audits were focused on the priority area of the public sector, namely, public sector services provided to the public; the audits also analyzed and evaluated the availability, efficiency and effectiveness of such services. Audit objects included some socially sensitive areas, such as services provided by family doctors, acquisition and use of expensive medical equipment, performance of children's socialization centers, prevention of corruption, supervision of movable cultural values, etc. (National Audit office of Lithuania 2011b, 2012b, 2013b, 2014b).

In 2011–2014, most audits were performed in the areas of public property, finance management, environmental protection, culture, education, healthcare and etc. (National Audit office of Lithuania 2011b, 2012b, 2013b, 2014b). Most of the

Table 2 Scope of performance audit

Year	Number of completed audits	Number of audited entities
2011	22	65
2012	22	72
2013	27	79
2014	25	78

Source: National Audit Office of Lithuania (2011b, 2012b, 2013b, 2014b)

deficiencies identified and pointed out by the auditors were related to the implementation of functions and powers of public administration institutions, such as inadequate regulation of certain processes and the activities of institutions, evidence of failure to comply with the predefined requirements, lack of efficient regulation of the activities, inefficient use of state budget and EU support funds, failure to create the required inter-institutional systems and infrastructures, institutions failing to exchange information, put in place common information systems, and significant delays in the implementation of their prescribed functions.

Similar study results were presented by Lakis and Nemanytė (2014); the two authors that the most frequent deficiencies and mistakes concerned inadequate regulation (29–39%), failure to comply with the established requirements (16–23%); failure to create an organizational system or the infrastructure, some institutions duplicate the same functions (8–15%); institutions inappropriately use budget funds (6–13%); the institutions fail to exchange information, submit the required reports or pass decisions without duly taking into account the relevant information (6–12%); the activities or functions of the institutions are performed with significant delays, slowly or in a fragmented manner (5–12%); the institutions have failed to perform an assessment or an analysis of specific activities or actions (4–12%). That eventually leads to a conclusion that the entities being audited and public authorities do not dedicate sufficient attention to the implementation of the recommendations submitted by auditors.

Results and impact of the performance audit are shown in Table 3, that present the recommendations issued to the audited entities in the performance audits completed in each year. Most of the recommendations (45.2%) were related to improving performance efficiency. By the end of each year, about 15% of these recommendations were fully or partly implemented.

One of the most important indicators of the results achieved by audits is the level of the implementation of the recommendations issued as a result of the public audits. In order to assess the impact of public performance audit, public auditors regularly monitor and analyze the implementation of the recommendations provided in audit reports. Their content and implementation deadlines are discussed with the audited entities. Public auditors monitor and analyze the implementation of the recommendations. Two years after the audit, reports on the implementation of the audit recommendations are prepared describing what has been made to carry out the recommendations and the impact of the public audit. Every year the data on the

Table 3 Results and impact of performance audit

Year	Number of recommendations issued (unit)	Share of recommendations implemented (%)
2011	131	83
2012	162	83
2013	218	86
2014	146	86

Source: National Audit Office of Lithuania (2011a, 2012a, 2013a, 2014a)

Table 4 Results of Seimas member and head of public institutions survey

The Seimas members (141 respondents)		Heads of public institutions, chief accountants and internal auditors used reports of the NAOL	
Read public audit reports "always" or "often"	over 52.0%	Used reports as a source of information	91.0%
Help in their work	87.5%	Contributed to improvement – Internal control and internal audit of public entities	93.0%
The NAOL contributes efficiently to ensuring of accountability in the public sector	87.5 %	– Property management, use and disposal	86.5%
		– Development of accounting and financial statements	85.0%

Source: National Audit Office of Lithuania (2004a, 2005a)

implementation of recommendations is analyzed in the annual report summarizing the implementation of the recommendations, which determines the implementation level, informs about the impacts of public performance audit, and identifies causes of the failure to carry out the recommendations.

Thus, performance audits undertaken by the Office provide an independent assurance to Parliament and the community that funds appropriated for particular activities are spent prudently and in accordance with Parliament's expectations. Performance audits reinforce the accountability of Ministers and public sector managers for their performance, as well as recognizing and advising the Parliament of management initiatives and achievements. As show Table 4, results of the work performed by the NAOL are required and used.

The NAOL is concerned with the execution of parliamentary supervision of the executive power. Especially close cooperation is with the Committee on Audit of the Seimas, which regularly considers reports of the National Audit Office and the implementation of its recommendations. The Committee on Audit considerably contributes to an implementation of recommendations of the NAOL. For example, on the basis of the NAOL audit results, the Government approved conception of reform of public sector accounting and financial statements system, the public property information system implementation concept and other was submitted to the Seimas. It is just a few examples showing that cooperation with the Committee on Audit of the Seimas substantially improved implementation of public audit recommendations and elimination of the weaknesses indicated in such recommendations. It contributes to formulate sound economic policies that lead to sustainable economic growth and development.

During 2011–2014, most recommendations issued by the auditors were addressed to the Government; the Government was in most cases recommended to establish or change some specific requirements, criteria, rules, initiate some changes in the regulation, appoint an institution responsible for addressing the key problems or other issues. Similar recommendations were submitted to the ministries. Thus, the publication of performance audit reports is a very important accountability mechanism since the reports are detailed descriptions or analysis of public sector performance, based on an independent access to documentation and information.

6 Conclusions

The ongoing public management reforms caused the appearance of a paradigm in public management, and the result-driven management perspective, thus triggering some cardinal changes in the area of performance assessment. Any assessment of activities in terms of the changes of financial performance proved to have become insufficient. Classical supervisory and control systems focusing merely upon financial statements and compliance with certain predefined norms could not meet the new requirements. This triggered a need for a different, comprehensive and all-inclusive model for performance assessment.

The practical realization of the presented performance audit model is based on the following provisions: appropriate selection of audit objects with a view to maximizing the value added to the society and the entity being audited, i.e., ensuring that the projected audit results (reports and recommendations) lead to important decisions; the areas designated as key in respect of performance audit should include the evaluation of the financial management and internal controls of an entity (perceiving public organizations as a tool of public authorities in pursuit of the objectives of the State); the process of performance audit should be viewed systemically, i.e., public organizations should be viewed as systems of interrelated functional and interactive components; public sector performance audit should be limited to fundamental and economically and socially important issues, i.e., the evaluation of materiality and risk assessment should be considered an inseparable part of performance audit.

The analyzed performance audits reports show that performance audits are indeed useful, particularly with regard to the management of public organizations. The benefits generally are of an operational nature, rather than of a strategic nature. The auditors referred, for example, to the improvement of systems and processes, the adoption of best practices, the identification of redundant jobs and the improvement of risk management within audited organizations.

Performance audit impact is important for the society and includes following aspects: better control over the use and the management of taxpayers' money; helps to get better value for money and improved delivery of public services; citizens can influence government spending via legislators. The performance audit reports are intended to contribute to improved operations in the audited entities. They can be used by the Parliament and its committees to hold the ministries to account for unsatisfactory performance, management practice or lack of compliance in their respective policy areas.

While referring to the interviews with members of the Seimas, the present paper reveals the usage of performance audit information by ministers, parliamentarians and end users. In addition to the big statements that are generally made about the importance of performance information for democracy, there is some evidence that these end users do indeed use this type of information.

Performance audit impact is important for the Parliament: NAOL audit findings provide an effective instrument for parliamentary scrutiny and control; it raises Parliament's profile in controlling the legality and reasonableness of public spending; increases confidence in the checks and balance in the democratic process; the Parliamentary control becomes more efficient and transparent. The performance audits are the tools to good public governance. They strengthen public governance by providing for accountability and protecting the core values of the government, i.e., ensuring that managers and officials conduct the public business transparently, fairly, and honestly, and with equity and probity.

References

Adamkus, V. (2012). *Notice to EU Supreme Audit Institutions* [online]. Accessed October 11, 2015, from http://adamkuslibrary.lt/category/isrchyvu/?lang=en

Barzelay, M. (2000). *The new public management: Improving research and policy dialogue*. Berkeley, CA: University of California Press.

Bourn, J. (2007). *Public sector auditing: Is it value for money?* West Sussex: Wiley.

Daujotaitė, D. (2010). *Performance audit model for modernization of public sector management*. Doctoral disertacijon, University of Mykolas Romeris, Vilnius.

European Court of Auditors (ECA). (2007). *Performance audit manual* [online]. Accessed November 23, 27, 2015, from http://www.eca.europa.eu/Lists/ECADocuments/PERF_AUDIT_MANUAL/PERF_AUDIT_MANUAL_EN.PDF

Funkhouser, M. (2011). Accountability, performance and performance auditing: Reconciling the views of scholars and auditors. In J. Lonsdale, P. Wilkins & T. Ling (Eds.), *Performance auditing: Contributing to accountability in democratic government* (pp. 209–230). Cheltenham: Edward Elgar Publishing Limited.

Hood, C., James, O., Scott, C., Jones, G. W., & Travers, T. (1999). *Regulation inside government: Waste-watchers, quality police, and sleaze-busters*. New York, NY: Oxford University Press.

INTOSAI. (1992). Auditing standards. Issued by the Auditing Standards Committee International Organization of Supreme Audit Institutions.

INTOSAI. (2004). *ISSAI 3000. Standards and guidelines for performance auditing based on INTOSAI's auditing standards and practical experience* [online]. Accessed November 23, 2015, from http://www.issai.org/media/13224/issai_3000_e.pdf

Lakis, V. (2007). *Audito sistema: Raida ir problemos [Auditing system: Problems and development]*. Vilnius: Vilnius University Press.

Lakis, V., & Nemanytė, J. (2014). *Rekomendacijų reikšmė užtikrinant veiklos audito rezultatyvumą viešajame sektoriuje [The significance of recommendations in ensuring the results of performance audit in public sector]* [online]. Accessed November 23, 2015, from http://www.zurnalai.vu.lt/informacijos-mokslai/article/viewFile/3104/2232

Leeuw, F. L. (1996). Performance auditing, new public management and performance improvement: Questions and answers. *Accounting, Auditing and Accountability, 9*(2), 92–102.

Lonsdale, J., & Bechberger, E. (Eds.). (2011). *Performance auditing: Contributing to accountability in democratic government*. Cheltenham: Edward Elgar Publishing.

Mackevičius, J. (2001). *Auditas: Teorija, praktika, perspektyvos [Auditing: Theory, practice, future]*. Vilnius: Lietuvos Mokslas.
Morin, D. (2001). Influence of value for money audit on public administrations: Looking beyond appearances. *Financial Accountability and Management, 17*(2), 99–117.
Morin, D. (2004). Measuring the impact of value-for-money audits: A model for surveying audited managers. *Canadian Public Administration, 47*(2), 141–164.
Morin, D. (2008). Auditors general's universe revisited. *Managerial Auditing Journal, 23*(7), 697–720.
Mulgan, R. (2001). Auditors-general: Cuckoos in the managerialist nest? *Australian Journal of Public Administration, 60*(2), 24–34.
National Audit Office of Lithuania. (2004). *Annual reports for 2004* [online]. Accessed November 29, 2015, from https://www.vkontrole.lt/en/docs/annual2004.pdf
National Audit Office of Lithuania. (2011a). *Annual reports for 2011* [online]. Accessed November 29, 2015, from https://www.vkontrole.lt/page.aspx?id=9
National Audit Office of Lithuania. (2011b). *Performance audit reports for 2011* [online]. Accessed November 14, 2015, from https://www.vkontrole.lt/audito_ataskaitos_en.aspx?tipas=15
National Audit Office of Lithuania. (2012a). *Annual reports for 2012* [online]. Accessed November 29, 2015, from https://www.vkontrole.lt/en/docs/Annual_Report_2012_NAOL.pdf
National Audit Office of Lithuania. (2012b). *Performance audit reports for 2012* [online]. Accessed November 11, 2015, from https://www.vkontrole.lt/audito_ataskaitos_en.aspx?tipas=15
National Audit Office of Lithuania. (2013a). *Annual reports for 2013* [online]. Accessed November 29, 2015, from https://www.vkontrole.lt/en/docs/Annual_Report_2013_NAOL.pdf
National Audit Office of Lithuania. (2013b). *Performance audit reports for 2013* [online]. Accessed November 11, 2015, from https://www.vkontrole.lt/audito_ataskaitos_en.aspx?tipas=15
National Audit Office of Lithuania. (2014a). *Annual reports for 2014* [online]. Accessed November 29, 2015, from https://www.vkontrole.lt/en/docs/Annual_Report_2014_NAOL.pdf
National Audit Office of Lithuania. (2014b). *Performance audit reports for 2014* [online]. Accessed November 14, 2015, from https://www.vkontrole.lt/audito_ataskaitos_en.aspx?tipas=15
Pollitt, C. (2003). Performance audit in Western Europe: Trends and choices. *Critical Perspectives on Accounting, 14*, 157–170.
Pollitt, C., Girre, X., Lonsdale, J., Mul, R., Summa, H., & Waerness, M. (1999). *Performance or compliance? Performance audit and public management in five countries*. Oxford: Oxford University Press.
Power, M. (1997). *The audit society: Rituals of verification*. Oxford: Oxford University Press.
Puškorius, S. (2004). *Veiklos auditas [Performance audit]*. Vilnius: Mykolas Romeris University Press.
Raudla, R., Taro, K., Agu, C., & Douglas, J. W. (2015). The impact of performance audit on public sector organizations: The case of Estonia. *Public Organization Review, 16*(2), 217–233.
Reichborn-Kjennerud, K. (2015). Resistance to control-Norwegian ministries' and agencies' reactions to performance audit. *Public Organization Review, 15*(1), 17–32.
Reichborn-Kjennerud, K., & Johnsen, Å. (2011). Auditors' understanding of evidence: A performance audit of an urban development program. *Evaluation, 17*(3), 217–231.
State Control Act. (2001). As last amended on 23 January 2014—No XII-766.
Tremblay, M. S., Malsch, B, 2015. *A review of performance audit literature* [online]. Accessed March 07, 2016, from http://irspm2015.com/index.php/irspm/IRSPM2015/paper/viewFile/1584/340

Van Loocke, E. & Put, V. (2011). The impact of performance audits: A review of the existing evidence. In J. Lonsdale, P. Wilkins & T. Ling (Eds.), *Performance auditing: Contributing to accountability in democratic government*. Cheltenham: Edward Elgar Publishing.

Waring, C., & Morgan, S. (2007). Public sector performance auditing in developing countries, Ch. 11. In A. Shah (Ed.), *Performance accountability and combating corruption*. Washington, DC: The World Bank.

Business Performance Assessment in the Customs Administrations Activity and Trade Facilitation Measures

Danutė Adomavičiūtė and Dalia Daujotaitė

Abstract Nowadays customs underlines the importance of investment as a means of making a considerable contribution to economic development and the protection of society from security threats. Customs administrations are implementing trade facilitation measures and began assessing the activities of the business companies, pursuing to contract the status of the authorized economic operator. In order to capture the overall view and variations on customs' capacities the need of the exploration of business performance appeared. Trade costs are growing in the value chain at every stage, when goods crossed state's borders multiple times. Reviewing the empirical literature of business performance assessment issues, it can be said that emphasize different researches aspects. This paper analyses the role of customs administrations to secure and facilitate legitimate trade in international supply chain and seeks to encourage a debate to consider the fundamental elements of business performance measurement systems.

Keywords Business performance assessment • Trade facilitation • Customs • AEO program

1 Introduction

The rise in the international trade is essential for the growth of globalization. Nowadays trade barriers such as tariff measures have decreased and new transportation technologies have diminished the distance between customers and sellers, however trading costs obtain high. High trading costs negatively affect the companies' performance results. Customs affect the growth of international trade and worldwide market expansion. In global supply chain customs procedures have a significant impact for trading costs. Customs procedures are very complex and

D. Adomavičiūtė • D. Daujotaitė (✉)
Faculty of Economics and Finance Management, Mykolas Romeris University, Vilnius, Lithuania
e-mail: adomaviciute.d@gmail.com; dalidauj@takas.lt

M.H. Bilgin et al. (eds.), *Empirical Studies on Economics of Innovation, Public Economics and Management*, Eurasian Studies in Business and Economics 6,
DOI 10.1007/978-3-319-50164-2_3

sometimes they result an irregular movement of goods, delay and time costs. Trade facilitation is one of the ways to reduce trade costs, which remain high despite a sharp decline in the transport costs and improvements in technology. On the one side, there is a necessity for effective control of international supply chains, while on the other side there are increasing requirements for facilitation of legitimate trade.

In December 2013, World Trade Organization (WTO) adopted a Trade Facilitation Agreement (TFA). This Agreement includes provisions for shipping the consignments, customs clearance of goods and measures for effective cooperation between customs and other appropriate authorities. The WTO has highlighted that the harmonization and simplification of international trade procedures through the measures proposed under the TFA has the capacity to generate some 400 billion to 1 trillion US dollars to the world economy to reduce trade costs by around 10–15%, increasing revenue accumulation. The realization of these benefits would be fundamental to determining the TFA's significance to the global trade community, and more broadly reaffirm the WTO's capacity to deliver on global prosperity (Ndonga 2015).

Customs appreciate the current international trade challenges, in the context of increased security requirements and discuss how tools could be efficiently implemented in the way that does not wreak the ongoing trade facilitation attempts. Under the global trade conditions customs activities are important for the protection of the public interests and the international supply network's security. From 2008, the EU customs administrations began assessing the performance of the business companies, which seek to gain the status of the authorized economic operator (AEO). In order to perform this, the need of the attention to the trade flows and the aspects of the international trade challenges as security of supply network appeared.

The object of research is business performance assessment. The aim of research is to identify the most important and the most hazardous and essential areas of business performance assessment carrying out customs audit. During the research, the analysis and systematization of the scientific literature were combined. In this article has been concentrated in the analysis of the literature on business performance assessment issues and customs legislation.

2 The Concepts of the Business Performance Assessment: Literature Review

The scientific literature reports a wide range of the concepts of the business performance assessment and performance indicators. As a result, nowadays there is a relatively wide range of the procedures evaluation models in the field of the business performance assessment. It is very important to analyze the ongoing changes in the business environment as well as to look for the effective models of the business companies' activities assessment. The field of business performance measurement (BPM) connects closely many subjects as strategy and operations management, financial management, human resources management, marketing, organizational behavior, accounting, control and etc.

The definitions of BPM system show the variety of the subject and each definition provides a different approach on this concept. Several authors describe BPM system from a different perspective. Strategic performance measurement process begins in ownership, including the organization's primary objectives (Atkinson 1998). According to Bititci et al. (1997), a performance measurement system is the information system which is of critical importance to the effective functioning of the performance management system. A balanced scorecard was created by Kaplan and Norton (2001) and escribed from four different measurement perspectives: financial, internal, customer, and learning and growth. This framework was analyzed by many scientists and was designed to measure the enterprise's strategy and to report on leading indicators. Instead of measuring anything, firms should measure those things that directly relate to the firm's strategy (Kaplan and Norton 2001).

Economic Value Added (EVA) system, developed by the Stern Stewart Corporation, is more suitable for the company's financial performance evaluation. EVA is a specific financial performance measure and the basis for a wider performance assessment framework (Otley 1999). According to its makers, EVA is developed to give managers more information to make decisions and is most directly linked to the creation of shareholder value (Stern Stewart Corporation 2002).

Activity-based costing (ABC) was created to provide wider understanding how overhead costs should be distributed to customers or suppliers. ABC appreciates the company's activities costs and is a way of measuring which of the company's activities generates the biggest amount of revenues and as a result ensures insight into what is really providing added value (Meyer 2002).

It can be stated that the business performance measurement systems can be divided into two groups. One measurement system's group, as balanced scorecard created by Kaplan and Norton, focuses on strategic assessment aspect, another group concentrates on the implementation of operations. Many scientists have considered the importance of performance measurement systems and their influence on the manager's decisions and the success. According to the research by Franco-Santos et al. (2007), it has been identified that there exist two opinions about characteristics of BPM systems: 53% of the respondents refer important performance measures and 35% propose goals as attributes of BPM systems.

BPM systems have been developed and companies have used BPM systems for different reasons to improve enterprises activities' internal control that traditional accounting methods had not allowed. Several approaches for creating and managing BPM systems have developed with the balanced scorecard as the mainstream framework in use nowadays.

After analyzing the business enterprises activities assessment's models, it can be stated, that present-day business activities' assessment systems include more indicators related with policy issues of organizations. During the evaluation process the companies' policies, tasks and objectives can be coordinated together. Most of the authors highlight the importance of enterprises' strategy and long-term goals and after analyzing, it was identified that the substantial influence is done by applying of non-financial indicators.

3 Trade Facilitation's Impact of Global Value Chain and WCO Initiative for Customs Administrations

Trade facilitation is an essential policy for customs. The facilitation of customs procedures brings benefits to the economic operators and trading partners. Trade facilitation pursues to reduce trade costs, which include all costs suffered from a producer of goods to a final consumer (Anderson and van Wincoop 2004). They include the costs of tariffs, the cost of time and transportation, customs taxes and duties, which were grown the costs of trade.

Some of more recent models have involved differences in the productivity of firms (Melitz 2003). Other models have concentrated on fragmented production and pronounced that trade costs are particularly harmful for business (Yi 2010). Supply chain models declare that the parts and components of goods are made in many different countries and in this situation the transport and trading costs of goods go up significantly, while the traditional trade theory declares that each final goods is produced entirely within one country.

While goods are in cross national borders process multiple times, costs of time and transportation are cumulated of the value chain several times and it means that trade costs have a bigger deterrent influence on international value chain. If trade costs are sizeable, it is not worthy to split up production between different countries. It can be noted, that trade facilitation is essential to the viability of international value chains, focusing specialization in countries which have a comparative advantage.

Export of goods from one country to another is subject for discussion to all the possible interferences that are operating on international trade. The following equation summarizes the approach and amounts trade costs in *ad valorem* tariff equivalents, i.e., as a percentage of the price:

$$Trade\ costs\ ij = \frac{(Domestic\ trade\ ii \times Domestic\ trade\ jj)^{Y}}{(Exports\ ii \times Exports\ jj)} - 1 \qquad (1)$$

The subscript ij shows a flow from country i to j and γ is a parameter accounting for the heterogeneity of products. The amount of the trade cost is proportional made of the domestic trade cost and exports cost. In the year 2000, Novy (2013) evaluated that trade costs between Germany and the United States were equivalent to a 70% tariff, whereas they compounded 25% tariff between the United States and Canada and these costs make from cargo costs (costs of time and transportation), quotas,

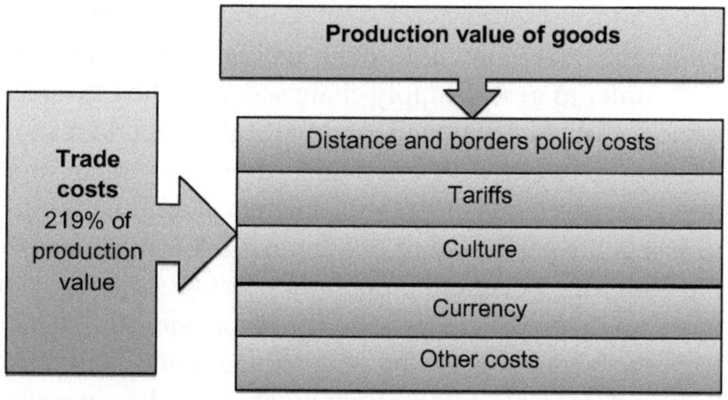

Fig. 1 Composition of trade costs. Source: compiled by the authors on the basis of Arvis et al. (2013)

cultural differences and other costs that can discourage trade process (World Trade Organization 2015).

Based on the Arvis et al. (2013) database, in 2010 trade costs in developing countries were equivalent to covering a 219% *ad valorem* tariff on international trade. This means that for each dollar it costs to produce a product, another US$2.19 will be supplemented with trade costs. Figure 1 indicates the dimension of trade costs and underlines their basic components. Production value of goods includes geographical features and borders policy costs, tariffs, culture, currency and other costs.

In order to reduce trade costs between countries and simplify international trade, on this point an important role pursue the World Customs Organisation (WCO). The WCO has established the Frameworks of Standards to Secure and Facilitate Global Trade (SAFE Framework) (World Customs Organization 2005) to trade facilitation and global supply chain security. The System includes two essential elements: customs to business enterprises and customs to customs. In 2015, the review of the SAFE Framework of Standards has been completed and now involves a new pillar customs to other government agencies which provides cooperation at three levels: multinational cooperation, cooperation within the government and cooperation between and among governments (World Customs Organization 2015). This instrument informed of present-day supply chain security standards and referred to a new approach about a closer collaboration between business and customs.

The WCO SAFE Framework of standards ensures the global standards for beginning an Authorized Economic Operator (AEO) program. The AEO program is acknowledged as a key driver for a customs and business partnership, transparent trading environment and in a wider context, leading to economic prosperity. Trade facilitation stimulates benefit both the governments and business community. The business community receives benefit by getting competitiveness in global markets due to decrease in delays and trade costs which are achieved with speedy movement of cargo across borders. In this way, supply chain security is strengthening while maintaining adequate customs controls and the facilitation of legitimate international trade balance. National customs administrations are capable to apply modern procedures to ensure efficient controls and at the same time promote to the economic development through increased international trade.

In order to global supply chain security, the European Commission implemented some measures developed to provide an effective response. These measures include the main concept with a new security management model. According the Community Customs Code (1992), the customs administrations of the EU countries started to assess the performance of the business companies, seeking to obtain the status of the authorized economic operator (AEO). AEO program proposes for customs an opportunity to divide its security responsibilities with the business sector. In this way, the business gets a lot of advantages and facilitation measures such as reduced levels of control, deferred payment, periodic reporting, reputational benefits and other benefit.

According the AEO program, it is important to assess the business companies' performance. The assessment of business enterprises' activities is carried out when the customs audit appreciates the activities of the economic operator and its compliance with the determinate parameters.

4 Analysis of Business Performance Assessment's Process in Customs Audit Field

Customs audit is a control process and the legal framework is being regulated by the Community Customs Code (1992). Customs audit can be attributed to effective trade facilitation measures because audit-based regulatory control allows for cargo flows quickly move across national borders. The customs audit examines business commercial registers and financial documents and in determining compliance with certain criteria, it is capable of delivering improvements of compliance.

After analyzing the scientific and practical literature, it is clear that the customs audit has features in common with other types of audit. According to the inspection area, it is closest to the audit of financial reports. However, it also features the operational audit as it carries out the verifications of enterprises' economic and commercial activities. Customs audit verifies the compliance with the Customs Code and other legal acts regulating customs activities and provisions—and these features are typical to the management audit. It can be stated that there is a correlation between the customs audit as well as the audit of financial reports, management audit and operational audit.

Customs auditors can take a variety of control forms, from random audits to verify compliance with regulatory requirements, to regularly scheduled audits with a focus on particular companies or industry sectors. What they all have in common is a legislative base that provides trained auditors with the power to enter premises and to inspect documents, either physically or electronically. Customs audit represents a move away from traditional approaches which focus on the physical inspection of cargo and the relatively ineffective documentary checks that restrict auditors to reviewing a very small percentage of a trader's overall transactions (Widdowson and Preece 2011). Customs audit rather is a focus on the business systems of the trader that generate and communicate transactions to the regulatory agencies, recognizing that good business systems with adequate controls will lead to high levels of regulatory compliance. In this context, risks to compliance can be mitigated if the audit process is used to identify enhancements to the trader's business systems and controls, thus working with the trader to improve future compliance.

Customs audit activities are designed to provide a clear indication of a company's level of compliance with regulatory requirements, and to highlight or confirm areas of potential risk where additional compliance or enforcement activity may need to be undertaken. However, customs audit results not only allow agencies to identify potentially unlawful conduct, but also to identify highly compliant traders that may be regarded as low-risk. Such entities can then be granted meaningful benefits such as 'fast-track' permissions and simplified procedures that contribute to facilitation outcomes while reducing costs to government. This concept forms the basis of the Authorized Economic Operator program that is being introduced by customs administrations worldwide. The AEO initiative, sometimes implemented as a 'trusted trader' program, is emerging as a central element of regulatory compliance management programs internationally.

A major difference between the conduct of customs audit and more traditional approaches to auditing is the skill set and knowledge required of the auditor. Customs audit has typically been based on a sound knowledge of customs law and technical skills in tariff, valuation and origin. Customs audit however requires an understanding of how a business operates and how this relates to its transactions with the broader spectrum of regulatory agencies. There is also an expectation from the trading community that the skill level of auditors is of an appropriately high standard, given that the customs audit process is designed to review their business systems and internal controls, assess the effectiveness of their compliance measures and make recommendations on enhancements or changes in order to improve future compliance.

Regarding supply chain logistics and trade data, the EU is one of the main players in the global field, near the United States and China, having a share of 15% in the world total (EU Customs Union 2015). In 2014, the value of EU trade with other countries near reached to 3.4€ trillion (1.70€ trillion for exports and 1.68€ trillion for imports). During 2014, near 278 million customs declarations were managed. 4.3 million business operators are registered in the customs Economic Operators Identification and Registration system (EORI) and carry out commercial activities related to importing and exporting goods in the role of consignee, declarant or representative (EU Customs Union 2015).

Using targeted management, customs has divided business into different categories. Steady efforts have been made to provide faster clearance services to businesses with a good record. According to Wu Hailong, the average waiting time for an export clearance was 1.5 h. Just over 99% of goods are now released within 24 h. The waiting time for an import clearance averages 17.9 h, with 64% of goods being released within 24 h. This improved efficiency has saved import and export companies nearly 80 billion Chinese Yuan (approximately 12.6 billion US dollars) in costs (World Custom Organization 2012).

The AEO status can be provided to economic operators who meet criteria, such as: (1) compliance with customs legislation and taxation rules and absence of criminal offences related to the economic activity, (2) appropriate record keeping, (3) financial solvency, (4) proven practical standards of competence or professional qualifications, and where relevant (5) appropriate security and safety measures. The number of valid AEO certificates in EU Member States was almost 14,000 at the end of 2015. The operators with the AEO status were involved in 54% of all imports and 68% of all exports and in 54% of transits (EU Customs Union 2015)

Essentially, an AEO is a member of the global trading community who is considered to comply with relevant regulatory requirements and standards. AEO's can generally expect to have their performance monitored, rather than having their activities scrutinized transaction by transaction. Their cargo is likely to be subjected to minimal intervention and they may be eligible to use simplified clearance processes. It is therefore vital that regulatory authorities ensure that assessments of traders' compliance levels are accurate. Customs audit is an essential tool in that regard.

Business performance assessment is relatively a new expression in the customs administrations activity and it requires managing challenges and for this cause, it is required to analyze this process. Therefore, it encourages creating a new business environment in the integrated market. Business environment consists of external and internal factors that influence and affect a business. Many new businesses work in a short-term. Customs auditors should find out the external and internal factors influencing the company's activities. After analyzing the models of the business performance evaluation, it has been identified that modern models include not only traditional indicators but also look at the operational procedures and the assessment of the whole global supply network.

According the AEO Guidelines (European Commission, Directorate-General Taxation and Customs Union 2012) the EU customs audit model, assessing the activities of business companies pursuing to achieve the AEO status, involve the following areas of enterprise's activities: evaluation of the available information about the company, company's accounting and logistics system, details about the requirements met, company's financial solvency, safety and security requirements. After performing the analysis of the EU model of the business enterprises activities' assessment and after analyzing theoretical models, it can be stated that the EU model does not include one of the important part of the indicators—the company's vision, strategy, objectives and related to these elements business risk's assessment. Recommended customs audit's model is depicted in Fig. 2.

The recommended model is complemented with new assessment part and appropriate performance measurement indicators: Internal control system (indicators to be evaluated: the control's environment, the business risk's assessment, the system of the information, control's activities, the monitoring of the control's procedures); business continuity management (indicators to be evaluated: an

Fig. 2 Model for assessment of business enterprises' activities

industry/a business sector, external and internal factors, the analysis of the most important financial indicators, a bankruptcy prediction, the analysis of the company's development).

The internal control system focuses on assuring achievement of an organization's objectives in operational effectiveness, appropriate financial reporting, and maintenance with laws, regulations and policies, and identifies the areas in which the greatest threat or risk of inaccuracies or loss exist. Business continuity management focuses on development and implementation of policies and strategies to assist a company manage a business disruption event. It is the capacity that assists in preventing and preparing from the impacts of a business disruption event. Disruption related risk includes physical and non-physical events such as financial crisis, natural disasters and other events. The analysis of the assessment's indicators in the model is performed by connecting these indicators with the company's vision, objectives and the implementation of the strategy.

An assessment area 'Responsibility and Profitability' is supplemented with new indicators of the property profitability, capital profitability and sales profitability. Following indicators are used to estimate a business's ability to earn income and manage costs. These additional indicators allow evaluating activities of companies deeply and wider. Also the developed and recommended model focuses on the realization of challenges today faced by the customs administrations. Further studies are required to investigate and create more specific models of trade facilitation that the flows of cargo will be conducted without disturbances.

5 Conclusions

Trade facilitation is an essential policy for customs. Simplification of customs procedures brings benefits to the economic operators and trading partners. Trade facilitation pursues to reduce trade costs, which include all costs suffered from a producer of goods to a final consumer. While goods are in cross national borders process multiple times, costs of time and transportation are cumulated of the value chain several times and it means that trade costs have a bigger deterrent influence on international value chain. In order to reduce trade costs between countries and simplify international trade, on this point an important role pursue the Frameworks of Standards to Secure and Facilitate Global Trade (SAFE Framework) (World Customs Organization 2005).

Customs audit can be attributed to effective trade facilitation measures because audit-based regulatory control allows for cargo flows quickly move across national borders. The assessment of business enterprises' activities is carried out when the customs audit appreciates the activities of the economic operator and its compliance with the determinate parameters. The customs audit examines business commercial registers and financial documents and in determining compliance with certain criteria, it is capable of delivering improvements of compliance.

After analyzing the theoretical business enterprises activities assessment's models and concepts, it can be stated, that present-day business activities' assessment systems include more indicators related with policy issues of organizations. During the evaluation process the companies' policies, tasks and objectives can be coordinated together. Most of the authors highlight the importance of enterprises' strategy and long-term goals and after analyzing, it was identified that the substantial influence is done by applying of non-financial indicators.

During the customs audit is very important to understand how a business operates and how this relates to its transactions with the other entities. There is also an expectation from the trading community that the skill level of auditors is of an appropriately high standard, given that the customs audit process is designed to review their business systems and internal controls, assess the effectiveness of their compliance measures and make recommendations on enhancements or changes in order to improve future compliance.

The analysis of the assessment's indicators in the recommended model is performed by connecting these indicators with the company's vision, objectives and the implementation of the strategy. Recommended customs audit's model was complemented with new assessment areas which allow evaluating in more detailed way.

References

Anderson, J. E., & van Wincoop, E. (2004). Trade costs. *Journal of Economic Literature, 42*(3), 691–751.

Arvis, J.-F., Duval, Y., Shepherd, B., & Utoktham, C. (2013). *Trade costs in the developing world: 1995–2010* (Policy Research Working Paper No. 6309). Washington, DC: World Bank.

Atkinson, A. A. (1998). Strategic performance measurement and incentive compensation. *European Management Journal, 16*(5), 552–561.

Bititci, U. S., Carrie, A. S., & Mcdevitt, L. (1997). Integrated performance measurement systems: A development guide. *International Journal of Operations and Production Management, 17* (5–6), 522–534.

Community Customs Code. (1992). *Council regulation (EEC) No 2913/92, European Commission* [online]. Accessed August 14, 2015, from http://eur-lex.europa.eu/LexUriServ/LexUriServ.do?uri=CONSLEG:1992R2913:20050511:LT

EU Customs Union. (2015). *Facts and figures*. EK. Accessed August 23, 2015, from http://ec.europa.eu/taxation_customs/resources/documents/customs/policy_issues/facts_and_figures/facts_figures_en.pdf

European Commission, Directorate-General Taxation and Customs union. (2012). *AEO guidelines* [pdf]. Accessed May 26, 2015, from http://ec.europa.eu/taxation_customs/resources/documents/customs/policy_issues/customs_security/aeo_guidelines2012_en.pdf

Franco-Santos, M., Kennerley, M., Micheli, P., Martinez, V., Mason, S., Marr, B., et al. (2007). Towards a definition of a business performance measurement system. *International Journal of Operations and Production Management, 27*(8), 784–801.

Kaplan, R. S., & Norton, D. P. (2001). *The strategy-focused organization*. Boston, MA: Harvard Business School Press.

Melitz, M. J. (2003). The impact of trade on intra-industry reallocations and aggregate industry productivity. *Econometrica, 71*(6), 1695–1725.

Meyer, M. W. (2002). Finding performance: The new discipline of management. In *Business performance measurement: Theory and practice*. Cambridge: Cambridge University Press.

Ndonga, D. (2015). *Single windows and trade facilitation. A tool for development*. Leiden: Wolters Kluwer.

Novy, D. (2013). Gravity redux: Measuring international trade costs with panel data. *Economic Inquiry, 51*(1), 101–121.

Otley, D. T. (1999). Performance management: A framework for management control systems research. *Management Accounting Research, 10*(4), 363–382.

Stern Stewart Corporation. (2002). *What is EVA?* Accessed November 21, 2014, from http://www.sternstewart.com/evaabout/whatis.shtml

Widdowson, D., & Preece, R. (2011). *Post clearance audit: Reference and implementation guide*. Washington, DC: World Bank. Accessed May 26, 2015, from http://siteresources.worldbank.org/INTRANETTRADE/Resources/239054-1305664393028/PostClearanceAudit_web.pdf

World Custom Organization. (2012, October). In the 21st century, economic globalization remains the main theme for world economic development. *WCO News*, N° 69 [Pdf]. Accessed June 07, 2016, from http://www.wcoomd.org/en/media/wco-news-magazine/~/media/CA4C731ECE724D46A3A99BA69F0CB13B.pdf

World Customs Organization. (2005). *Framework of standards to secure and facilitate global trade*. Brussels: World Customs Organization.

World Customs Organization. (2015). *Framework of standards to secure and facilitate global trade*. Brussels: World Customs Organization.

World Trade Organization. (2015). *World trade report 2015. Speeding up trade: Benefits and challenges of implementing the WTO Trade Facilitation* [pdf]. Accessed November 21, 2015, from https://www.wto.org/english/res_e/booksp_e/world_trade_report15_e.pdf

Yi, K.-M. (2010). Can multistage production explain the home bias in trade? *American Economic Review, 100*(1), 364–393.

The Determinants of Lending to Customers: Evidence from Italy Between 2008 and 2012

Franco Tutino, Giorgio Carlo Brugnoni, Concetta Colasimone, and Luca Riccetti

Abstract Over the period between 2008 and 2012 the loans to customers trend, the quality deterioration of the loans to customers portfolios and the interest return on the lending to customers activity showed in Italy relevant heterogeneities by bank size and by juridical connotation. This paper, based on financial statements data between 2008 and 2012 from about 500 Italian banks, adopts a panel data analysis to investigate if the heterogeneities showed in the loans to customers trend, in the quality deterioration of the loans to customers portfolios and in the interest return on the lending to customers activity are effectively significant and to what extent they could be explained by the differences that could be identified in the main features of the intermediation model adopted by banks. Moreover, this paper investigates the existing relationship between the loans to customers development and the credit quality deterioration and to what extent they both contribute to affect the economic return of the lending to customers activity.

Keywords Lending to customers • Credit quality • Income effects • Bank size • Juridical connotation • Intermediation model

1 Introduction

Over the period between 2008 and 2012, the lending to customers activity of Italian banks showed a significant slowdown and a relevant credit quality deterioration, affected by the global financial crisis, by the sovereign debt crisis and by the economic downturn which followed. Although basically widespread, this phenomenon took on significant heterogeneities by bank size and by juridical connotation. Smaller banks, cooperative intermediaries and popular banks showed a more intense loans to customers development in comparison to larger banks and commercial intermediaries, although they experienced a more relevant credit quality deterioration.

F. Tutino • G.C. Brugnoni (✉) • C. Colasimone • L. Riccetti
Department of Management, Sapienza University of Rome, Rome, Italy
e-mail: franco.tutino@uniroma1.it; giorgiocarlo.brugnoni@uniroma1.it; concetta.colasimone@uniroma1.it; luca.riccetti@uniroma1.it

M.H. Bilgin et al. (eds.), *Empirical Studies on Economics of Innovation, Public Economics and Management*, Eurasian Studies in Business and Economics 6,
DOI 10.1007/978-3-319-50164-2_4

This paper, based on financial statements data between 2008 and 2012 from about 500 Italian banks, investigates if the heterogeneities showed in the loans to customers trend and in the quality deterioration of the loans to customers portfolios are effectively significant and to what extent they could be explained by the differences that could be identified in the main features of the intermediation model adopted by banks. The underlying idea is that the credit supply policies adopted by banks are influenced also by the specificities of the intermediation models of reference and by the related underlying management strategies. Indeed, to different funding and lending policies, as well as to differentiated balance sheet assets and liabilities composition strategies, could correspond different vulnerabilities to exogenous factors and different financial and capital constraints on the credit supply. Moreover, this paper investigates the existing relationship between the loans to customers trend and the credit quality deterioration, in order to verify if and how to more dynamic loans to customers developments corresponds a more relevant credit quality deterioration and to what extent the credit quality of the loans to customers portfolios matter in conditioning the loans to customers trend itself. Finally, the research looks also at the economic return of the lending to customers activity, in order to investigate its heterogeneity by bank size and by juridical connotation, to what extent it could be explained by the main intermediation model features and how it results conditioned by the loans to customers development and the by credit quality deterioration.

The paper is structured as follows. The next section reviews the literature, identifying the significance of our research and its main contributions. Third section illustrates the dataset and the sample of banks analyzed. Fourth section shows the main descriptive empirical evidence by bank size and by juridical connotation—focusing on the loans to customers trend, on the quality deterioration of the loans to customers portfolios, on the interest return on the lending to customers activity and on the main the intermediation model features between 2008 and 2012—and formulates the hypotheses of research to be verified through the econometrical estimations. Fifth section specifies the methodology adopted. Sixth section reports and comments the results of the econometrical estimations. The last section concludes the paper, summarizing the main findings and expressing some closing remarks. Luca Riccetti's contribution to this paper regards the application of the econometrical techniques described in section "Methodology".

2 Literature Review, Significance of the Research and Main Contribution

The impacts of the global financial crisis, of the sovereign debt crisis and of the economic downturn which followed on the lending activity contributed to increase researching interests in order to investigate the main features and determinant factors. Some studies analyse the role played by the demand and supply factors in affecting the loans to customers development (Panetta and Signoretti 2010; Del Giovane et al. 2010, 2011, 2013; De Bonis et al. 2014). Other contributions investigate the significance of certain specific banking features and intermediation model characteristics (as bank size, capitalization, funding, liquidity, risk, profitability, customer relationship) in affecting the banking credit supply policies and the loans to customers trend (Albertazzi and Marchetti 2010; Bonaccorsi di Patti and Sette 2012; Kapan and Minoiu 2013; Gambacorta and Mistrulli 2014; Miani et al. 2012; De Mitri et al. 2010; Albertazzi et al. 2012; Bofondi et al. 2013; Felici et al. 2012; Morelli et al. 2013; Albertazzi and Bottero 2013; Albertazzi and Bottero 2014; Altunbas et al. 2010; Gambacorta and Marques-Ibanez 2011; Tutino et al. 2013, 2014). Finally, other contributions look more in details at the banking intermediation models features in terms of impacts on risk, stability and performance (Altunbas et al. 2011; Ayadi et al. 2011, 2012; Chiaramonte et al. 2013; Cosma and Gualandri 2014). Table 1 summarizes the main investigated aspects by the studies reviewed. Overall, the research significantly develops the studies conducted in Tutino et al. (2013), in Tutino et al. (2014) and in Brugnoni (2014).

Although the empirical literature on the lending to customers activity and of the banking intermediation models is doubtless ample—confirming the relevance of the subject—the study of the loans to customers trend, of the quality deterioration of the loans to customers portfolios and of the interest return on the lending to customers activity, looking at the main heterogeneities by bank size and at the significance of the relationship with the main banking intermediation model features, seems to be absolutely interesting and need to be deepen furthermore, especially dealing with the Italian banking system. Understanding how the recent financial crisis affected the lending to customers activity, investigating the main differences showed among banks of different size and characterized by different intermediation model features, could help to identify the main constraints and determinant factors which effectively affected the lending to customers activity in Italy over the global financial crisis, the sovereign debt crisis and the economic downturn which followed, giving some elements possibly useful to think over the development of banking strategies to give new impulse to the real economy financing. In particular, this research aims to contribute also to the academic and the institutional debate on the identification of a way of doing banking activities able to combine the fundamental role of banking intermediaries in financing the real economy with the necessary stability of banks and of the financial and banking system more in general.

This paper differs from other contributions in the literature for the size, the composition and the relevant representativeness of the sample, for the specific focus on the bank size and on the juridical connotation and for the significance of the period analysed and of the specific focus on the Italian banking system. About the sample—size, composition, representativeness—refer to section "Data and Sample". As for the bank size factor, is identified according to the specific classification criteria designed by the Bank of Italy (Table 2), while in the literature it is generally identified by the total assets volume (Albertazzi and Bottero 2013, 2014) or by its natural logarithm (Altunbas et al. 2010, 2011; Gambacorta and Marques-Ibanez 2011;

Table 1 Literature review: synthesis of the main aspects investigated

Loans to customers development: demand and supply factors							
	Period of reference			Investigated aspects		Determinant factors	
	Pre-crisis	Global financial crisis 2007–2009	Sovereign debt crisis 2011–2012	Credit trend	Cost of credit	Demand factors	Supply factors
Panetta and Signoretti (2010)		X		X	X	X	X
Del Giovane et al. (2010)		X		X	X	X	X
Del Giovane et al. (2011)		X		X	X	X	X
Del Giovane et al. (2013)		X	X	X	X	X	X
De Bonis et al. (2014)		X	X	X	X	X	X

Loans to customers development and specific banking features

	Period of reference			Investigated aspects		Determinant factors						
	Pre-crisis	Global financial crisis 2007–2009	Sovereign debt crisis 2011–2012	Credit trend	Cost of credit	Bank size	Capitalisation	Funding	Liquidity	Risk	Profitability	Customer relationship
Albertazzi and Marchetti (2010)		X		X		X	X		X			
Bonaccorsi di Patti and Sette (2012)		X		X	X		X	X	X	X		
Kapan and Minoiu (2013)		X		X			X	X	X			
Gambacorta and Mistrulli (2014)		X			X	X	X		X			X
Miani et al. (2012)		X			X		X					
De Mitri et al. (2010)		X		X		X						X
Albertazzi et al. (2012)			X	X	X	X						
Bofondi et al. (2013)			X			X	X	X		X		
Felici et al. (2012)		X		X		X						

(continued)

Table 1 (continued)

Loans to customers development and specific banking features												
	Period of reference			Investigated aspects		Determinant factors						
	Pre-crisis	Global financial crisis 2007–2009	Sovereign debt crisis 2011–2012	Credit trend	Cost of credit	Bank size	Capitalisation	Funding	Liquidity	Risk	Profitability	Customer relationship
Morelli et al. (2013)			X	X						X		
Albertazzi and Bottero (2013)		X		X		X	X	X	X	X	X	
Albertazzi and Bottero (2014)		X		X		X	X	X	X	X	X	
Altunbas et al. (2010)	X			X		X	X		X	X		
Gambacorta and Marques-Ibanez (2011)		X		X		X	X	X	X	X	X	

Intermediation model, risk, performance and stability of banks									
	Period of reference			Investigated aspects			Determinant factors		
	Pre-crisis	Global financial crisis 2007–2009	Sovereign debt crisis 2011–2012	Profitability	Risk	Stability	Bank size	Juridical connotation	Intermediation model
Altunbas et al. (2011)		X					X		X
Ayadi et al. (2011)		X		X	X				
Ayadi et al. (2012)		X		X	X				X
Chiaramonte et al. (2013)	X	X				X	X	X	X
Cosma and Gualandri (2014)		X	X						X

Source: Own elaboration

Table 2 Bank size classification

		Bank of Italy criteria	
			Average intermediated funds[a]
BANK SIZE	Larger banks	Major banks	More than 60 billion/€
		Large banks	Between 26 and 60 billion/€
	Medium banks	Medium banks	Between 9 and 26 billion/€
	Smaller banks	Small banks	Between 1.3 and 9 billion/€
		Minor banks	Less than 1.3 billion/€

Source: Bank of Italy (2011)
[a]Weighted average of the intermediated funds from the last five quarter before the valuation date, assigning weight 1 to the final quarters and weight 2 to the middle quarters. The lower weighting assigned to the final quarters of the year enables to mitigate the influence of distortions related to the typical seasonality of the data in December (Bank of Italy 2011). Volume of intermediated funds means volume of total assets

Bofondi et al. 2013; Chiaramonte et al. 2013). As for the juridical connotation, our analysis takes into account and compares all the three different juridical typologies of banks existing in the Italian Banking System (*commercial banks, popular banks* and *cooperative banks*). Complete studies on the lending to customers activity and on the main intermediation model features by juridical connotation are not widespread. Regarding the relevance of the period analysed, years between 2008 and 2012 look quite significant as they result affected by the global financial crisis, by the sovereign debt crisis and by the economic downturn which followed. In particular: between 2008 and 2009 the global financial crisis developed, with relevant effects on the Italian real economy and on the lending to customers activity of banks; in 2010 the loans to customers trend moderately increased, reflecting the slowdown of the financial turbulences and a slow economic recovery; in 2011 and 2012 the effects of the sovereign debt crisis, the economic downturn which followed and the consequent credit quality deterioration caused a significant credit tightening. Finally the specific focus on the Italian banking system in analyzing the loans to customers development by bank size and by juridical connotation takes on a significant relevance for different reasons. First of all, as the Italian financial system is notoriously bank-based, distortions in the credit supply typically have sizeable impacts on the real economy (Gambacorta and Mistrulli 2014). Second, the structure of the Italian banking system is characterized by a significant heterogeneity by bank size—several small local banks coexist with few larger and multi-national banks—and by juridical connotation—several cooperative banks, fewer popular and commercial banks. Moreover, as the lending activity of banks are inevitably strongly affected by the country specific economic environment and by the specificities of the financial and banking system of reference, looking at a specific banking system—in this case the Italian one– enables to identify relevant specificities, that could be more hard to let emerge by transnational analyses. The underlying idea is that we could positively contribute to the international literature, not necessary by analyzing transnational samples or by comparing different banking systems, but also analyzing in deep a certain reality, identifying its relevant specificities, strengths and weaknesses and spreading the main evidence at an international level, sharing in this way the possible best practices identified.

3 Data and Sample

The analysis is based on individual financial statements data from around 500 Italian banks in the period between 2008 and 2012. Data are extracted from ABI Bilanci FAST. This database, supplied by the Italian Banking Association, collects individual and consolidated financial statements data from almost all the banks and the banking groups belonging to the Italian banking system, except for data related to branches of foreign banks. In order to conduct the analysis by bank size and by juridical connotation, the sample is divided into three size classes (larger banks, medium banks, smaller banks)—according to the classification criteria designed by the Bank of Italy (Table 2)[1]—and into the three different juridical typologies of banks existing in the Italian Banking System (commercial banks, popular banks and cooperative banks). The sample is designed considering the same intermediaries throughout the years analyzed, trying to manage as best as possible any event of change (mergers and acquisitions, placement under special administration,[2] transformations from banks into financial intermediaries[3]). In this way, it results basically homogeneous over time and, therefore, more significant for the purposes of the research. Moreover, we pay particular attention to ensure that the incidence of the different classes of banks in terms of the number of intermediaries included in the sample would be as consistent as possible with respect to the Italian banking system. Table 3 reports information about the composition and the representativeness of the sample. Table 4 splits the composition of the sample by bank size. Table 5 splits the composition of the sample by juridical connotation. The sample represents between 68.21 and 79.24% of the Italian banking system in terms of number of intermediaries, between 75.93 and 83.83% in terms of loans to customers volume and between 60.42 and 75.73% in terms of total assets volume. The

[1]From 2012 the methodology adopted by the Bank of Italy to classify banks by size has been changed, moving from an individual approach to a consolidated one. To classify the sample by bank size, the classification of banks by size in 2012 followed t. The robustness of this simplification has been verified for each bank of the sample applying the criteria specified in Table 3.1 at the average of the total assets of banks between 2012 and 2011 and between 2011 and 2010, analysing and modifying each incongruity.

[2]As specified by the article 70 of the Legislative Decree 385/1993 and subsequent amendments (the Italian Consolidated Law on Banking) among the norms on the crisis management procedures (Title IV).

[3]As specified by the article 107 of the Legislative Decree 385/1993 and subsequent amendments (the Italian Consolidated Law on Banking) among the norms on the entities operating in the financial sector (Title V).

Table 3 Sample: composition and representativeness

	Sample	Italian banking system	Sample representativeness[a] (%)	Sample	Italian banking system	Sample representativeness[a] (%)
	2012			2009		
Number of banks	500	631	79.24	500	712	70.22
Loans to customers (billion/€)[b]	1551	2042	75.93	1533	1848	82.93
Total assets (billion/€)[b]	2544	4211	60.42	2795	3691	75.73
	2011			2008		
Number of banks	500	665	75.19	500	724	69.06
Loans to customers (billion/€)[b]	1560	2018	77.32	1517	1809	83.83
Total assets (billion/€)[b]	2553	4035	63.29	2722	3635	74.88
	2010			2007		
Number of banks	500	689	72.57	500	733	68.21
Loans to customers (billion/€)[b]	1569	1994	78.69	1371	1724	79.50
Total assets (billion/€)[b]	2525	3759	67.17	2413	3332	72.43

Source: Own elaboration on data from *ABI Bilanci Fast*

[a]Ratio, respectively, between the number of banks included in the sample and the total number of banks in the banking system and between the total assets volume of the banks from the sample and the total assets volume of the banks of the banking system

[b]Aggregated data on the loans to customers and on the total asset regarding the Italian banking system as a whole—elaborated on data from the *Statistical Database* managed by the Bank of Italy available online on http://www.bancaditalia.it/statistiche/basi-dati/bds/index.html

Table 4 Sample: composition by bank size

	2012		2011		2010		2009		2008		2007	
	Number	%	Number	%	Number	%	Number	%	Number	%	Number	%
	Sample											
Larger banks	10	2	10	2	10	2	10	2	10	2	10	2
Medium banks	21	4	21	4	21	4	21	4	21	4	21	4
Smaller banks	469	94	469	94	469	94	469	94	469	94	469	94
Total	500	100	500	100	500	100	500	100	500	100	500	100
	Italian banking system											
Larger banks	13	2	14	2	15	2	19	3	19	3	20	3
Medium banks	27	4	27	4	30	4	31	4	32	4	35	5
Smaller banks	588	93	624	94	644	93	662	93	673	93	678	92
Total	628[a]	100	665	100	689	100	712	100	724	100	733	100

[a]The number of total banks at 31 December 2012 differs from 631 cause for the intermediaries it was not possible to identify a specific size class cause they were registered but not yet operating

Table 5 Sample: composition by juridical connotation

	2012		2011		2010		2009		2008		2007	
	Number	%	Number	%	Number	%	Number	%	Number	%	Number	%
	Sample											
Commercial banks	106	21	106	21	106	21	106	21	106	21	106	21
Popular banks	29	6	29	6	29	6	29	6	29	6	29	6
Cooperative banks	365	73	365	73	365	73	365	73	365	73	365	73
Total	500	100	500	100	500	100	500	100	500	100	500	100
	Italian banking system											
Commercial banks	199	32	216	32	235	34	252	35	252	35	252	34
Popular banks	37	6	37	6	38	6	38	5	39	5	39	5
Cooperative banks	395	63	412	62	416	60	422	59	433	60	442	60
Total	631	100	665	100	689	100	712	100	724	100	733	100

composition of the sample by bank size and by juridical connotation results enough coherent with the Italian banking system composition.

4 Main Descriptive Evidence and Hypotheses of Research

4.1 Credit Trend

Between 2008 and 2012, the trend of loans to customers slowed down significantly, in spite of a slight recovery in 2010 (Table 6). The slowdown in the trend of loans to customers emerged as particularly intense in 2009, when the effects of the financial crisis manifested more significantly on the real economy (Bank of Italy 2010). After a slight recovery in 2010, reflecting the increased demand of loans cause of the bettered conditions of the productive sector (Bank of Italy 2011), the lending to customers activity of banks contracted in 2011 and in 2012, mainly cause of the ongoing economic downturn, deepen by the negative effects of the sovereign debt crisis on the financial system and on the real economy (Bank of Italy 2012a, 2013a). Looking at the loans to customers development by bank size and by juridical connotation (Table 6), interesting heterogeneities emerge. In 2009, while larger intermediaries and commercial banks registered a contraction of the loans to customers, smaller banks, cooperative intermediaries and popular banks continued to perform positively in terms of lending to customers. In 2010, in a context of generalized recovery of the lending to customers development, smaller banks, cooperative intermediaries and popular banks still registered higher growth rates than larger banks and commercial intermediaries, although showing a decreasing performance in comparison to the previous years. In 2011 and in 2012, while larger intermediaries registered a significant contraction of the loans to customers, smaller banks performed better in terms of lending to customers, although at growth rate close to stability and significantly lower than in the past. Cooperative banks performed better than commercial banks in 2011, while they registered a contraction in 2012, although less significant than commercial banks. On the contrary, popular banks registered a higher contraction than commercial banks in 2011, while they performed better than commercial banks and cooperative intermediaries in 2012. More in general, over the period between 2008 and 2012, smaller intermediaries, cooperative banks and popular intermediaries registered a positive loans to customers trend, while larger intermediaries and commercial banks registered a significant contraction. Overall, the heterogeneities by bank size and by juridical connotation emerged in the loans to customers development determined a significant change in the market share. Comparing 2008 with 2012, smaller banks, cooperative intermediaries and popular banks registered a significant increase in their market share, while larger intermediaries and commercial banks decreased.

Table 6 Loans to customers trend

	Loans to customers growth rate[a]						Market share[b]				
	2012	2011	2010	2009	2008	2008–2012	2012	2011	2010	2009	2008
Total	−0.60	−0.55	2.33	1.07	10.64	2.25	100.00	100.00	100.00	100.00	100.00
Larger banks	−0.37	−2.31	0.44	−0.18	10.97	−2.42	56.77	56.63	57.66	58.74	59.48
Medium banks	−2.94	2.99	5.87	−1.06	11.34	4.71	19.08	19.54	18.87	18.24	18.64
Smaller banks	0.77	0.95	4.35	6.29	9.18	12.83	24.15	23.82	23.47	23.02	21.89
Commercial banks	−1.09	−0.72	1.32	−1.56	11.71	−2.03	70.62	70.97	71.09	71.81	73.73
Popular banks	1.75	−1.20	4.59	11.63	5.77	17.38	17.93	17.52	17.64	17.26	15.62
Cooperative banks	−0.49	2.42	6.26	6.16	10.44	14.97	8.25	8.24	8.00	7.71	7.34

Source: Own elaboration on data from *ABI Bilanci Fast*

[a] $\Delta\%LC_t = \frac{\text{Loans to customers}_t - \text{Loans to customers}_{t-1}}{\text{Loans to customers}_{t-1}}$ (for further details see section "Methodology")

[b] $\Delta\%LC_t = \frac{\text{Loans to customers}_{it}}{\text{Loans to customers}_{t-1}}$ i = larger banks, medium banks, smaller banks, commercial banks, popular banks, cooperative banks, total

Data on the loans to customers trend basically show a significant heterogeneity by banks size and juridical connotation. In order to conquer higher market shares and not to endanger their customer relationship and strong local roots, smaller intermediaries, cooperative banks and popular intermediaries might have adopted less restrictive lending policies, although in a period of general financial and economic distress, then exposing themselves to greater current and prospective credit quality deterioration credit risks. Therefore, this evidence lead to investigate also about the credit quality deterioration over the period analysed and about its possible heterogeneity by banks size and by juridical connotation. Indeed, banking intermediaries which between 2008 and 2012 adopted more expansive credit policies—smaller banks, cooperative intermediaries and popular banks—could have registered a more relevant credit quality deterioration.

4.2 Credit Quality

Data on the gross deteriorated loans to customers incidence and on the gross loans to customers rate of deterioration between 2008 and 2012 show a relevant credit quality deterioration, with significant heterogeneities by bank size and by juridical connotation (Table 7). The gross deteriorated loans to customers incidence reached 12.70% in 2012 from 5.24% in 2008, with significant increases between 2008 and 2009—when the effects of the global financial crisis caused a deep economic distress—and between 2011 and 2012—when the effects of the sovereign debt crisis contribute to deepen the economic downturn—while in 2010 the general economic recovery could have contributed to partially slowdown the quality deterioration of the loans to customers. These evidence emerge also looking at data on the gross loans to customers rate of deterioration, which confirms a more relevant credit quality deterioration between 2008 and 2009 and between 2011 and 2012.[4] As for data by bank size and by juridical connotation, interesting heterogeneities emerge. Between 2008 and 2012 smaller banks and cooperative intermediaries experienced a higher credit quality deterioration than larger banks and commercial intermediaries, both in terms of gross deteriorated loans to customers incidence and gross loans to customers rate of deterioration. About popular banks, although they show a gross deteriorated loans to customers incidence basically similar to commercial banks, they experienced a higherloans to customers rate of deterioration, between cooperative banks and commercial banks.

[4]Looking at the credit quality deterioration between 2011 and 2012, however, we need to take into account that it could also reflect the possible increase of the volume of past due exposures in comparison to 2011, cause of the change in the requisites for their identification. Indeed, from 2012 all the credit exposures have to be classified as past due after 90 days of delay, while before 2012 for some kind of credit exposure the limit was 180 days.

Table 7 Credit quality

	Gross deteriorated loans to customers incidence[a]						Gross loans to customers rate of deterioration[b]					
	2012	2011	2010	2009	2008	2008–2012	2012	2011	2010	2009	2008	2008–2012
Total	12.70	10.11	8.78	7.69	5.24	8.91	2.91	1.48	1.45	2.73	0.63	8.55
Larger banks	11.92	9.63	8.35	7.13	4.38	8.28	2.56	1.25	1.40	2.91	−0.44	7.93
Medium banks	13.27	10.56	9.33	8.50	6.82	9.70	2.75	1.75	1.54	1.76	2.98	7.94
Smaller banks	14.08	10.89	9.40	8.48	6.22	9.81	3.89	1.82	1.48	3.07	1.54	10.82
Commercial banks	12.73	10.20	8.84	7.62	5.08	8.89	2.80	1.49	1.50	2.62	0.43	8.20
Popular banks	12.16	9.49	8.48	7.87	5.42	8.69	3.17	1.12	1.10	3.58	1.21	9.62
Cooperative banks	13.56	10.59	8.96	8.01	6.55	9.54	3.39	2.13	1.66	2.12	1.45	10.01

Source: Own elaboration on data from *ABI Bilanci Fast*

[a] $\Delta\%GDLC_t = \frac{\text{Gross deteriorated loans to customers}_t}{\text{Gross loans to customers}_{t-1}}$ (for further details see section “Methodology”)

[b] $\%GDLC_t = \frac{\text{Gross deteriorated loans to customers}_t - \text{Gross deteriorated loans to customers}_{t-1}}{\text{Gross inbonis loans to customers}_{t-1}}$ (for further details see section “Methodology”)

Data on the credit quality between 2008 and 2012 confirm that banks which performed more intensely in terms of lending to customers trend—smaller banks, cooperative intermediaries and popular banks—experienced a more significant credit quality deterioration. At the same time, however, the credit quality deterioration which interested smaller banks, cooperative banks and popular banks could have negatively influenced their credit strategies in order to adopt more prudent and restrictive credit policies, causing a contraction of the credit development. Similar evidence emerge also in Di Battista and Nieri (2012): banks which between 2007 and 2008 registered a loans to customers development above the average, in 2010 showed a more relevant deterioration. Therefore, the expansive lending policies adopted by the more dynamic banks in lending to customers may have been destabilizing in the mid-long term in terms of excessive risk taking, affecting banks strategies in the direction of more restrictive lending policies. Consequently, it is possible that banks could be forced to slow down their lending to customers in order to deal with the excessive risks taken during the financial crisis. Indeed, as stated by Altunbas et al. (2010), all other factors being equal, the deterioration of credit exposures leads to an inevitable negative impact on the credit supply, since it reduces profits and erodes banks' capital. Moreover, for banks perceived as more risky, it may be difficult to raise unsecured debt or equity funds to finance their lending activities or to meet capital requirements, thereby making credit providing more difficult and costly. The Bank of Italy (2013a, p. 212) highlights that "The growth rate of lending is negatively correlated with the default rate. Declining credit quality entails larger loan losses, which reduces profitability and consequently the profits that can be set aside to increase banks' capital. An increase in non-performing loans also reinforces banks' risk aversion, prompting them to adopt more prudent lending policies in order to limit further losses in the future". A first evidence of this phenomenon could be caught looking at the dynamic of the loans to customers by smaller banks, by cooperative banks and by popular banks separately between 2009 and 2010 and between 2011 and 2012. While until 2010 these banks provided loan to customers at a more intense rate, from 2011 they registered a relevant slowdown. The banks which showed a more dynamic lending activity over the first part of the crisis, may have changed their lending policies in a more restrictive direction in the second part of the crisis. Evidence from the Regional Bank Lending Survey (RBLS)[5] confirm that, while in the period immediately after

[5]The *Bank Lending Survey* (BLS) is conducted quarterly by the Bank of Italy on behalf of the Eurosystem on a sample of the eight major Italian banking groups, accounting for more than two-thirds of the Italian lending market. It provides qualitative information on the supply and demand factors affecting the loans to customers trend. The *Regional bank Lending Survey* (RBLS) is conducted every 6 months by the Bank of Italy on a sample of round 400 Italian banks, accounting for more than 80% of the Italian lending market and more representative of the composition of the Italian banking system by bank size. Therefore, it enables to deepen the analysis of the credit supply and demand factors also by bank size. For further information on the *Bank Lending Survey* (BLS) refer to the methodological notes available on (www.bancaditalia.it/statistiche/tematiche/moneta-intermediari-finanza/intermediari-finanziari/indagine-credito-bancario), to Berg et al. (2005) and to European Central Bank (2003).

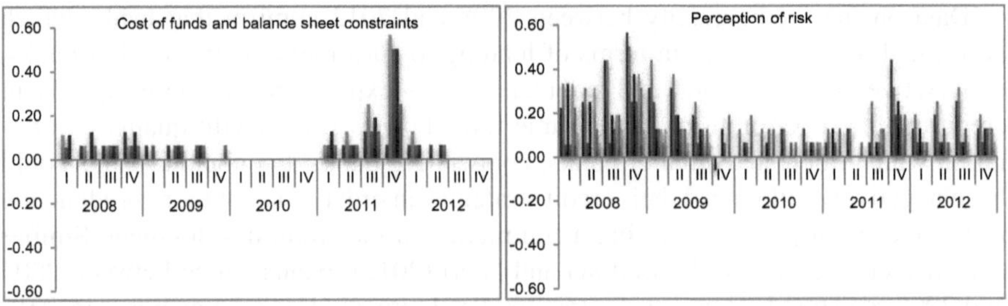

Fig. 1 Credit supply: determinant factors (diffusion index)[a]. Source: Own elaboration on results for Italy from the *Bank lending Survey* (BLS), available online (www.bancaditalia.it/statistiche/tematiche/moneta-intermediari-finanza/intermediari-finanziari/indagine-credito-bancario/index.html). [a]The diffusion index is the weighted average of the numerical values assigned to the different possible qualitative answers, with weights equal to the frequency observed for any possible answer. For questions concerning the supply of credit the values assigned to the qualitative answers are the following: 1 = tightened considerably, 0.5 = tightened somewhat, 0 = basically unchanged, −0.5 = eased somewhat, −1 = eased considerably

the financial crisis started in 2008 the more restrictive lending policies mainly interested larger intermediaries, from the second half of 2011 the tightening of the supply criteria have been more similar by bank size, looking relatively more relevant for smaller banks (Bank of Italy 2012b). In particular, while larger banks look to have eased progressively their credit supply conditions, smaller banks showed more caution in providing loans to customers. If in 2011 larger intermediaries suffered more for the turbulences caused by the sovereign debt crisis, mainly cause of their higher recourse to the international wholesale funding markets, the slowdown in the loans to customers trend registered in 2011 and 2012—more homogeneous by bank size and by juridical connotation—could reflect also the more generalized deterioration of the credit quality, which interested more or less intensively all the categories of banks. In 2012, indeed, the more restrictive credit supply conditions would be mainly due to perception of risk in a period characterised by a progressive deterioration of the economy, in particular for smaller banks (Bank of Italy 2013b). Moreover, data from the results for Italy of the *Bank Lending Survey (BLS)* regarding the main determinant factor affecting banks' credit supply (Fig. 1), confirm the significance of the perception of risk in conditioning the tightening of the lending supply policies adopted by banks, in particular in the first part of the crisis (2008–2009) and in the second one (2011–2012). The relevance of deepening the analysis of the relationship between the loans to customers development and the credit quality deterioration emerges clearly, in order to verify, from one side, if a more intense credit quality deterioration effectively followed a more dynamic credit development, on the other side, the significance of the credit quality deterioration in affecting the lending policies adopted by banks and, consequently, the loans to customers trend.

4.3 Income Effects

The slowdown in the loans to customers trend and the credit quality deterioration emerged between 2008 and 2012 inevitably had income effects. From one side, the slowdown in the loans to customers development and the generalized decrease in the interest rates caused a relevant negative impact on income through a contraction of the interest income from the lending to customers activity. From the other side, the credit quality deterioration negatively affected the income statement through the increasing impairment losses on the credit exposures in portfolio.

Data on the net interest return on loans to customers show a significant decrease between 2008 and 2012 and a relevant heterogeneity by bank size and by juridical connotation (Table 8). Smaller banks and cooperative banks show higher interest return on loans to customers than larger banks and commercial banks, both on average and each year considered separately. About popular banks, they show lower returns than cooperative and commercial banks, except for 2012, when they performed better then commercial banks, but worse than cooperative banks. Looking at its main component, the gross interest return on loans to customers is always higher for smaller banks and cooperative intermediaries than larger intermediaries and commercial banks, while the cost of credit risk on loans to customers is generally higher for larger intermediaries and commercial banks than for smaller banks and cooperative intermediaries.

These evidence suggest that smaller banks and cooperative intermediaries could have registered higher returns, possibly cause of higher interest rates charged on the loans to customers, but also thanks to lower loans loss provisions. However, as these categories of banks also experienced a more significant credit quality deterioration, this evidence lead to think that these banks maybe do not properly charged their income statement with loans loss provisions as larger intermediaries did. Overall, data on the income effects from the lending to customers activity between 2008 and 2012 show that banks which performed more intensely in terms of lending to customers trend—smaller banks, cooperative intermediaries and popular banks—and which, at the same time, experienced more significant credit quality deterioration, registered higher returns.

4.4 Intermediation Model Features

Data on the main intermediation model features of banks (Table 9) basically show that smaller banks and cooperative banks are generally characterized by the prevalence of the loans to customers among the investments and of the direct funding among liabilities, by more equilibrated financial structures (lower dependence on the interbank market as a source of funding, lower loans to customers to funding ratio, higher leverage ratio), by the prevalence of the net interest income among the operating income. Popular banks, however, show intermediation model features more similar to the ones of the commercial banks. The loans to customers and the direct funding represent a lower

Table 8 Income effects

	Net interest return on loans to customers[a]					
	2012	2011	2010	2009	2008	2008–2012
Total	1.47	2.51	2.14	2.71	5.12	2.79
Larger banks	1.24	2.26	2.01	2.56	5.04	2.62
Medium banks	1.45	2.76	2.35	2.76	5.05	2.88
Smaller banks	2.03	2.92	2.27	3.08	5.40	3.14
Commercial banks	1.34	2.47	2.16	2.96	5.07	2.80
Popular banks	1.66	2.40	2.06	1.51	4.99	2.52
Cooperative banks	2.23	3.09	2.11	2.80	6.00	3.25

	Gross interest return on loans to customers[b]						Cost of risk on loans to customers[c]					
	2012	2011	2010	2009	2008	2008–2012	2012	2011	2010	2009	2008	2008–2012
Total	2.95	3.38	2.89	3.59	5.79	3.72	−1.48	−0.87	−0.76	−0.87	−0.67	−0.93
Larger banks	2.70	3.21	2.81	3.47	5.67	3.57	−1.46	−0.96	−0.80	−0.92	−0.62	−0.95
Medium banks	2.91	3.45	3.07	3.61	5.83	3.78	−1.46	−0.69	−0.72	−0.86	−0.78	−0.90
Smaller banks	3.57	3.72	2.97	3.86	6.09	4.04	−1.54	−0.79	−0.70	−0.78	−0.69	−0.90
Commercial banks	2.84	3.38	2.95	3.85	5.71	3.75	−1.50	−0.90	−0.79	−0.89	−0.64	−0.94
Popular banks	3.12	3.15	2.75	2.44	5.83	3.46	−1.46	−0.75	−0.69	−0.94	−0.84	−0.94
Cooperative banks	3.61	3.87	2.72	3.40	6.53	4.03	−1.38	−0.78	−0.61	−0.60	−0.53	−0.78

Source: Own elaboration on data from *ABI Bilanci Fast*

[a] $NIRLC_t = \frac{\text{Loans to customers interest income}_t - \text{Loans to customers loss provisions}_t}{\frac{\text{Loans to customers}_t + \text{Loans to customers}_{t-1}}{\text{Loans to customers}_{t-1}}}$ (for further details see section "Methodology")

[b] $GIRLC_t = \frac{\text{Loans to customers interest income}_t}{\frac{\text{Loans to customers}_t + \text{Loans to customers}_{t-1}}{\text{Loans to customers}_{t-1}}}$

[c] $CR_t = \frac{\text{Loans to customers loss provisions}_t}{\frac{\text{Loans to customers}_t + \text{Loans to customers}_{t-1}}{\text{Loans to customers}_{t-1}}}$

Table 9 Intermediation model features

	Assets composition						Liabilities composition					
	Loans to customers/Total assets						Direct funding[a]/Total assets					
	2012	2011	2010	2009	2008	Average 2008–2012	2012	2011	2010	2009	2008	Average 2008–2012
Total	60.95	61.10	62.13	54.85	55.73	58.95	60.38	59.41	61.60	58.71	57.26	59.47
Larger banks	57.92	55.94	56.79	47.62	49.06	53.47	57.08	55.23	57.75	52.27	51.29	54.72
Medium banks	66.30	68.38	68.96	68.11	68.72	68.09	59.78	60.19	60.34	66.56	65.51	62.48
Smaller banks	64.80	70.37	73.24	71.47	70.40	70.06	69.51	71.23	74.88	76.85	73.37	73.17
Commercial banks	60.52	59.96	61.70	52.34	54.13	58.39	58.53	57.23	59.90	56.63	54.72	58.12
Popular banks	58.87	58.74	57.18	57.21	54.57	57.32	60.63	59.14	59.06	56.65	57.70	58.64
Cooperative banks	64.15	72.09	73.75	71.77	72.50	70.85	71.65	76.60	80.40	81.11	79.03	77.76

	Financial structure											
	Net interbank position[b]/Total assets						Loan to direct funding ratio[c]					
	2012	2011	2010	2009	2008	Average 2008–2012	2012	2011	2010	2009	2008	Average 2008–2012
Total	−8.55	−6.50	−4.45	1.26	−0.08	−3.66	100.96	102.85	100.86	93.42	97.31	99.08
Larger banks	−9.09	−6.41	−4.44	0.91	−0.49	−3.91	101.48	101.29	98.33	91.12	95.65	97.57
Medium banks	−8.78	−8.80	−8.57	0.87	−0.42	−5.14	110.90	113.60	114.29	102.34	104.90	109.20
Smaller banks	−6.96	−4.83	−0.93	2.91	1.82	−1.60	93.22	98.80	97.80	93.01	95.95	95.76
Commercial banks	−9.35	−8.01	−6.85	0.66	−1.54	−4.64	103.39	104.78	102.99	92.41	98.93	100.41
Popular banks	−7.77	−3.17	1.06	1.11	2.79	−1.20	97.10	99.33	96.80	100.99	94.58	97.76
Cooperative banks	−6.57	−2.43	2.46	4.96	5.21	0.73	89.52	94.11	91.73	88.48	91.73	91.11

(continued)

Table 9 (continued)

	Leverage ratio[d]					
	2012	2011	2010	2009	2008	Average 2008–2012
Total	8.87	8.59	10.04	9.38	9.01	9.18
Larger banks	9.29	8.70	10.65	9.48	9.06	9.44
Medium banks	7.90	7.83	8.18	8.19	7.68	7.95
Smaller banks	8.50	8.90	9.69	10.00	9.98	9.42
Commercial banks	8.90	8.47	9.83	8.85	8.42	8.90
Popular banks	8.30	8.47	10.70	11.40	11.29	10.03
Cooperative banks	9.64	9.69	10.54	10.93	11.09	10.38

	Income composition											
	Net interest margin/Operating income						Net fee/Operating income					
	2012	2011	2010	2009	2008	Average 2008–2012	2012	2011	2010	2009	2008	Average 2008–2012
Total	54.18	56.15	56.23	60.33	65.75	58.53	31.46	31.91	32.04	28.83	26.72	30.19
Larger banks	46.75	47.76	49.45	55.24	58.67	51.57	34.42	32.97	32.74	30.08	28.74	31.79
Medium banks	59.81	62.99	63.48	65.23	71.04	64.51	31.58	32.14	32.73	29.66	27.32	30.69
Smaller banks	62.46	67.40	65.06	67.30	77.49	67.94	26.49	29.62	30.01	25.49	21.67	26.66
Commercial banks	51.39	53.88	54.76	60.32	63.87	57.26	32.47	32.63	32.42	29.71	28.22	31.22
Popular banks	55.22	53.55	52.62	53.11	62.53	55.41	32.89	32.62	33.57	28.93	25.26	30.66
Cooperative banks	68.88	76.15	74.27	73.37	84.46	75.43	19.87	23.12	23.57	20.03	16.63	20.64

Source: Own elaboration on data from *ABI Bilanci Fast*

[a]Direct funding = Deposits from customers + Debt securities in issue

[b]Net interbank position = Loans to banks − Deposits from banks

[c]Loans to customers to direct funding ratio = Loans to customers/Direct funding

[d]Leverage ratio = Equity/Total asset (for further details see section "Methodology")

percentage of the total assets than for cooperative banks and net fees incidence on operating income is higher. Only regarding the financial structure, popular banks look more similar to cooperative banks, showing a dependence on the interbank market relatively lower, a lower loans to customers to funding ratio and a higher leverage ratio.

Between 2008 and 2012, banks which performed more intensely in terms of lending to customers trend, that experienced a more significant credit quality deterioration and which registered higher return on the lending to customers activity—in particular smaller banks and cooperative intermediaries—are generally characterized by intermediation models more traditionally focused on the credit intermediation with customers. A positive relationship between the more or less traditional characteristic of the intermediation model adopted and the dynamism in the lending to customers seems to emerge. The difficulties in terms of funding affected banks in varying intensities during the financial crisis, and this surely played a significant role in influencing their credit supply. The liquidity crisis and the operational difficulties which characterized the wholesale interbank market in the most acute years of the financial crisis undoubtedly affected the business of larger intermediaries, whose financing significantly depends on this funding channel (Bonaccorsi di Patti and Sette 2012). On the contrary, smaller banks, which typically mainly collect funds from retail customers, were able to support their lending activity thanks to an availability of funds less affected by the consequences of the international financial turmoil. Banks which during the financial crisis supported the development in loans to customers with a greater intensity are also those generally characterized by a net positive position on the interbank market, a higher incidence of deposits from retail customers on total assets and a higher growth rate of this component of the liabilities (Di Battista et al. 2010). As the incidence of credit intermediation activity increases compared to the other operating areas (financial and securities intermediation, provision of services, interbank intermediation) the availability and the interest to provide loans in times of crisis increase, with the likely intent of preserving the core business, maintaining unchanged the relationship with customers.

Similar considerations are outlined also in Di Battista et al. (2010) and in Di Battista and Nieri (2011). Evidence from the Regional Bank Lending Survey (RBLS) and data from the results for Italy of the Bank Lending Survey (BLS) regarding the main determinant factor affecting banks' credit supply (Fig. 1) confirm the significance of the funding costs and balance sheet constraints in affecting the credit supply policies adopted by banks, giving significance to the analysis conducted in this research, aimed to investigate the significance also of the main intermediation model features in explaining the heterogeneities emerged in the loans to customers development, in the credit quality deterioration and in the returns on the lending activity.

4.5 Hypotheses of Research

The descriptive evidences emerged above and the main considerations which followed lead to formulate the following hypotheses of research, to be verified through the estimation of regressions (1), (2) and (3) as specified in section "Methodology".

5 Methodology

In order to verify the hypotheses of research discussed in section "Main Descriptive Evidence and Hypotheses of Research" (Table 10), we estimate the following three regressions, with the aim to explain the loans to customers development, the credit quality deterioration and the return on the lending activity with the bank size, the juridical connotation, the main intermediation model features and with the credit development and the credit quality themselves.

5.1 Credit Trend

To verify if a significant relationship between the loans to customers development, the bank size, the juridical connotation, the main characteristics of the intermediation model and the credit quality does exist, we specify the following regression (1), which enables to verify hypothesis 1 to hypothesis 5 (Table 10).

$$\overbrace{\Delta\%LC_t}^{\text{Credit trend}} = \underbrace{a_t + b_{it}BS_{it}}_{\text{Bank size}} + \overbrace{c_{jt}JC_{jt}}^{\text{Juridical connotation}} + \underbrace{d_{kt}AC_{kt} + f_{lt}LC_{lt} + g_{mt}FS_{mt} + h_{nt}IC_{nt}}_{\text{Intermediation model}} + \overbrace{h_{ot}CQ_{ot}}^{\text{Credit quality}} + \varepsilon_t \tag{1}$$

The dependent variable is the loans to customers growth rate ($\Delta\%LC_t$) (Table 11). The explanatory variables (Table 12) are the bank size dummy variables (BS_{it}), the juridical connotation dummy variables (JC_{jt}), the assets composition variables (AC_{kt}), the liabilities composition variables (LC_{lt}), the financial structure variables (FS_{mt}), the income composition variables (IC_{nt}) and the credit quality variables (CQ_{ot}). The bank size dummy variables (BS_{it}) identify banks by size according to the classification designed by the Bank of Italy following the criteria reported in section "Data and sample" (Table 2). In particular, we consider in the model the larger banks dummy variable (LA_t) and the smaller banks dummy variable (SM_t), in order to verify the significance of the heterogeneity by bank size emerged in the loans to customers trend and if smaller banks effectively performed better than larger banks in lending to customers (hypothesis 1). Therefore, according to the descriptive evidences analyzed in section "Main Descriptive Evidence and Hypotheses of Research", we expect a negative significance (−) of

Table 10 Hypotheses of research: credit trend, credit quality, income effects

Credit trend			(1)
1	Smaller banks showed a more intense loans to customers trend than larger banks	Bank size	
2	Cooperative banks showed a more intense loans to customers trend than commercial banks.	Juridical connotation	
3	Popular banks showed a more intense loans to customers trend than commercial banks		
4	Credit quality deterioration, affecting banks' credit supply policies, had a negative impact on the loans to customers trend	Credit quality	
5	Banks which showed a more intense loans to customers trend are characterized by a more traditional intermediation model	Intermediation model	
Credit quality			(2)
6	Smaller banks showed a more intense loans to customers quality deterioration than larger banks	Bank size	
7	Cooperative banks showed a more intense loans to customers quality deterioration than commercial banks	Juridical connotation	
8	Popular banks showed a more intense loans to customers quality deterioration than commercial banks		
9	Banks which showed a more intense loans to customers trend registered a more relevant quality deterioration	Credit trend	
10	Banks which showed a more intense loans to customers quality deterioration are characterized by a more traditional intermediation model	Intermediation model	
Income effects			(3)
11	Smaller banks showed a higher return on the lending activity than larger banks	Bank size	
12	Cooperative banks showed a higher return on the lending activity than commercial banks	Juridical connotation	
13	Banks which showed a more intense loans to customers trend registered a higher return on the lending activity	Credit trend	
14	Credit quality deterioration, affecting banks' credit supply policies, had a negative impact on the return on the lending activity	Credit quality	
15	Banks which showed a higher return on the lending activity are characterized by a more traditional intermediation model	Intermediation model	

Source: Own elaboration

Table 11 Dependent variables

Credit trend	$\Delta\,\%\,LC_t$	*Loans to customers growth rate* $\frac{\text{Loans to customers}_t - \text{Loans to customers}_{t-1}}{\text{Loans to customers}_{t-1}}$
Credit quality	$\Delta\,\%\,GDLC_t$	*Gross loans to customers rate of deterioration* $\frac{\text{Gross deteriorated loans to customers}_t - \text{Gross deteriorated loans to customers}_{t-1}}{\text{Gross bonis loans to customers}_{t-1}}$
Income effects	$NIRLC_t$	*Net interest return on loans to customers* $\frac{\text{Loans to customers interest income}_t - \text{Loans to customers loss provisions}_t}{\frac{\text{Loans to customers}_t + \text{Loans to customers}_{t-1}}{2}}$

Source: Own elaboration

Table 12 Explanatory variables

Bank size		BS_{it}	LA_t	*Larger banks*
			SM_t	*Smaller banks*
Juridical connotation		JC_{jt}	CB_t	*Cooperative banks*
			PB_t	*Popular banks*
Intermediation model characteristics	Assets composition	AC_{jt}	LC_TA_t	*Loans to customers to total assets ratio* $\frac{\text{Loans to customers}_t}{\text{Total assets}_t}$
	Liabilities composition	LC_{lt}	DF_TA_t	*Direct funding to total assets ratio* $\frac{\text{Direct funding}_t}{\text{Total assets}_t}$
	Financial structure	FS_{mt}	NIP_TA_t	*Net interbank position to total assets ratio* $\frac{\text{Net interbank position}_t}{\text{Total assets}_t}$
			LC_DF_t	*Loans to customers to direct funding ratio* $\frac{\text{Loans to customers}_t}{\text{Direct funding}_t}$
			LR_t	*Leverage ratio* $\frac{\text{Equity}_t}{\text{Total assets}_t}$
	Income composition	IC_{nt}	NIM_OI_t	*Net interest margin to operating income ratio* $\frac{\text{Net interest margin}_t}{\text{Operating income}_t}$
			NF_OI_t	*Net fee to operating income ratio* $\frac{\text{Net fee}_t}{\text{Operating income}_t}$
Credit quality		CQ_{ot}	$\%GDLC_{t-1}$	*Gross deteriorated loans to customers incidence (t − 1)* $\frac{\text{Gross deteriorated loans to customers}_{t-1}}{\text{Gross loans to customers}_{t-1}}$
			$\Delta\,\%\,GDLC_t$	*Gross loans to customers rate of deterioration (t)* $\frac{\text{Gross deteriorated loans to customers}_t - \text{Gross deteriorated loans to customers}_{t-1}}{\text{Gross bonis loans to customers}_{t-1}}$
			$\Delta\,\%\,GDLC_{t-1}$	*Gross loans to customers rate of deterioration (t − 1)* $\frac{\text{Gross deteriorated loans to customers}_{t-1} - \text{Gross deteriorated loans to customers}_{t-2}}{\text{Gross in bonis loans to customers}_{t-2}}$
Credit trend		CT_{pt}	$\Delta\,\%\,LC_t$	*Loans to customers growth rate (t)* $\frac{\text{Loans to customers}_t - \text{Loans to customers}_{t-1}}{\text{Loans to customers}_{t-1}}$
			$\Delta\,\%\,LC_{t-1}$	*Loans to customers growth rate (t − 1)* $\frac{\text{Loans to customers}_{t-1} - \text{Loans to customers}_{t-2}}{\text{Loans to customers}_{t-2}}$

Source: Own elaboration

the larger banks dummy variable (LA_t) and a positive significance (+) of the smaller banks dummy variable (SM_t). The juridical connotation dummy variables (JC_{jt}) distinguish banks by juridical connotation. In particular, we consider in the model the cooperative banks dummy variable (CB_t) and the popular banks dummy variable (PB_t), in order to verify if cooperative banks and popular banks registered a loans to customers development effectively more intense than commercial banks (hypothesis 2 and hypothesis 3). Therefore, according to the descriptive evidence analyzed in section "Main Descriptive Evidence and Hypotheses of Research", we expect a positive significance (+) both of the cooperative banks dummy variable (CB_t) and of the popular banks dummy variable (PB_t). The cooperative banks dummy variable, in particular, could add interesting elements of analysis in explaining the significance of the heterogeneity by juridical connotation emerged in the loans to customers development. As known, cooperative banks are typically characterized by smaller size, traditional intermediation models and typical strong relationships with the surrounding environment. These characteristics could have positively influenced the trend of loans to customers over the financial crisis, as these kind of banks could have continued to adopt expansive credit policies in order to maintain strong customers relationships. However, as most of the cooperative banks are smaller banks, these features could also be already caught by the smaller banks dummy variable. The assets composition variables (AC_{kt}), the liabilities composition variables (LC_{lt}), the financial structure variables (FS_{mt}) and the income composition variables (IC_{nt}) identify the main characteristics of the intermediation model adopted by banks. These variables enable to distinguish banks between the ones more traditionally focused on the credit intermediation with customers—prevalence of loans to customers among the investments and of direct funding among liabilities, more equilibrated financial structure (lower dependence on the interbank market as a source of funding, lower loans to customers to funding ratio, higher leverage ratio), prevalence of net interest income among the operating income—and the ones characterized by more diversified intermediation structures. In this way, it could be possible to verify if the intermediation model matters in explaining the heterogeneities emerged in the trend of loans to customers. In other words, if banks characterized by more traditional intermediation models registered a loans to customers development effectively more intense than banks characterized by more diversified intermediation models (hypothesis 5). The underlying idea is that credit supply policies adopted by banks are influenced by the specificities of the intermediation models of reference and by the related underlying management strategies. To different funding and lending policies, as well as to differentiated balance sheet assets and liabilities composition strategies, correspond different vulnerabilities regarding the exogenous conditionings and also different financial and capital constraints on the credit supply. Therefore, according to the descriptive evidences analyzed in section "Main Descriptive Evidence and Hypotheses of Research", we expect a positive significance (+) of the loans to customers to total assets ratio (LC_TA_t) and of the direct funding to total assets ratio (DF_TA_t), a negative (−) significance of the loans to customers to direct funding ratio (LC_DF_t), a positive significance (+) of the net interbank position to total assets ratio (NIP_TA_t) and of the leverage ratio (LR_t), a positive significance (+) of the net interest margin to operating income ratio (NIM_OI_t) and a negative (−) significance of the net fee to operating income ratio (NF_OI_t). Finally, the credit quality variables (CQ_{ot}) allow to verify if and how the credit quality and its deterioration had a negative impact on the loans to customers trend (hypothesis 4). Indeed, the loans to customers development could reflect credit supply policies affected by the quality of the loans to customers portfolio at the end of the previous year ($\%GDLC_{t-1}$) and by its rate of deterioration over the same year ($\Delta\%GDLC_t$) and the previous one ($\Delta\%GDLC_{t-1}$). Therefore, according to the descriptive evidences analysed in section "Main Descriptive Evidence and Hypotheses of Research", we expect a negative significance (−) of the gross deteriorated loans to customers incidence in $t-1(\%GDLC_{t-1})$, of the gross loans to customers rate of deterioration in $t(\Delta\%GDLC_t)$ and of the gross loans to customers rate of deterioration in $t-1(\Delta\%GDLC_{t-1})$. In the model we do not consider the gross deteriorated loans to customers incidence in $t(\%GDLC_t)$, first of all because of its possible endogeneity with the dependent variable and multicollinearity with the other three credit quality independent variables considered, but also because the credit policies and the relative effects in terms of credit development could be effectively conditioned by the stock of deteriorated loans at the beginning of the year, than at the end of the year.

Regression (1) develops the one estimated in Tutino et al. (2014), adding also the credit quality variables as explanatory variables and considering the banks size variable, the juridical connotation variables and the intermediation characteristics variables in a different way. For further details on the comparison between regression (1) and the one analyzed in Tutino et al. (2014) refer to Table 13.

5.2 *Credit Quality*

To verify if a significant relationship between the credit quality deterioration, the bank size, the juridical connotation, the main characteristics of the intermediation model does exist and if and how it could be affected by the loans to customers trend, we specify the following regression (2), which enables to verify hypothesis 6 to hypothesis 10 (Table 10).

$$\overbrace{\Delta\%GDLC_t}^{\text{Credit quality}} = \underbrace{a_t + b_{it}BS_{it}}_{\text{Bank size}} + \overbrace{d_{jt}JC_{jt}}^{\text{Juridical connotation}} + \underbrace{e_{kt}AC_{kt} + f_{lt}LC_{lt} + g_{mt}FS_{mt} + h_{nt}IC_{nt}}_{\text{Intermediation model}} + \overbrace{h_{pt}CT_{pt}}^{\text{Credit trend}} + \varepsilon_t \qquad (2)$$

The dependent variable is the gross loans to customers rate of deterioration ($\Delta\%GDLC_t$) (Table 11). In this regression, to the explanatory variables already considered in the previous one (1)—the bank size dummy variables (BS_{it}), the juridical connotation dummy variables (JC_{jt}), the assets composition variables (AC_{kt}), the liabilities composition variables (LC_{lt}), the financial structure variables (FS_{mt}), the

Table 13 Comparison between regressions (1) and the regression estimated in Tutino et al. (2014)

	Regression (1)				Tutino et al. (2014)			
Bank size		BS_{it}	LA_t	Larger banks		BS_{it}	MA_t	Major banks
							LG_t	Large banks
			SM_t	Smaller banks			SM_t	Small banks
							MI_t	Minor banks
Juridical connotation		JC_{jt}	CB_t	Cooperative banks		JC_{jt}	CB_t	Cooperative banks
			PB_t	Popular banks				
Intermediation model characteristics	Assets composition	AC_{jt}	LC_TA_t	Loans to customers/Total assets	Assets composition	CA_{jt}	LC_TA_t	Loans to customers/Total assets
							FA_TA_t	Financial assets/Total assets
					Interbank position	PIN_{kt}	$NPIP\_TA_t$	Net positive interbank position/Total assets
							$NNIP\_TA_t$	Net negative interbank position/Total assets
	Liabilities composition	LC_{lt}	DF_TA_t	Direct funding/Total assets	Liabilities composition	LC_{lt}	DC_TA_t	Deposits from customers/Total assets
							TC_TA_t	Debt securities in issue/Total assets
	Financial structure	FS_{mt}	NIP_TA_t	Net interbank position/Total assets	Financial structure	FS_{mt}	FA_DF_t	Financial assets to direct funding ratio
			LC_DF_t	Loans to customers to direct funding ratio			LC_DF_t	Loans to customers to direct funding ratio
			LR_t	Leverage ratio			LR_t	Leverage ratio
	Income composition	IC_{nt}	NIM_OI_t	Net interest margin/Operating income	Income composition	IC_{nt}	NIM_OI_t	Net interest margin/Operating income
			NF_OI_t	Net fees/Operating income			NF_OI_t	Net fees/Operating income

(continued)

Table 13 (continued)

	Regression (1)				Tutino et al. (2014)			
Credit quality		CQ_{ot}	Δ % $GDLC_t$	Gross deteriorated loans to customers incidence (t − 1)				
			% $GDLC_{t-1}$	Gross loans to customers rate of deterioration				
			Δ % $GDLC_{t-1}$	Gross loans to customers rate of deterioration (t − 1)				

Source: Own elaboration

income composition variables (IC_{nt})—in spite of the variables identifying the credit quality (CQ_{ot}), we add the variables identifying the credit development as independent variables (CT_{pt}) (Table 12)—looking at the loans to customers growth rate, both in the same year ($\Delta\,\%\,LC_t$) and in the previous one ($\Delta\,\%\,LC_{t-1}$)—in order to analyze the relationship between the loans to customers growth rate and the quality deterioration of the loans to customers portfolio (hypothesis 9). Therefore, according to the descriptive evidence analyzed in section "Main Descriptive Evidence and Hypotheses of Research", we expect a positive significance (+) of the loans to customers growth rate in t and in t − 1. As for the other explanatory variables, the bank size dummy variables (BS_{it}) allow to verify the significance of the heterogeneity by bank size emerged in the loans to customers deterioration and if smaller banks effectively registered a more intense quality deterioration than larger banks in lending to customers (hypothesis 6). Therefore, according to the descriptive evidences analyzed in section "Main Descriptive Evidence and Hypotheses of Research", we expect a negative significance (−) of the larger banks dummy variable (LA_t) and a positive significance (+) of the smaller banks dummy variable (SM_t). The juridical connotation dummy variables (JC_t) enable to verify if cooperative banks and popular banks registered a more intense quality deterioration than commercial banks (hypothesis 7 and hypothesis 8). Therefore, according to the descriptive evidence analyzed in section "Main Descriptive Evidence and Hypotheses of Research", we expect a positive significance (+) both of the cooperative banks dummy variable (CB_t) and of the popular banks dummy variable (PB_t). The intermediation model variables enable to verify if banks characterized by more traditional intermediation models registered a quality deterioration effectively more intense than banks characterized by more diversified intermediation models (*hypothesis 10*). Therefore, according to the descriptive evidence analyzed in section "Main Descriptive Evidence and Hypotheses of Research", we expect a positive significance (+) of the loans to customers to total assets ratio (LC_TA_t) and of the direct funding to total assets ratio (DF_TA_t), a negative (−) significance of the loans to customers to direct funding ratio (LC_DF_t), a positive significance (+) of the net interbank position to total assets ratio (NIP_TA_t) and of the leverage ratio (LR_t), a positive significance (+) of the net interest margin to operating income ratio (NIM_OI_t) and a negative (−) significance of the net fee to operating income ratio (NF_OI_t).

5.3 Income Effects

Regarding the main income effects, in order to verify if a significant relationship does exist with the bank size, the juridical connotation, the main characteristics of the intermediation model and if and how it could be affected by the loans to customers trend and by the credit quality deterioration (hypothesis 11 to hypothesis 15) (Table 10), we specify the following regression (3).

$$\overbrace{\text{NIRLC}_t}^{\text{Return}} = \underbrace{a_t + b_{it}\text{BS}_{it}}_{\text{Bank size}} + \overbrace{c_{jt}\text{JC}_{jt}}^{\text{Juridical connotation}} + \underbrace{d_{kt}\text{AC}_{kt} + e_{lt}\text{LC}_{lt} + f_{mt}\text{FS}_{mt} + g_{nt}\text{IC}_{nt}}_{\text{Intermediation model}} + \overbrace{h_{ot}\text{CT}_{ot}}^{\text{Credit trend}} + \underbrace{h_{pt}\text{CQ}_{pt}}_{\text{Credit quality}} + \varepsilon_t \tag{3}$$

The dependent variable is the net interest return on loans to customers ($NIRLC_t$) (Table 11), ratio between the volume of interest income netted by the loan loss provisions and the average volume of loans to customers. This variable basically enables to consider the average interest return charged by banks on loans to customers—approximated by the *gross interest return on loans to customers* ($GIRLC_t$), ratio between the volume of income interests and the average volume of loans to customers—taking into account also the negative contribution related to the loans to customers quality deterioration—caught by the *cost of credit risk* (CR_t), ratio between the loans loss provisions and the average volume of loans to customers. While the gross interest return on loans to customers could enable to obtain indicative information about the pricing policies adopted by banks, it could not be considered as an appropriate indicator to analyze the profitability of the lending to customers activity as a whole, as it does not take into account the funding from customers cost and the impairment losses on loans to customers. The net interest return on loans to customers partially resolves one of the limits of the gross interest return indicator, as it considers also the losses coming from the loans to customers quality deterioration, although it does not take into account the funding from customers cost. As for the explanatory variables, in this regression we included all the variables considered in the previous regressions (1) and (2). The bank size dummy variables (BS_{it}) allow to verify the significance of the heterogeneity by bank size emerged in the net interest return on loans to customers and if smaller banks effectively registered a more intense return on the lending activity than larger banks (hypothesis 11). Therefore, according to the descriptive evidence analyzed in section "Main Descriptive Evidence and Hypotheses of Research", we expect a negative significance (−) of the larger banks dummy variable (LA_t) and a positive significance (+) of the smaller banks dummy variable (SM_t). The juridical connotation dummy variables (JC_t) enable to verify if cooperative banks registered a more intense return on the lending activity than commercial banks (hypothesis 12). Therefore, according to the descriptive evidence analyzed in section "Main Descriptive Evidence and Hypotheses of Research", we expect a positive significance (+) of the cooperative banks dummy variable (CB_t). The credit trend variables (CT_{ot})—the loans to customers growth rate, both in the same year ($\Delta\,\%\,LC_t$) and in the previous one ($\Delta\,\%\,LC_{t-1}$)—enable to analyze the relationship between the loans to customers growth rate and the net interest return on loans to customers (*hypothesis 14*). Therefore, according to the descriptive evidence analyzed in section "Main Descriptive Evidence and Hypotheses of Research", we expect a positive significance (+) of the loans to customers growth rate both in t ($\Delta\,\%\,LC_t$) and in $t-1(\Delta\,\%\,LC_{t-1})$. The credit quality variables (CQ_{pt}) allow to verify if and how the credit quality and its deterioration had a negative impact on the net interest return on loans to customers (*hypothesis 15*). Therefore, according to the descriptive evidence analyzed in section "Main Descriptive Evidence and Hypotheses of Research", we expect a negative significance (−) of the gross deteriorated loans to customers incidence in t − 1 ($\%GDLC_{t-1}$), of the gross loans to customers rate of deterioration in t($\Delta\,\%\,GDLC_t$) and of the gross loans to customers rate of deterioration in t − 1($\Delta\,\%\,GDLC_{t-1}$).

Regressions (1), (2) and (3) are estimated adopting a pooled ordinary least squares approach (POLS) and a static panel approach, both with random effects (RE) and with fixed effects (FE). First of all, we add the year dummies in order to catch possible common time effects due to the different phases in the evolution of the crisis (global financial crisis and economic downturn between 2008 and 2009, slow economic recovery in 2010, sovereign debt crisis and economic downturn between 2011 and 2012). Despite the presence of year dummies, our residuals present heteroscedasticity problems pointed out by all the heteroscedasticity tests (Breusch-Pagan, White, Modified Wald test for groupwise heteroscedasticity). Moreover, Wooldridge test for autocorrelation highlights the presence of autocorrelation. Given the presence of heteroscedasticity and autocorrelation, we choose to use cluster-robust standard errors. After the estimation, we have to choose the favorite model among pooled ordinary least squares regression (POLS), panel data with random effects (RE) approach and panel data with fixed effects (FE) approach. In order to choose between pooled ordinary least squares regression (POLS) and panel data with random effects (RE) approach, we use the Breusch and Pagan Lagrangian Multiplier test for random effects and, in every case, the test reject the null hypothesis (with a p-value below 1%), therefore the panel data with random effects (RE) approach has to be preferred. To select the best model between the pooled ordinary least squares regression (POLS) and the panel data with fixed effects (FE) approach, we perform the F-test on all the dummies for the subject-specific effects (the fixed effects). We always reject (with a p-value well below 1%) the null hypothesis that all dummies are jointly non-significant, therefore the panel data with fixed effects (FE) approaches to be preferred. In order to choose between the panel data with random effects (RE) approach and the panel data with fixed effects (FE) approach, we employ the Hausman test (to be precise, we perform the Hausman test by using a procedure based on auxiliary regressions, by following the Mundlak's approach 1978). In this case we find that the data with fixed effects (FE) approaches to be used for regressions (1) and (3), while the panel data with random effects (RE) approach can be used for regression (2). We also check for problems due to multicollinearity and outliers. About multicollinearity, there are not variables that present a variance inflation factor (VIF) above 10; moreover, with a backward process (that is deleting the less significant variable, till all variables have a p-value below 10%) we delete from the chosen—panel data with fixed effects (FE) approach for regressions (1) and (3) and panel data with random effects (RE) approach for regression (2)—the variables that are not significant with a further reduction of the VIF values of the variables. The restricted regressions (RE-Rand FE-R) usually confirm the results of the full model, showing the robustness of the results to possible multicollinearity problems. About outliers, for each regression we repeat the estimation after deleting the banks that present, in the pooled regression, a high value of both leverage and Cook's distance in at least 1 years. All estimates are very robust: we do not observe changes in which variables are significant and in the signs of these significant variables. Given that in two of the three analyses we select the FE approach, given that the presence of subject-specific fixed effects implies the need to remove all the dummies that groups banks in size classes or with different juridical connotation, and given the importance of the dimensional heterogeneity for our analysis, we decide to interact the dimensional dummies with the continuous explanatory variables in order to understand if the size can influence the coefficient of these variables. In other words, to understand if the size has a relevant impact in modifying the relationships between these explanatory variables and the dependent variable. In the specification with a size dummy interacted with the continuous explanatory variables, both the F test on fixed effects and the Hausman test reject their null hypothesis, selecting the FE specification for all the three analyses. Wecallthese estimations FE-DUM.

6 Results of the Estimations

6.1 Credit Trend

According to the results of tests used to select the best model between pooled ordinary least squares regression (POLS), panel data with random effects (RE) and panel data with fixed effects (FE), the panel data with fixed effects (FE) approach resulted the unbiased estimator for regression (1). Table 14 reports the results of the estimations of regression (1) for the pooled ordinary least squares (POLS) approach, for the panel data with random effects (RE) approach, for the panel data with fixed effects (FE) approach and for the panel data with fixed effects interacted with the smaller banks dummy variable (FE-DUM).

About the bank size and the juridical connotation, the panel data approach with fixed effects (FE) do not allow to estimate the significance of the relating dummy variables in explaining the loans to customers growth rate. However, according to the results of the pooled ordinary least squares regression (POLS), the major and large dummy variable results significantly negative, the smaller banks dummy variable significantly positive and the popular banks dummy variable significantly positive. About the cooperative dummy variable, it results positive, but not significant. Therefore, the pooled ordinary least squares regression (POLS) would suggest to accept hypothesis 1 and hypothesis 3. Instead, given that the cooperative bank dummy variable could be strongly correlated with the smaller banks dummy variable, as most of the smaller banks are cooperatives, the significance of the cooperative bank dummy variable could be affected by this collinearity aspect.

According to the panel data with fixed effects (FE) estimation, no one of the variables considered about the credit quality look significant in conditioning the loans to customers growth. Therefore, *hypothesis 4* could not be accepted.

Table 14 Results of the estimations—Regression (1)—Credit trend

		POLS	RE	FE	0FE-R	FE-DUM
LA_t	Larger banks (t)	−0.03169	−0.02682	(Omitted)	(omitted)	
		0.0295	0.0867			
SM_t	Smaller banks (t)	0.02631	0.02824	(Omitted)	(omitted)	
		0.0034	0.0566			
CB_t	Cooperative banks (t)	0.00124	0.00317	(Omitted)	(omitted)	
		0.8130	0.7161			
PB_t	Popular banks (t)	0.03521	0.03655	(Omitted)	(omitted)	
		0.0000	0.0019			
LC_TA_t	Loans to customers/ Total assets (t)	−0.13902	−0.09549	0.35288	0.37776	0.07606
		0.0000	0.0611	0.0004	0.0000	0.7582
DF_TA_t	Direct funding/Total assets (t)	0.09171	0.07793	−0.11427	−0.15657	0.02193
		0.0131	0.1668	0.2287	0.0064	0.9551
NIP_TA_t	Net interbank position/ Total assets (t)	−0.04452	−0.05763	−0.06260		0.05628
		0.0765	0.1057	0.2181		0.7715
LC_DF_t	Loans to customers to direct funding ratio (t)	−0.00133	−0.00200	−0.00351		−0.08750
		0.9345	0.9481	0.9441		0.3069
LR_t	Leverage ratio (t)	−0.06470	0.00721	0.20764		−0.34219
		0.2133	0.9180	0.4419		0.5341
NIM_OI_t	Net interest margin/ Operating income (t)	−0.00023	−0.00206	0.00255		−0.04883
		0.9725	0.7809	0.8559		0.2302
NF_OI_t	Net fee/Operating income (t)	0.00321	0.00264	−0.03686		0.06465
		0.8858	0.9396	0.5656		0.7174
$\%GDLC_{t-1}$	Gross deteriorated loans to customers incidence (t − 1)	−0.26226	−0.23506	0.00126		−0.16471
		0.0000	0.0000	0.9934		0.5910
$\Delta\%GDLC_t$	Gross loans to customers rate of deterioration (t)	0.08450	0.06138	0.03045		−0.70056
		0.0122	0.4575	0.6982		0.1634
$\Delta\%GDLC_{t-1}$	Gross loans to customers rate of deterioration (t − 1)	0.01405	−0.00261	−0.04852		0.22817
		0.6968	0.9292	0.1479		0.5149
2010	Year 2010	0.00973	0.00799	−0.00569	−0.00752	
		0.0422	0.0631	0.2277	0.0747	
2011	Year 2011	−0.03453	−0.03658	−0.05350	−0.05436	
		0.0000	0.0000	0.0000	0.0000	
2012	Year 2012	−0.06141	−0.06206	−0.06473	−0.06287	
		0.0000	0.0000	0.0000	0.0000	
C	Constant	0.09283	0.06389	−0.09355	−0.06600	−0.01881
		0.0019	0.2376	0.2010	0.0980	0.7871

Source: Own elaboration on data from *ABI Bilanci Fast*

However, according to the results of the *pooled ordinary least squares regression* (POLS), the gross deteriorated loans to customers incidence in t − 1 result significantly negative, while the gross loans to customers rate of deterioration in t is positively significant and the gross loans to customers rate of deterioration in t − 1 is not significant. Therefore the coefficient of the gross deteriorated loans to customers incidence in t − 1 supports *hypothesis 4*, and the positive sign of the gross loans to customers rate of deterioration could not defeat our hypothesis because the loans to customers trend could be affected by credit deterioration with a lag in time. Finally, all the 3 year dummies result negatively significant in explaining the loans to customers growth rate. Moreover, as their coefficients are higher and higher in absolute value as the year increase, the estimations suggest that effectively the slowdown in the loans to customers trend was relatively more relevant in 2011 and in 2012 than in the previous years. As for regression (1) the estimation of the model interacted with the smaller banks dummy variable do not add anything more to the analysis.

Among the variables considered to capture the main intermediation model features, only the loans to customers to total assets and the direct funding to total assets are significant. The loans to customers to total assets is positively related to the loans to customers growth rate. Consistently with hypothesis 5, banks characterized by an assets composition more traditionally oriented towards lending to customers registered a more intense loans to customers trend. On the contrary, the direct funding to total assets variable result negatively related to the loans to customers growth rate: banks characterized by a liabilities composition more traditionally based on direct funding performed less intensely in lending to customers. This evidence, however, looks in contrast with the descriptive evidence supporting *hypothesis 5*, with the POLS estimate, and with the evidence emerged in Tutino et al. (2014) and in Gambacorta and Marques-Ibanez (2011). According to Tutino et al. (2014), the more traditionally focused is the funding structure, the more stable it results in sustaining the loans to customers providing. However, Tutino et al. (2014) present a cross-section analysis with an OLS estimate, that is consistent with the POLS estimate of this paper, and restrict the analysis to 2008–2011, in a period characterized by the peak of the liquidity crisis. According to Gambacorta and Marques-Ibanez (2011), banks characterized by a higher incidence of deposits form customers on total liabilities show higher in supporting the credit trend. Indeed, the financial crisis showed that banks characterized by a financial structure excessively dependent on short term funding on the interbank market had been affected by turbulences on the interbank market in a more relevant way, letting emerge a higher vulnerability of the financial structure and, consequently, registering more significant impacts in terms of credit supply. However, the net interbank position results not significant, therefore it does not support this consideration. As for the leverage ratio, it does not result significant in explaining the loans to customers growth rate. In Tutino et al. (2014), however, it results negatively significant, in contrast with the expectation. Similar evidence emerged in Gambacorta and Marques-Ibanez (2011). According to the authors, the negative sign of the relationship lead to doubt about the significance of the indicator in capturing the effect of capitalisation of the bank on the dynamic of credit. As highlighted in Tutino et al. (2014), the leverage ratio itself typically looks at the quantitative aspect of the financial structure, without dealing with its quality. What is really relevant is not the level of equity compared to the total assets volume, but the whole structure of the funding and of the assets: their composition, their vulnerability and—as already highlighted—their stability in sustaining the lending activity of banks.

6.2 Credit Quality

As for the estimation of regression (2), according to the acceptance of the Hausman test, we can use the *panel data with random effects* (RE) approach. In this way, we gain efficiency in the estimate compared the *panel data with fixed effects* (FE), and we are not forced to delete the bank size and the juridical connotation dummy variables. Table 15 reports the results of the estimations of regression (2) for the *pooled ordinary least squares* (POLS) approach, for the *panel data with random effects* (RE) approach, for the *panel data with fixed effects* (FE) approach and for the *panel data with fixed effects* interacted with the smaller banks dummy variable (FE-DUM).

About the *bank size*, the results of the estimations lead to accept *hypothesis 6*: the smaller banks dummy variable is positively related to the *gross loans to customers rate of deterioration*, but only for the restricted random effect regression (RE-R). Between 2008 and 2012 smaller banks effectively showed a more intense loans to customers quality deterioration than larger banks.

As for the *juridical connotation*, the cooperative bank dummy variable results negatively significant in explaining the *gross loans to customers rate of deterioration*, while the popular banks dummy variable does not result significant. Over the period analyzed cooperative banks showed a less intense loans to customers quality deterioration than commercial banks and popular banks with the same size and features. Therefore the estimations do not enable to verify *hypothesis 8* and, as the sign of the relationship results in contrast with our expectation, lead to refuse *hypothesis 7*. However, as the cooperative bank dummy variable could be strongly correlated with the smaller banks dummy variable, as most of the smaller banks are cooperatives, the significance of the cooperative bank dummy variable could be affected by this aspect.

About the significance of the loans to customers trend in affecting the credit quality deterioration, the estimations lead to accept *hypothesis 9*. The loans to customers growth rate variable result positively significant at 10% in relation to the *gross loans to customers rate of deterioration*. Banks which showed a more intense loans to customers trend registered a more relevant quality deterioration. In particular, the estimations interacted with the smaller banks dummy variable let emerge that the positive effect of the loans to customers growth rate on the credit quality deterioration is significantly higher for larger banks. However, the

Table 15 Results of the estimations—Regression (2)—Credit quality

		POLS	RE	RE-R	FE	FE-DUM
LA_t	Larger banks (t)	−0.00267	−0.00202		(Omitted)	(omitted)
		0.7826	0.7747			
SM_t	Smaller banks (t)	0.01144	0.01113	0.01223	(Omitted)	(omitted)
		0.0553	0.0552	0.0285		
CB_t	Cooperative banks (t)	−0.01295	−0.01311	−0.01027	(Omitted)	(omitted)
		0.0002	0.1170	0.0331		
PB_t	Popular banks (t)	−0.00279	−0.00282		(Omitted)	(omitted)
		0.6022	0.6895			
LC_TA_t	Loans to customers/ Total assets (t)	0.01074	0.00853		0.05356	0.26274
		0.5558	0.6845		0.4963	0.0200
DF_TA_t	Direct funding/Total assets (t)	−0.00307	0.00375		0.06885	−0.09589
		0.9003	0.8593		0.1127	0.3631
NIP_TA_t	Net interbank position/Total assets (t)	−0.00917	−0.00435		0.05890	0.07045
		0.5824	0.7661		0.4636	0.4657
LC_DF_t	Loans to customers to direct funding ratio (t)	−0.00075	−0.00251		0.02930	−0.03682
		0.9442	0.8526		0.2103	0.1293
LR_t	Leverage ratio (t)	−0.16765	−0.16854	−0.15206	−0.23897	−0.69907
		0.0000	0.0000	0.0000	0.0727	0.0610
NIM_OI_t	Net interest margin/ Operating income (t)	0.00903	0.00927		0.01615	0.01280
		0.0417	0.1768		0.2897	0.5505
NF_OI_t	Net fee/Operating income (t)	−0.03230	−0.03325		−0.06112	−0.03816
		0.0295	0.2517		0.3750	0.7119
$\Delta\%LC_t$	Loans to customers growth rate (t)	0.02674	0.02934	0.03607	0.02763	−0.11822
		0.0950	0.2636	0.0826	0.3898	0.0544
$\Delta\%LC_t$	Loans to customers growth rate (t _ 1)	0.01477	0.01139		−0.01307	−0.01160
		0.2536	0.3695		0.2725	0.7122
2010	Year 2010	−0.01001	−0.01001	−0.00829	−0.01000	
		0.0018	0.0012	0.0000	0.0002	
2011	Year 2011	−0.00589	−0.00545		−0.00166	
		0.0763	0.1577		0.6821	
2012	Year 2012	0.01067	0.01141	0.01327	0.02173	
		0.0039	0.0100	0.0000	0.0113	
C	Constant	0.03522	0.02888	0.03230	−0.06866	−0.05075
		0.0754	0.1863	0.0000	0.3598	0.4792

Source: Own elaboration on data from *ABI Bilanci Fast*

estimations do not enable to verify if the quality deterioration resulted effectively lagged in time. Indeed the loans to customers growth rate in the previous year results as not significant. Finally, among the 3 year dummies, the 2010 results negatively significant and the 2012 positively related to the *gross loans to customers rate of deterioration*, while the 2011 does not result significant, confirming that in 2010 the credit deterioration is less intense, while in 2012 it increases significantly.

Among the variables considered to capture the main intermediation model features, only the *leverage ratio* shows a statistically significant negative relationship with the *gross loans to customers rate of deterioration*. Banks characterized by a lower incidence of equity on total assets registered a more intense credit quality deterioration. This evidence, in contrast with *hypothesis 10*, could be biased by a possible endogeneity of the leverage ratio. In fact, as the loans to customer deteriorate, provisions reduce profits, with negative effect on the equity. According to the estimation of the model interacted with the smaller banks dummy variable, the leverage ratio remains negative for smaller banks and it becomes positive for larger banks and the loans to customers to direct funding ratio becomes significantly positive for larger banks, still in contrast with *hypothesis 10*. Only the loans to customers to total assets ratio, negatively significant for larger banks and positively for smaller banks, looks in line with *hypothesis 10*. For smaller banks, a traditional intermediation model feature as the prevalence of the loans to customers among the investments could effectively explain the higher credit quality deterioration.

6.3 Income Effects

As for regression (1), the *panel data with fixed effects* (FE) results to be the unbiased estimator to estimate regression (3) in comparison to the *pooled ordinary least squares* (POLS) and *panel data with random effects* (RE) approaches. Table 16 reports the results of the estimations of regression (3) for the *pooled ordinary least squares* (POLS) approach, for the *panel data with random effects* (RE) approach, for the *panel data with fixed effects* (FE) approach and for the *panel data with fixed effects* interacted with the smaller banks dummy variable (FE-DUM).

About the *bank size* and the *juridical connotation*, the *panel data approach with fixed effects* (FE) do not allow to estimate the significance of the relating dummy variables in explaining the *net interest return on loans to customers*. Therefore, the estimations do not enable to verify *hypothesis 11* and *hypothesis 12*. However, according to the results of the other two approaches—the *pooled ordinary least squares regression* (POLS) and the *panel data with random effects* (RE)—the *cooperative banks dummy variable* and the *popular banks dummy variable* result significantly negative, while the *larger banks dummy variable* and the *smaller banks dummy variable* still do not result significant. Therefore, although probably biased, these estimations would suggest to refuse *hypothesis 12*.

Table 16 Results of the estimations—Regression (3)—Income effects

		POLS	RE	FE	FE-R	FE-DUM
LA_t	Larger banks (t)	−0.00039	−0.00042	(Omitted)	(omitted)	
		0.9126	0.8945			
SM_t	Smaller banks (t)	0.00077	0.00092	(Omitted)	(omitted)	
		0.7218	0.6854			
CB_t	Cooperative banks (t)	−0.00389	−0.00437	(Omitted)	(omitted)	
		0.0021	0.0148			
PB_t	Popular banks (t)	−0.00474	−0.00474	(Omitted)	(omitted)	
		0.0145	0.0535			
LC_TA_t	Loans to customers/Total assets (t)	−0.04445	−0.03529	0.00697		0.01363
		0.0000	0.0001	0.5850		0.7296
DF_TA_t	Direct funding/ Total assets (t)	0.04999	0.04431	0.01631	0.02495	−0.00498
		0.0000	0.0001	0.3194	0.0081	0.9077
NIP_TA_t	Net interbank position/Total assets (t)	0.01672	0.01842	0.02270		−0.01961
		0.0059	0.1919	0.2843		0.5731
LC_DF_t	Loans to customers to direct funding ratio (t)	0.01661	0.01390	0.00528		−0.00554
		0.0000	0.0089	0.4641		0.6007
LR_t	Leverage ratio (t)	0.00283	0.01769	0.14652	0.18572	0.21660
		0.8226	0.4125	0.0065	0.0000	0.0184
NIM_OI_t	Net interest margin/Operating income (t)	0.00545	0.00601	0.00769		0.02962
		0.0007	0.0009	0.1140		0.0008
NF_OI_t	Net fee/Operating income (t)	−0.01996	−0.02623	−0.03667	−0.00839	−0.12468
		0.0002	0.0004	0.0821	0.0694	0.0024
$\Delta\%LC_t$	Loans to customers growth rate (t)	0.04115	0.03644	0.02391	0.02449	−0.01768
		0.0000	0.0000	0.0021	0.0040	0.3346
$\Delta\%LC_t$	Loans to customers growth rate (t − 1)	0.01385	0.01178	0.00256		0.00324
		0.0039	0.0134	0.4929		0.6488
$\% GDLC_{t-1}$	Gross deteriorated loans to	−0.00106	−0.02437	−0.09362	−0.10528	0.10722

(continued)

Table 16 (continued)

		POLS	RE	FE	FE-R	FE-DUM
	customers incidence (t − 1)					
		0.9051	0.0518	0.0001	0.0000	0.1681
$\Delta\%GDLC_t$	Gross loans to customers rate of deterioration (t)	−0.01984	−0.02427	−0.03633	−0.03585	0.10531
		0.0149	0.1601	0.0833	0.0903	0.0203
$\Delta\% GDLC_{t-1}$	Gross loans to customers rate of deterioration (t − 1)	−0.00657	−0.00330	0.00066		−0.03526
		0.4531	0.6412	0.8895		0.3750
2010	Year 2010	−0.00596	−0.00564	−0.00523	−0.00620	
		0.0000	0.0000	0.0007	0.0000	
2011	Year 2011	0.00505	0.00543	0.00652	0.00564	
		0.0000	0.0000	0.0008	0.0000	
2012	Year 2012	−0.00161	−0.00090	0.00152		
		0.2336	0.6820	0.6244		
C	Constant	0.00796	0.01031	0.00211	0.00236	−0.00572
		0.2705	0.2096	0.8767	0.7918	0.7016

Source: Own elaboration on data from *ABI Bilanci Fast*

Regarding the relationship between credit development and the *net interest return on loans*, the results of the estimation lead to accept *hypothesis 13*. Banks which showed a more intense loans to customers trend registered a higher return on the lending activity. Moreover, also the loans to customers growth rate registered the previous year results positive, even if not significant, while it results significantly positive according to both to the *pooled ordinary least squares* (POLS) and *panel data with random effects* (RE) approaches, suggesting that the positive effects of the loans to customers trend on the net interest return on loans result also lagged in time.

As for the impact of the credit quality deterioration on the performance of the lending activity, estimations confirm that the more the credit quality deteriorate, the lower is the net interest return on loans to customers. Both the gross deteriorated loans to customers incidence in t − 1 ($\%GDLC_{t-1}$) and the gross loans to customers rate of deterioration in t($\Delta\% GDLC_t$) results negatively significant in affecting the net interest return on loans to customers. Therefore *hypothesis 14* is verified: credit quality deterioration, affecting banks' credit supply policies, had a negative impact on the return on the lending activity. Given that the estimation of regression (2) leads to accept *hypothesis 9*, the findings regarding *hypothesis 13* and *hypothesis 14* seem to be in contrast. However, the estimation of the model interacted with the smaller banks dummy variable contributes to interpret this evidence. In fact, the negative effects of the gross loans to customers rate of deterioration in t(Δ % $GDLC_t$) result significantly stronger for larger banks than for smaller intermediaries. This estimation looks consistent with the descriptive evidence emerged in section "Main Descriptive Evidence and Hypotheses of Research". Smaller banks, although they registered a higher credit quality deterioration, registered a lower cost of risk than larger banks, which impacted less strongly on the return of the lending activity. This evidence lead to suppose that maybe smaller banks had been less prudent in loan loss provisioning than larger banks. Moreover, the estimation of regression (2) interacted with the smaller banks dummy variable let emerge that the positive effect of the loans to customers growth rate on the credit quality deterioration is significantly higher for larger banks. This evidence lead to think over possible negative impacts on the return of the lending activity in the future. As smaller banks registered a higher credit quality deterioration, with relatively lower negative income effect, they could face higher losses in the future, while larger intermediaries anticipated, charging the income statement with higher loans loss provisions in the past.

Finally, regarding the intermediation model features, among the variables considered in the model, only the *direct funding to total assets* variable, the *leverage ratio* variable and the *net fee to operating income* variable show a statistically significant relationship with the *net interest rate of return*. Banks characterized by a more customer oriented funding structure, by a lower incidence of net fee on operating income and by a higher incidence of equity on total assets registered higher returns. However, the leverage ratio could present an endogeneity problem, as higher returns contribute to let the equity and the leverage ratio increase. The *net interest margin on operating income* results positive even if not significant, while it results significantly positive according to both to the *pooled ordinary least squares* (POLS) and *panel data with random effects* (RE) approaches. These results lead to conclude that effectively banks characterized by more traditional intermediation models—as the smaller banks are, according to the descriptive evidence discussed in section "Main Descriptive Evidence and Hypotheses of Research"—could have experienced higher returns (*hypothesis 15*). The estimation of the model interacted with the smaller banks dummy variable, in accordance to the descriptive evidence discussed in section "Main Descriptive Evidence and Hypotheses of Research", lead to support this conclusion. Indeed, the leverage ratio is positive only for smaller banks, the loans to costumers to funding ratio is significantly positive for larger banks, the *net fee to operating income* is positive for larger banks and negative for smaller banks, while the net interest margin to operating income ratio is negative for larger banks and positive for smaller banks. According to the estimations, for smaller banks, the more traditional intermediation model features, effectively contribute to guarantee higher returns on the lending to customers, while for larger banks estimations do not lead to conclude the same.

7 Conclusions

Over the period between 2008 and 2012 the loans to customers trend, the quality deterioration of the loans to customers portfolios and the interest return on the lending to customers activity showed in Italy relevant heterogeneities by bank size and by juridical connotation. The analysis conducted in this paper, based on financial statements data between 2008 and 2012 from about 500 Italian banks, investigated if the heterogeneities showed in the loans to customers trend, in the quality deterioration of the loans to customers portfolios and in the interest return on the lending to customers activity are effectively significant and to what extent they could be explained by the differences that could be identified in the main features of the intermediation model adopted by banks. Moreover, it looked the existing relationship between the loans to customers trend and the credit quality deterioration and to what extent they conditioned the economic return of the lending to customers activity.

About the analysis of the loans to customers trend, the estimations confirm that over the period analyzed banks characterized by an assets composition more traditionally oriented towards lending to customers registered a more intense loans to customers trend. In particular, consistently with the descriptive evidence, the slowdown in the loans to customers development resulted effectively more relevant in 2011 and in 2012 than in the previous years. As for the other investigated factor, the estimations do not clearly lead to further conclusions.

Regarding the credit quality deterioration, the analysis basically confirms that smaller banks effectively showed a more intense loans to customers quality deterioration than larger banks. Moreover, the estimations confirm that banks which showed a more intense loans to customers trend registered a more relevant quality deterioration, especially in the case of larger banks. In particular, consistently with the descriptive evidence, in 2010 the credit quality deterioration was relatively less intense, while in 2012 it increased significantly. About the other aspects analyzed, the results of the estimations do not enable to conclude further more.

Finally, regarding the return on the lending activity, the analysis shows that banks characterized by a more customer oriented funding structure, by a lower incidence of net fee on operating income and by a higher incidence of equity on total assets registered higher returns. In particular, for smaller banks, the more traditional intermediation model features effectively contribute to guarantee higher returns on the lending to customers. Moreover, consistently with the descriptive evidence, the results of the estimations confirm that banks which showed a more intense loans to customers trend registered a higher return on the lending activity and that, at the same time, the more the credit quality deteriorates, the lower is the net interest return on loans to customers. Therefore, the credit quality deterioration results to have a negative impact on the return on the lending activity. However, although smaller banks experienced a higher credit quality deterioration, they registered a lower cost of risk than larger banks, which impacted less strongly on the return of the lending activity. This evidence leads to suppose that maybe smaller banks had been less prudent in loan loss provisioning than larger banks. Moreover, as the estimation regarding the credit quality deterioration let emerge that the positive effect of the loans to customers growth rate on the credit quality deterioration is significantly higher for larger banks, this evidence lead to think over possible negative impacts on the return of the lending activity in the future.

Overall, although the results of the estimations do not allow to confirm all the investigated aspects, the analysis clearly leads to conclude that over the period analysed banks which performed more intensely in terms of lending to customers trend effectively experienced a more significant credit quality deterioration, with significant negative impact in terms of return on the lending activity. In particular, as smaller banks registered a higher credit quality deterioration, with relatively lower negative income effect, they could face higher losses in the future, while larger intermediaries anticipated, charging the income statement with higher loans loss provisions in the past.

References

Albertazzi, U., & Bottero, M. (2013, July). *The procyclicality of foreign bank lending: Evidence from the global financial crisis* (Working Papers, 926). Bank of Italy.

Albertazzi, U., & Bottero, M. (2014). Foreign bank lending: Evidence from the global financial crisis. *Journal of International Economics*, *92*(Supplement 1), S22–S35.

Albertazzi, U., & Marchetti, D. J. (2010, April). *Credit supply, flight to quality and evergreen: An analysis of bank-firm relationships after Lehman* (Working Papers, 756). Bank of Italy.

Albertazzi, U., Ropele, T., Sene, G., & Signoretti, F. M. (2012, September). *The impact of the sovereign debt crisis on the activity of Italian banks* (Occasional Papers, 133). Bank of Italy.

Altunbas, Y., Gambacorta, L., & Marques-Ibanez, D. (2010). Bank risk and monetary policy. *Journal of Financial Stability, 6*(3), 121–129.

Altunbas, Y., Manganelli, S., & Marques-Ibanez, D. (2011, November). Ba*nk risk during the financial crisis. Do business models matter?* (Working Paper series, 1394). European Central Bank.

Ayadi R., Arbak E., & De Groen, W. P. (2011). *Business models in European banking. A pre- and post-crisis screening*. Brussels: Centre for European Policy Studies (with a contribution from Llewellyn, D. T.).

Ayadi, R., Arbak, E., & De Groen, W. P. (2012). *Regulation of European banks and business models: Towards a new paradigm?* Brussels: Centre for European Policy Studies (with a contribution from Llewellyn, D. T.).

Bank of Italy. (2010). *Annual report 2009*. Rome: Bank of Italy.

Bank of Italy. (2011). *Annual report 2010*. Rome: Bank of Italy.

Bank of Italy. (2012a). *Annual report 2011*. Rome: Bank of Italy.

Bank of Italy. (2012b, July). *Geographical breakdown of credit supply and demand.* Bank of Italy, Regional Economies, 23.

Bank of Italy. (2013a). *Annual report 2012*. Rome: Bank of Italy.

Bank of Italy. (2013b, July). *Geographical breakdown of credit supply and demand.* Bank of Italy, Regional Economies, 22.

Berg, J., Van Rixtel, A., Ferrando, A., De Bondt, G., & Scopel, S. (2005, February). *The bank lending survey for the Euro Area* (Occasional Paper Series, 23). European Central Bank.

Bofondi, M., Carpinelli, L., & Sette, E. (2013, April). *Credit supply during a sovereign debt crisis* (Working Papers, 909). Bank of Italy.

Bonaccorsi di Patti, E., & Sette, E. (2012, January). *Bank balance sheets and the transmission of financial shocks to borrowers: Evidence from the 2007–2008 crisis* (Working Papers, 848). Bank of Italy.

Brugnoni, G. C. (2014). *Creditoallaclientela e caratteristiche di fondo del modello di intermediazione delle banche italiane: evidenze empiriche per dimensione e categoria giuridica di banca tra il 2008 e il 2012 [Loans to customers and main intermediation model features of Italian banks: empirical evidence by bank size and juridical connotation between 2008 and 2012]*. Ph.D. Dissertation, Sapienza University of Rome.

Chiaramonte, L., Poli, F., & Oriani, M. (2013). On the relationship between bank business models and financial stability: Evidence from the financial crisis in OECD countries. In J. Falzoned (Ed.), *Bank stability, Sovereign debt and derivatives*, Palgrave Macmillan Studies in Banking and Financial Institutions (pp. 7–30). Basingstoke: Palgrave Macmillan.

Cosma, S., & Gualandri, E. (2014). Crisi del debito sovrano e modello di intermediazione delle banche italiane [The sovereign debt crisis: The impact on the intermediation model of Italian banks]. *Bancaria, 2*, 48–60.

De Bonis, R., Nuzzo, G., & Stacchini, M. (2014). Andamenti e determinanti del credito nell'area dell'euro [Lending in the Euro Area: trends and determinant factors]. In A. Zazzaro (Ed.), *Le banche e il credito alle imprese durante la crisi [Banks and lending to firms during the crisis]* (pp. 63–96). Il Mulino: Bologna.

De Mitri, S., Gobbi, G., & Sette, E. (2010, September). *Relationship lending in a financial turmoil* (Working Papers, 772). Bank of Italy.

Del Giovane, P., Eramo, G., & Nobili, A. (2010, June). *Disentangling demand and supply in credit developments: a survey-based analysis for Italy* (Working Papers, 764). Bank of Italy.

Del Giovane, P., Eramo, G., & Nobili, A. (2011). Disentangling demand and supply in credit developments: a survey-based analysis for Italy. *Journal of Banking & Finance, 35*(10), 2719–2732.

Del Giovane, P., Nobili, A., & Signoretti, F. M. (2013, November). *Supply tightening or lack of demand? An analysis of credit developments during the Lehman Brothers and the sovereign debt crises* (Working Papers, 942). Bank of Italy.

Di Battista, M. L., & Nieri, L. (2011). Un'indagine sulle differenze nelle politiche del credito delle banche italiane nella recente crisi finanziaria [Lending policies in Italian banks during the financial crisis]. *Bancaria, 3*, 11–19.

Di Battista, M. L., & Nieri, L. (2012). Crisi finanziaria e politiche creditizie delle banche in Italia: Un aggiornamento [Financial crisis and lending policies in Italian banks: An update]. *Osservatorio Monetario*, Associazione per lo Sviluppo degli Studi di Banca e Borsa (ASSBB), 41–50.

Di Battista, M. L., Nieri, L., & Patarnello, A. (2010). Gli effetti della crisi sull'offerta di credito da parte delle banche [Effects of the crisis on the lending supply by Italian banks], *Osservatorio Monetario*, Associazione per lo Sviluppo degli Studi di Banca e Borsa (ASSBB), 1, 42-56.

European Central Bank. (2003). *A bank lending survey for the euro area* [pdf]. Accessed January 3, 2016, from https://www.ecb.europa.eu/pub/pdf/other/pp65_75_mb200304en.pdf

Felici R., Manzoli, E., & Pico, R. (2012, July). *La crisi e le famiglie italiane: un'analisi microeconomica dei contratti di mutuo* [*Crisis and Italian households: A microeconomic analysis of mortgage contracts*] (Occasional Papers, 125). Bank of Italy.

Gambacorta, L., & Marques-Ibanez, D. (2011, May). *The bank lending channel. Lessons from the crisis* (Working Paper series, 1335). European Central Bank.

Gambacorta, L., & Mistrulli, P. E. (2014). Bank heterogeneity and interest rate setting: What lessons have we learned since Lehman Brothers? *Journal of Money, Credit and Banking, 46*(4), 753–778.

Kapan, T., & Minoiu, C. (2013, May). *Balance sheet strength and bank lending during the global financial crisis* (Working Paper, WP/13/102). International Monetary Fund.

Miani, C., Nicoletti, G., Notarpietro, A., & Pisani, M. (2012, September). *Banks' balance sheets and the macroeconomy in the Bank of Italy quarterly model* (Occasional Papers, 135). Bank of Italy.

Morelli, P., Pittaluga, G. B., and Seghezza, E., 2013. Credit supply and the rise in sovereign debt risk in the eurozone. In J. Falzon (Ed.), *Bank stability, sovereign debt and derivatives*, Palgrave Macmillan Studies in Banking and Financial Institutions (pp. 93–114). Basingstoke: Palgrave Macmillan.

Mundlak, Y. (1978). On the pooling of time series and cross section data. *Econometrica, 46*(1), 69–85.

Panetta, F., & Signoretti, F. M. (2010, April). *Domanda e offerta di credito in Italia durante la crisi finanziaria* [*Credit demand and supply in Italy during the financial crisis*] (Occasional Papers, 63). Bank of Italy.

Tutino, F., Colasimone, C., & Brugnoni, G. C. (2013). Credit development, quality deterioration and intermediation model: does bank size matter? Evidence from Italy between 2006 and 2010 financial crisis. In J. Falzon (Ed.), *Bank stability, sovereign debt and derivatives*, Palgrave Macmillan Studies in Banking and Financial Institutions (pp. 57–92). Basingstoke: Palgrave Macmillan.

Tutino, F., Colasimone, C., Brugnoni, G. C., and Riccetti, L., 2014. Intermediation model, bank size and lending to customers: is there a significant relationship? Evidence from Italy between 2008 and 2011. In T. Lindblom, S. Sjögren & M. Willesson (Eds.), Governance, regulation and bank stability, Palgrave Macmillan Studies in Banking and Financial Institutions (pp. 201–241). Basingstoke: Palgrave Macmillan.

Possibilities of Exotic Options Application in the Pro-ecological Investments Efficiency Assessment

Dziawgo Ewa

Abstract Environmental degradation is a global problem of modern civilisation. It is a challenge to contemporary enterprises to combine economic benefits and social responsibility with pro-environmental activities. Traditional methods of evaluation of investment projects may result in undervaluing some of the analysed pro-environmental projects. Hence, there is a need for new methods of investment project assessment which would enable active project management. The method of analysing real innovation enables valuation of flexibility embedded in a project. This is of particular importance in assessing pro-ecological projects. Some types of financial option and models of their valuation can facilitate pro-environmental management of the company value. This paper presents selected types of financial exotic-flexible options and models of their valuation. Their application can make it significantly easier to manage the pro-environmental investment projects of a company. The aim of the study is to present the possibility of transferring financial option pricing models of to the area of pro-ecological investment projects. This is of key importance in investments management.

Keywords Pricing models of options • Investment management • Risk management

1 Introduction

Modern society has an obligation to prevent degradation of the natural environment, which results from managing renewable and non-renewable resources in an irrational and improper manner. Adverse climate change, loss of biodiversity, unsustainable use of natural resources, decrease in the planet's ability to absorb pollution and waste necessitate the implementation of solutions aimed at reducing the system degradation. Solving environmental issues requires international cooperation. Environment degradation issues are widely discussed at many international

---

D. Ewa (✉)
Department of Econometrics and Statistics, Nicolaus Copernicus University, Toruń, Poland
e-mail: dziawew@umk.pl

M.H. Bilgin et al. (eds.), *Empirical Studies on Economics of Innovation, Public Economics and Management*, Eurasian Studies in Business and Economics 6,
DOI 10.1007/978-3-319-50164-2_5

forums, especially within the UNO and the EU. Of key importance in this regard is to develop a strategy and to implement green economy programmes. This is a type of economy which has a positive effect on people's welfare and social equality, while at the same time reducing environmental risks and the consumption of natural resources (Figge and Hahn 2012).

Green growth is a new, revolutionary paradigm of development, which sustains economic growth while at the same time ensuring climatic and environmental permanence (Jänicke 2012). While taking into account the future consequences of its actions, contemporary society should respect frugal production and consumption and recycle waste (Coddington 1993).

A key role in the concept of eco-development is played by enterprises. Increasing awareness in the society of the need to prevent environment degradation makes enterprises combine economic benefits and social responsibility with pro-environmental actions. Taking into account environmental issues improves a company's image. New factors which affect creating value in a company are associated with seeking innovative methods which can be used to evaluate the pro-environmental projects implemented by the company. The concept of financial exotic options analysis and models of pricing their options can be transmitted (with certain limitations) on area of estimate of efficiency of investment. The purpose of this paper is to present the applicability of exotic-flexible options in the assessment of the pro-ecological projects.

2 Implementation of the Assumptions of Pro-environmental Policy by Enterprises

The state has some environmental protection tools which it can use to control environmental protection processes:

- Legal instruments: emission standards, regulations regarding licensing certain kinds of activities, regulations which necessitate that environmental protection requirements should be met, principles of eco-development as a criterion of land development, regulations concerning carrying out an environmental impact assessment, an official list of hazardous waste.
- Economic instruments: ecological fees, environmental penalties, product fees, subsidies and emission trading (Poskrobko 1998).

Instruments of social impact are also important in the system of environmental management. Their aim is to influence individuals and social groups, both directly and indirectly, with an intention of encouraging them to act pro-environmentally. Ecological education of the society should ensure proper perception of the environment and processes that take place within it.

The environmental policy of the authorities, legal and administrative environmental regulations, international regulations as well as an increase in the society's awareness of the need to prevent degradation of the natural environment—all this helps to modify economic activities in companies, as a consequence of which companies try to combine economic benefit and social responsibility with environmentally friendly actions. It is desirable, when seeking permanent partners and strategic investors, to take into account both good financial results and implementation of various elements of social and pro-environmental policy (Dziawgo and Dziawgo 2016).

Taking into account environmental aspects contributes to improvement of environmental parameters of a company operation. Examples of implementation of environmental priorities by companies include: minimising resource- and energy-intensity of production and storage, implementation of environmentally-friendly changes in manufacturing technology, reducing environmental nuisance caused by the products offered by a company, reduction of pollution and waste generated directly by the company, creating conditions which favour recovery of raw materials, recycling, using waste as an additional source of energy, carrying out and sponsoring of research work devoted to launching new pro-environmental products and improvement of manufacturing processes, sponsoring programmes of environmental education.

Scientific and innovative pro-environmental research is of key importance in the process of making companies pro-environmental. Implementation of low-waste and no-waste technologies should frequently be accompanied by existing technologies, which—for various reasons—cannot be replaced with more environmentally friendly ones. If new products are launched or if changes are made in existing ones, it is necessary to limit the harmful effect on the environment in all phases of the product life cycle. This means that the amount of waste should be reduced or minimised at every stage of the process of the product manufacture, sale, consumption and at the post-consumption stage (Common and Stagl 2005).

Waste recycling and its reduction at the source are the main methods of minimising waste applied in production companies. Waste reduction at source can be achieved by changing the raw material used in production or by a change of the production process. Implementation of pro-environmental projects can bring tangible benefits for a company, such as: material and energy savings, increasing the use of raw materials and energy by limiting losses and increasing efficiency of production processes, reducing environmental fees, avoiding penalties for violation of environmental protection regulations, an increase in economic effectiveness of a company and, in consequence, in its competitive edge, reduction of production costs, an improvement of the company image thanks to offering environmentally friendly products.

3 Real Options in the Analysis of Pro-ecological Projects

The net present value (NPV) method is one of the most commonly used ones in the investment account (Myers 1984). According to this method, such investment projects should be accepted for which the NPV has a positive value. An assessment of an investment project by the NPV method can undervalue certain projects as it does not value the decision flexibility of certain investment projects.

When an investment decision is taken, concerns may arise about the date of starting an investment, about expanding the scale of the project, temporary suspension of the project or its discontinuation (Amram and Kulatilaka 1999). The real option analysis method enables valuation of the ability to react swiftly to changes in the environment. Therefore, it is an analytical tool which facilitates active management of an investment project (Dziawgo 2014).

Real innovation is a right (but not an obligation) to change a decision within an investment project if new factors appear that affect its execution (Trigeorgis 2001). For some investment projects, several types of real options can occur simultaneously (Fig. 1).

Defer option means that the project execution is delayed in order to examine more closely the changing market environment. If there are any circumstances which can have an adverse effect on the company, defer option helps to avoid unprofitable investments and suffering losses. On the other hand, if the project is executed later (in more advantageous market conditions), it can generate profits.

One of such examples of defer option is an investment project which involves the acquisition of land with mineral deposits. Before excavation is started, a series of additional analyses should be carried out to explore the contents of the deposit better.

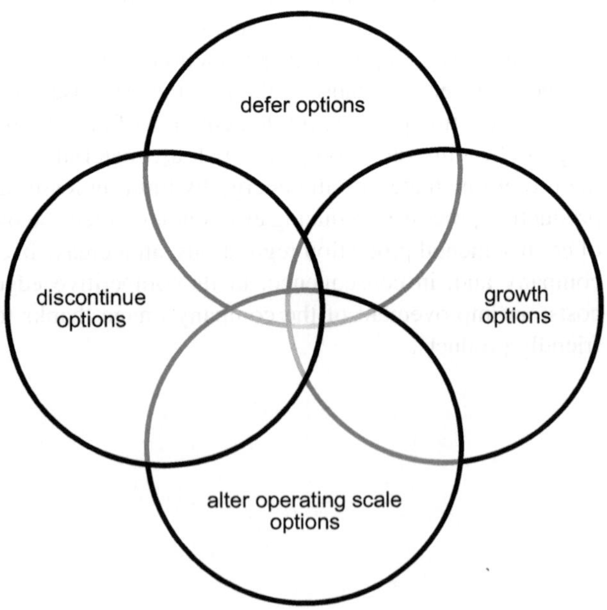

Fig. 1 Real options in the investment projects

The results of such analyses can affect the decisions to assign sufficient resources in order to reduce the amount of waste or to increase the degree of waste reuse.

Discontinue option enables one to discontinue a project if disadvantageous market conditions occur or if technical analyses give negative results. Examples of pro-environmental projects in which discontinue option is applied include: taking into account environmental characteristics when purchasing goods, carrying out R&D work aimed at obtaining materials by recycling or from new sources, participation in the transfer of environmental techniques and technologies.

Growth option enables a company to carry out more projects. A company uses its resources and carries out an investment project to ensure expansion of its activities by new products and modern technologies. The following pro-environmental projects can be considered within the growth option: placing new pro-environmental products on the market, implementation of new technologies in the production process, in which materials recovered by recycling are used, applying technologies which reduce the consumption of raw materials and minimise the amount of waste produced, implementation of energy-saving technologies, placing new technologies to minimise the amount of waste.

Owing to alter operating scale option, it is possible to differentiate production scale depending on the changing market conditions. Projects undertaken in the company can be temporarily reduced or suspended and re-launched. The production scale can be periodically increased or reduced. This option improves the effectiveness of the operating activities. The option of altering operating scale can include undertakings aimed at reducing the resources consumption rate, including materials obtained from recycled waste in the production process, reducing materials and energy consumption.

The value of real options is dependent on the following factors: the current value of the benefits of the investment project, investment layouts, the expiry time of the investment project, the discount rate being the risk-free rate, volatility of cash flows, and the cash flows lost (Fig. 2).

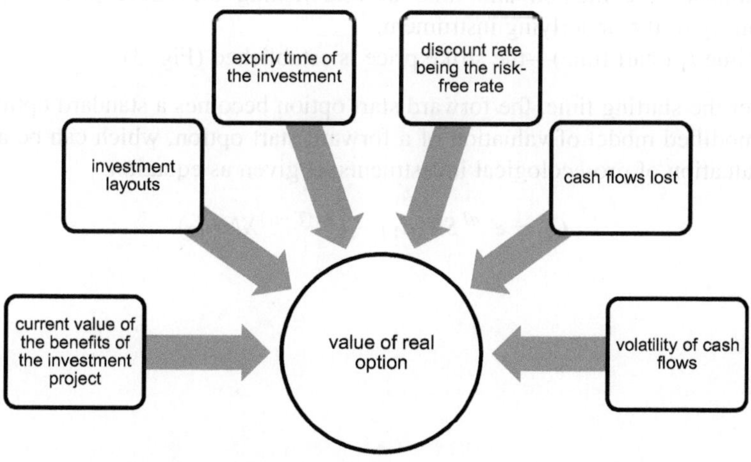

Fig. 2 Factors which effect on the value of real options

4 The Exotic-Flexible Options in the Assessment of Pro-ecological Investments

There are certain similarities between real and financial innovations. The buyer of the financial call/put option has the right (but not the obligation) to buy/sell a specific underling instrument at the certain time (the expiration date) for a certain price (the strike price). Financial options are issued on the interest rate, currency, economic index, shares (Hull 2003; Dziawgo 2003). Both financial and real options are implemented if they bring benefits to the buyer. It is also typical of both option types that they are applied in a risky environment and that they enable a choice of alternative solutions. The main differences between real and financial options include the possibility of an active reaction of the buyer of a real option to the factors which affect its value, the real options' being characterised a longer time to expiry and absence of the exclusive right to implement a real option. A real option can be implemented by a competitor that is carrying out a similar investment.

Exotic options are characterized by the income structure different from the structure of standard options (Zhang 2001; Dziawgo 2013). Flexible options are the time-dependent options in the class of exotic options. The buyer their options is entitled to selection of some option features in the future. The flexible options are the following (Rubinstein 1991): forward start option, chooser options (simple and complex).

4.1 *Forward Start Option*

Parameters of the forward start option are established at two moments:

- At time t_0 (beginning of the option life cycle) an agreement is concluded, which establishes the method and time of establishing the strike price, type and quantity of the underlying instrument.
- At time t_1 (start time)—the strike price is established (Fig. 3).

After the starting time, the forward start option becomes a standard option.

A modified model of valuation of a forward start option, which can be applied for evaluation of pro-ecological investments, is given as equation:

$$C_f = e^{-qT} SN(d_1) - e^{-r(T-t_1)} XN(d_2) \tag{1}$$

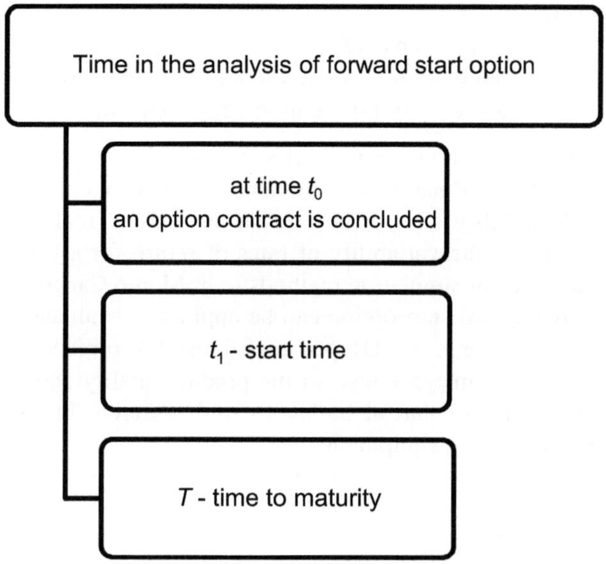

Fig. 3 Time and forward start options

where:

C_f Value of the call forward start option

S Value of future pecuniary income from the investment project, re-valued for year t_1 $S = \sum_{i=0}^{n} S_{\tau_i}(1+\mu)^{-\tau_i}$, S_{τ_i} Pecuniary income from the investment project in year τ_i

n The period of the investment project (years)

μ Discount rate

r Risk-free interest rate

X Investment outlay in year t_1

T Time to the option maturity

σ Coefficient of volatility of the cash flows generated by the investment

q Lost cash flows

$N(d)$ Cumulative probability function for a standard normal variable distribution

$$d_1 = \frac{\ln\left(\frac{S}{X}\right) + \left(r - q + 0{,}5\sigma^2\right)(T - t_1)}{\sigma\sqrt{T - t_1}} \quad d_2 = d_1 - \sigma\sqrt{T - t_1}.$$

The financial effectiveness of the investment in terms of real options is:

$$ROV = C_f - I \tag{2}$$

where:

ROV Real options value

I Value of initial investment in research and development—value of updated cash flow (until the moment of beginning)

other designations remain the same as in formula (1).

If the *ROV* has a positive value, the investment is profitable.

Variability of cash flow in an analysis of real options can be determined by estimating the variability of rates of return for a twin instrument, from historical data or from simulation methods (e.g. Monte Carlo).

A forward start option can be applied to evaluate the financial effectiveness of two-stage (e.g. R&D) pro-environmental projects, whose first stage involves research in improvement of the product quality and manufacturing processes and the second—financial outlay for the research, but also purchase of appropriate manufacturing equipment.

4.2 Chooser Options

In the case of a chooser option, the option's strike price, expiration time and the so-called chooser time are determined on the contract date. At the chooser time the buyer of the option decides whether the possessed option will be a call option or a put option with a predetermined strike price and expiration time (Fig. 4).

If the chooser option is simple, then the strike price and the times to maturity for the call and the put option are identical. In the case of a complex chooser option the strike price and/or the times to maturity for the call and the put option are different.

A modified model of valuation of a simple chooser option, which can be applied for evaluation of pro-environmental investments, is given as formula:

$$C_s = S\left(e^{-qT}N(d_1) - e^{-qt'}N\left(-\widetilde{d}_1\right)\right) - Xe^{-rT}\left(N(d_2) - N\left(-\widetilde{d}_2\right)\right) \quad (3)$$

where:

C_s Value of the simple chooser option

t' Chooser time

$t' \in [0; T], X$ Investment outlay in year *t'*,

$$d_1 = \ln\frac{\frac{S}{X}+\left(r-q-0{,}5\sigma^2\right)T}{\sigma\sqrt{T}}, \quad d_2 = \ln\frac{\frac{S}{X}+\left(r-q+0{,}5\sigma^2\right)T}{\sigma\sqrt{T}}, \quad \widetilde{d}_1 = \ln\frac{\frac{S}{e^{-r(T-t')}X}+\left(r-q-0{,}5\sigma^2\right)t'}{\sigma\sqrt{t'}},$$

$$\widetilde{d}_2 = \ln\frac{\frac{S}{e^{-r(T-t')}X}+\left(r-q+0{,}5\sigma^2\right)t'}{\sigma\sqrt{t'}},$$

other designations remain the same as in formula (1).

The financial effectiveness of the investment is:

Fig. 4 Time and chooser options

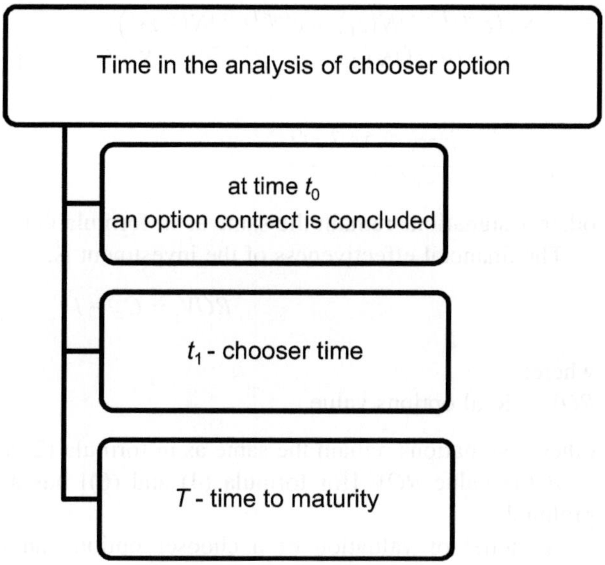

$$ROV = C_s - I \tag{4}$$

where:

ROV Real options value

other designations remain the same as in formula (2) and (3).

A modified model of valuation of a complex chooser option, which can be applied for evaluation of pro-ecological investments, is:

$$\begin{aligned} C_c = {} & S(e^{-qT_1}N_1(x, y_1, \lambda_1) - e^{-qT_2}N_1(-x, -y_2, \lambda_2)) - \\ & -X_1e^{-rT_1}N_1\left(x - \sigma\sqrt{t'}, y_1 - \sigma\sqrt{T_1}, \lambda_1\right) + X_2^{-rT_2}N_1\left(-x + \sigma\sqrt{t'}, -y_2 + \sigma\sqrt{T_1}, \lambda_2\right) \end{aligned} \tag{5}$$

where:

C_c	Value of the complex chooser option
$N(a, b, \lambda)$	Bivariate normal function
T_1	Time to the call option maturity
T_2	Time to the put option maturity
X_1	Investment outlay in year t' (for call option)
X_2	Investment outlay in year t' (for put option),

$$x = \frac{\ln\frac{Se^{-qt'}}{S_{cr}e^{-rt'}}}{\sigma\sqrt{T}} + 0,5\sigma^2T,\ y_i = \frac{\ln\frac{Se^{-qT_i}}{X_i\, e^{-rT_i}} + 0,5\sigma^2T_i}{\sigma\sqrt{T_i}},\ \lambda_i = \frac{\sqrt{t'}}{T_i},\ \text{for } i = 1, 2,$$

S_{cr} is the solution to following equation:

$$S_{cr}\left(e^{-q(T_1-t')}N(z_1)+e^{-q(T_2-t')}N(-z_2)\right)-$$
$$-X_1e^{-r(T_1-t')}N\left(z_1-\sigma\sqrt{T_1-t'}\right)-X_2{}^{-r(T_2-t')}N\left(-z_2+\sigma\sqrt{T_2-t'}\right)=0$$

$$z_i=\frac{\ln\frac{S_{cr}e^{-q(T_i-t')}}{X_ie^{-r(T_i-t')}}+0,5\sigma^2(T_i-t')}{\sigma\sqrt{T_i-t'}},$$

other designations remain the same as in formula (1).

The financial effectiveness of the investment is:

$$ROV=C_c-I \tag{6}$$

where:

ROV Real options value,

other designations remain the same as in formula (2) and (5).

If the value *ROV* [for formula (4) and (6)] has a positive, the investment is profitable.

A model of valuation of a chooser option can be applied to evaluate the effectiveness of two-stage pro-environmental (e.g. R&D or bearing a high risk) projects with the following properties:

- The first stage involves a series of tests.
- Taking actions included in the second stage depends on the test results from the first stage and the variability of the cash flows generated by the investment project.

5 Conclusion

For highly predictable and poorly flexible projects, the NPV method (as well as other discount methods) is a sufficient analytical tool for evaluation of the financial effectiveness of a project.

Application of a concept of real options in evaluation of investment projects is justified for projects with high risk and flexibility. Real options can be used to pricing the flexibility embedded in a project. The method of real option analysis is an alternative and complement to conventional methods of evaluation of investment project effectiveness.

In many pro-environmental projects, the outcome is highly uncertain; reaction to changing market conditions is also possible. Frequently, considerable financial outlays must be made at the initial stage of execution of pro-environmental projects. However, in a long term, pro-environmental projects can considerably increase the company value.

If financial effectiveness of pro-environmental two-stage investment projects is evaluated, a model of valuation of the forward option and the chooser option is commonly used. The structure of these options contains time-dependence. Considering this feature, models of valuation for these options can be transferred to the area of valuation of pro-ecological projects, which consists of two stages and from which options of deferring, growth, discontinuation and altering the operation scale can be isolated. Considering the possibility of project valuation with respect to a selected moment and type of investment, flexible options can help company management to take a decision regarding carrying out a pro-ecological investment project.

References

Amram, M., & Kulatilaka, N. (1999). *Real options: managing strategic investment in an uncertain world*. Boston, MA: Harvard Business School Press.

Coddington, W. (1993). *Environmental marketing: Positive strategies for reaching the green consumer*. New York: McGraw-Hill.

Common, M., & Stagl, S. (2005). *Ecological economics: An introduction*. New York: Cambridge University Press.

Dziawgo, E. (2003). *Modele kontraktów opcyjnych* [Models of the options]. Toruń: UMK.

Dziawgo, E. (2013). *Wycena opcji egzotycznych* [Exotic options pricing]. Toruń: UMK.

Dziawgo, E. (2014). Real options in the assessment of the company's pro-ecological investments. *Copernical Journal of Finance and Accounting, 3*(1), 61–73.

Dziawgo, L., & Dziawgo, E. (2016). Ecological evolution of financial market: Ecologically responsible investment. In: M. H. Bilgin, H. Danis, E. Demir, & U. Can (Eds.), *Business Challenges in the Changing Economic Landscape-Vol. 1: Proceedings of the 14th Eurasia Business and Economics Society Conference* (pp. 167–178). Basel: Springer.

Figge, F., & Hahn, T. (2012). Is green and profitable sustainable? Assessing the trade-off between economic and environmental aspects. *International Journal of Production Economics, 140*(1), 92–102.

Hull, J. C. (2003). *Options, futures and other derivatives*. Upper Saddle River, NJ: Prentice Hall.

Jänicke, M. (2012). Green growth: From a growing eco-industry to economic sustainability. *Energy Policy, 48*(8), 13–21.

Myers, S. C. (1984). Finance theory and financial strategy. *Interfaces, 14*(1), 126–137.

Poskrobko, B. (1998). *Zarządzanie środowiskiem* [Environmental management]. Warszawa: PWE.

Rubinstein, M. (1991). Pay now, choose later. *Risk, 4*(2), 44–47.

Trigeorgis, L. (2001). Real options: An overview. In E. S. Schwartz & L. Trigeorgis (Eds.), *Real options and investment under uncertainty: Classical readings and recent contributions* (pp. 103–134). Cambridge: MIT Press.

Zhang, P. G. (2001). *Exotic options. A guide to second generation options*. Singapore: World Scientific.

Weather Derivatives: Another Need for India

Nidhi Choudhary and Girish K. Nair

Abstract The weather derivatives are comparatively new instruments which were launched only in 1997 for the first time in USA. The instrument since then has developed huge market in USA and Europe. This paper is an attempt to understand the working of the instrument and then conclude if the instrument is a good product for India. The need analysis of weather derivatives in India will be done as per the three sectors of the Indian Economy, namely Primary or the agriculture and allied activities sector, secondary or the manufacturing sector and tertiary or the service sector. The analysis will be done in terms of threat faced by these sectors from uncertain weather in India and how can weather derivatives help in controlling the loss in this condition. The paper is an analysis of sectoral need of weather derivatives. The paper will also discuss the major challenges which Indian economy can face while introducing weather derivatives.

Keywords Weather • Derivatives • Risk management • Sectors of Indian Economy

1 Introduction

The Oxford dictionaries (n.d.) define weather as 'the state of the atmosphere at a particular place and time as regards heat, cloudiness, dryness, sunshine, wind, rain, etc.' The atmospheric condition or rather the weather conditions have always stood as an important aspect of running any business. More importantly it is defined as an important aspect of uncontrollable or the systematic risk. Weather conditions like rain, storms, hurricanes, tsunamis etc. pose a big threat to business activities. Mist,

N. Choudhary (✉)
FMS-WISDOM, State Bank of India School of Commerce and Banking, Banasthali University, Vanasthali, Rajasthan, India
e-mail: nidhic10@gmail.com

G.K. Nair
International Hospitality Management, Stenden University, Doha, Qatar
e-mail: GNair@stenden.edu.qa

M.H. Bilgin et al. (eds.), *Empirical Studies on Economics of Innovation, Public Economics and Management*, Eurasian Studies in Business and Economics 6,
DOI 10.1007/978-3-319-50164-2_6

storm, hail, visibility, moisture, high pressure, low pressure, heat, etc. can be critical for a business at times. These unpredictable conditions pose a serious threat to business turnovers of small and medium segment businesses to giant empires to multinational corporations etc. It is also argued that the developing nations are more exposed to weather risk than developed countries. According to an approximation by meteorological research institutions, more than 80% of the business activities in the world are weather dependent (Müller and Grandi 2000). Fundamentally each sector of the economy is openly or incidentally subject to the effect of the weather directly or indirectly.

One of the very usual ways of covering these risks was insurance. But the concept of insurance covers the losses caused by high risk event (like hurricane) which have a low probability of occurrence. The amount of claim is restricted to the limit of the loss incurred. But the business is more impacted by less riskier events (like higher or lower than average rainfall or snow, etc.) which have a higher likelihood of existence. In such a scenario, the weather derivatives are blessings for the business houses. An innovation of financial engineering, weather derivatives are business tools that can be utilized by organizations or individuals as measure of a risk management policy to reduce their risk linked with adversarial or sudden weather conditions. The underlying for these derivative contracts is the weather condition. The stakeholder who trades a weather derivative decides to endure this risk for a premium. If weather is good and nothing adverse happens, he takes a profit for himself. However, in case of turn of events and adverse weather conditions, the company who buys the derivative instrument is entitled to the agreed amount. The weather derivatives are very different from insurance contracts which cover low-probability events like cyclones and windstorms. On the other hand, weather derivatives are shield against high-probability events like a colder-than-expected winter, etc. The insurance claim is dependent on valuation of losses instigated by the definite variables but in event of weather derivatives, the clearing of the claim rest on the existence of the adverse weather condition. Hence, the entire process of valuation of loss is eliminated which reduces the costs by leaps and bounds. In other words, there will not be uncertainties in association with the initiation of payment to the economic operators. Furthermore, since only the value of the weather derivative is associated with the meteorological variable, the inconveniences regarding the information asymmetry can be excluded.

More specifically, a financial weather derivative contract may be defined as a weather liable contract whose settlement will be in an amount of cash which will be calculated on the bases of future weather events. The disbursement value in this case will be determined from a weather index, expressed as values of a weather variable, measured at a specified location. Table 1 summarizes the difference between weather insurance and weather derivatives.

Table 1 Weather insurance vs. weather derivatives

Weather insurance	Weather derivatives
The payment is subject to the loss incurred by insurer due to adverse weather conditions	The payment is not subjected to any business loss. It is based on weather index
There should be insurable interest to buy a weather insurance policy	The purchase of a weather derivative can be even out of speculative motive
The policies are not tradable	The derivative contracts are traded on exchange
Used to cover high risk low probability events	Used to cover low risk high probability events

2 Working of Weather Derivatives

Weather risk products appear to be relatively new in the market which was introduced only in 1997. The first weather derivative contract was entered between Enron and Koch Industries which was aimed at transferring the risk of adverse weather. These contracts are not linked to prices of any underlying asset or index, but they are connected to weather indices which are generated from data obtained from meteorology stations. The underlying index can be of wind speed, snowfall, precipitation, temperature, or a combination of two or more. A wide majority of weather derivative contracts are either temperature-related (98%), rain-related (0.9%), snow (0.5%), and wind (0.2%). Figure 1 presents categorization of weather based derivative products.

One of the primer features of the derivative contract is that the contract will have the maximum pay-out specified which is also called 'Limit' or the 'Notional Value'. Similarly, the contract will also have a 'Trigger or Strike Level' which is the pre-set weather index level at which contract initiates to pay out. The contract can be a put, call, collar, swap, straddle, etc. in structure. The pay-off of this contract is determined by the performance of the index comparative to an initiated value and not on the real loss. However, the maximum payment is 'capped' and indicated in the contract. The logic is that the purchaser of such a derivative would be reimbursed by the amount for which his cash flows are unfavorably impacted by the weather.

For example, most derivative contracts in the US are based on Heating Degree Days (HDD) index for winter protection and Cooling Degree Days (CDD) index for summer protection. They are calculated as follows:

$$\text{HDD} = \text{Max}(0, 65^{\circ}\text{F minus average temperature in a day}) \qquad (1)$$

$$\text{CDD} = \text{Max}(0, 65^{\circ}\text{F minus average temperature in a day}) \qquad (2)$$

The threshold temperature for CDD and HDD has conventionally been 65 °F. The main reason behind is that most of the consumers are likely to use extra energy to warm their homes when the temperature is under 65 °F and when it is beyond 65 °F, they tend to use energy on cooling. As discussed, the pay-off is defined as a

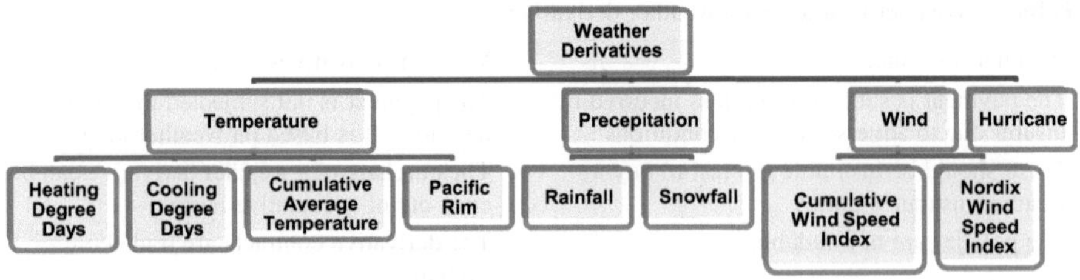

Fig. 1 Categorization of weather derivatives

Table 2 Example of contract

Temperature	Degrees
Maximum	84
Minimum	62
Average	73
Base Temperature	65
CDD	8

specific dollar amount and 'capped' in the contract. Let there be a contract of \$500 per degree day capped at \$15,000.

In case of the contract represented in Table 2,

$$\text{CDD} = 65^\circ \text{ minus Average temperature in a day}$$
$$\text{CDD} = 65^\circ - 73^\circ = -8^\circ$$

The payment in such situation $= 8^\circ \times 500 =$ \$4000.

3 Objective of the Study

The main objective of the study is to comment on the need of weather derivative contracts in various sectors of Indian economy after understanding the working of the contract. The study has done a thorough review of literature and highlighted the success of the instrument in various countries.

4 Literature Review

The weather derivatives have attained high attention from academicians, press and financial experts in the western countries but the product has failed to gain the required attention in Indian economy. A lot of studies have been done about the need and usefulness of the product in the various economies of the world including

India. The following section presents some of the relevant studies for the current research.

Chen et al. (2006) scrutinized the prospective of weather derivatives in evading against livestock profit risk, which mainly concerns the profit risk from heat stress in hot and humid summers in US economy. With the access to conjectural weather derivatives and reduced equipment, the producer's ideal portfolio choice of these two instruments is derived in a "mean-variance utility maximization framework". The study concludes that weather derivatives can work as a standby for abatement technologies. Further, the study suggested that the concurrent usage of them is more profitable than using them alone.

Stoppa and Hess (2003) analyzed the case of rainfall index insurance with the help of weather derivatives in agriculture policies with reference of Morocco. They concluded that the weather derivatives can be beneficial to take care of the general part of agricultural risk, implying the possible applications in separate arrangements of agricultural risk disclosure.

Hurduzeu and Constantin (2008) emphasized that one of the features that had an important influence on the economic development was characterized by climatic change. The issue of the weather risk management holds a priority position for Governments at international level, corporate houses impacted by weather and the insurance companies. The authors further tried to discourse a more appropriate tactic than the traditional insurance policies on the issue of weather risk management by offering a novel unusual risk management explanation denoted by weather derivatives. Additionally, they also focused upon agriculture as an important economic sector and emphasized the need of employing weather derivatives in agriculture.

In one of the unique study, Paul (2013) has made an attempt to comment on the feasibility of weather derivatives in India. He concluded that the weather derivatives in India have a very long way to go and the instrument will see the light of the day due to loopholes found in insurance programs. But there are certain issues on the awareness, technical, infrastructure and on legislative end to make them work in India.

Another research (Sharma and Vashishtha 2007) studied the risk hedging prospects of weather derivatives in agriculture and power sector in India. The research indicated that the traditional methods of risk hedging tools and methods have proved to be costly and insufficient for the vast economy like India. The research further suggested that weather derivative might prove to be more malleable, maintainable and efficient for Indian economy. Agarwal (2002) has also commented that a derivative product offers more than an insurance product. An insurance product is just capable of providing a cover but a weather derivative is not only capable of providing a cover but also provides more options like 'trade feasibility' and 'flexibility'.

Therefore, weather derivatives are beautiful creations of financial engineering. The instrument is a need of the hour for all Indian economy. The presented research is an attempt to do a more detailed analysis for the requirement of the instrument in India.

5 Global Turnover of Weather Derivative Market

The derivative market is one of the fastest growing markets in the world. The weather section of the derivative market is not deprived of this Midas touch. The open interest in the market has shown an exponential growth since 2002 (Fig. 2). However, the markets could not escape the impact of recession in 2009 and the market size is negatively sloping since then. But it cannot be denied that the market has shown a tremendous growth over the years as shown in Fig. 3. The bulk of deals

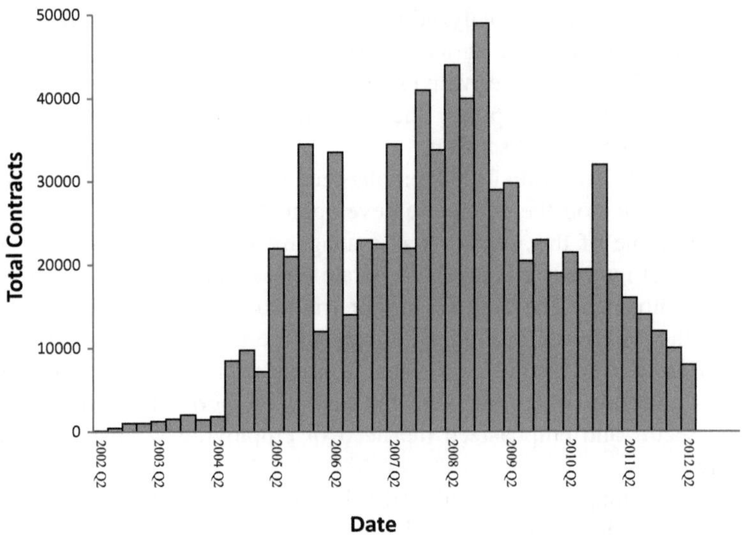

Fig. 2 Open interests in global weather derivatives market. Source: Pricewaterhouse Coopers (2011)

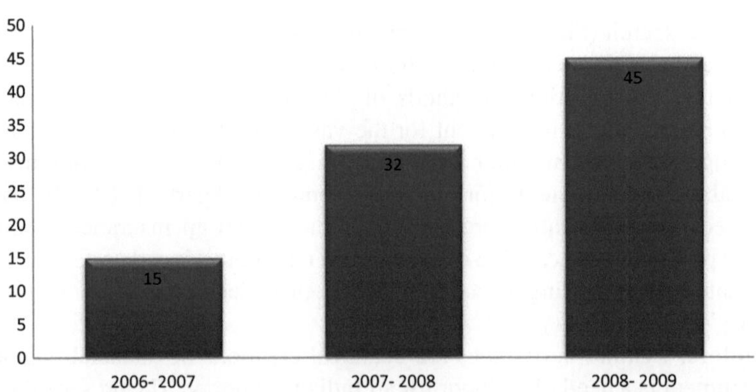

Fig. 3 Turnover of global weather derivative market (in billion dollars). Source: Pricewaterhouse Coopers (2011)

in weather derivative are still on-going in the US, but there is an emerging market within Europe which is concentrated in France, UK, Scandinavia and Germany. The dealings in European market are primarily over-the-counter (OTC) and not exchange traded contracts. The market is dominated by energy players, insurers and reinsurers

6 Weather Derivatives for Various Sectors of Indian Economy

The present study has done the need analysis of weather derivatives in India as per the three sectors, namely Primary Sector (Includes agriculture and allied activities like horticulture, animal husbandry, fishing, etc.), Secondary Sector (Includes various manufacturing and its sub sector.) and Tertiary Sector (Includes service like retail, healthcare, education, etc.)

6.1 Weather Derivatives for Indian Primary Sector

Despite the fact that agribusiness, including unified exercises, represented just 18 for every penny of the GDP at steady (2011–2012) costs in 2013–2014 as provided in the Economic Survey of India (Ministry of Finance 2015), its part in the nation's economy is much greater with its offer altogether job as indicated by the 2001 evaluation, keeping on being as high as 47% (The World Bank 2013). The declining offer of the farming and unified segment in the nation's GDP is predictable with ordinary advancement direction of any economy, however quick agrarian development stays crucial for employments, livelihoods, and the sustenance security (Ministry of Finance 2015). Farming in India relies on upon rainfall in light of the fact that watering system offices are not completely created. On the off chance that the rain comes up short or it rains intensely or troublesome, it ruins agriculture output. Agribusiness is likewise a bet with temperature. Too high a temperature contrarily influences the efficiency of a yield. The present protection framework in India does not provide food much for any loss of product because of unfavorable and unavoidable climatic conditions.

The crop insurance on a large scale was introduced in India in 1985. However, even till today, crop insurance in India is not available for all crops in all state. This is a major gap wherein weather derivatives can be of big help. Further, the red tapism and the 'Babu' system in Indian governance is a major problem in implementation of the insurance system (Kumar 2016). The weather derivatives however are more transparent in this context. Further, owing to the features of weather derivatives, they fill up the gap of requirements which is created by the current features of crop insurance.

Table 3 Key indicators of agriculture sector

#	Item	2011–2012	2012–2013	2013–2014	2014–2015
1	Growth in GDP in agriculture and allied sectors	–	1.2	3.7	1.1
	Share of agriculture and allied sectors in total GDP	18.4	18	18	N/A
	Crops	12	11.7	11.8	
	Livestock	4	4	3.9	
	Forestry and logging	1.6	1.5	1.4	
	Fishing	0.8	0.8	0.9	
2	Share of agriculture and allied sectors in total GCF	8.6	7.7	7.9	
	Crops	7.4	6.5	6.6	
	Livestock	0.8	0.7	0.7	
	Forestry and logging	0.1	0.1	0.1	
	Fishing	0.4	0.4	0.5	
3	GCF in agriculture and allied sectors as per cent to GDP of the sector (at current 2011–2012 prices)	18.3	15.5	14.8	

Source: Ministry of Finance (2015)

Table 4 Performance of monsoon 2003–2012 (June–September)

Year	Number of meteorological subdivisions			Percentage of districts with normal/excess rainfall	Percentage of long period average rainfall for the country as a whole
	Normal	Excess	Deficient/ scanty		
2003	23	8	5	76	102
2004	23	0	13	56	87
2005	24	8	4	72	99
2006	21	6	9	60	100
2007	18	13	5	72	106
2008	31	2	3	76	98
2009	11	3	22	42	78
2010	17	14	5	70	102
2011	26	7	3	76	101
2012	22	1	13	58	92

Source: Ministry of Finance (2012), http://indiabudget.nic.in/es2012-13/echap-08.pdf

The agriculture sector in India is an important source of employment for a majority of population. Moreover, the sector has a very important source of food, food products and even provide raw material for the various industrial sectors. The variation of the monsoon from the average numbers is a big problem for the sector. The performance of the monsoon (as shown in the Tables 3 and 4) is unpredictable

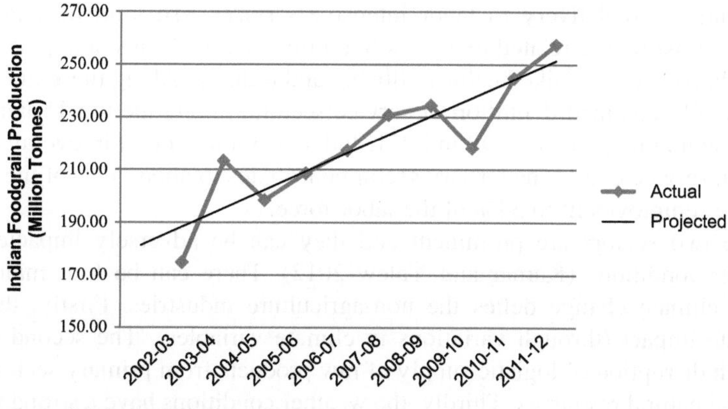

Source: (Ministry of Finance , 2015)

Fig. 4 Actual and projected Indian food grain productions

and uncertain. This adds to the problem of actual vs. projected food grain production in the country (Fig. 4). The fluctuations in the expected food grain production have led to various other problems like inflation, black marketing of food grains, etc.

In such a situation, the weather derivatives can prove to be an effective tool for the sector. The scope for the growth of weather derivatives in India is well highlighted by the facts presented. As pointed by Panagariya et al. (2009), India is highly vulnerable to climate change. This uncertainly calls for sufficient preparation for adaptation to possible extreme weather change effects. This makes weather derivatives in India a need to fight against the variations in temperatures, rainfall, snow, etc.

6.2 Weather Derivatives for Secondary and Service Sector

The secondary sector is the manufacturing sector in an economy. The sector is one of the dominant sectors of the economy, which acts like the backbone of development. The industrial sector in the economy consists of engineering, mining, electricity and production activities. The sector accounts for 27.6% of the GDP and provides employment to 14% of the total workforce (Ministry of Finance 2015). Today India holds some key commercial ventures in the areas like steel, designing and machine instruments, gadgets, petrochemicals, and so on. Significance has likewise been given to enhance the framework of the nation.

The service sector covers a wide exhibit of services extending from service given by the most modern segments like information transfers, satellite mapping, and PC programming to basic services like those performed by the hair stylist, the craftsman, and the handyman; exceedingly capital intensive services like aeronautics and delivery to labor intensive services like tourism, and housing; heavy infrastructure related exercises like railroads, roadways, and ports to social part related exercises like health wellbeing and training. Along these lines, there is no formally confined definition of service sector. Among the top 15 nations with most astounding general GDP in 2011, India positioned ninth in overall GDP and tenth in service GDP. The tertiary sector contributes to about 57% of the GDP and provides employment to 34% of the labor force.

The two sectors are prominent and they can be adversely impacted by the weather conditions (Kumar and Yalew 2012). There can be four main lines in which climate change defies the non-agriculture industries. Firstly, there is an absolute impact (through variations in climate variables). The second impact is through disruption of logistic supply of raw products from primary sector, cultivation and natural resources. Thirdly, the weather conditions have a strong impact on the productivity of labor and migration of labor (Viswanathan and Kumar 2015). Research indicates that weather erraticism is a significant positive element of labor migration. Lastly, the secondary and tertiary sectors are impacted ultimately through markets which bear the impact of weather. This include crucial factor like hazard and protection premium, new market prospects, and new taste and preferences and demand of the customers, etc. These findings can be summarized in the Fig. 5.

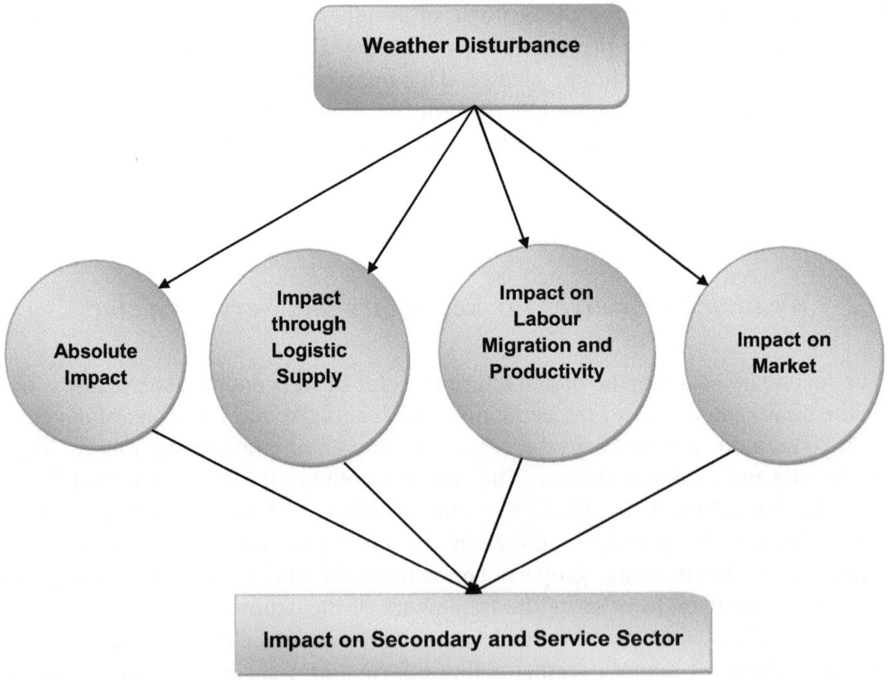

Fig. 5 Various ways in which weather can impact secondary and tertiary sector of Indian economy

Table 5 Hedgeable weather risks for various economic sectors

Economic sector	Hedgeable weather risks
Energy	Reduced and/or excessive demand
Hedge Funds[a]	Making profits on volatile markets
Agriculture	Crop yield, handling, storage, pests
Offshore	Storm frequency/severity
Insurance	Increased claims, premium diversification
Entertainment	Postponements, reduced attendance
Retailing	Reduced demand of weather-sensitive products
Construction	Delays, incentive/disincentive clauses
Transportation	Budget overruns, delays
Manufacturing	Reduced demand, increased raw material costs
Governments	Budget overruns

Source: CME Group (2011)
[a]Speculators in weather include hedge funds and others interested in capitalizing on these volatile markets

By looking at the factors, one can easily judge that the threats posed by the weather to these sectors are small and uninsurable. But the overall impact of these factors can be strong and can adversely impact the profit status of the firm. The companies can not only hedge against these conditions but also make profit from the weather conditions with the help of weather derivatives.

7 Potential Market Makers of Weather Derivatives in India

The existing markets of weather derivatives consist of various market players which hedge themselves against the adverse weather conditions with the help of these contracts. Table 5 provides the details of hedgeable weather risks for various economic sectors.

8 Conclusion

The three sectors of the Indian economy are drastically impacted by the weather conditions, the agriculture sector being the worst hit. There is a need to introduce weather derivatives on Indian exchanges and more importantly, there is a need to introduce them to the most affected classes, i.e. the farmers. The weather derivatives would not only act as a substitute for crop insurance for the farmers but also it is a step ahead in this direction where the farmers can not only overcome the losses but make a lot of money by simply betting on weather. The other two sectors may require a less aggressive approach but their need cannot be underestimated. Hence, it is high time that the Government of India should introduce the product in the market on a high scale. Though the Multi Commodity Exchange of India has introduced the rainfall index so that the over the counter market on rainfall weather derivatives can develop but that is just a minor step towards the scope and arena of weather derivatives in India. The contract should be launched with very aggressive education campaign for the target class. The Government of India should not delay in introducing the solution to year's old problem.

References

Agarwal, A. (2002). A new approach and model for weather derivative instrument based on water table for floods, droughts and rainfall. *Finance India, 16*(3), 877–914.

Chen, G., Roberts, M. C., & Thraen, C. (2006). Managing dairy profit risk using weather derivatives. *Journal of Agricultural and Resource Economics, 31*(3), 653–666.

CME Group. (2011). The weather derivatives markets at CME group: A brief history [online]. Accessed January 6, 2016, from https://www.cmegroup.com/education/files/Weather_Derivatives_Markets_at_CME_Group.pdf

Hurduzeu, G., & Constantin, L. (2008). Several aspects regarding weather and weather derivatives. *The Romanian Economic Journal, 11*(27), 187–202.

Kumar, N. (2016). Why crop insurance schemes fail poor farmers when they are needed the most. *Economic Times*. [online]. Accessed October 17, 2015, from http://articles.economictimes.indiatimes.com/2015-04-26/news/61542788_1_crop-insurance-scheme-insurance-fraud-kisan-credit-card

Kumar, S., & Yalew, A. (2012). Economic impacts of climate change on secondary activities: A literature review. *Low Carbon Economy, 3*, 39–48.

Ministry of Finance. (2012). *Agriculture and food management* [pdf]. Accessed December 22, 2015, from http://indiabudget.nic.in/es2012-13/echap-08.pdf

Ministry of Finance. (2015). Union budget and economic survey 2014–15. Accessed July 20, 2015, from http://indiabudget.nic.in/budget2014-2015/survey.asp

Muller, A., & Grandi, M. (2000). Weather derivatives: A risk management tool for weather-sensitive industries. *Geneva Papers on Risk and Insurance, 25*(2), 273–287.

Oxford Dictionaries. (n.d.). Weather definition [online]. Accessed July 20, 2015, from http://www.oxforddictionaries.com/us/definition/american_english/weather

Panagariya, A. (2009). Climate change and India: Implications and policy options. In S. Bery, B. Bosworth, & A. Panagariya (Eds.), *India policy forum 2009–10* (pp. 73–153). New Delhi: SAGE Publications India Pvt Ltd.

Paul, J. (2013). A study on the feasibility of weather derivatives in India. *PARIPEX-Indian Journal of Research, 2*(1), 14–15.

Pricewaterhouse Coopers. (2011). Weather risk derivative survey, weather risk management association [online]. Accessed 20 July 2015, from http://wrma.org/members_survey.html

Sharma, A., & Vashishtha, A. (2007). Weather derivatives: Risk-hedging prospects for agriculture and power sectors in India. *The Journal of Risk Finance, 8*(2), 112–132.

Stoppa, A. and Hess, U. (2003). Design and use of weather derivatives in agricultural policies: The case of rainfall index insurance in Morocco. In *International Conference Agricultural Policy Reform and the WTO: Where Are We Heading?* Capri: WTO.

The World Bank. (2013). World development indicators 2013 [online]. Accessed October 20, 2015, from http://databank.worldbank.org/data/download/WDI-2013-ebook.pdf

Viswanathan, B., & Kumar, K. (2015). Weather, agriculture and rural migration: Evidence from state and district level migration in India. *Environment and Development Economics, 20*(4), 469–492.

Part II
Economics of Innovation

Global Competitiveness of World Superpowers: Education, Talents and Innovations

Antanas Buracas and Vytas Navickas

Abstract The study below evaluates the impact of knowledge determinants on global competitiveness of the USA, Japan, China and India based on multiple criteria assessment methodology and their empirical evaluation. The indices for complex evaluations are determined mostly by the global education and innovation parameters published in the international comparisons. Their comparative assessment promotes the effective resource distribution and investment policy both in education and innovative business. It is important to discuss the reliability of criteria determining the impact of abilities, talents and productive innovations development on the economic competitiveness. The multiple criteria evaluation is focused on the education and innovation interdependencies with global output determinants as well as other criterial systems used for the education and innovation strategies and their comparative evaluations.

Keywords Global competitiveness • Multiple criteria evaluation • Assessment of innovation impact • Education impact on innovations

1 Introduction. Presumptions and Criteria of Measurement

The approach in the research under review concerns the detailing and comparison of criterial systems for evaluation of the education potential and innovation determinants in the countries determining world economic development with account of multicriteria decision making system. The main evaluating systems applied by the international institutions for comparisons of development potentials of world superpowers are duplicating in some degree one another but anyway can be used as effective analytical instrument for global management of intellectual resources (knowledge and talents), also distributing financial and manual resources, for stimulating investments into productive innovations; anticipating some shortages

A. Buracas (✉) • V. Navickas
Faculty of Social Education, Lithuanian University of Educational Sciences, Vilnius, Lithuania
e-mail: antanas@buracas.com; vytas.navickas@leu.lt

M.H. Bilgin et al. (eds.), *Empirical Studies on Economics of Innovation, Public Economics and Management*, Eurasian Studies in Business and Economics 6,
DOI 10.1007/978-3-319-50164-2_7

in employment of highly skilled labor as indicator for necessary changes in national education systems (Carayannis 2013). The practical evaluation of the comparisons in the global knowledge and innovation pillars for some selected countries revealed the applicability of the most analytical criteria used for evaluating their comparative growth determinants and importance to deepen the qualitative research of their competitiveness.

As empirical basis for international comparisons of the intellectual development indices, the data series published by the WEF and INSEAD on knowledge-based economy were analyzed.[1] The advantage of the so-called intellectual economy determinants as integral competitiveness indicators used by WEF is their wide international comparability. Sometimes their significances are different in various international reports published as a result of differently detailed analytical tasks in the process of different expert evaluation of regional or sectorial peculiarities[2]; but mostly their comparisons are useful (Evans et al. 2011; EIU 2011; Hüsing et al. 2013; IMF 2015; OECD 2013; WEF 2010; Guloglu and Tekin 2012).

The criteria used by authors for selection of main superpower states were not adequate: in first group—combined economic and intellectual potential (USA, Japan) and second group—combined economic and manpower potential (China, India). The EU was not included so as the published expert evaluations do not present the comparable aggregated data suitable for the selected purposes.

The innovations lead to much more intensive technical and economic growth: the differences between leading powers as the USA and Japan and second group of mega population countries (China, India) by GTCI and GII levels, also UNDP *Human Development Reports* Education index (HDR EI) are lower than their GDP per capita (PPP) differences (Table 1).

Besides, the HDR EI (UNDP 2015) adjusted to income inequality again shows deep distance between rich and poor countries; according to the OECD approach, the efficiency of countries' skills strategy evaluates their developing, activating and using outcomes (Bilbao-Osorio et al. 2015). The knowledge creation index for China is even higher (67.1) than for Japan (52.8), its GII knowledge impact index is highest between selected superpowers. But the differences in Human development index and Social progress index levels still remain rather bright. Both these indices can be comparable with a bridge between global social progress and economic competitiveness so as access to knowledge, information and education (incl.

[1]In particular, the Global Innovation Index (GII), Network Readiness Index (NRI), also Global Information Technology Index (GITI) were reviewed. Some of them are interconnected with Global Talent Competitiveness Index (GTCI) developed by joint efforts of the World Intellectual Property Organization (WIPO), Cornell University, and Human Capital Leadership Institute (Buracas et al. 2012).

[2]P. ex., the capacity for innovation for USA and Japan are evaluated equally by their network readiness index (NRI 5.6); but relevant NRI values in *Global Competitiveness Report* (GCR) are 5.9 and 5.4; the difference was resulting, possibly, from inadequate evaluation time or other expertizing peculiarities (WEF 2014).

Table 1 Comparative macro data and scores for selected states

Comparative macro data	USA	Japan	China	India
Total GDP (PPP, billion $)	18,125	4843	18,976	7997
GDP per capita (PPP, $)	53,142	36,315	11,903	5410
GDP (PPP, $) as % of world total	19.31	5.4	15.4	5.83
NRI value	5.61	5.41	4.05	3.85
GTCI overall score	68.32	58.01	45.21	34.12
GTCI rank (out of 93)	4	20	41	78
GII overall score	60.01	52.41	46.57	33.70
Social progress index	84.62	86.54	62.10	53.92
Human development index	0.91	0.89	0.72	0.59
HDR Education index (EI)	0.89	0.81	0.61	0.47
Inequality adjusted HDR EI	0.83	0.65	...	0.27

Source: IMF (2015), Bilbao-Osorio et al. (2015), UNDP (2015), Porter et al. (2016)
Note: The data on indices are comparable only by lines

advanced) is one of the basic presumptions of innovative society and innovative economics.

It is important, first, to evaluate the structural changes in the renewed production functions, with the changing productive contribution of the intellectual resources within different business sectors and regions. Second, it is necessary to integrate the more important estimates of professional competency determining the value of intellectual resources, their talents and intellectual capital of the firms into national social accounts. Third, the strategic development insights of the intellectual potential have to stimulate the alternative managerial solutions, to contribute to the general social and economic transformations and to diminish the emerging risks of innovations. At the same time, the concept of intellectual production in those interconnected nets is mostly oriented to human capital or, more exactly, to knowledge skills, a. o. pillars measured by GII and NRI determinant systems.

The components of professional abilities and competencies, talents, innovations, and network readiness are overlapping and interdependent to some degree; talents are grown within some family a/o social traditions, cultivated by changing educational systems, and their social significances depend on their successful contacts with entrepreneurship and best practices, also on network readiness. As a result, the global human potential and its competitiveness strongly depend on partnership between skillful talented people, business, educational system and the government.

Most of the countries apply lifelong learning, many of them are promoting geographical mobility of innovative competencies, services and products what in some cases influence substantially their global national significance. The distribution between branches and sectors of economic activity is also one of the actual directions of social policy when aiming to ameliorate the impact of talents and innovations on economic competitiveness. It is clear that adequate structure of creative potential can be developed mostly by big advanced economies, and the smaller countries have to cooperate when developing and retaining the necessary

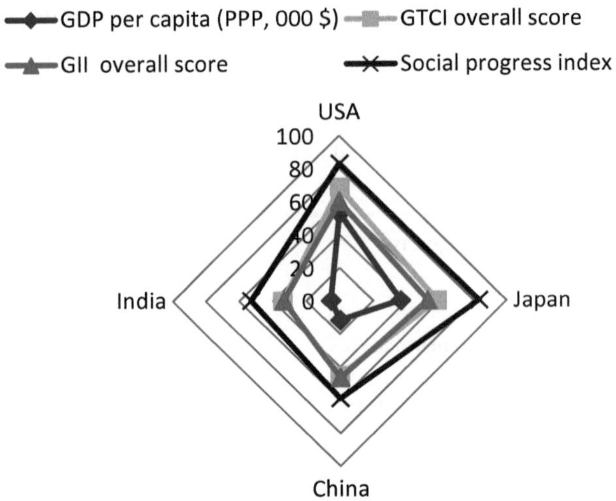

Fig. 1 Some comparative levels of superpowers' macro indices

availability of highly skilled workers and talent pool. As a result of accelerated progress in the world creative potential and modern intellectual technologies, the part of world inhabitants below the poverty line diminished even with accelerated growth of population in less developed countries.[3]

The business investments in knowledge-based capital contributed up to 34% average labor productivity growth in the EU and the US (OECD 2013) were revealed. The framework of World Bank's Knowledge Assessment Methodology (KAM) identifies four pillars to innovation processes: economic incentive and institutional regime (policies and institutions for the protection of intellectual property, the rule of law, the ease of starting a business, etc.), education (human capital), innovation (universities, firms, and research institutes), and ICT (physical capital). The GTCI approach was carefully audited by Joint Research Centre, the EC, also by some professionals from the World Bank Institute. So, our approach is an effort to clarify some additional methodological aspects when applying the GTCI techniques for particular comparative cases.

The macroeconomic potential per capita measured by PPP (in USD) of the US is about 1.5 times higher than that of Japan, nearly 5 times higher than in China and nearly 10 times higher, comparing with India. However, as was mentioned, their GII and GTCI determinants vary less than their comparative GDP per capita revealing the trend to diverge their competitive potency determining some perspective cultural and educational resources to global competitiveness (Fig. 1).

The measurement of the GTCI, as an analytical tool, is oriented, first of all, to implement the human resource management policies. In fact, it is simplified and mostly based on the knowledge and practical experience (training etc.) to apply productively the necessary high-level skills, or global knowledge (GK) skills. It is

[3]From 52% in 1981 up to 22% in 2008 (Lanvin and Evans 2015).

substantial if these skills are linked to entrepreneurship, or leadership, and innovation of production and its products. Another most significant component of GTCI is the labor and vocational (LV) skills (necessary for employment) besides their formal training measured by labor productivity. Both these integrated indicators are substantially dependent on the dimensions of the social progress index as access to basic knowledge, access to advanced education, tolerance and inclusion determinants, also satisfaction of basic human needs.

Some researchers tried to establish world indicators of skills for employment database (in collaboration with the World Bank, ETF, ILO and UNESCO) but the reports under review still does not cover India and China. The conceptual framework is oriented to detail the range of factors driving LV skills from their industrial requirements to acquisition in education and training process matching to level required by the labor market and as a result to economic and social outcomes (OECD 2015).

On the one side, the essential skills for innovation can be developed in the learning process and necessary infrastructure to be formed adequately. As a result, on the other side, the developing of innovation-friendly environment is a substantial presumption of talent competitiveness. Their efficiency and adequacy can be evaluated as a result of more detailed comparisons of real differences and similarities in such main characteristics as dimensions of social and economic policies, cultural and historical development, size of economies, their GDP per capita, regional peculiarities etc. For example, the brain drain of competent specialists (identified as talents) mostly goes from less developed countries to high developed ones (especially the US), and this migration of potentially innovative resources is substantially slowing down the convergence of potential national innovation indices and GTCI of selected countries. But the specifics of India and China are that their state policy stimulating return of innovative brains helped to return this trend and about equalize the outflows and inflows of qualified labor force (Bilbao-Osorio et al. 2015).

The selected global indices characterizing the business-oriented learning and building of innovation infrastructure do not account some specific differences of compound factors in selected countries connected with education traditions (p. ex., artes liberales in Western countries, or early development of child abilities in Eastern countries). The criteria used in popular international rating systems of university and professional institutes are based on international education standards[4] and partly accounted in the KAM, GTCI a/o systems dedicated to comparative evaluations of intellectual economy infrastructure and knowledge potential.

[4]See, p. ex., International Education Standards and Assessment, Program for the International Assessment of Adult Competencies (PIAAC), Program for International Student Assessment (PISA) a/o (Carayannis 2013).

2 Comparative GTCI Determinants and Parameters

According to the study under review, most of the resulting indices of education services and intellectual economics, such as the talent competitiveness input, output and sub-indices of GTCI, are compared and analyzed both aggregated and by components for selected countries. The value of GTCI is average of the scores obtained on levels of those input and output pillars; the input sub-index is determined by institutional enablers for talent development, also other means to attract, grow and retain talent; and the output sub-index evaluates GK and LV skills. As a total, 48 benchmarking indicators were included in the international comparative evaluation of the GTCI for 103 countries producing 96.7% of the world's GDP.

It is possible to suppose that interactions between the GK and LV skills, on the one side, innovativeness and competitiveness of the economies, on the other, are mutual. So, the skills determining talents usually require of innovative economy and strong education infrastructure; but higher levels of the GK and LV skills usually allow expecting the better possibility for growth of economic potential, more innovative and higher-quality education (Table 2).

For China, according to GTCI score, the most substantial achievement is in global knowledge level between upper middle income group countries (in Asia and Oceania according to the WB classification), and for India the most substantial retardation—at retain level (within lower middle income group), but it is much lower than in USA and Japan. For Japan the retardation is in attract level (within high income group of countries, Fig. 2).[5]

The talent impact is the resulting measure determined by innovation output (GII, Table 3) and new product entrepreneurial activity (% of entrepreneurs producing new products or services). As concerns innovation output, it is derived from aggregating knowledge and technology output (it covers knowledge creation, impact and diffusion) and creative output (the last one includes creative intangibles, creative goods and services and online creativity). The knowledge creation itself is measured by such parameters of inventive and innovative activities, as patent applications and recognized (cited) scientific publications. The knowledge impact is measured by innovations impact on real economy, such as increases in labor productivity, also by entry of new firms, by certifications and international standardization (Dutta et al. 2015): the economies are more dependent on technology transfer than they are on original R&D.

From the Table 3, even now the significance of GII knowledge impact and especially GITI talent impact levels for China are evaluated higher than for USA or Japan, and the level of GII knowledge creation for China and USA is about similar; GII creative outputs are on similar levels for Japan and China. At the same time, the biggest difference between both superpower groups concern the GITI levels of highest skills and competencies, also rather specific are significant

[5]Importance measures for variables at various levels of the GTCI structure are presented: Lanvin and Evans (2015).

Table 2 Comparison of selected GTCI input and output sub-Index determinants directly determining innovation effect in world Superpowers

Ranks by determinants and scores	USA	Japan	China	India
GII overall score, 2015	60.01	54.00	47.50	31.70
NRI value	5.61	5.41	4.05	3.85
GTCI score	68.32	58.01	45.21	34.12
Input[a]	70.59	63.42	48.01	44.08
Enablers	78.87	74.97	51.67	46.96
Attract	68.07	45.46	43.68	38.95
Growth	72.93	52.85	48.15	34.22
Retain	73.26	66.45	41.62	24.25
Output[a]	61.56	52.82	38.8	23.8
Labor and vocational	57.14	59.66	42.22	36.88
Global knowledge	59.64	48.68	43.88	23.45

Notes: all sub-index rankings are between 0 and 100. [a]2013. In 2014 for US input score 73.28 (higher), output—58.39 (lower). Expert evaluations are taken from the source: Dutta et al. (2015), Bilbao-Osorio et al. (2015)

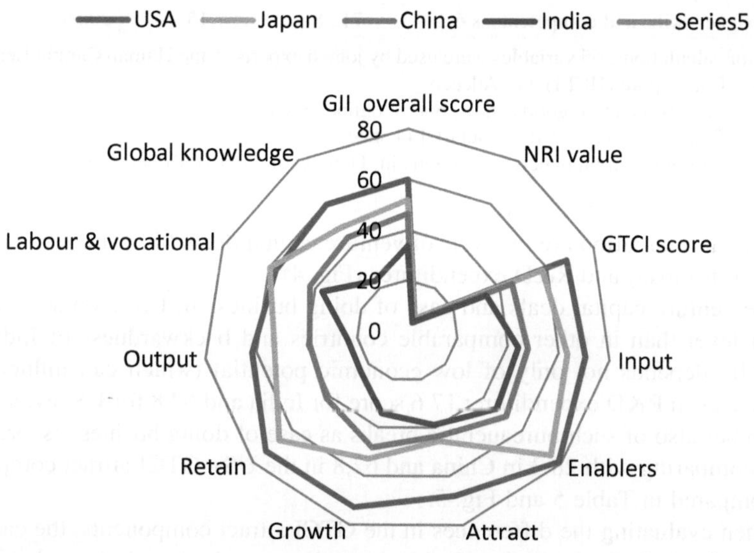

Fig. 2 Comparative levels of GTCI input and output determinants

differences between the selected countries by their GITI levels of vocational enrolment (also Fig. 3).

The consecutive detailing of GTCI enablers by their components (Table 4) for comparable country groups revealed that Japan achieved highest levels by managing business-government relations and R&D expenditures. In this group of determinants, the especially deep differences between both group of countries and most

Table 3 Comparison of GTCI pillars determining talent effect, 2014

Selected scores by determinants	USA	Japan	China	India
GII knowledge creation	68.5	52.8	67.1	18.4
GII knowledge absorption	41.3	32,3	35.5	20.2
GII knowledge impact	56.7	40.5	65.7	34.1
GII knowledge diffusion	49.0	48.2	44.3	44.1
GII innovation linkages	46.4	46.3	30.5	38.9
GII creative outputs[a]	46.5	38.1	35.7	28.6
NRI[b]	5.6	5.4	4.1	3.8
NRI readiness sub index	6.3	5.8	4.8	4.6
NRI usage sub index	5.6	5.7	3.9	3.4
NRI impact sub index	5.4	5.1	3.7	3.6
ICT access	72.4	77.3	43.6	25.0
R&D expenditure	81.3	74.8	45.0	32.0
GITI Talent impact	47.7	40.2	67.07	25.08
GITI Vocational enrolment	n/a	24.18	42.81	1.67
GITI Lifelong learning	70.44	61.53	68.72	45.02
GITI Employable skills 5.1	54.05	61.07	39.72	38.59
GITI Higher skills and competencies 6.1	71.58	57.15	20.69	21.82

Notes: for calculations, 65 variables were used by joined experts of the Human Capital Leadership Institute of Singapore (HCLI) and Adecco
[a]Intangible assets, creative goods and services, online creativity
[b]Network Readiness Index (NRI)—out of 144 states
Own elaboration based on expert evaluations in: Dutta et al. (2015), Bilbao-Osorio et al. (2015)

substantial retardation are in levels of venture capital deals (they are also underdeveloped in Japan) and R&D expenditures (Fig. 4).

The venture capital deals and ease of doing business in US is on substantially higher level than in other comparable countries and backwardness of India substantially depends not only of low economic potential (which can influence the differences in R&D expenditure: 17.6 score for India and 62.8 for US, even 74—in Japan) but also of such bureaucratic breaks as ease of doing business (score 7.7 in India comparing with 28.3 in China and 62.8 in the US). GTCI attract components are compared in Table 5 and Fig. 5.

When evaluating the differences in the GTCI attract components, the caste and feudal relics in India determines its biggest differences by female-to-male earnings ratio (13.1 comparing with 95.2 in USA, 57.4—China and 48.8—Japan). India does not also present data concerning part of female graduates. It is interesting to mention the latest tendency of equalization of brain inflows (gain) and outflows (drain) in USA, India and China (Fig. 5).

The components determining the innovation and GTCI growth are important as a result of main interstate differences dependent of cultural and education traditions (especially in lifelong learning, also vocational enrolment which is most popular in China and in access to growth opportunities; Table 6). It is interesting to mention that minor differences are when comparing the quality of management schools in

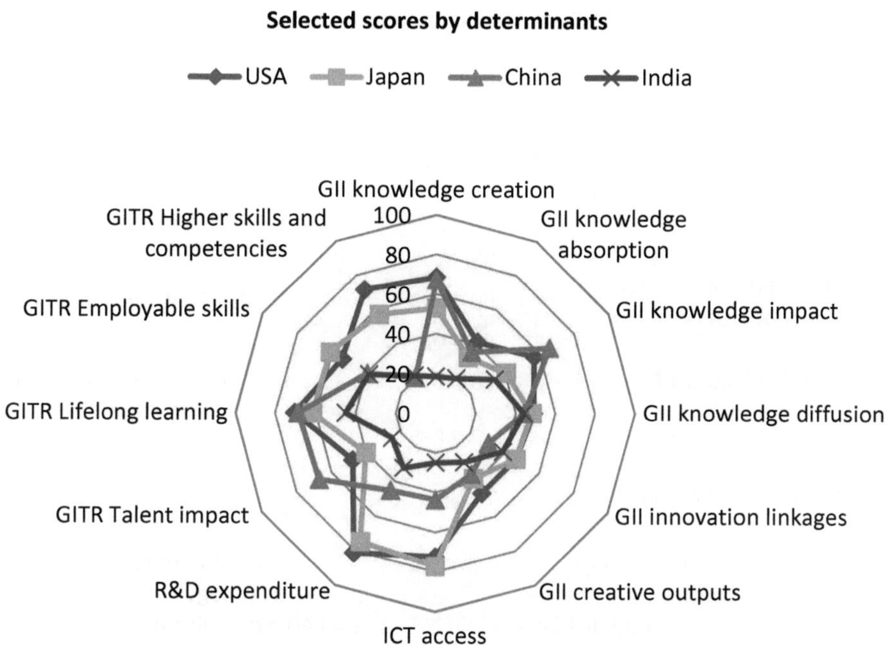

Fig. 3 Comparison of GII and GITI determinants in selected superpowers

Table 4 GTCI enablers' scores by components

GTCI scores by components	USA	Japan	China	India
1 Enablers	78.87	74.97	51.67	46.96
1.1 Regulatory landscape	69.07	78.67	50.15	47.07
1.1.1 Government effectiveness	79.85	76.57	36.73	31.36
1.1.2 Business-government relations	53.69	70.8	61.36	57.33
1.1.3 Political stability	81.21	88.63	52.35	35.17
1.2 Market landscape	83.26	68.73	40.93	32.22
1.2.1 Intensity of local competition	80.31	87.37	71.05	75.86
1.2.2 Venture capital deals	98.02	6.63	4.70	12.01
1.2.3 Firm-level technology absorption	83.23	84.4	61.49	67.48
1.2.4 R&D expenditure	62.79	74	41.38	16.59
1.2.5 ICT access	77.32	83.89	38.66	13.69
1.2.6 Ease of doing business	97.9	76.1	28.30	7.7
1.3 Business landscape	84.27	77.51	63.94	61.60
1.3.1 Difficulty of hiring	100	89	89	100
1.3.2 Difficulty of redundancy	100	70	50	30
1.3.3 Labor-employer cooperation	60.98	76.1	56.69	56.63
1.3.4 Reliance on professional management	76.1	74.95	60.08	59.76

Note: Own elaboration based on expert evaluations in: Bilbao-Osorio et al.

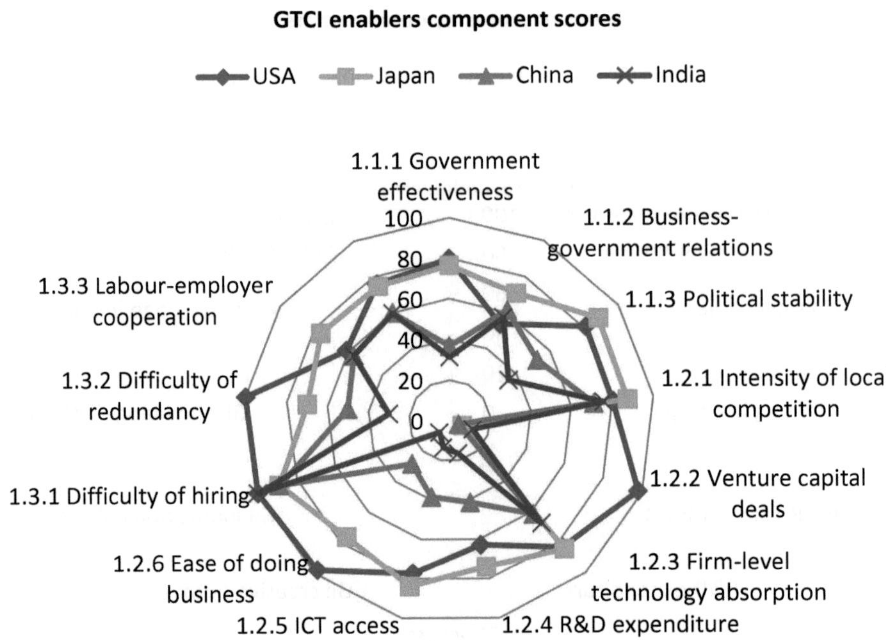

Fig. 4 Comparison of components for GTCI enablers of world superpowers

Table 5 GTCI attract scores by components for world superpowers

GTCI attract scores by components	USA	Japan	China	India
Attract	68.07	45.46	43.68	38.95
2.1 External openness	52.79	33.62	34.49	33.01
2.1.1 FDI inflow	12.18	5.12	15.09	14.27
2.1.2 FDI and technology transfer	64.51	63.03	59.02	67.37
2.1.3 Prevalence of foreign ownership	67.43	66.65	56.17	55.23
2.1.4 Brain gain	79	38.67	56.50	45.33
2.1.5 Brain drain	78	55.17	54.67	46.33
2.2 Internal openness	83.35	57.29	52.87	44.89
2.2.1 Tolerance to minorities	88.96	58.21	59.01	79.05
2.2.2 Tolerance to immigrants	87.25	60.65	47.05	26.47
2.2.3 Female graduates	68.84	41.88	45.36	n/a
2.2.4 Female-to-male earnings ratio	95.24	48.81	57.14	13.10
2.2.5 Social mobility	76.46	76.93	55.79	60.95

Note: Own elaboration based on expert evaluations in: Bilbao-Osorio et al. (2015)

selected countries; the evaluations of China and Japan are on similar levels, and its much higher level in India comparing with Japan is perhaps determined by traditional interconnections between metropolis G.B. and India.

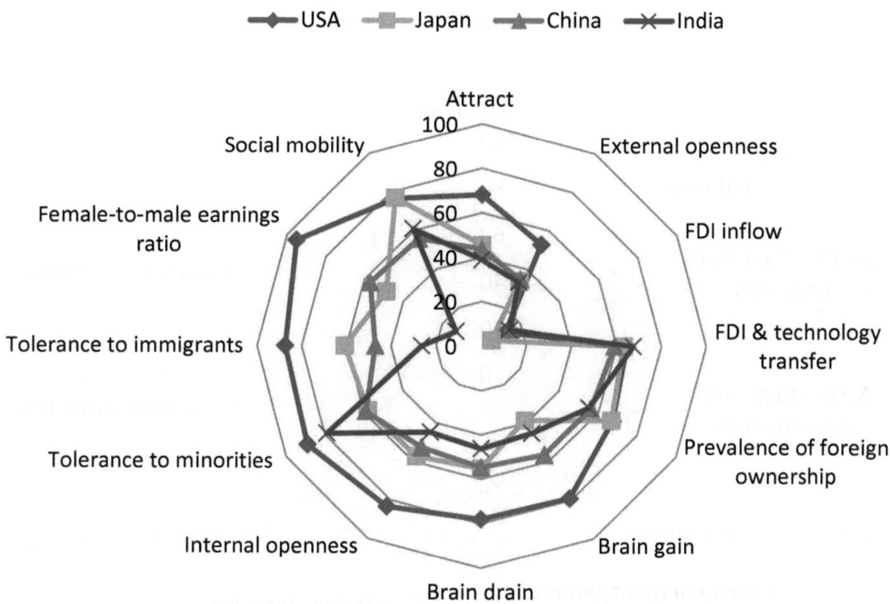

Fig. 5 Comparison of GTCI attract components

Table 6 Evaluation of GTCI growth scores by components for world superpowers

GTCI growth scores by components	USA	Japan	China	India
Grow index	72.93	52.85	48.15	34.22
3.1 Formal education	66.18	52.17	48.28	16.94
3.1.1 Vocational enrolment	n/a	24.18	42.81	1.67
3.1.2 Tertiary enrolment	94.35	57.74	20.93	19.84
3.1.3 International students inflow	15.53	17.95	0	0
3.1.4 University ranking	99.76	83.15	77.69	46.24
3.2 Lifelong learning[a]	70.44	61.53	68.72	45.02
3.2.1 Quality of management schools	74.8	50.59	51.90	67.09
3.2.2 Extent of staff training	66.08	72.46	54.26	52.71
3.3 Access to growth opportunities	82.18	44.86	27.45	40.7
3.3.1 Use of virtual social networks	89.8	78.72	62.15	72.56
3.3.2 Number of LinkedIn users	100	1.91	0	7.55
3.3.3 Willingness to delegate authority	69.97	57.87	47.63	47.8

Source: Own elaboration based on expert evaluations in Bilbao-Osorio et al. (2015)
Note: [a]Further education and training climate (Bilbao-Osorio et al. 2015). Some expert evaluations or selected determinants, as: firms offering formal training etc., are incommensurable

Substantial differences in tertiary enrolment (USA—94.35 and India 19.8, China 20.9) and international students' inflow as well as numbers of LinkedIn users are mostly dependent on inadequate economic and technical potential of the compared countries (Fig. 6). Besides, in the last case (numbers of LinkedIn users) it is

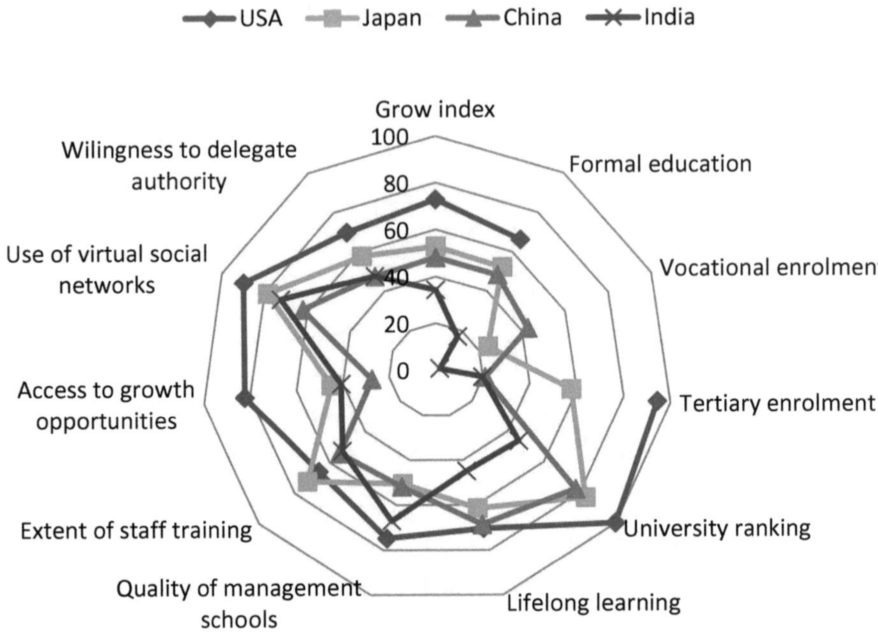

Fig. 6 Comparison of GTCI growth components

necessary to mention substantial difference also between the USA and Japan (respectively 100% and 2%) what first-of-all shows the different social approaches to personal privacy.

Between retain components, most substantial differences are revealed in the coverage by pension systems—when they are evaluated at 95 scores in Japan and 92 scores in USA, the comparative level in China achieved only 33 scores and about 10 in India (Table 7).

Naturally, similar differences concern lifestyle comparisons (especially sanitation and environmental performance levels, see Fig. 7).

The vocational and labor skills have direct and especially substantial impact on economic competitiveness of selected superpower potential (Table 8). The deep difference in labor productivity per employee is one of synthetic indices integrally determining the technical retardation of India (4.6 scores) and China (nearly 11 scores) from the USA (nearly 70) and Japan (46 scores). At the same time the differences in educating the employable skills are not so significant (61—for Japan and 54—for USA, when nearly 40 for China and 39—for India). Some specific differences are in expert evaluations of secondary-educated workforce: USA has lower level of it (about 29 scores, when 52—for Japan, 39—for India); but USA has more comparable 63 scores of secondary-educated population and, as a result, is leading in tertiary enrolment.

The comparative components of GTCI labor and vocational components are better seen in cobweb diagram, Fig. 8.

Table 7 Evaluation of GTCI retain components for world superpowers

GTCI retain scores by components	USA	Japan	China	India
4 Retain	73.26	66.45	41.62	24.25
4.1 Sustainability	78.52	60.72	32.45	23.55
4.1.1 Pension system	92.13	95.35	33.23	9.87
4.1.2 Extent and effect of taxation	52.02	43.51	50.79	45.22
4.2 Lifestyle	67.99	72.18	50.80	24.95
4.2.1 Environmental performance	67.53	75.31	28.02	9.06
4.2.2 Safety at night	73.59	78.75	86.99	56.51
4.2.3 Physicians density	38.42	33.82	28.53	9.27
4.2.4 Sanitation	99.54	100	59.65	24.97

Note: Own elaboration based on expert evaluations in Bilbao-Osorio et al. (2015)

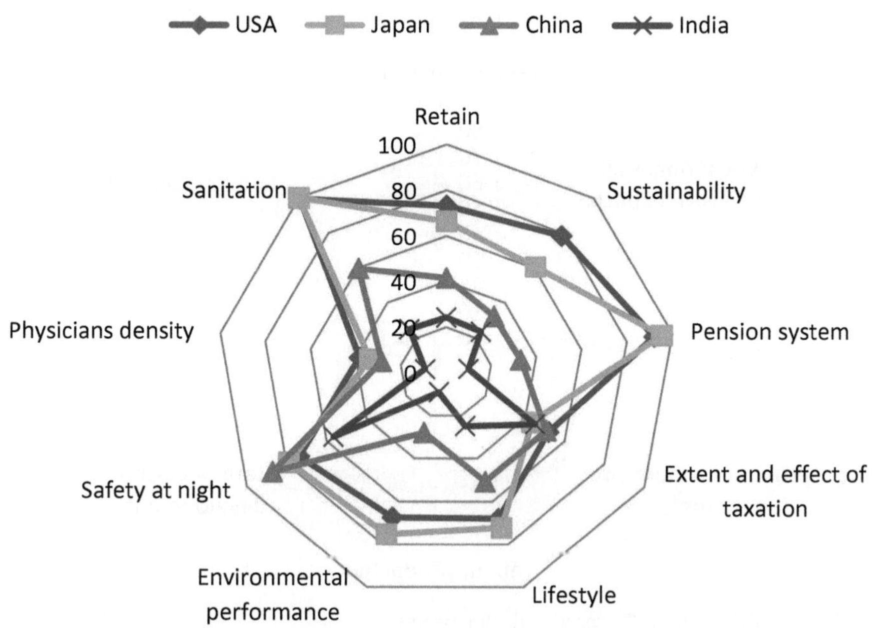

Fig. 7 Comparison of GTCI retain components for world superpowers

The integral index of global knowledge summarizes the educational and entrepreneurial drive of selected superpowers: it is 2.5 times higher for the USA than for India, but the level of China (44) is converging to Japan level (49 scores, see Table 9). At the same time, talent impact of China was evaluated by experts (67 scores) even higher than that in the USA (48 scores) or Japan (40 scores) what was determined mostly by sophisticated exports and new product development; the achievements in the innovation output were nearly 1.5 times much higher in the USA.

Table 8 Evaluation of GTCI vocational scores by components for world superpowers

GTCI vocational scores by components	USA	Japan	China	India
5 Labor and vocational skills	57.14	59.66	42.22	36.88
5.1 Employable skills	54.05	61.07	39.72	38.59
5.1.1 Secondary-educated workforce	28.79	51.84[a]	19.23	39.12
5.1.2 State of cluster development	70.57	70.3	60.21	64.7
5.2 Labor productivity	60.23	58.24	44.73	35.17
5.2.1 Labor productivity per employee	69.56	46.08	10.99	4.64
5.2.2 Relationship of pay to productivity	63.22	61.46	60.01	51.21
5.2.3 Vocational skill-intensive exports	47.92	67.19	62.18	49.68

Note: Own elaboration based on expert evaluations in Bilbao-Osorio et al. (2015)
[a]Secondary-educated population

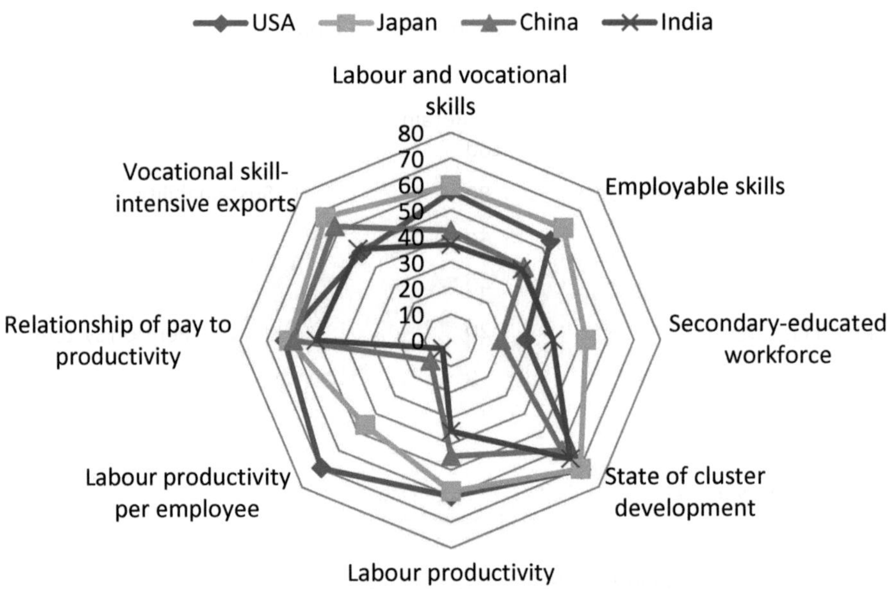

Fig. 8 Comparison of GTCI vocational components

These structural peculiarities of selected superpowers are better seen in web diagram characterizing their global knowledge component levels (Fig. 9).

For a summarizing review, main innovation and competency (or talents) determinants can be selected from parallel expert evaluation systems (mostly NRI and GCR) into Table 10 and their scores compared. So, China and India are lagging by intellectual property protection more than by availability of latest technologies. Comparing totality of indicators, all the superpowers have lower scores for venture capital availability, and Japan has lowest between selected countries. The differences in quality of education systems and use of virtual social networks in selected superpowers are indecisive but Japan is leading by its sophisticated system of

Table 9 Evaluation of GTCI global knowledge scores by components

GTCI global knowledge scores by components	USA	Japan	China	India
6 Global Knowledge	59.64	48.68	43.88	23.45
6.1 Higher skills and competencies	71.58	57.15	20.69	21.82
6.1.1 Tertiary-educated workforce	100	65.49	n/a	12.29
6.1.2 Tertiary-educated population	67.66	49.71	5.95	n/a
6.1.3 Professionals	63.72	n/a	16.77	10.98
6.1.4 Researchers	50.91	56.41	10.39	1.32
6.1.5 Quality of scientific research institutions	82.58	78.21	55.06	58.14
6.2 Talent impact	47.7	40.2	67.07	25.08
6.2.1 Innovation output	70.73	51.94	56.71	42.18
6.2.2 New product entrepreneurial activity	45.95	59.46	66.22	36.49
6.2.3 Sophisticated exports	26.43	49.03	78.29	21.26

Note: Own elaboration based on expert evaluations in Bilbao-Osorio et al. (2015)

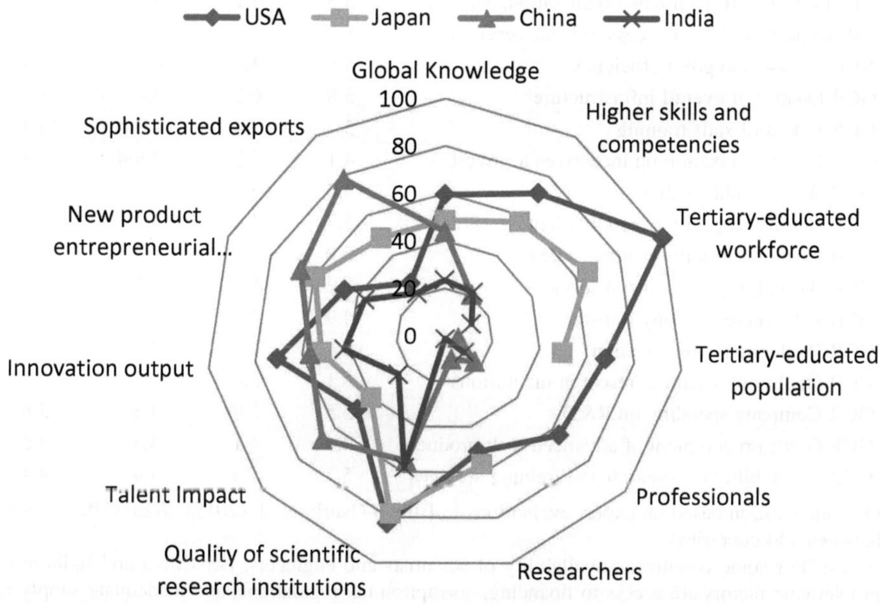

Fig. 9 Comparison of GTCI global knowledge components for world superpowers

primary education. Naturally, the country capacity to retain talented specialists is highest in USA.

Main comparative similarities and differences of innovation and competency indicators determining the competitivity of the selected countries are graphically presented in Figs. 10 and 11.

The analysis done in this section of our review also revealed the premises for a GTC approach to strategic programming of sustainable economic expansion so as it

Table 10 Selected indicators determining innovations and their competitiveness

Scores by selected indicators	USA	Japan	China	India
NRI Intellectual property protection	5.2	5.7	3.9/4	3.7
NRI Availability of latest technologies	6.4	6.3	4.4	5.2
NRI Venture capital availability	4.3	3.1	3.8/3.9	3.3
NRI Accessibility of digital content	6.2	6.2	5.2	4.8
NRI Quality of the education system	4.6	4.1	4	4.4
GCR Quality of primary education	4.7	5.5	4.2	3.6
NRI Use of virtual social networks	6.4	5.7	4.7	5.4
NRI Firm-level technology absorption	6	6.1	4.7	5
NRI Capacity for innovation	5.6	5.6	4.2	4
GCR Capacity for innovation	5.9	5.4	4.2	4
NRI Extent of staff training	5	5.3	4.3/4.3	4.2
NRI Gov't success in ICT promotion	5	4.7	4.8	4.9
NRI Impact of ICT on new services and products	5.3	5.2	4.6	4.8
NRI Impact of ICT on new organization. Models	5.3	4.7	4.7	4.6
NRI Impact of ICT on access to basic services	5.2	5.1	4.7	4.3
NRI ICT use and gov't efficiency	4.6	4.8	4.6	4.4
GCR Quality of overall infrastructure	5.8	6.2	4.4	3.7
GCR Extent of staff training	5	5.4	4.3	3.9
GCR Effect of taxation on incentives to invest	4.1	3.7	2.9/4	3.9
GCR Buyer sophistication	4.5	5.3	4.3	3.8
GCR Country capacity to retain talent	5.7	4.4	4.2	3.9
GCR Country capacity to attract talent	5.8	3.3	4.2	3.8
GCR Availability of financial services	6.2	5.3	4.5	4.2
GCR FDI and technology transfer	4.9	4.7	4.5	4.2
GCR Production sophistication	6.1	6.4	4.1	4
GCR Quality of scientific research institutions	6.1	5.8	4.3	4
GCR Company spending on R&D	5.5	5.8	4.3	3.8
GCR Gov't procurement of advanced tech products	4.4	4.1	4.3	3.5
GCR Availability of research and training services[a]	5.3	5.4	4.4	4.4

Own elaboration based on expert evaluations in Bilbao-Osorio et al. (2015), WEF (2014) (ranks between 144 countries)

Notes: [a]For some countries—availability of scientists and engineers. For China and India most problematic factors are access to financing, corruption tax regulations, and inadequate supply of infrastructure, for Japan—tax rates, restrictive labor regulations, insufficient capacity to innovate and government bureaucracy, for US—tax rates and their regulation, also insufficient government bureaucracy, access to financing etc.

exposed the more weak and strong determinants or pillars in national innovation and talent competitiveness development.

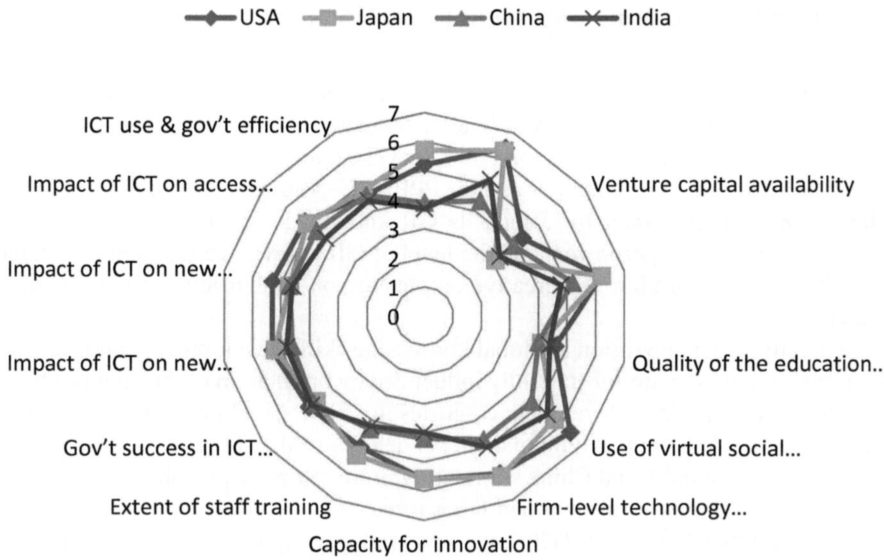

Fig. 10 Comparison of NRI indicators determining innovations and talents competitiveness

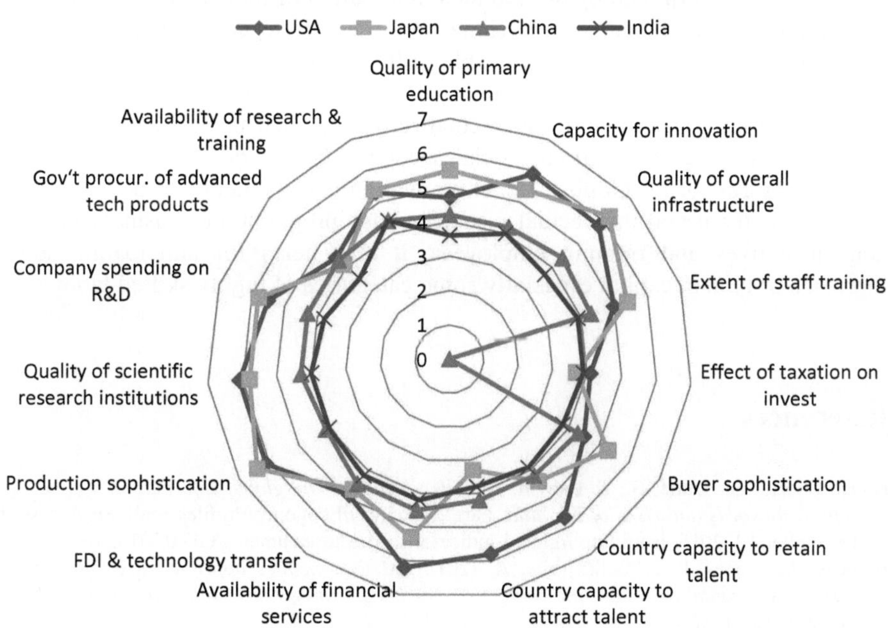

Fig. 11 Comparison of NRI indicators determining innovations and talents competitiveness

3 Some Conclusions and Generalizations

The GTCI analysis confirms that economies are more dependent on technology transfer than on their original R&D. The differences between the USA and Japan, on the one side, China and India, on other, by GTCI and GII levels are much lower than their differences in GDP per capita (PPP). The knowledge creation index for China is even higher than for Japan, its GII knowledge impact index is highest among the selected superpowers and the level of GII knowledge creation for China and USA is about similar; GII creative outputs are on similar levels for Japan and China.

Logically, the competition in global knowledge skills development and levels of their implementation are substantially influenced by brain drain of the talents which mostly goes from less developed countries to high developed ones, and that influence some deviations within main dependencies of the GTCI model. However, the state policy in India and China stimulating brain return helped about to equalize the outflows and inflows of qualified labor force.

The correlation between GTCI scores and GDP per capita, also between national economic competitiveness and global talent indices is weaker than expected by approach based on GTCI model. The deep difference in labor productivity per employee was determined by the technical retardation of India and China comparing with USA and Japan. At the same time the differences of both groups of superpowers in educating the employable skills are not so significant.

It is necessary to integrate of more important estimates of professional competency determining the value of intellectual resources, their talents and intellectual capital of the firms into national social accounts. In general, GII and GTCI are useful measures for developing global innovation management, for better distributing the material and intellectual resources, also programming business innovations incentives and training employees. It also helps for anticipating some shortages of human capital especially some categories of highly skilled labor.

References

Bilbao-Osorio, B., Dutta, S., & Lanvin, B. (Eds.). (2015). *The global information technology report. Rewards and risks of big data*. Part 2: Country/Economy Profiles [online]. Accessed December 12, 2015, from http://global-indices.insead.edu/documents/GITR2014.pdf

Buracas, A., Lopes, I. T., & Zvirblis, A. (2012). *Metaeconomics approach and intellectual resources evaluation. Multiple objective methods: Integrating into decision making*. Saarbrucken: LAP.

Carayannis, E. G. (Ed.). (2013). *Encyclopedia of creativity, invention, innovation and entrepreneurship*. New York: Springer-Verlag.

Dutta, S., Lanvin, B., & Wunsch-Vincent, S. (Eds.). (2015). *The global innovation index 2015. Effective innovation policies for development*. Appendix II: Data Tables [online]. Accessed August 10, 2016, from https://www.globalinnovationindex.org/gii-2015-report

EIU. (2011). *The global talent index report: The outlook to 2015*. [online]. Accessed August 10, 2016, from http://www.globaltalentindex.com/pdf/Heidrick_Struggles_Global_Talent_Report.pdf

Evans, P., Pucik, V., & Bjorkman, I. (2011). *The global challenge: International human resource management*. New York: McGraw-Hill.

Guloglu, B., & Tekin, R. B. (2012). A panel causality analysis of the relationship among research and development, innovation, and economic growth in high-income OECD countries. *Eurasian Economic Review, 2*(1), 32–47.

Hüsing, T., Korte, W. B., Fonstad, N., Lanvin, B., Cattaneo, G., Kolding, M.et al. (2013). *e-Leadership: e-Skills for competitiveness and innovation. Vision, roadmap and foresight scenarios*. Empirica, IDS, INSEAD [online]. Accessed August 10, 2016, from http://eskills-vision.eu/fileadmin/eSkillsVision/documents/VISION%20Final%20Report.pdf

IMF. (2015, April). *World economic outlook: Uneven growth—short- and long-term factors*. Washington. [online]. Accessed August 10, 2016, from https://www.imf.org/external/pubs/ft/weo/2015/01/pdf/text.pdf

Lanvin, B., & Evans, P. (Eds.). (2015). *The global talent competitiveness index. Talent attraction and international mobility* INSEAD, Fontainebleau. [Online]. Accessed August 10, 2016, from http://global-indices.insead.edu/gtci/documents/INSEAD_2015-16_Full_Book_Ebook.pdf

OECD. (2013). *Supporting investment in knowledge capital, growth and innovation*. Paris: OECD Publishing. Accessed August 10, 2016, from http://dx.doi.org/10.1787/9789264193307-en

OECD. (2015). *Building effective skills strategies at national and local levels. Better policies for better lives*. Accessed December 22, 2015, from http://skills.oecd.org/documents/Building-effective-skills-strategies-project-brochure.pdf

Porter, M. E., Stern, S., & Green, M. (2016). *Social progress index*. Social Progress Imperative, US. Accessed August 10, 2016, from http://13i8vn49fibl3go3i12f59gh.wpengine.netdna-cdn.com/wp-content/uploads/2016/06/SPI-2016-Main-Report1.pdf

UNDP. (2015). *Human development reports*. [online]. Accessed December 22, 2015, from http://hdr.undp.org/en/content/

WEF. (2010). *Stimulating economies through fostering talent mobility*. With The Boston Consulting Group, Cologny/Geneva [online]. Accessed November 8, 2015, from http://www3.weforum.org/docs/WEF_PS_TalentMobility_report_2010.pdf

WEF. (2014). *The global competitiveness report 2014–2015: Full Data Edition*. K. Schwab (Ed.). Accessed October 17, 2015, from http://www.weforum.org/docs/WEF_GlobalCompetitivenessReport_2014_15.pdf

[illegible]

OECD. (2015). [illegible]

[illegible]

Energy Security: Is It a Strategic Cause of Conflicts or Peace Among States/Actors in the Global Nexus?

Pantelis Sklias, Spyros Roukanas, and Floros Flouros

Abstract The aim of this article is to study certain aspects related to energy security, which is of great importance globally. A number of conceptual frameworks regarding the issue of energy security are examined to understand the relationships between relevant parameters and then to investigate their implications for the national security of countries in the Eastern Mediterranean region under the broader consideration of the international political economy. Megatrends are major, transformative forces that affect the global future. They have a far-reaching impact on economies, industries, societies and individuals. Today's world is in constant motion and goods, capital and labor are moving globally at a faster pace than ever, with overall energy-related issues becoming increasingly important for societies and states. Economic power is continuing to shift eastwards and it is thus of considerable interest to study energy security in the broader area of the Eastern Mediterranean and its effect on the national security of the countries located in the region. Research needs to examine whether energy security is a threat to the national security of such countries and/or an opportunity for them. In this study, the theory of economic nationalism is employed for the analysis as it emphasizes the primary importance of the state and national security, whereas realism is essentially a political ideology and mercantilism is an economic one.

Keywords Megatrends • Energy security • International political economy

P. Sklias (✉) • F. Flouros
Department of Political Science and International Relations, University of Peloponnese, Corinth, Greece
e-mail: pantelis@uop.gr; floros.flouros@ntualumni.org.uk

S. Roukanas
Department of International and European Studies, University of Piraeus, Piraeus, Greece
e-mail: sroukana@unipi.gr

M.H. Bilgin et al. (eds.), *Empirical Studies on Economics of Innovation, Public Economics and Management*, Eurasian Studies in Business and Economics 6,
DOI 10.1007/978-3-319-50164-2_8

1 Introduction

In this paper, we examine the issue of energy security related to the current megatrends that characterize the global environment and that ultimately affect states and actors in the short and long term. According to the European Environment Agency (EEA 2013), it is well known that societies mainly rely on a few basic resources, such as food, water, energy and materials, to satisfy their needs. Following Kruyt et al. (2009), the nexus that exists between energy security and critical global issues of high risk, such as environmental problems and the economic relationships among players in the markets, has resulted in energy security issues being found and considered in ever wider scope. Economies are related to major investments in infrastructure and energy resources, while energy is a driving force for communities and energy security is of the utmost importance for them. The depletion of resources can cause scarcity in the markets and eventually lead to social problems in communities (EY 2015). Within creasing urbanization, it is estimated that the 750 largest cities will contribute 60% of global gross domestic product (GDP) by 2030 (Oxford Economics 2015); thus, urban regions and states will need sustainable solutions to optimize resources and ensure the well-being of their citizens.

As El-Badri (2015), the Secretary General of the Organization of Petroleum Exporting Countries (OPEC), points out, there have been tremendous changes in the world and consequently in the energy industry since the organization was established in 1960. Although many aspects and characteristics of energy have changed, energy security is one issue that holds the same degree of importance.

OPEC's World Oil Outlook 2014 estimates that oil-related investment requirements will approach $10 trillion (in 2013 dollars) in the period between 2014 and 2040. The security of supply and security of demand cannot be decoupled and a comprehensive examination of energy security is needed over the short-, medium- and long-term timescales.

Energy security means "different things to different people, particularly the 1.3 billion people without access to electricity and the 2.7 billion people relying on biomass for their basic needs". It is very important that "the proposed seventh goal of the United Nations Sustainable Development Goals will call for countries to ensure access to affordable, reliable, sustainable and modern energy for all" (El-Badri 2015). Energy can influence the foreign policy of a state and also it can be a potential tool for it, while at the same time politics may influence the use of energy resources (Leigh 2014).

2 The International Political Economy and Energy Issues

The international political economy (IPE) approach can contribute to gaining an in-depth understanding of several issues related to policy, economics, society and technology and thus facilitate their study as it includes specialized sciences, such as politics, economics and international relations (IR). IPE can help us perceive the way that politics shape the economy and the way that economy shapes politics. It was developed on the basis that several global issues could not be explained within a conventional framework of knowledge (Sklias 2011). As Waltz (1991, p. 22) noted, "theory is just representing things that had happened and it only portraitures events" and claimed that a theory can "construct a reality, but no one can ever say that it is the reality.

IPE has very quickly become one of the main areas of IR, within the broader area of political sciences. It is seen as one of the most challenging and promising areas of IR, being able to describe and explain the international system through a "holistic interpretation". IPE is considered a science with dual characteristics: it concerns economic science, which covers the knowledge fields of micro-and macroeconomics up to international trade, while at the same time it relates to the political science of IR. The strong relationship between IPE and economic theory is also one of the main contributions that IPE makes to international studies. There has been a great deal of discussion concerning whether the theory of IR includes IPE or the other way around. The latter may be more likely in the case that economists include IR theory in their analyses (Ifestos 2015).

According to Guzzini (1998, p. 142), "if International Political Economy has a birth date, then it was the 15 August 1971", when the then United States (US) president, Nixon, tried "to suspend the Bretton-Woods monetary system". This decision changed the way in which the international monetary system run and "the US officially declared its power position as challenged". It is helpful here to make a brief reference to the basic theoretical approaches of IPE as the political economy (PE) of IR is complicated and at the same time it is necessary to protect national interests within a balanced power system (Sklias 2011).

Liberals and realists, while arguing about the role of the state and markets in the economic and political system, agree to accept the capitalist production system as the dominant economic-political system (Sklias 2011). Table 1 illustrates the three basic theories of the IPE in a synoptic and comprehensive way.

Of the three main approaches presented above, the theory of realism is the one adopted for the analysis herein as it interprets with higher clarity the real economic and political world. It is seen that "Realism emphasizes the primary importance of the state and the national security" and is essentially a political ideology, whereas statism (mercantilism) is an economic ideology (Sklias 2011, p. 53).

There are four main reasons why realism has such staying power as an ideology (Rosenberg 1994). Even though no clear definition of the term "international" exists, however "the distinctive social form of the modern state has to be addressed theoretically". Secondly, realism sounds "plausible" because "it articulates

Table 1 Classic IPE approaches

• Realism	• Hamilton, List, Krasner, Gilpin, Strange • Level: state, individual • Human nature: aggressive • Units: states • Confrontation of state: unionist • Confrontation of international companies: harmful • Behavioural dynamics: state as rational actor • Market relations: negative • Game simulation: zero sum • Hegemony: importance of a sovereign state • International organizations: not important	• Liberalism	• Smith, Ricardo, Kant, Wilson, Keynes, Hayek, Keohane, Nye • Level: pluralism, individualism • Human nature: cooperative • Units: state, company, NGO • Confrontation of state: pluralistic • Confrontation of international companies: harmful • Behavioural dynamics: individual as rational actor • Market relations: positive • Game simulation: positive sum (win–win) • Hegemony: post-hegemonic cooperation • International organizations: important	• Constructivism	• Marx, Lenin, Frank, Cox • Level: global structure • Human nature: ductile • Units: planet, globalization, sex, class • Confrontation of state: class representation • Confrontation of international companies: harmful • Behavioural dynamics: within societies • Market relations: exploitative • Game simulation: zero sum • Hegemony: hegemony on state and society • International organizations: serving interests of wealth (state, companies and classes)

Source: Sklias (2011)

commonly held common-sense assumptions about world politics". Third, to the extent that IR remains an American social science "the persistence of realism seems assured". Finally, "it consists of the absence of any well-known alternative conceptualization of the political structure of the global system to the one extrapolated from normative political theory and the behavior of the critics of realism".

Realists point out that the development of unusual strategies to end war would not be possible to succeed, since they did not take into consideration basic laws of human nature and behavior (Vasquez 2004). The realist tradition is considered by many scholars as a definitive tradition in the field of international relations (Schmidt 1998). The idea of energy security is open for manipulation and interpretations and even more complex, a person's individual perspective colors the extent to which he perceives risks to energy security and opportunities to enhance it Fischhendler and Nathan (2014).

Several scholars claim that social sciences—and more particularly international relations—tend not to focus greatly on technological systems and if they do so, it is mostly in a superficial and uncritical way. At the same time, it is also argued that politics should pay attention to the "carrying capacity of the earth". It is important to note that technological systems are driven by energy which is the master resource (Litfin 2014). First of all, it is important to evaluate critically the available literature and thus to be able to undertake a work of synthesis (Knopf 2006). According to Dixon (2006, p. 47), "Energy is the lifeblood of all societies; just as we can understand fundamental things about the human body by tracing its flow of blood, we can understand much about a society's activities by tracing its flows of energy". Energy is "a re-emerging domestic and foreign policy field" (Kuzemco 2014, p. 58) and the energy policy of a country is considered to be "a highly politicized topic" (Kaveshnikov 2010, p. 585).

Energy security is enhanced provided that any solution will consider the necessity to balance geopolitical, economic (energy interdependence) and environmental (climate changes) implications of energy (Pascual and Elkind 2010). More specifically:

The geopolitical aspects of energy security are firstly related to the coordination of "energy-related relations" such as competing energy suppliers; energy suppliers versus consumers; competing consumer countries; and a country that seeks to take advantage of energy-related power to command other aspects vis-à-vis another country; secondly, the economic importance of energy and thirdly, risks due to the interruption of supply linkages. Energy inter dependencies related to producers seeking high prices in the market, while ensuring that demand is not diminished and consumers depending on a continuous and smooth supply to secure enough energy for their economies. Finally, climate change, which is the most important "challenge for the human race" and it is considered to be a "threat multiplier".

The literature predominantly concerns energy security as: a concept, a policy process, related to the accessibility of energy services and interplay in the global market (Fischhendler and Nathan 2014). A next step is to define the parameters and factors that comprise energy security and related risks. In addition, there are "different severity filters" found in the literature to define a threshold that affects have to exceed in order to count as a threat to energy security (Wizner 2012).

The theory of economic nationalism is used for the analysis, mainly because it emphasizes the primary importance of the state and national security, while realism is essentially a political ideology and mercantilism an economic one. There are two main principles that characterize economic nationalism: the fact that the international system is not governed by any authority (anarchy), while the role that the state plays appears central and sovereign for the world political and economic environment (Roukanas and Diamantis 2014).

3 Energy Changes and Outlook: 1990–2040

Strong supply growth has gained the upper hand over geopolitical concerns in shaping oil price trends. Exceptional growth in non-OPEC countries, especially in the US, now sees global oil supply growth running at more than double the pace of demand growth. Thus, oil prices have declined dramatically from the level of US $110 (Brent), which was quite stable from beginning of 2011 until autumn 2014; in early 2015, the price was at the US$50 level and at the end of 2015 it fell below the level of US$40 per barrel. Table 2 presents the proven oil reserves for Organization for Economic Cooperation and Development (OECD) and non-OECD countries, as well as for OPEC and non-OPEC members.

It is important to note that the countries that hold most of the proven oil reserves are not OECD members, while proven reserves increased at almost the same rate among OPEC and non-OPEC countries over the period 1994–2014. Figures 1 and 2 present the oil production and consumption of the different groups of countries. There was a greater increase in non-OECD countries, where production changed by around 42%, followed by OPEC countries, which experienced an increase of around 37% during the same period.

At the same time, as shown in Fig. 2, non-OECD countries almost doubled their oil consumption, whereas consumption remained relatively stable in OECD countries.

Table 2 Proven oil reserves (in thousand million barrels)

	End 1994	End 2014	Δ (%)
OECD	148.4	248.6	68
Non-OECD	969.5	1451.5	50
OPEC	778.9	1216.5	56
Non-OPEC	216	341.7	58

Source: BP (2015)

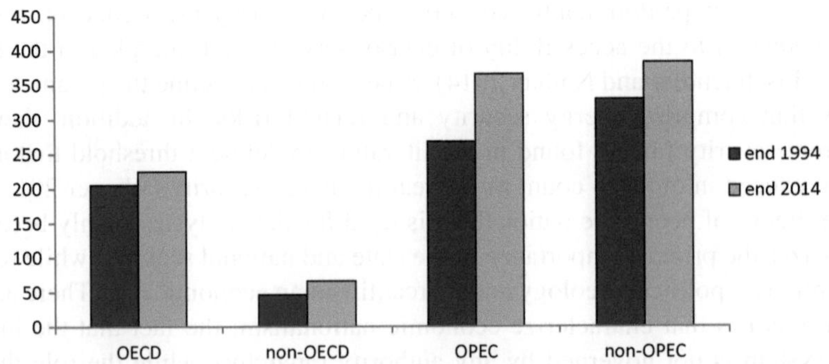

Fig. 1 Oil production in OECD/non-OECD and OPEC/non-OPEC countries, 1994–2014 [in million tons per annum (MTPA)]. *Source*: BP (2015)

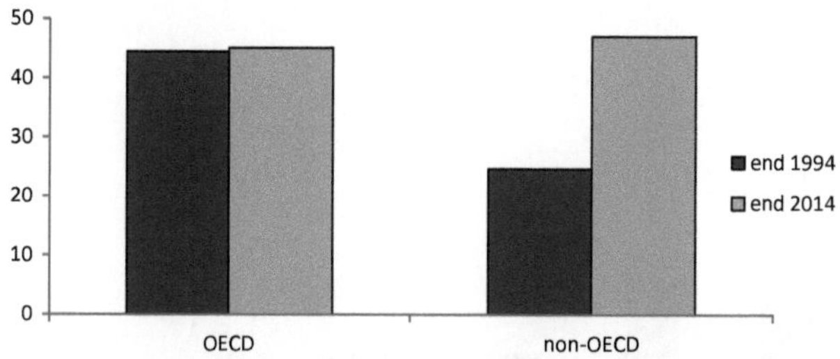

Fig. 2 Oil consumption in OECD/non-OECD countries, 1994–2014 (in MTPA). *Source*: BP (2015)

Table 3 Regional oil production and consumption, 1994–2014

	Oil production ('000 bpd)			Oil consumption ('000 bpd)		
	End 1994	End 2014	Δ (%)	End 1994	End 2014	Δ (%)
North America	138.1	187.2	36	21.3	23.3	9
South America	5.3	7.6	43	4.3	7.1	65
Europe and Eurasia	136.5	171.9	26	199.3	182.5	−8
Middle East	201.2	285.5	42	4.4	8.7	98
Africa	7	8.2	17	2.1	3.8	81
Asia-Pacific	7.1	8.3	17	17.1	30.8	80

Source: BP (2015)

It is expected that global fundamentals will continue to shape long-term prices, while short/medium-term volatility has returned. The strongest growth will continue in the developing nations of Asia, the Middle East and Latin America; however, due to the competitive advantages derived from shale gas, growth will be strong in North America, whereas Europe and Japan are expected to lag behind (Blake 2014).

In Table 3, the regional allocation of both oil production and consumption from the year 1994–2014 is given. It is important to note that North America has been producing more than it has consumed for the last two decades, while the opposite has occurred in the Asia-Pacific region, where consumption has increased to a much greater extent than production over the same period. Finally, Europe and Eurasia are the only regions that show a decline in the consumption rates; all the other regions exhibit increases, from around 10% in the case of North America to almost 100% in the case of the Middle East.

Based on the annual outlook report issued by British Petroleum (BP 2015), there are some very important indications related to global energy issues, summarized as follows:

First, there will be a "regional imbalance" (production–consumption) in every geographical region until 2040, which is expected to affect the energy trade and consequently the energy security of the regions and countries. Secondly, North America will become a net exporter from 2016/2017, while the Asian countries will

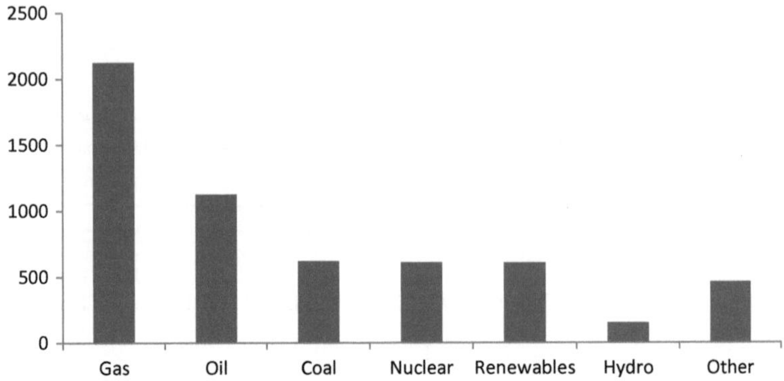

Fig. 3 Global growth in demand by source of energy, 2014–2040 (in MTPA). *Source*: Blake (2014)

continue to grow in terms of energy needs, "accounting for around 70% of inter-regional net imports by 2035". Finally, the Middle East will continue to be the largest energy exporter, even if its share will decline "from 46% in 2013 to 36% in 2035".

Energy issues, which are strongly related to economics, can exacerbate or ease tensions or conflicts of a political nature, depending on the willingness of the actors involved. Economic power continues to shift eastwards and thus it is of great interest to study energy security in the broader area of the East Mediterranean and its effect on the national security of the countries located there. Figure 3 shows the primary energy demand, which is expected to be driven mainly by liquefied natural gas (LNG), followed by oil and coal. More specifically, the demand for LNG will be around 2300 MTPA while that for oil will be 1250 MTPA and Coal around 600 MTPA.

4 Energy Resources as a Means of Power for States/Actors

Since 2008, energy and food markets—those most fundamental to human existence—have been in turmoil. Resource scarcity has had a much bigger global impact in recent years than was predicted, with ongoing volatility a sign that the world is only partway through navigating a treacherous transition in the way it uses resources. Scarcity and perceptions of scarcity increase political risk, while geopolitical turmoil exacerbates shortages and complicates the search for solutions.

The new politics of strategic resources examines the political dimensions of strategic resource challenges at the domestic and international levels. For better or worse, energy and food markets are shaped by perceptions of national interest and do not behave in the same way as traditional market goods. Thus, while markets are an essential part of any response to tighter resource supplies, governments will also play a key role (Steven et al. 2014).

It is well known that oil and gas "play a vast and vital role in our society as it is organized today". Oil and gas are not only two of the most important energy sources for meeting the needs of human society, but also represent the feedstock for several consumer goods, thus playing a growing and relevant role in people's lives (Mariano and La Rovere 2014). States can react to any evolving situation in the energy market, adopting reflexive strategies and taking each other into account (Correlje and van der Linde 2005). Moreover, it has been observed in relation to previous incidents in the energy market that "the state of the world" concerns the oil and gas industry.

Energy is one of the most important resources on which human existence and development depends. Oil and gas exploration gives rise to several socio-economic concerns for "host governments, local communities and project proponents". If these are not properly and effectively addressed, they can result in "significant non-technical risk to projects such as local backlash, delays in project approvals, missed opportunities for delivery of benefits and reduced scope to prevent and/or mitigate and negative impacts". Such issues are most important if "resource extraction projects are developed in remote, socially or environmentally sensitive regions" (Wagner et al. 2014).

Independent socio-economic impact studies can provide early identification of socio-economic, cultural and strategic environmental issues as part of corporate planning, due diligence and risk management. From the stakeholder's perspective, it is of relevance to consider the interconnections between them, particularly those related to the oil and gas industry.

The resources on which societies rely to satisfy their basic needs can be divided into four major categories: food, water, energy and materials. Ecosystems are necessary to contribute to and support the availability of such resources and also to provide a range of other ecosystem services that affect human health and well-being. It is often the case that the economy is given priority in policies and the environment is considered as separate from human societies. However, as argued in the sustainable development theory, the above elements are "interconnected, with the economy dependent on society and the environment while human existence and society are dependent on, and within the environment"(Giddings et al. 2002).

The social impacts of oil and gas activities can be positive and negative (Consiglio et al. 2006). They claim that negative impacts, such as "resource use and the movement of people", can be balanced by positive impacts, such as "the promotion of employment, socio-economic development and improvements in infrastructure". Differences have arisen between the state and stakeholder communities regarding the legitimacy of use of land and the natural resources in it. The state considers that it owns the natural resources and thus state agencies are authorized to decide the path of the best possible exploration option that can contribute to the country's economy, whereas local communities usually attach more than economic definitions to land (Akpan 2005).

Finally, the prevailing approach in IPE considers the world in terms of regions and states, with the dividing parameters that define the spheres of influence mainly being political and military strategies, combined with regionalism. This yields, for example, the US, the European Union, Russia and Asia as such spheres of influence. Concerns related to the national security of the state tend to prevent economic cooperation and integration among these spheres; rather, they implement protective rules and regulations related to their people, capital, goods and flows (Correlje and van der Linde 2005).

5 Contemporary Megatrends

Megatrends are major, transformative forces that affect the global future. They have a far-reaching impact on economies, industries, societies and individuals. Today's world is in constant motion, with goods, capital and labor moving globally at a faster pace than ever. In other words, global megatrends are "a manifestation of a vast number of processes and changes across the world" (EEA 2015). In Europe, two different means are employed to deal with such megatrends: first, shaping global change in ways that mitigate and manage risks and create opportunities: this can be done using both "unilateral and multilateral efforts to mitigate environmental pressures or facilitate trade, or through using foreign aid mechanisms to invest in education and poverty alleviation". Second, finding ways to adapt to global trends, for example by looking to anticipate and avoid harm "by increasing the resilience of social, environmental and economic systems".

In 2010, the EEA produced an assessment of emerging global trends (EEA 2015), summarizing 11 global megatrends grouped into five clusters: social, technological, economic, environmental and governance. The data and results of the EEA (2015) report are based on reliable and comparable environmental information from both the EEA itself and the European Environment Information and Observation Network (Eionet), which is a network of 39 European countries. The issues defined in such clusters are expected to contribute to a discussion about "how Europe should monitor and assess future changes in order to better inform environmental policymaking". The 11 megatrends have different kinds of impact on the resource categories (EEA 2013). These are then addressed in turn in the following sub-sections.

5.1 Diverging Global Population Trends

The EY (2015) report indicates that this parameter will be one of the main megatrends observed within the next 20–30 years as it foresees an increasing population, especially in underdeveloped and developing countries. The global population is expected to surpass 9.6 billion by 2050, even though the rate of growth is slowing and most of the population increase will take place in the urban areas of developing countries. The use of resources and consequently the environment is expected to be affected by such an increasing population in the developing world, as well as the global growth of an affluent middle class and the increase in ageing populations in developed countries (EEA 2015).

5.2 Towards a More Urban World

Urban regions in developing countries are expected to absorb most of the increase in global population within the coming years and it can be observed that 67% of people will be living in cities by 2050. Organized and well-designed cities could be an appropriate, efficient and environmentally sustainable means of ensuring the welfare of a growing population and for this reason "smart planning provides for the efficient re-use and mixed-use of urban space" (EEA 2015, pp. 29–35). Urbanization and the increase in the number of megacities all around the world are considered to comprise an important megatrend, while at the same time sizable migration flows to developed countries are expected to take place, which will initially affect the demographics of those societies (EY 2015). According to Oxford Economics (2015), world urbanization is centered particularly around 750 major cities, which will contribute 60% of global GDP by 2030. Thus, urban regions and states will need sustainable solutions to optimize resources and assure the well-being of their citizens.

5.3 Changing Disease and Risks of Epidemics

Non-communicable diseases now outweigh the risk from communicable diseases globally, mainly due to "increased ageing and rapidly changing economic and social conditions". The danger of "global pandemics continue", especially during the easier movement of populations, while "around a quarter of the burden of disease and deaths are attributable to environmental causes" (EEA 2015, pp. 37–43).

5.4 Accelerating Technological Change

It is no longer possible to project technological changes; these provide increasing options and opportunities to minimize humanity's impact on the environment and reliance on non-renewable natural resources and at the same time to improve lifestyles to stimulate innovation and green growth (EEA 2015).

5.5 Continued Economic Growth

It is predicted that economic results globally will experience a threefold increase by 2050, even though development may slow down in various countries as they become more prosperous. High economic development has led to reductions in global poverty and increases in well-being but it is also linked to growing inequality and escalating environmental pressures. However, there are issues in terms of measurement as GDP is typically used as a measurement of growth; specifically, the constraints of GDP as a means of measuring human well-being and the sustainability of growth have prompted international efforts to identify better indicators of societal progress (EEA 2015).

5.6 An Increasingly Multipolar World

Developing regions in the world are rapidly increasing their share of global economic output, trade and investment. The main reasons for this are structural changes, trade liberalization and rapidly increasing workforces. The appearance of a more different mixture of major economic powers can confuse global efforts to coordinate governance and thus any growing economic interdependence will not contribute to manage the social and environmental impacts related to production and consumption systems (EEA 2015).

5.7 Intensified Global Competition for Resources

Since the beginning of the twentieth century, the global use of material resources has increased around 10 times; moreover, it is expected to double by 2030. Due to the continuous increasing demand for material resources, there is the potential for endangering access to certain necessary resources and engendering environmental problems. As noted by the EEA (2015, pp. 69–75), even though increasing "scarcity and rising prices should incentivize investments in technologies to alleviate supply risks, such innovations will not necessarily reduce environmental pressures". According to the US Energy Information Administration (EIA 2013), global energy demand is expected to be around 30–40% higher by 2040 or even earlier.

5.8 Growing Pressures on Ecosystems

The aforementioned increasing population gives rise to additional effects in terms of the type of consumption of food, mobility and energy that seriously affect the

"Earth's ecosystems and their life-supporting services". Such changes lead to serious concerns regarding food, such as meat-heavy diets, as well as strategies for bioenergy production. Moreover, the consequences of ecosystem degradation on poverty and inequality outside of Europe will increase the immigration to Europe (EEA 2015).

5.9 *Increasingly Severe Consequences of Climate Change*

Climate change and its effects at the socio-economic level are expected to cause other consequent problems (EY 2015). Climate change is seen to exert continuous effects at higher rates in terms of "natural ecosystems and their biodiversity, slow economic growth, erode global food security, threaten human health and increase inequality". The risks of irreversible effects could potentially be reduced by emissions abatement and adaptation measures, building on actions in Europe (EEA 2015).

5.10 *Increasing Environmental Pollution*

The levels of air pollution and releases of nutrients from agriculture and wastewater are still high. They bring soil acidification, eutrophication of aquatic ecosystems and losses in agricultural yield, while during the coming years total pollution is expected to reach even higher levels, especially in the region of Asia (EEA 2015).

5.11 *Diversifying Approaches to Governance*

It has been noted that governmental authorities are trying to address the long-term, systemic challenges facing society and their limited focus and powers. The need for aligned action globally is seen in the proliferation of international agreements and the role of business and civil society in governance. Thus, it is necessary to have a "diversification of governance", however this can give rise to questions related to coordination and effectiveness, and the replacement of government authority by less transparent non-state actors (EEA 2015).

6 Energy and Conflicts/Peace Among States

There are many analysts and theorists who consider that energy security issues are closely related to what is called "escalating geopolitical tensions in oil-producing regions", combined with the new energy consumers in Asia, the "over-reliance on oil" and "an expected depletion of fossil fuels" (Fischhendler and Nathan 2014, p. 152). As Leigh (2014) notes, there are quite a lot conflicts, foreign interventions and wars that have occurred due to the struggle for resources, more often in oil-rich areas such as the Middle East, but also throughout the world. He mentions that "access to energy resources is a major determinant of certain international developments", while Shaffer (2009) states that energy interests affect the mapping of geostrategic interests.

Correlje and van der Linde (2005) classify the different kinds of disruptions and thus conflicts related to energy in three main categories as follows: disruptions and conflicts that can occur due to a "political decision" not to supply markets, or an "international military conflict", or a reason related to technical aspects; slowly emerging supply gaps as an effect of "lagging investments in production and/or transportation" and finally results of ideological differences between the governments of supply countries.

There are six factors that affect stability of supply relations and consequently to disrupt them to achieve foreign policy goals as following: degree and relative dependence on supply; overall political and economic relations between states; the domestic supply situation of the producer and transit states; the decision-making process affecting the oil and gas policy in each state; the involvement of transit states in the fuel supply and finally the commercial benefits of continued supply to the actors involved (Shaffer 2013).

There have been several incidents in recent history in which energy and energy security issues have been linked to national security issues and tensions/conflicts among the actors involved, for example in the following instances:

- In World War I the British government decided to change the type of fuel used by the navy from coal to oil to gain a tactical/strategic advantage as a country (Yergin 1988).
- In World War II all military operations relied on oil as the main and basic means of fuel, so energy security became a wider concept that also included industrialized services, which were more reliant on motorized transportation (Cherp and Jewell 2011).
- In the 1970s, most of the oil industries in the Middle East were nationalized and an oil embargo was put in place which caused threats to industrialized countries as it put their development and political stability at huge risk (Yergin 1988).
- With the Iranian revolution in 1979–1980, oil prices "skyrocketed", as a result of which "US growth plunged sharply again" (Nivola and Carter 2010, p. 107).
- In Egypt, energy security is seen as an issue related to access to oil supplies as the state suffered to secure regular and accessible services (Fischhendler and Nathan 2014).

- In the Kingdom of Saudi Arabia, the country with the largest oil reserves in the world, it has been recognized that there might be energy independence for Western countries in the future and thus it has started looking for more "sustainable methods for development and maintaining energy independency with foreign nations" (Fischhendler and Nathan 2014, p. 154).
- In Israel, the Tzemach Committee, which is involved in the country's energy policy design, has been seeking a linkage between energy security in the country's economy and local competition in the market, as well as geopolitical advantages for the state in the region (Tzemach Committee 2012).
- In Cyprus and Turkey, the recent discoveries of hydrocarbons in the eastern Mediterranean region have caused tensions. It is yet to be seen how this will end, also bearing in mind the Cypriot problem that still prevails in the island (Ogurlu 2012).
- In Jordan, the International Monetary Fund (IMF) considers the energy issue to be an area of weakness in the country's economy (Fischhendler and Nathan 2014, p. 154).
- In Lebanon, the government has expressed concerns about the intentions and actions of its neighbor state of Israel, accusing it of stealing Lebanon's oil and arguing that this will cause serious problems for the wealth of its economy in the near future (Abdel-Kader 2011).
- In the US, Hillary Clinton, when Secretary of State, stated at a NATO meeting that "energy security and supply disruptions should be viewed as threats to the alliance" (Shaffer 2013, p. 1). On another occasion, the government under the Obama leadership announced its intention to "implement at Energy Security Trust, which will address some of the insecurities that climate-change poses" and the same time to reduce "the influence that foreign oil producers have on national decisions" (Fischhendler and Nathan 2014, p. 152).
- In 2006 and 2009, Russia and Ukraine failed to reach agreement on the price of gas, which was one of the factors that led to the crisis, although not the only one, due to "Russian's exploitation of energy needs as an instrument of state power" (Elkind 2010, p. 136).
- In China, the National Oil Companies (NOCs) are seen as the "arms of the Chinese government that are aggressively snapping up exploration and production assets around the world to enhance China's energy security at the expense of that of other consumers" (Downs 2010, p. 73).

It is also important to note that almost one out of three civil wars is due to oil (Ross 2008). The supply of energy is referred to as a "weapon and supply disruptions as threats or attacks on a state". The disruption of supplies can be initiated not only by suppliers, but also by consumer and transit countries. Even though alliances are considered to be vehicles that bring participating member states close to the security of their suppliers, they are not the norm or the usual scenario. Concerning the causes of intentional disruptions, most have been linked to Russia (Shaffer 2013).

7 Conclusions

Based on the analysis in this paper, it is clear that states need to revisit their energy policies and design a new vision for the future. For this reason, they need to understand the oncoming megatrends that will have serious implications for the globe, at the same time considering those critical success factors that will contribute to sustainable investment and an innovative approach. Political will is required to solve conflicts and to bring about strategic realignments (Leigh 2014). Furthermore, cooperation on technical issues which are related to energy production will help to build confidence and attenuate risks of confrontation over claims. However, very little has been done and achieved so far regarding effective coordination across borders on energy issues and this needs to change, otherwise it will not be possible for national governments to develop and sustain energy policies (Florini 2010).

Energy security through consideration of the major factors drives energy policy decisions, including the actions of other nations, a changing climate, and the quest for energy independence (Pascual and Elkind 2010). After the 1970s oil crisis, for most Middle Eastern oil producers the energy security concept entailed the capability of inflicting political and economic hardship on Western nations dependent on petroleum, as the oil embargoes effectively operated as 'oil weapons' (Yergin 1991).

The energy security issue together with various other policy issues can be considered an umbrella term for international security, economic development and political relations (Ciuta 2010). Energy security will be significantly enhanced if solutions are found that take into consideration the need to balance the geopolitical, economic and environmental implications of energy (Yergin 2010).

Acknowledgement The publication of this paper has been supported in part by the University of Piraeus Research Center.

References

Abdel-Kader, N. (2011). Potential conflict between Lebanon and Israel over oil and gas resources—A Lebanese perspective. *National Defense Magazine*, *78* [online]. Accessed January 29, 2016, from http://www.lebarmy.gov.lb/en/content/potential-conflict-between-lebanon-and-israel-over-oil-and-gas-resources-%E2%80%93-lebanese

Akpan, W. (2005). Putting oil first? Some ethnographic aspects of petroleum-related land use controversies in Nigeria. *African Sociological Review*, *9*(2), 134–152.

Blake, E. (2014). *World energy outlook. 9th Annual GPCA Forum*. Dubai: IHS.

BP. (2015). *BP energy outlook. Outlook to 2035*. British Petroleum [online]. Accessed December 25, 2015, from http://www.bp.com/en/global/corporate/energy-economics/energy-outlook-2035.html

Cherp, A., & Jewell, J. (2011). The three perspectives on energy security: Intellectual history, disciplinary roots and the potential for integration. *Current Opinion in Environmental Sustainability, 3(4)*, 202–212.

Ciuta, F. (2010). Conceptual notes on energy security: Total or banal security? *Security Dialogue, 41*(2), 123–144.

Consiglio, M., Witchalls, B., Armstrong, K., Stampa, M., Madec, A., Abdullah, M., et al. (2006, April 2–4). *A guide to social impact assessment in the oil and gas industry*. SPE International Health, Safety & Environment Conference, Abu Dhabi, UAE.

Correlje, A., & Van der Linde, C. (2005). Energy supply security and geopolitics: A European perspective. *Energy Policy, 34*(5), 532–543.

Dixon, T. H. (2006). *The upside of the down: Catastrophe, creativity, and the renewal of civilization*. Washington, DC: The Island Press.

Downs, E. (2010). Who's afraid of China's oil companies? In C. Pascual & J. Elkind (Eds.), *Energy security: Economics, politics, strategies and implications* (pp. 73–102). Washington, DC: Brookings Institution Press.

EEA. (2013). *Environmental indicator report 2013—Natural resources and human well-being in a green economy*. Copenhagen: European Environment Agency.

EEA. (2015). *The European environment state and outlook 2015: Assessment of global megatrends*. Copenhagen: European Environment Agency.

EIA. (2013). *Eastern Mediterranean region* (Full report online). US Energy Information Administration [online]. Accessed December 25, 2015, from http://www.eia.gov/todayinenergy/detail.cfm?id=12611

El-Badri, A. S. (2015). *Security of energy supplies inextricably linked with demand* [online]. Accessed October 31, 2015, from http://www.opec.org/opec_web/en/3013.htm

Elkind, J. (2010). Energy security: Call for a broader agenda. In C. Pascual & J. Elkindeds (Eds.), *Energy security: Economics, politics, strategies and implications* (pp. 119–148). Washington, DC: Brookings Institution Press.

EY. (2015). *Megatrends 2015: Making sense of a world in motion* [online]. Accessed November 25, 2015, from http://www.ey.com/GL/en/Issues/Business-environment/ey-megatrends-that-will-shape-our-future-4-global-marketplace

Fischhendler, I., & Nathan, D. (2014). In the name of energy security: The struggle over the exportation of Israeli natural gas. *Energy Policy, 70*, 152–162.

Florini, A. (2010). Global governance and energy. In C. Pascual & J. Elkind (Eds.), *Energy security: Economics, politics, strategies and implications* (pp. 149–181). Washington, DC: Brookings Institution Press.

Giddings, B., Hopwood, B., & O'Brien, G. (2002). Environment, economy and society: Fitting them together into sustainable development. *Sustainable Development, 10*(4), 187–196.

Guzzini, S. (1998). *Realism in international relations and international political economy: The continuing story of a death foretold*. London: Routledge.

Ifestos, P. (2015). *International political economy* [online]. Accessed October 31, 2015, from http://www.ifestosedu.gr/94%CE%94%CE%B9%CE%B5%CE%B8%CE%BD%CE%AE%CF%82%CE%A0%CE%BF%CE%BB%CE%9F%CE%B9%CE%BA%CE%BF%CE%BD%CE%BF%CE%BC%CE%AF%CE%B1.htm

Kaveshnikov, N. (2010). The issue of energy security in relations between Russia and the European Union. *European Security, 19*(4), 585–605.

Knopf, J. W. (2006). Doing a literature review. *Political Science and Politics, 39*(01), 127–132.

Kruyt, B., Vuuren, D. P., Vries, H. J. M., & Groeneberg, H. (2009). Indicators for energy security. *Energy Policy, 37*(6), 2166–2181.

Kuzemco, C. (2014). Ideas, power and change: Explaining EU–Russia energy relations. *Journal of European Public Policy, 21*(1), 58–75.

Leigh, M. (2014). Energy—A geopolitical game changer? *The International Spectator, 49*(2), 1–10.

Litfin, K. (2014). Gaia theory, eco villages, and IR taking material limits seriously: An interview with Karen Litfin. In M. Mayer, M. Carpes, & R. Knoblich (Eds.), *The global politics of science and technology* (Vol. 1, pp. 259–265). Heidelberg: Springer.

Mariano, J., & La Rovere, E. (2014). Environmental impacts in the oil industry in petroleum engineering downstream. In Encyclopedia of Life Support Systems (EOLSS) (Ed.), *Developed under the auspices of UNESCO*. Paris: Eolss Publishers. http://www.eolss.net
Nivola, P., & Carter, E. (2010). Making sense of "energy independence". In C. Pascual & J. Elkind (Eds.), *Energy security: Economics, politics, strategies and implications* (pp. 105–118). Washington, DC: Brookings.
Ogurlu, E. (2012). *Rising tensions in the Eastern Mediterranean: Implications for Turkish foreign policy* (IAI Working Papers 12/04). Instituto Affari Internazionali.
Oxford Economics. (2015). *Future trends and market opportunities in the world's largest 750 cities* [online]. Accessed December 22, 2015, from http://www.oxfordeconomics.com/cities/report
Pascual, C., & Elkind, J. (2010). Introduction. In C. Pascual & J. Elkind (Eds.), *Energy security: Economics, politics, strategies and implications* (pp. 1–6). Brookings: Washington, DC.
Rosenberg, J. (1994). *Empire of civil society—A critique of the realist theory of international relations*. London: Verso.
Ross, M. (2008). *Blood barrels—Why oil wealth fuels conflict*. Foreign Affairs. Accessed Februay 2, 2016, from https://www.foreignaffairs.com/articles/2008-05-03/blood-barrels
Roukanas, S., & Diamantis, G. (2014). BRICs in the global economy under the prism of economic nationalism of IPE. *International Journal of Economic Sciences and Applied Research, 7*(1), 51–67.
Schmidt, B. (1998). *The political discourse of anarchy*. Albany, NY: Stake University of NY Press.
Shaffer, B. (2009). *Energy politics*. Philadelphia, PA: University of Pennsylvania Press.
Shaffer, B. (2013). Natural gas supply stability and foreign policy. *Energy Policy, 56*, 114–125.
Sklias, P. (2011). *Political economy of international relations: The Copenhagen summit for climate change*. Athens: Papazisi (in Greek).
Steven, D., O'Brien, E., & Jones, B. (2014). *Fueling a new order? The new geopolitical and security consequences of energy* (The Brookings Institute, Paper, April 15, 2014).
Tzemach Committee. (2012). *The recommendations of the Inter-Ministerial Committee to examine the government's policy regarding natural gas*. State of Israel: Ministry of Energy and Water Resources.
Vasquez, J. A. (2004). *The power of power politics: From classical realism to neotraditionalism*. Cambridge: Cambridge University Press.
Wagner, J., Dowse, S., & Jones, M. (2014, March 17–19). *Managing socio-economic risk in frontier areas: A case study from the Falkland Islands*. SPE International Conference on Health, Safety, and Environment, Long Beach, CA, USA.
Waltz, K. (1991). Realist thought and neorealist thought. In R. Rothstein (Ed.), *The evolution of theory in international relations* (pp. 21–38). Columbia, SC: University of South Carolina (1992).
Wizner, C. (2012). Conceptualizing energy security. *Energy Policy, 46*, 36–48.
Yergin, D. (1988). Energy security in the 1990s. *Foreign Affairs, 67*(1), 110–132.
Yergin, D. (1991). *The prize: The epic quest for oil, money, and power*. New York, NY: Simon and Schuster.
Yergin, D. (2010). Foreword. In C. Pascual & J. Elkind (Eds.), *Energy security: Economics, politics, strategies and implications* (pp. 7–8). Brookings: Washington, DC.

The Organizational Cyberspace: E-trainerism. The Model of Advanced ICT and Augmented Reality in Sports Enterprises

Wojciech Cieśliński, Kazimierz Witkowski, Zbigniew Piepiora, and Paweł Piepiora

Abstract The aim of the study is to verify the theoretical basis of advanced ICT and Augmented Reality in the organizational development and sports clubs to improve their sports performance. The methodology of the article is based on setting the computer designed system. The study includes the preparation and implementation of a system to manage a sports club and augmented reality technologies in the improvement of sports training system remotely and in real time. After conducted analysis, the following conclusions can be drawn. The use of ICT and AR enables the implementation of mechanisms of organizational learning of sports enterprises (process of collecting, diffusing and sharing the knowledge in the organization in terms of cyber, using the model of negative feedback). An important contribution of described results of research and implementation projects is the development of knowledge concerning the area of research. It is the implementation based on the process approach and organizational learning in the field of management tasks and the tasks of sports training through applications of technologically advanced information systems that improve the organizational effectiveness of sports clubs and the effectiveness of sports training.

Keywords Global competitiveness • Organizational cyberspace • E-trainerism • ICT • Augmented reality • Sports • Club • Enterprise

---

W. Cieśliński
Department of Communication and Management in Sport, University School of Physical Education in Wrocław, Wrocław, Poland
e-mail: wojciechbcieslinski@gmail.com

K. Witkowski • P. Piepiora
Department of Sport Teaching, University School of Physical Education in Wrocław, Wrocław, Poland
e-mail: kazimierz.witkowski@awf.wroc.pl; pawelpiepiora@gmail.com

Z. Piepiora (✉)
Departmentof Spatial Economy, Wrocław University of Environmental and Life Sciences, Wrocław, Poland
e-mail: zbigniew.piepiora@up.wroc.pl

M.H. Bilgin et al. (eds.), *Empirical Studies on Economics of Innovation, Public Economics and Management*, Eurasian Studies in Business and Economics 6,
DOI 10.1007/978-3-319-50164-2_9

1 Introduction

The aim of the study is to verify the theoretical basis of advanced ICT and Augmented Reality in the organizational development and sports clubs to improve their sports performance. The consequence of theoretical assumptions is to develop a technologically advanced system in the company's organizational cyberspace sport or the design of a prototype of E-trainterism.

E-trainerism is an integrated system of managing the sports, coaching and managerial development and the improvement using the predictive model of managing the data, information and knowledge (the cyberspace) and the extended reality to generate new values in the field of the sports development of competitors and the development of coaching staff and managers of the sports enterprises.

The design studies shall concern designing the functionality of the mobile data communications system for a sports club (the e-AZS platform), implementing the e-AZS platform, designing the mathematical model of traffic in the teaching techniques of judo, designing the software for computer-assisted modeling of traffic, the trial test of the software using the augmented-reality technology, designing the system of managing the organizational cyberspace of the sports enterprises with the use of the advanced information technologies (ICT AR). It is pointed out that the development of organizational cyberspace of enterprises, including sports, is possible and necessary for the reason that the virtual space is now the largest area of coaching, managerial and sports development opportunities. No use of development trends in the high technology sector causes the uncompetitive market in the provision of services in the field of sport of children and youth, professional or amateur, and elderly.

2 Research Predicates

The Organizational Cyberspace is a space which is defined as a system of connections and interactions between events generated running in virtual space. The basis for definition and description of such space is to identify the processes that take place in this space generated and triggered by virtual events or events generated by computer.

As it can be seen in Fig. 1, a description of cyberspace must involve two objects, processes and virtual events. After the literature review (Hammer and Stanton 1994; Kaplan and Norton 1996; Krupski 2005; Kasprzak 2005; Perechuda and Cieśliński 2008; Cieśliński 2007b; Cieśliński et al. 2015), We state the predicates research on this issue: the process approach and the implementation of information

virtual EVENT → virtual PROCESS → virtual EVENT

Fig. 1 The model of managing cyberspace

systems, focusing on processes and organizational development of enterprises; business processes in the company and building a system of raising organizational efficiency; the process approach and the functional areas of the enterprise; structural-systemic and interactive paradigm for managing and controlling processes recognition system; interpretative cognitive science management and process management description; process orientation and configuration of the organizational structure of enterprises; turbulent and laminar processes of economic tools and operation conditions; focusing on the structure design and outsourcing as a tool for restructuring activities in the organization; corporate strategy and business process architecture; economic processes and levels of referral and their use in modeling and organizational designing, the process approach and the requirements of logistics systems; processes' management and 'knowledge' and 'event-driven' paradigm of modern enterprise activities, in particular economic networks; the dynamics of economic networks; events initiating and ending mileage processes; virtual events are generated and controlled by computer; the use of advanced information technologies (ICTs and augmented reality), is a condition for sport clubs to compete in the market for sports.

In particularly, we recognized: lack of consistency management systems, caused by the lack of relationship between the enterprise's development strategy and the evolution of the architecture of business processes in networks; negative impact of implemented systems on organizational culture (including means of communication); generate and implement their own foreign technology and products with innovative process-oriented organizations in the conditions of existence of strong systemic disturbances in economic networks; the space computer generated and controlled computational technology creates cyberspace; the need to identify the functionality of the e-AZS and the functionality of the e-trainer with the use of augmented reality technology is the basis for creating a cyberspace organization and training in sports clubs; development of cyberspace organization of sports enterprises, through computerization of their processes and the use of augmented reality; the space organization of sports clubs is real space, and virtual media and their expanded version, which is augmented reality, mediality and virtuality, trainersim as a modern idea of competence development executives and coaching of clubs and players.

3 The Trainerism: A Modern Idea of Functioning Organization of Work of Sports Club

Trainerism combines the idea of managerial training, coaching and training system for personnel of enterprises, taking into account the training system and the programming burden in such a way as to continually improve (achieve continuous growth—supercompensation) ability to exercise in teamwork, intellectual and emotional. Trainerism is the idea of using practical experience and theory and the

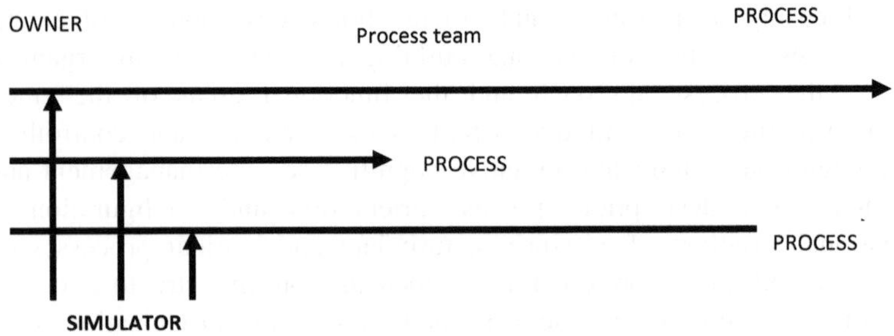

Fig. 2 The model approach to managing the organization of work and sports training by simulator. Source: Own study on the basis of (Hammer and Champy 2006)

theory of sports training and experience of team sports for development and improvement of human capital enterprises, including in particular the development and improvement of team work process (Cieśliński 2006, 2007a, b, 2009).

As we can see in Fig. 2, the essence of trainerism boils down to that you program cycles, training and recreation of employees in such a way as to improve the efficiency of their interaction and personal development. In sport, fitness is achieved not during training (working for employees) but when by the work optimally done during previously selected holiday. We assume that research (experiment conducted on employees of the company) confirm the hypothesis about the need to take into account the improvement of human capital strategy, enterprise-cyclical workloads, improvement-training and leisure.

Trainer, as a person who plans to work his ward, should consider not only the existing development needs and satisfying them, but also on the effect of training load. He must know that the accumulated quantitative work lowers the efficiency of each people. It is only thanks to the relaxation you can get increased capacity for learning. The awareness of this tool should be an essential element in the planning of micro, meso and macrocycles training. We can see an example of microcycle in the Table 1.

Supercompensation is increasing the efficiency of own work, through the appropriate selection of ratio between the period of work and rest. It cannot be lengthened the rest because it leads to weakness—the forgetfulness of conducted training, often lowering the efficiency to the level before the test. It is often repeated error, in design terms, of led workouts. One isolated in its themed training, without further reinforcements, and raising the level, will be forgotten. Trainerism is a process and it is the effectiveness, built on the effect of supercompensation.

As we can see in Fig. 3, the idea of trainerism has its origins in sport training. The simulator is a person on the one hand developing their workers through proper selection of volume and intensity of work and leisure. The organization, which is the basis of this approach is process oriented approach and implementation of mechanism of organizational learning. The efficiency of such a system is determined by the extent to which this is possible the cooperation of the managerial and training staff with IT systems. It is assumed the need to project for a system that

Table 1 An example of microcycle

	Type of work			Type of training			Type of leisure		
Day of week	Work planning	Organizing	Control	Motivation to work	Conceptual thinking	Interpersonal thinking	Operating thinking	Passive leisure	Leisure
Monday	x	x			x			x	
Tuesday			x	x		x			x
Wednesday	x	x						x	
Thursday			x		x				x
Friday			x				x	x	
Saturday					x	x			x
Sunday								x	x

Source: Own study on the basis (Witkowski et al. 2016)

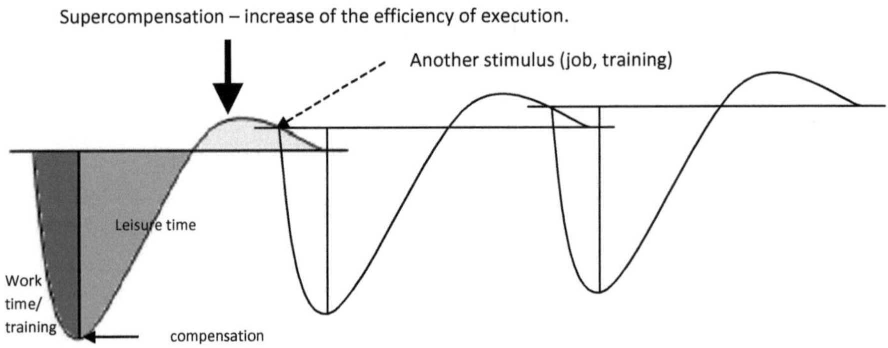

Fig. 3 A model of building the state of high alert for the tasks. Source: Own study based on Cieśliński (2006)

virtualizes certain areas of organizational sports clubs and their areas that are associated with the development staff and players (trainerism, the idea in which there are distinguished three roles; trainer, manager and couch). The following describes issues related to virtualization of these three roles; or organizational system virtualization and sports training system and the executive.

4 The Methodology

4.1 The Virtualization of Organizational Functions and Training in a Sports Club

Sports Club is a system of organization and training. Seeking the improvement of organizational effectiveness and training generates new opportunities to compete in the market for sports. Thus, nowadays sports clubs are sports enterprises. Assumptions of the project are: to develop the functionality of organizational system of a sports club (e-AZS), to design the functionality of e-simulator prototype. The following describes the features that were subject to virtualization both in terms of organization and training.

The contemporary space organizations create events and their permutations, or processes. Events which constitute the space can be generated in real space creating material values, in virtual space, creating intangible assets and in the media, creating the media (Cieśliński et al. 2016a, b). Space can therefore be defined in several dimensions. In addition to the above-mentioned dimension (the event takes place in the real, virtual and medial world), one can talk and describe events depending on what sector of the economy event occurs (public, private or governmental space).

Augmented Reality (Expanded Reality) is, on the one hand, technology (augmented reality, virtuality, mediality) on the other hand, the idea indicating the ways of mixing reality using relationships between events that occur in the organizational sphere of public, private and NGO. Expanding the fact it is so permutation of events, which is a process, which features an overlapping of real processes, e-processes and media processes. The idea of expanding reality boils down to is that events in the real space are imposed on a computer-generated event (event virtual) and/or the media (media events). You can also talk about the process reverse. The events of the virtual space and media are levied on real events. Such processes form an expanded reality (augmented reality), virtuality (augmented virtuality) and mediality (augmented mediality).

4.2 *Setting the Computer Designed System*

The information environment of the proposed system includes schemes administered by AZS AWF Wroclaw and systems outside the administration of AZS AWF Wroclaw. Schemes administered by AZS AWF Wroclaw consist of the website AZS AWF Wroclaw (http://azs.awf.wroc.pl) (including documents associated with a module repository) and the financial and accounting system (including data associated with the budgeting module).

Systems outside the administration of AZS AWF Wroclaw consist of: the AZS system (including http://www.azs.pl and ID AZS system with information about the members of AZS—needed in the task (module) of conducting of players and teams of athletes), computer systems Ministry of Sport and Tourism (including 'passports of competitors'—needed in the module of conducting players and teams of athletes), systems of associations of sports disciplines, for example, the Polish Athletics Association (PZLA)—including website (http://www.pzla.pl) with fixture list—needed in the module of planning training camps and competition results of individual professions—need in the module of conducting of players and teams of athletes, data of athletes—need in the module of conducting of players and teams of athletes.

5 The Case Study

5.1 *The Model of the Functionality of the e-AZS and Augmented Reality in the Construction of a Prototype e-Simulator*

The study includes the preparation and implementation of a system to manage a sports club and augmented reality technologies in the improvement of sports training system remotely and in real time. The following describes the operation of the organizational system KS AZS AWF Wrocław. The organizational structure AZS AWF Wrocław (according to its statute) is actors and tasks.

5.2 Actors of System

Table 2 summarizes the actors system, resulting from the organizational structure of the sports club AZS AWF Wroclaw and the objectives of the implemented system.

5.3 Tasks of the KS AZS AWF Wrocław

Tasks of the KS AZS AWF Wrocław are planning training camps and competitions, conducting (and monitoring) players and teams of athletes (team games), organizing sports events, human resources management, real estate and movable. Tasks allocated under AZS AWF Wroclaw are assigned to duties of secretary.

Table 2 Actors of the ICT system of the AZS AWF Wrocław

Actor	Role
IT administrator	The person responsible for managing the system, granting privileges to individuals, setting and deleting user accounts, and also responsible for the technical aspects of the system
President	A person with insight into accounting data and reports, as well as plans starts, trips
Director	A person with insight into accounting data and reports, as well as booking rooms/fields and other facilities
Chief accountant	The person responsible for accounting records and their introduction to the system
Secretary	The person responsible for personal matters, possibly the collection of data from groups of recruited players
Director of training	Coordinates the budgeting process (plan and settlement), and the proper assignment of points for the club
Coordinating trainer	Coordinates the planning process clusters and takeoffs, as well as planning and budget implementation, training and performance
Trainer	Responsible for organizing training sessions, their conduct and evaluation (fill in diaries training), as well as plans to cluster and starts, plans and implements the budget, supplemented by data in the "athlete passport", collects the results of the competition
Competitor	From the system point of view, this is a person who has access to data concerning him or her training diary, plans groupings and take-offs, as well as the results of the competition and the data contained in their 'passport player'
Guest	From the system point of view, this is a person who has access to a fixture, training camps and races, as well as the results achieved athletes in competition

Task 1 is planning training camps and competitions—this module should allow the formation of groupings plan for training and competing in competitions for individual players and teams. In particular, functionality should include entering data on competitions (schedule), in particular; the term of competitions, the venue, the planned competition, the deadline for applications athletes, the fees associated with the start player, the additional requirements, planning starts in the competition by assigning players to the competition contained in the schedule indicating the possibility of competition planned to start player, modifying the plan starts in the competition, coordinating starts in the competition between the coaches, reminding the need to make notifications or meeting additional requirements, reminding upcoming rides occupations, starting the relationship with the corresponding items in the financial plan (fees associated with starts in the competition, the fees related to housing and transport) and inputting the results for each player taking part in the competition (including a list of competitors which competed, the results obtained, occupied space)—acquisition results of organizer information system (usually—sports association) with the possibility of supplementing them with additional data manually and automatically (or semiautomatically).

Task 2 is Conducting (and monitoring) players and team athletes (team games). One of the tasks of the club is to conduct and monitor athletes of different sports disciplines (individual and team). For this purpose, coaches are hired and their basic tasks are defining training exercises, doing training plans, implementing training plans, evaluating the players' achievements, keeping diaries of players, planning training camps, planning starts in competitions, creating a list of documents required from the player to compete, creating a list of documents required from the player to participate in training camps, budgeting, accounting for the implementation of the planned budget, collection of results of matches, supplementing the data in the ‚passport of athlete' and monitoring the documents submitted by players.

Task 3 is organizing sports events (e.g. the competitions) of the club. The main tasks in this area include defining a list of activities in the area of organizing an event with selection of actors those are responsible for the execution of tasks and coordination of the event, defining a mailing list to send invitations, defining the information about the availability of sports facilities, defining the budget for the executing event, accounting for the budget, getting the contact details for the relevant departments and for the cooperating media within the framework of the event, finding sponsors and partners, supporting the organization (voluntarily), the promotion, handling of calls of players, collecting and sharing the results of players (competitors).

Task 4 is human resources management. As part of the administrative duties of the club, the following tasks stand out in the area of Human Resource Management: records of trainers, records of other employees.

6 Conclusion

The aim of the study was to verify the theoretical basis of advanced ICT and Augmented Reality in the organizational development and sports clubs to improve their sports performance. Nowadays, most sports enterprises go through a phase of orientation for processes as a condition for further development in the direction of orientation for events which may provide a basis for the development in the direction of virtual networks and implementation of ICT systems and augmented reality (including mediality and virtuality) and the same to configuration of own organization in the direction of orientation for events and building the organizational cyberspace of sports clubs.

The use of ICT and AR enables the implementation of mechanisms of organizational learning of sports enterprises (process of collecting, diffusing and sharing the knowledge in the organization in terms of cyber, using the model of negative feedback). The implementation of organizational learning mechanisms is associated with three main areas of action: the configuration of features of the organizational structures of sports enterprises in the direction of orientation on the processes of development in the direction of orientation on events; development of enterprise's IT maturity towards the implementation of advanced ICT and augmented reality, sports enterprises are influenced by modern information technologies.

An important contribution of described results of research and implementation projects is the development of knowledge concerning the area of research'. It is the implementation based on the process approach and organizational learning in the field of management tasks and the tasks of sports training through applications of technologically advanced information systems that improve the organizational effectiveness of sports clubs and the effectiveness of sports training.

Acknowledgement This study is financed from funds earmarked for research in 2013–2016 and 2015–2017, by the Ministry of Science and Higher Education, supervised by dr hab. Kazimierz Witkowski, prof. at AWF Wrocław, and dr hab. Wojciech B. Cieśliński, prof. at AWF Wrocław, grant number: 0014/RS2/2013/52, 'e-AZS Platform' and 2015–2017—'the AZS-AWF Wrocław Sports Club and applications related to Augmented Reality in judo (prototyping an educational trainer)', grant number: 0011/RS3/2015/53.

References

Cieśliński, W. (2006). Wykorzystanie doświadczeń treningu sportowego do rozwoju menedżerów w organizacjach [The use of sports training experiences to the development of managers in organizations]. In T. Listwan, & K. Witkowski (Eds.), *Sukces w zarządzaniu kadrami: kapitał ludzki w organizacji międzynarodowej* [Success in human resources management: Human capital in an international organization] (pp. 15–23). Wrocław: AE.

Cieśliński W. (2007a). Procesowa a informacyjna dojrzałość przedsiębiorstw – wyniki badań [Process and enterprise information maturity – Results of research]. In A. Szewczyk (Ed.),

Problemy społeczeństwa informacyjnego [Problems of information society] (ch. 1). Szczecin: Uniwersytet Szczeciński.

Cieśliński, W. (2007b). Trenadżeryzm – procesowe ujęcie doskonalenia kapitału ludzkiego przedsiębiorstw [Trainerism – process approach to improve the human capital of companies]. In A. Potocki (Ed.), *Społeczne aspekty przeobrażeń organizacyjnych* [Social aspects of organizational transformation] (ch. 1). Warszawa: Difin.

Cieśliński, W. (2009). Procesowa dojrzałość przedsiębiorstw – wyniki badań empirycznych [Process maturity of enterprises – Results of empirical research]. In S. Nowosielski (Ed.), *Procesowa orientacja przedsiębiorstw* [Process oriented businesses] (ch 1). Wrocław: AE

Cieśliński, W. B., Witkowski, K., Głowicki, P., Piepiora, P. A., & Sobecki, J. (2015). Applying advanced ICT technologies and augmented reality to generate future events on the example of organization and education in sports methodological assumptions. *IJRITCC, 3*(10), 5967–5971.

Cieśliński, W. B., Witkowski, K., Piepiora, Z., Piepiora, P. A., & Bernat, P. (2016a). The safety engineering of mass sports events – The model of emergency management of logistics processes with using of advanced technologies (Augmented Reality, GPS and ICT). In *Proceedings of the 2016 International Conference on Intelligent Control and Computer Application in Advances in Computer Science Research.* Paris: Atlantis Press. Accessed March 28, 2016, from http://www.atlantis-press.com/php/pub.php?publication=icca-16

Cieśliński, W. B., Sobecki, J., Piepiora, P. A., Piepiora, Z. N., & Witkowski, K. (2016b). Application of the augmented reality in prototyping the educational simulator in sport – The example of judo. *Journal of Physics: Conference Series, 710*, 1–8.

Hammer, M., & Champy, J. (2006). *Reengineering the corporation: A manifesto for business revolution (Collins Business Essentials).* New York, NY: Harper Business Rev Upd edition.

Hammer, M., & Stanton, S. (1994). *The reengineering revolution: A handbook.* New York, NY: Harper Business.

Kaplan, R. S., & Norton, D. P. (1996). *The balanced scorecard: Translating strategy into action.* Boston: Harvard Business Review Press.

Kasprzak, T. (2005). *Modele referencyjne w zarządzaniu procesami biznesu* [Reference models in the management of business processes]. Warszawa: Difin.

Krupski, R. (2005). *Zarządzanie przedsiębiorstwem w turbulentnym otoczeniu* [Business management in turbulent environment]. Warszawa: PWN.

Perechuda, K., & Cieśliński, W. (2008). Zarządzanie procesami – perspektywa tworzenia wartości [Process Management – The perspective of value creation]. In K. Krzakiewicz (Ed.), *Problemy pracy kierowniczej* [The problems of managerial work]. Poznań: TNOiK.

Witkowski, K., Piepiora, P. A., Cieśliński, W. B., & Piepiora Z. (2016). Quality management versus process approach. In P. Jedlička (Ed.), *Hradec Economic Days 2016.* Double-Blinded Peer-Reviewed Proceedings of the International Scientific Conference Hradec Economic Days 2016, February 2th and 3th, vol. III, Gaudeamus: University of Hradec Králové.

Part III
Management & Marketing

Unexpected Industries with Consumer Power

Renata Beata Dylkiewicz and Paulina Katarzyna Dylkiewicz

Abstract The contemporary business structures are shaped by various economic indicators and highly influenced by dominating industries. It can be clearly indicated that there is an evident difference between industries being more required by the customers, having more power over them, and thereby involving more capital investments and more capital gains. While certain industries satisfy the basic needs of customers and are naturally on the growth due to particular business and economic circumstances, there are other industries that can be viewed as less powerful and less needed. These are the line businesses that are often seen as those that do not serve the most sufficient needs of customer groups. Despite the fact that the products produced in those fields are not the key needed products, there is a lot of consumer power and thereby spending involved. This article aims to analyze what are the industries that are growing and gaining more of the spending from the increasing disposable incomes of consumers in Asia, as compared to European consumers.

Keywords Industries • Unexpected industries • Consumer power

1 Introduction

The majority of economies are shaped by various economic indicators and influenced by dominating industries. These industries can be called the traditional industries that build up any market economy. There are however industries that are often overlooked and not taken into any economical discussions and considerations, still having a lot of power and grasping more and more of the consumer spending. The lookout for the unexpected industries with consumer power in this article will be focused within the markets of China and India. The choice of these two markets can be explained by their fast growth, being largest emerging market economies. These two countries also have very interesting population projections and

R.B. Dylkiewicz • P.K. Dylkiewicz (✉)
Faculty of Economic Sciences, Koszalin University of Technology, Koszalin, Poland
e-mail: dylkiewicz@interia.pl; paulina.dylkiewicz@hotmail.com

M.H. Bilgin et al. (eds.), *Empirical Studies on Economics of Innovation, Public Economics and Management*, Eurasian Studies in Business and Economics 6,
DOI 10.1007/978-3-319-50164-2_10

increasing GDP per head, which also explain the choice of those markets to be looked at. The lead towards discovering the powerful industries can be based upon the market trends, growth projections, consumer engagement and consumer spending, as well as current market trends. It has to be underlined however that this discussion looks only at selected industries, which further overlaps and neglects some of other potential industries with such power. This delimitation results from limited scope of this article, however can be an indication for further research and analyses.

2 Consumer Power and an Industry

This analysis aims to look into industries with consumer power; therefore there is a need for a detailed definition of the term 'industry'. An industry can be simply explained as a group of companies correlated through their business activities. The strength of an industry is influenced by consumer power, it is therefore interesting to look into the relationship between the resource exchange and power. Basically it is the relationship between buyers and suppliers around a process of a resource exchange. Suppliers need to obtain money through sales revenue, while buyers need to obtain products that are not currently supplied by them. These needs are transformed by the buyer into purchase specifications offered by suppliers. The activities of specification generation as well as the evaluation are iterative. The power here plays a significant part. The purchasing power grows out of the interdependence of the suppliers and buyers. The extent of buyers' potential power is a combination of the attributes defined as attractiveness and availability of the resources (Ramsay 1995). And while it is discussed that the consumers have power related to the particular resources, this can be broadened into entire product categories, and thereby industries. That also explains the linkage between the consumer power and the potential of an industry, as the industries that produce products those customers need, have clearly higher potential of succeeding in economical terms. Logically then, industries that supply products of basic needs could be seen as those with stronger potential to thrive in the market, however this analysis aims to show that there are industries that increasingly gain popularity among consumers, while still being underestimated.

2.1 The Markets of China and India

The key countries to be looked at in this discussion are China and India. Both are considered as the BRIC countries (Brazil, Russia, India and China), with fast growth and emerging market economies. China and India in the context of analyzed industries are very interesting markets to be looked at. Furthermore, despite differences, there are also some similarities when analyzing the topic more in-depth—it is additional argument for the choice of China and India as the countries of focus in the discussion of powerful industries.

2.2 *Delimitations*

The delimitations of this article arise from limitations in the scope of this study, and from conscious inclusionary and exclusionary decisions undertook by the researchers throughout the development of the study (Simon and Goes 2013). Focusing on the key topic of this discussion, there are numerous related aspects that have been excluded from the consideration. This relates to other potential industries that could have consumer power in the view as explained previously. Other countries that could play an important role within this topic have also been screened off from the discussion, as the sole focus remains on China and India. These indications have been excluded to restricted timeframe and scope of this article. However it is indeed a potential topic to be further research, especially in terms of the industries that have similar power or other countries where such phenomena takes place.

3 Power in China and India

One of the previous chapters has shown the reason for key interest around China and India. There are, however, other interesting projections that underline the importance of those two countries in current economic outlook. Some of most interesting statistics relate to the population projections and the GDP per head. Table 1 presented shows that China and India, as compared to Japan, United Kingdom and the United States, have most significant growth projections and will easily outnumber other countries. In relation to the population projections, the GDP projections (Table 2) make this analysis even more valued, as the GDP per head in China and India also are estimated to steadily grow, and thereby play an important role in the state of economies in those two countries.

In the context of growing numbers of the population, as well as increasing GDP per head, it can be indicated that there will be visible consequences of such statistics in the economies of China and India. This could be taken further into analysis what is the linkage between those projections and the core industries, as well as the state of the economy on the whole. This article however, aims to look into industries that are often overlooked, but still can play an important role in the economies of China and India. These industries to be discussed include the luxury products industry, tourism industry and healthcare industry.

Table 1 Population projections (in millions)

Country	2005	2010	2015	2020
China	1312	1354	1396	1431
India	1131	1214	1294	1367
Japan	127	127	126	124
United Kingdom	60	62	64	65
United States	303	318	332	346

Source: United Nations Population Database, http://www.un.org/

Table 2 GDP per head in US$

Country	2005	2010	% change 2010 vs. 2005	2015	% change 2015 vs. 2010	2020	% change 2020 vs. 2015
China	1761	4280	143.0	9120	113.3	17,180	88.4
India	765	1370	79.0	2620	91.2	4310	64.5
Japan	35,704	41,140	15.2	49,230	19.7	59,800	21.5
United Kingdom	37,886	35,740	−5.7	45,900	28.4	54,500	18.7
United States	42,736	48,230	12.9	57,070	18.3	76,190	33.5

Source: Deloitte (2015)

3.1 Luxury Industry

Luxury is a commonly used term to describe products, services and lifestyle, also seen as a culture and philosophy. Thereby the actual definition of this industry is rather wide (Wiedmann et al. 2007). There are several segments that compose the luxury goods industry. The typology of luxury industry by Boroian and De Poix (2010) focused mainly on the personal luxury goods. Here, the core of the business is the fashion industry. Luxury goods include so-called ready-to-wear, jewelry, watches, shoes, leather goods, silk products. Brand diversification is wide—many of luxury companies enter extents outside their traditional specialty. In this view luxury products also include cosmetics, perfumes, pens, gifts, eyewear, sportswear, furniture, mobile phones, cigarettes, mobile phones, flowers or even pet accessories (Boroian and De Poix 2010). Bain and Company (2014) has created wider compilation of luxury products that lie within the luxury industry and presented it in a form of a graph (Fig. 1). It shows that personal luxury goods strongly overlap with the travel and hospitality related products, as well as food and drinks among others.

The power of the luxury industry lies also in the statement that it is relatively insulated from economic changes and crises. The market of luxury has been doing well compared to other industry segments. This is explained, as the customer base of luxury is believed to have the best financial security. Those customers also keep on purchasing habits despite global economic instabilities (Walker 2009). In modern economy, the world of luxury and affluence is also a rare example of a case

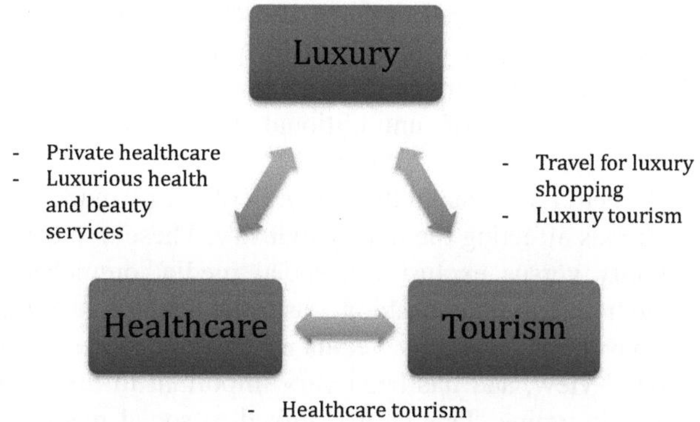

Fig. 1 Luxury, tourism and healthcare interlinked

strongly resistant to disinflation. In this case, prices are rising rather than dropping as they target consumers' aspirations (Yeoman and McMahon-Beattie 2006). As it has been shown, luxury industry is a complex notion, believed to be different than other industries, with high dependency on many factors and contexts. It is also assumed that the meaning of luxury will continue to transform regarding to its meaning and the scope of good it includes, but also to the markets, customers and key users. The industry of luxury for years has been linked to places such as Paris, London, New York, Milan and Tokyo. And while the mature markets are still significant when it comes to share of sales, there is an evident move towards nontraditional luxury markets (Bellaiche et al. 2010).

In 2014 China was the world's fifth largest luxury market. China could be described as a miracle when it comes to growth of luxury market, as luxury market was almost nonexistent 20 years ago (Hoffmann and Coste-Manière 2012). The growth of the market came from the increasing wealth of Chinese population. This includes increasing number of Chinese billionaires, growth of the wealthy class, but also rapid increases in household disposable incomes, which not only relates to the highest income segment, but also the high income and upper middle income class. All of which had high luxury spending (Fung Business Intelligence Centre 2013). While currently the Chinese economy has slowed down, the luxury market depends on consumer market and growth of the upper income class (Deloitte 2014). Economic instabilities and governmental actions might affect the growth of Chinese luxury market, however already achieved strong position in the luxury spending, China as one of key markets in the luxury segment. In comparison, India has been estimated to have the fastest growing luxury market in the Asia Pacific region, the numbers show that this growth is even faster than in China (Deloitte 2014). India has an increasing number of millionaires, growing purchasing power in the upper class, and increasing brand awareness among Indians. Indian consumer spending is expected to grow steadily. This growth can be assigned to increasing incomes and aspirations of Indian consumers. Again the economic, industrial and often cultural reasons for such speedy growth only confirm that the markets in China and India in terms of luxury spending have a strong potential. Many of economic studies and researches look only at the luxury products in the traditional typology of them. There is a lot more to consider when extending the view of luxury products towards other categories of untraditional luxury products as it has been explained previously.

To better understand the potential of luxury market, there is a need to investigate the trends affecting the luxury industry. These trends include phenomena named as ubiquity versus exclusivity, social media, omnichannel, globalization, tourism, democratization, fast fashion, custom and bespoke initiatives, from communication to conversion. Ubiquity versus exclusivity relates to the value of luxury in customers' view, and has been very important in the growing trend of luxury being available online. This is also linked to social media, where customers have new voice and increase their power. E-commerce is further related to omnichannel or channel agnostic distribution strategies that luxury brands are adopting to keep pace with consumer expectations. Luxury brands already acknowledge that the internet has radically changed the traditional shopping trends of customers. Globalization also impacts the expending global middle class in the emerging markets that is supporting growth in the luxury sector and is projected to continue growing. Those emerging middle classes in the new markets also influence the economies of the United States and Europe. One of the examples is the emerging markets' middle class travelling to western countries on the purpose of shopping for luxury products. Here tourism is believed to be strong lever for the growth of luxury spending. The transformational forces of globalization and information are driving the democratization of luxury. Here exclusivity is replaced with mass availability, increasing access to new markets, as well as to new customers. On the other side of that, luxury companies start to cooperate with other brands, try new strategies, combine their forces, adopt channels etc. Such promotion to mass audience by luxury brands is often a risk of a diminution of brand status. Here, a thread to luxury brands is a growing strength of fast fashion. Deloitte (2014) suggest that luxury brands should be able to keep their exclusivity by introducing more custom made products, limited editions and other exclusive initiatives. They should be constantly on the lookout for new strategies and actions, especially regarding the social media and e-commerce, with the focus on communication and conversion (Deloitte 2014). All of these trends are indicated to have an effect on the luxury industry, both in the mature markets and the emerging ones. The scale of those trends, however, is hardly measurable. Here, the customers play the most important role. There are many factors coming out from customers that can have affect on the perceived value of luxury goods and thereby the customer spending on such products. That is why the luxury industry is believed to be an industry with such potential.

3.2 Tourism Industry

Tourism industry in this discussion has been defined interchangeably with the hospitality industry. It needs to be underlined though that hospitality industry is a broader term. One of the most defining aspects of the hospitality industry is that it focuses on customer satisfaction, and this can be extended not only to travel and tourism, but also further to other activities and leisure time. This sector includes hotels, and other forms of accommodation, restaurants, bars, cafeterias, etc.; establishments for the provision of meals and refreshments of industrial and institutional catering, as well as travel agencies, tourists guides, tourism information offices, conference and exhibition centers. Wider definitions also include visitors attractions into this sector, particularly natural, cultural and heritage sites, as well as museums, zoos etc. (ILO 2010). Hospitality industry, traditionally focused on the physical product, is believed to be walking up to a consumer demanding consistent delivery. This also related to the upscale to luxury segments.

Deloitte (2015) on hospitality foresees that emerging markets of China and India, where rise of the middle classes continues, will generate an increase in demand for business and leisure travel. While a lot of the development up until now has focused on the luxury market for the upscale customer, the biggest potential in the markets of China and India lies in the growth of the mid-market and budget products, those aimed at the domestic traveler (Deloitte 2015). Knowing that hospitality is such a broad term, the hospitality industry needs to be looked at through new lenses. The influences of the industry have been graphically expressed below.

There are a lot of factors currently surrounding the hospitality industry, and all of these factors play an important role in shaping the industry. These aspects are very different when it comes to diverse markets, and also dramatically vary when being connected to different fields of hospitality. The core of the hospitality industry, particularly the travel and tourism activity can serve as a base for the discussion about the ongoing trends in the markets of China and India. Table 3 shows that markets in China and India, as compared to the United States, United Kingdom and Japan, have the most dramatic increase in the expenditure on travel and tourism activity. Another conclusion that can be drawn is that this spending has a continuous pattern and a very steady growth.

Other statistical data sheets also show that the tourism industry in China has greatly expanded over the last years. Domestic tourism has been growing annually by 10% on average, while inbound tourism has also increased by 10% in total over similar period. Here, the largest growth was taking place in China's outbound tourism industry (EUSME 2014). Despite such incredible growth, China's travel industry is highly influenced and regulated by the government. There are regulations prohibiting any foreign travel agencies based in China to operate in services related to outbound travel for Chinese nationals. However, it can be also indicated that there are opportunities for foreign actors in the Chinese market, especially

Table 3 Amounts spent on travel and tourism within key markets

Country	Travel and Tourism activity (2000 US$ billions)[a]	2005	2010	% change 2010 vs. 2005	2011	2012	2013	2013	2015	% change 2015 vs. 2010
United States	Personal	626	609	−2.7	624	650	677	701	724	18.9
	Business	211	196	7.8	199	209	220	232	242	24.2
United Kingdom	Personal	141	128	9.3	130	135	139	144	149	16.4
	Business	28	24	−13.7	25	26	27	28	30	21.9
Japan	Personal	279	273	−2.0	274	282	290	298	304	11.4
	Business	72	71	−0.6	72	74	78	81	83	17.1
China	Personal	74	108	44.7	118	133	151	169	185	73.5
	Business	26	36	38.8	39	44	49	55	62	73.2
India	Personal	38	54	40.5	58	63	70	76	82	53.1
	Business	7	9	18.3	9	10	11	13	14	63.1

Source: World Travel and Tourism Council, http://www.wttc.org, Economic Data Tool
Note: [a]US$ billion, expressed at 2000 prices and exchange rates (excludes the effect of price changes)

regarding the untapped niche markets, including high end or luxury markets (EUSME 2014).

India's tourism industry experiencing such strong period of growth can be acclaimed not only to the increasing population of Indian middle class, but also to growth in high spending of foreign tourists, and intense government campaigns to promote India as tourist destination. India's interesting history and rich culture combined with its diversity highly appeal to international tourists. According to Asha (2013), India's travel and tourism industry is one of the most profitable in the country. Tourism in India is being seen as an engine of growth for the Indian economy, and also as a key employment generator. In 2011 it was predicted that the annual growth to be almost 9 percent between 2011 and 2021. Such forecast gives India the fifth rank among countries, which have the fastest growing tourist industry. The World Tourism Organization is estimating that India will take the lead in South Asia with an outstanding number of 8.9 million arrivals by 2020 (Asha 2013).

It has been estimated that penetration of the domestic travel markets in China and India will lead to the greatest long term returns for internationally known brands, while the local brands will still dominate the mid-market and budget sectors. Also, that both China and India are at the risk of having an over-supply of luxury hotels in most popular cities, and this will have consequences, at least in the short run. The trends for the Chinese traveler mainly related to the domestic travel being more attractive and affordable option in the short term. However, the outbound travel sector in China does have a lot of potential. Tourism expenditure forecasts are rising. The Indian traveler has great appetite for travel, with the greatest impact coming from domestic and regional tourism markets. International travel is expected to grow. The World Tourism Organization (UNWTO) forecasts that India will account for around 50 million outbound tourists by year 2020 (Deloitte 2015).

To be ahead in the hospitality industry, especially to meet the needs of the new customers, companies need to prepare their response to new consumer behaviors and general trends. When it comes to the customer, it can be indicated that the global budget hotel brands will have a stronger focus towards emerging market strategies. This strongly applies to China and India. Game changers should move quickly to take advantage of economic growth prospects in those markets, as well as to consider the supply shortages in those countries. Another important action for companies is to engage customers into loyalty programs, which should influence the industry across all segments. Brands should try to understand different generational needs and values, as different markets, especially the culturally diverse ones have different key segments with potential in the hospitality industry. Brand marketing, as lifestyle brands, embracing the power of social media and the capabilities on the whole, as well as developing a multi-channel approach with use of smart phone technology are also trends that travel brands would leverage on in grasping the emerging consumers (Deloitte 2015).

The value of the brand in the eyes of the consumer, the growth in emerging markets, especially with the focus on China and India, the importance of technology that is more consumer facing, as well as the sourcing, development and preservation of human capital are the aspects that have shaped the hospitality industry in the last 5 years. These key characteristics have to be looked at in the new perspective of growing importance of the sustainability agenda, as well as exogenous evens and cycles. These are strongly believed to be the key trends that will influence, and define the success of the marketplace in the upcoming years.

3.3 Healthcare Industry

Healthcare industry is the last industry to be looked at in this discussion. It comprises of providers of diagnostics, remedial, preventive and therapeutic services. It involves doctors, nurses, hospitals and other private, public, and voluntary organizations. It involves hospital activities, medical and dental practice activities and other human health activities. It also relates to the delivery of healthcare services, from primary, secondary and tertiary levels of care. Medical tourism is a rapidly growing practice of international travelling to obtain healthcare. The healthcare industry is claimed to be one of the world's largest and fastest growing industries (KFF 2006).

Healthcare spending in China is on a rapid increase. The estimation of country's annual expenditure indicates growth at average rate of 11.8% a year, each year up to 2018. This should lead to reaching $892 billion by 2018. Such high spending is going to be driven by increasing disposable incomes of consumers and public healthcare reforms by the government (Deloitte 2015). Medical tourism is also expected to become a growth industry in China, driven by favorable government policies, current health care reform efforts, relatively low medical costs, and highly qualified medical personnel.

India's healthcare sector has been growing speedily driven by a number of factors. Total healthcare spending in India is projected to rise at annual rate of 12%, to reach projected $195.7 billion in 2018 (Deloitte 2015). Factors influencing such predictions include increasing the average life expectancy and average income level and rising awareness for health insurance. Healthcare has become one of the India's largest sectors both in terms of revenue and employment. Here, similarly as in the case of previously presented industries, the raising middle class who can afford quality healthcare plays the biggest role. Another important fact is that India's reputation as a global health care destination is also growing. This is thanks to the advances in medical research but also investments in the private sector. It is also believed that private sector accounts for more of all outpatient care in India as compared to the public sector. It has also been underlined that the Indian government is planning to invest heavily in the Indian health care sector (Asha 2013).

The healthcare industry and its potential are covered the least in this discussion. This is due to strong influence of the government both in China and India; thereby the growth of this industry will also be dependent on the actions taken by the governments there. Knowing that consumer power is less significant as opposed to the luxury and hospitality industries, however as it has been explained, the healthcare industry should not be neglected as it has a strong growth potential and a lot of unforeseen power. Furthermore the healthcare industry can be linked to the luxury industry and the hospitality industry, which will be explained in the following chapter. The interconnectedness of powerful industries can only bring more opportunities both for the consumers and the brands.

4 Conclusion

The markets of China and India are emerging markets rapidly on the growth. Current economical circumstances have a lot of power for different industries to thrive. While there are many traditional industries which will take advantage of the economic setting in those two countries, there are other industries that are often overlooked, but do have a lot of potential. These include the luxury, tourism and healthcare industries. All of these industries have been forecasted to grow and play important roles for consumers in China and India. What is also interesting is that these three industries strongly overlap. This has been presented in the Fig. 1.

Luxury, tourism and healthcare industry are highly interconnected. There are trends of travel for luxury shopping, the luxury tourism, healthcare tourism and also high-end private healthcare and luxurious health and beauty services. All of these notions overlap, and it is often difficult to estimate the engagement of consumers in each of those industries. However, it has been shown that all of these industries are strong already and will get stronger with increasing consumer engagement; thereby they should not be overlooked anymore but included as strong ingredients in the economies in China and India.

References

Asha. (2013). Emerging sectors of Indian Economy. *Global Journal of Management and Business Studies, 3*(5), 491–496.

Bain & Company. (2014). Luxury goods worldwide market study fall-winter 2014. *The Rise of the Borderless Consumer* [pdf]. Accessed February 17, 2015, from http://www.bain.com/bainweb/PDFs/Bain_Worldwide_Luxury_Goods_Report_2014.pdf

Bellaiche, J., Mei-Pochter, A., & Hanish, D. (2010). *The new world of luxury: Caught between growing momentum and lasting change*. The Boston Consulting Group, December 2010.

Boroian, M., & De Poix, A. (2010). *India by design: The pursuit of luxury & fashion*. Singapore: John Wiley & Sons (Asia) Pte. Ltd.

Deloitte. (2014). *Global powers of luxury goods. In the hands of the consumer*. London: The Creative Studio at Deloitte.

Deloitte. (2015). *Hospitality. Game changers or spectators?* London: The Creative Studio at Deloitte.

EUSME. (2014). *Tourism market in China*. Beijing: The EU SME Centre.

Fung Business Intelligence Centre. (2013). *Luxury market in China: Huge growth potential ahead* [pdf]. Accessed February 17, 2015, from http://www.funggroup.com/eng/knowledge/research/-china_dis_issue109.pdf

Hoffmann, J., & Coste-Manière, I. (2012). *Luxury strategy in action*. Hampshire: Palgrave MacMillan.

International Labour Organization (ILO). (2010). Developments and challenges in the hospitality and tourism sector. Global Dialogue Forum for the Hotels, Catering, Tourism Sector, 23—24 November 2014.

KFF. (2006). *Snapshots: Comparing projected growth in health care expenditures and the economy* [online]. Accessed February 17, 2015, from http://kff.org/health-costs/issue-brief/snapshots-comparing-projected-growth-in-health-care-expenditures-and-the-economy/

Ramsay, J. (1995). Purchasing power. *European Journal of Purchasing and Supply Management, 1*(3), 125–138.

Simon, M. K., & Goes, J. (2013). *Dissertations and scholarly research: Recipes for success*. Seattle, WA: Dissertation Success LLC.

Walker, A. (2009). Luxury brands lose none of their shine. *Luxury Goods Marketing Feature*, 32–33.

Wiedmann, K., Hennings, N., & Siebiels, A. (2007). Measuring consumers' luxury value perception: A cross-cultural framework. *Academy of Marketing Science Review, 2007*(7), 1–12.

Yeoman, I., & McMahon-Beattie, U. (2006). Luxury markets and premium pricing. *Journal of Revenue and Pricing Management, 4*(4), 319–318.

Brand Meanings in the Context of Luxury Fashion: A Projective Study in China

Sonja Lahtinen and Pekka Tuominen

Abstract The purpose of this study is to describe and analyze brand meanings in the context of luxury fashion among young Chinese women. The theoretical framework for this study is built from two streams of literature. The first part elucidates the concept of luxury and further introduces the three dimensions of luxury brands based on previous research: the functional, the experiential and the symbolic. In the second part semiotics is applied to explain the structure of brand meanings, and the model of interactive transfer among three elements—the culture, the brand and the individual—is introduced to demonstrate how these brand meanings are co-created in the marketplace. The qualitative data was generated through the projective Zaltman Metaphor Elicitation Technique (later ZMET) in China. Based on the various and heterogeneous brand meanings that respondents associated with luxury fashion brands, eight meaning orientations were formed, which organize respondents' beliefs and emotions towards the luxury fashion brands. The interpretive repertoire of Chinese respondents extends the meanings far beyond the ones that brands have created by themselves and those that have been recognized by prior research. This shows considerable sophistication and dedication from the consumers in the interpretation and co-creation of brand meanings. The findings may assist brand managers in developing global brand strategies that are sensitive to local differences and focus on creating personally meaningful brand experiences.

Keywords Brand meanings • Luxury fashion brands • ZMET-method

1 Introduction

The market for luxury goods is continuing to grow globally, despite macroeconomic uncertainty. In the year 2014 worldwide sales of personal luxury goods reached 223 billion euros, a growth rate of 5% (Bain and Company 2014). The

S. Lahtinen • P. Tuominen (✉)
School of Management, University of Tampere, Tampere, Finland
e-mail: sonja.lahtinen@uta.fi; pekka.tuominen@uta.fi

M.H. Bilgin et al. (eds.), *Empirical Studies on Economics of Innovation, Public Economics and Management*, Eurasian Studies in Business and Economics 6,
DOI 10.1007/978-3-319-50164-2_11

growth in the luxury market is mainly driven by changing socio-economic and demographic factors in the global environment. Thus, while Europe has been the clear leader in luxury consumption for centuries, the main drivers of growth are now coming from the rising middle class of the emerging markets, such as Brazil, India, Russia and China (Bain and Company 2014; Christodoulides et al. 2009).

Asia-Pacific represents today the biggest market for luxury. While other emerging countries in this region, such as India, Malaysia and Indonesia are contributing to the rising sales figures, the growth is predominantly due to the Chinese middle class, which is increasingly brand aware and willing to invest in luxury (Li et al. 2012). The importance of Chinese luxury consumers is further fueled by the growing tourism. Bain and Company (2014) estimated that last year Chinese consumers purchased 47% of all the luxury purchases worldwide, spending three times more on luxury purchases abroad than they spent locally. Thus, understanding Chinese consumers and their brand consumption becomes critical also outside the country.

The important role of brands in contemporary consumer cultures can be considered as the embodiment of the immaterial world (Turunen and Laaksonen 2011). We use brands to send messages to others about who we are and what we are like (Berger 2010). On the one hand, brands separate and differentiate us from others; on the other hand, they integrate us into the society and into the subcultures with which we share similar tastes (Chan et al. 2012). Thus, when people buy a luxury item, they are buying not just the product, but a complete package that comprises the product and a set of intangible benefits that appeal to emotional, social and psychological levels of their being (Okonkwo 2007).

There is a level at which these brands are universal—if not, they would never achieve strong equity across different markets—but there is also a level at which the cultural factors lead consumers to interpret these brands differently (Oswald 2012). Luxury brands are now facing the diversity of the world and the various interpretations of their multicultural consumers. For example, Chinese luxury consumers may not follow the trends of the Italians, since Chinese, as well as Italians, perceive luxury brands in terms of their unique cultural backgrounds. Since globalization makes luxury brands readily available in diverse cultural contexts, these brands are now challenged to find a balance with the special characteristics of each of their markets (Okonkwo 2007).

Existing research has explored many aspects of luxury branding, but some areas of this field of study are ripe for further exploration. First of all, much of the luxury brand literature has taken a managerial perspective and neglected the consumer point of view (Turunen 2015). The research topics cover a variety of areas: the nature and definition of luxury goods (e.g., Vigneron and Johnson 2004; Vickers and Renand 2003; Tynan et al. 2010), the competitive structure of luxury markets (e.g., Chadha and Husband 2006), issues relating to the democratization of luxury (e.g., Silverstein and Fiske 2003), market segmentation (e.g., Dubois et al. 2005), conspicuous consumption (e.g., Shukla 2010) and counterfeiting (e.g., Bian and Veloutsou 2007; Turunen and Laaksonen 2011), just to mention few of the main ones. In spite of this broad literature on the luxury market, the field needs more theoretical understanding about the brand meanings attached to luxury fashion brands and how they are constructed in a culture.

A specific stream of research under consumer behavior, Consumer Culture Theory (CCT), has been trying to break away from the managerial focus of the branding literature, by examining consumption from the cultural perspective (e.g., Cayla and Eckhardt 2008; Joy and Li 2012). CCT is defined as a family of theoretical perspectives, studying the dynamic relationships among the consumers' actions, the marketplace and the cultural meanings (Arnould and Thompson 2005). Each research area under CCT provides a unique way to study consumption behavior: (a) consumer identity projects, (b) marketplace cultures, (c) the socio-historical patterning of consumption and (d) mass-mediated marketplace ideologies and consumers' interpretive strategies (Arnould and Thompson 2005). This study aims to open up new possibilities to understand consumer culture in China, and shows relevance on several of the aforementioned research areas.

The purpose of this study is to describe and analyze brand meanings in the context of luxury fashion among young Chinese women. To achieve this purpose, the study has two research questions:

1. What kind of brand meanings do young women attach to luxury fashion in China?
2. How do the cultural and social factors contribute to the construction of these meanings?

The target group consists of young female adults, aged between 20–35 years old. This target group was chosen, since consumers for luxury brands are relatively young in Asia; in most Asian markets the biggest spenders on luxury brands are young women between the ages of 20 and 30 (Chadha and Husband 2006). In addition, the brand meanings are not studied among the whole demographic group of young women, but among the group of young female consumers who actually buy and use luxury fashion brands. This research is concentrating only on luxury *fashion* brands. This is because from the semiotic point of view, some products are more important for people as a means of forming and expressing their identity, such as fashion accessories and clothes (Berger 2010).

2 Theoretical Framework

2.1 *The Concept of Luxury Brands*

The concept of luxury is multifaceted, and the idea of luxury naturally contributes to the concept of luxury brands (Turunen and Laaksonen 2011). Researchers have found that consumers have difficulty identifying what makes a brand luxurious and that they typically define luxury by listing what they consider to be luxury brands, such as Louis Vuitton, Hermes, and Chanel (Roper et al. 2013). This vagueness of luxury holds true not only for the consumers but also for academics. An additional confusion is created when researchers do not differentiate between the concepts of luxury and luxury brands. Some researchers have focused on examining the overall concept of luxury, whereas other researchers have investigated luxury as a property of brands (Brun and Castelli 2013). This paper concentrates only on examining the meanings of luxury brands, that is, the concept of luxury in the marketing context.

Despite the lack of an operational definition of luxury brands, the review of the broad literature reveals that there are certain external features that are commonly attached to luxury brands. Nueno and Quelch (1998) describe luxury brands as those whose ratio of functionality to price is low, while the ratio of intangible and situational utility to price is high. The concept of exclusivity is also well documented in the luxury literature (Wiedmann et al. 2007). In addition to the elements of price and exclusivity, luxury brands feature excellent quality, design, and craftsmanship (Brun and Castelli 2013).

Although these aforementioned perspectives are pervasive in the contemporary literature, luxury brands cannot be characterized only by their external attributes but also by their emotional appeal and symbolic features. Thus, instead of narrowly associating luxury with certain brand features, there has been a call for an integrative perspective on luxury brands (Berthon et al. 2009; Tynan et al. 2010; Shukla and Purani 2012; Roper et al. 2013).

Few researchers have already answered this call. Vigneron and Johnson (2004) classify two major dimensions of luxury value perception: personal perceptions (hedonic value and extended self) and non-personal perceptions (conspicuousness, uniqueness and quality). Wiedmann et al. (2007) extend this framework by using four dimensions: social, functional, individual, and financial value. Vickers and Renand (2003) differentiate between luxury and non-luxury brands in three dimensions: functionalism, experientialism and symbolic interactionism. Berthon et al. (2009) also conceptualize luxury goods with similar value-based dimensions: the objective (material), the subjective (individual) and the collective (social).

Based on these indicators argued in the contemporary literature, three dimensions of luxury brands are suggested: symbolic, experiential and functional. First, luxury brands have a strong symbolic dimension that includes both the self and others. Second, the experiential dimension is relating luxury to pleasure, emotions and sensory stimulation. Thirdly, luxury brands are associated with greater quality and functionality and also with higher price. It is suggested that for a brand to be considered as a luxury brand, each of these dimensions is necessary, but not sufficient on their own.

2.2 *The Semiotic Structure and Interactive Transfer of Brand Meanings*

Brand meanings permeate much of consumers' lives in various ways (Mick and Oswald 2006). Brand meanings are one of the most significant signs we—as

Fig. 1 The binary structure of signs in semiotics (adapted from Oswald 2012, p. 52)

Signified	Status, style, wealth
Signifier	Louis Vuitton logo

consumers—use in our everyday lives to construct our identities, to communicate our self-concepts and to interpret messages sent by other consumers and companies alike. The basic unit of meaning is a sign, which is regarded as something that stands for something else, such as a spoken or written word, or a material object unified in the mind with a particular cultural concept (Berger 2010).

From a semiotic perspective, brands are cultural signifiers (Berger 2010). The signifier/signified relationship is structured by codes associating a material signifier (word, image, etc.) with a signified (cultural concept). The relation between these two is arbitrary and based on convention (Oswald 2012). For example, the meaning of a Louis Vuitton bag is not intrinsic to the object itself, but is codified by habit and convention. The logo is then a sign for the broader world of cultural codes, rituals and consumer experiences, as illustrated in Fig. 1 (Oswald 2012). Since the signifier/signified association is ruled by social convention and cultural habit, this relationship is context-related and can change over time (Berger 2010).

McCracken's model (1986) of meaning transfer is probably the most widely used approach in the marketing literature to explain how the meanings are created in the marketplace (Batey 2008). In his analysis of meaning movement, McCracken (1986) suggests that cultural meaning is drawn from a culturally constituted world and transferred to consumer goods through advertising and fashion system. Then the meaning is transferred from the object to an individual consumer through a number of personal rituals, such as possession, exchange, grooming and divestment rituals. Although McCracken's model has been widely used, it has been criticized for assuming that meanings are primarily handed down to consumers by cultural intermediaries (e.g., Thompson and Haytko 1997; Ligas and Cotte 1999; Batey 2008; Bengtsson 2002).

Rather than characterizing the meaning transfer as a top-down process, Thompson and Haytko (1997) suggest the dynamic poststructuralist approach, in which meanings are constructed across diffuse social contexts. The interactive perspective proposes that consumers are using creative ways to combine, adapt, or even create brand meanings to fit their own life goals (Ligas and Cotte 1999). This interactive perspective acknowledges that brand meanings are not perceived similarly by all consumers, but are interpreted personally, linking the brand, the socio-cultural environment and the individual together (Holt 1997; Thompson and Haytko 1997; Ligas and Cotte 1999; Bengtsson 2002). Meaning is thus always in flux among three different elements: the culture, the individual and the object (Turunen and Laaksonen 2011). In Fig. 2, the two-directional arrows depict the reciprocal movement of the meanings between these elements and represent the dynamic process of meaning development.

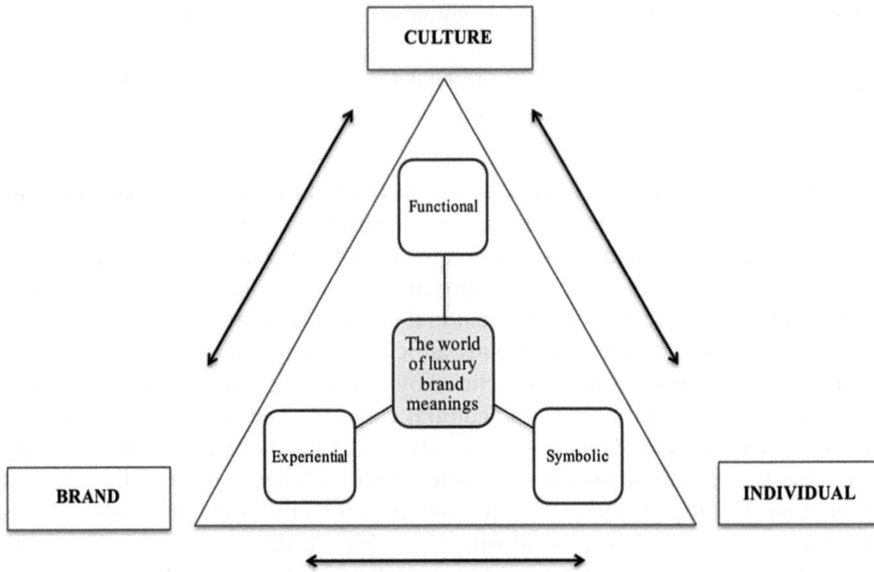

Fig. 2 The meanings for luxury brands

3 Conducting the Study

Philosophically, this study is based on the social constructionist paradigm. Since brand meanings are subjective, context-related and formed through social interaction, constructionism serves as an appropriate philosophical basis for the study. The study is qualitative in nature and adopts a novel projective technique, the Zaltman Metaphor Elicitation Technique (ZMET). It is shown by prior studies that most marketing research tools are verbo-centric, relying on literal language to collect, analyze and report data, although people are better able to convey their thoughts in nonverbal terms (Catchings-Castello 2000). Based on the two fundamental assumptions that thoughts are image-based and mostly subconscious, Zaltman (1997) suggests that research that is strictly based on written or verbal interactions might be missing some critical details. The so-called "depth deficit" (Mulvey and Kavalam 2010), typical for contemporary consumer studies, can be overcome with the use of the ZMET.

Data was generated using a convenience sample of six respondents in China. The participants differed in their backgrounds, and their ages ranged between 20 and 35. Respondents were asked to collect images that represent their thoughts and feelings about luxury fashion brands and to bring the pictures to the interviews. The in-depth interviews followed the eight steps in the ZMET method: storytelling, missed images, sorting, construct elicitation, the most representative image, opposite image, sensory images and the mental map (Zaltman 1997). In all of the steps, participants described the content of each picture in their own words, and the interviewer tried to understand the associated ideas and relevant connections among different constructs. The analysis of the generated data started already during this process, and tentative conclusions were drawn from the notes and drawings produced during the interviews.

The more formal data analysis began with the coding of the transcribed interviews. Transcripts were coded with individual colors representing each idea or construct. After similar codes started to emerge, they were grouped into "code families" representing specific categories of meaning. After no new constructs emerged, an individual mental map was created to illustrate the meanings identified with each participant and finally these maps were combined as an aggregated map that represents the collective mental model across participants.

With six respondents in this study, the targeted completeness of the integrated consensus map was met, since according to Zaltman (1997), data from four or five participants, at most, is required to generate all of the constructs in a consensus map. He argues this by stating that the mind is not the possession of the individual, but it grows from interactions within the socio-cultural world. According to Christensen and Olson (2002), in order to keep the aggregated map intelligible but still meaningful, the researcher has to find a balance between detail and interpretability. In practice, many different versions of the consensus map were created, with different cutoff levels. The final consensus map includes eight central constructs and 36 minor constructs. This is roughly in line with the rule Zaltman (1997) has created that a completed consensus map should include between 25 and 30 constructs and represent 85% of the constructs mentioned by any one participant.

4 Findings and Discussion

4.1 The Brand Meanings for Luxury Fashion Among Young Chinese Women

The aggregated consensus map reveals eight meaning orientations for luxury fashion brands shared among Chinese respondents. These eight meaning orientations are (1) pursuing hedonistic pleasure; (2) driving force in life; (3) appreciating beauty, art and quality; (4) daydreaming and fantasy world; (5) connecting and expressing the self; (6) seeking connection to others; (7) matter of investment; and (8) valuing sustainability. As seen in Fig. 3, each of the meaning orientations includes several more detailed sub-meanings. Some of them are closely related to each other and the connections are illustrated with the dotted lines in the map. Next, these eight meaning orientations are examined in more detail.

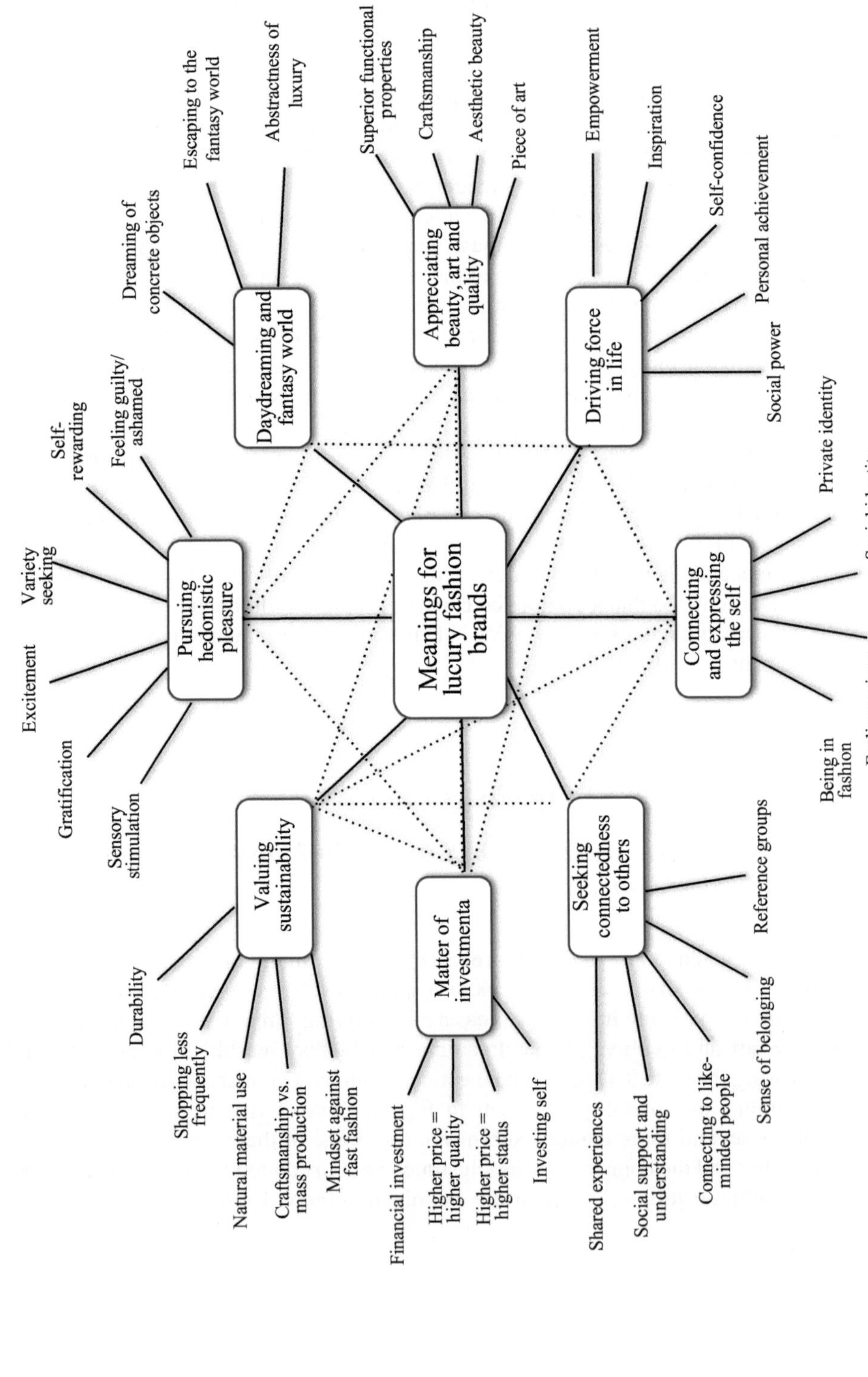
Meanings for lucury fashion brands
Pursuing hedonistic pleasure
Variety seeking
Excitement
Gratification
Sensory stimulation
Self-rewarding
Feeling guilty/ ashamed
Daydreaming and fantasy world
Dreaming of concrete objects
Escaping to the fantasy world
Abstractness of luxury
Appreciating beauty, art and quality
Superior functional properties
Craftsmanship
Aesthetic beauty
Piece of art
Driving force in life
Empowerment
Inspiration
Self-confidence
Personal achievement
Social power
Connecting and expressing the self
Private identity
Social identity
Feeling unique
Being in fashion
Seeking connectedness to others
Reference groups
Sense of belonging
Connecting to like-minded people
Social support and understanding
Shared experiences
Matter of investmenta
Investing self
Higher price = higher status
Higher price = higher quality
Financial investment
Valuing sustainability
Durability
Shopping less frequently
Natural material use
Craftsmanship vs. mass production
Mindset against fast fashion

4.1.1 Pursuing Hedonistic Pleasure

Certain products and brands carry an emotional meaning and provide intrinsic enjoyment in addition to their more tangible benefits (Wiedmann et al. 2007). In the literature, these subjective and intangible aspects of consumption are referred to as hedonistic consumption (Hirschman and Holbrook 1982). Here, hedonism describes the perceived subjective utility and intrinsically attractive properties (Wiedmann et al. 2007) acquired from the purchase and consumption of luxury fashion brands. Respondents referred to this kind of hedonistic pleasure when they talked about luxury fashion brands; they brought out concepts such as sensory pleasure, gratification, aesthetics and excitement. For example, luxury fashion brands were used as tools of variety seeking and self-rewarding.

4.1.2 Daydreaming and Fantasy World

According to Astous and Deschenes (2005), consumers often realize part of the consumption in their minds; they imagine, dream or fantasize that they possess some desired object, or that they live certain experiences. In addition of dreaming about certain products, the dreaming itself was seen as important, and respondents referred to constructs such as "escaping to the fantasy world." Because luxury fashion was seen as far from reality, it offered a perfect destination for dreaming. Hansen and Wänke (2011) suggest that the association between luxury and abstractness is based on the psychological distance of luxury. Psychological distance manifests itself in many ways; luxury is exclusive and socially distant, and purchases are seldom and often only hypothetical (Hansen and Wänke 2011).

4.1.3 Appreciating Beauty, Art and Quality

Various studies in the field show that superior quality is one of the most mentioned attributes when talking about luxury fashion brands (Vigneron and Johnson 2004; Dubois et al. 2005; Wiedmann et al. 2007; Turunen 2015). For respondents, the utilitarian considerations, such as materials, fitting, details, finishing, durability and resistance, contributed to the image of excellent product quality. Although respondents were more focused on functional, product-related quality, they were still talking about the aesthetics and the image of the craftsmanship. There was underlying a more profound significance composed of deeper meanings about feeling oneself worthy of good quality.

> In luxury fashion, the quality is the most important thing, you don't spend money to get a thing that is not durable, that's the basic need. But also the design and the materials are very important. Like leather, or cashmere, materials must be natural (Source: Respondent B).

4.1.4 Driving Force in Life

Among the many tasks brands can perform, they can help consumers achieve goals that are motivated by the self. Brands may act as symbols of personal accomplishment, provide self-esteem and help people through life transitions (Escalas and Bettman 2003). Many of the respondents viewed luxury fashion brands as being a driver of moving forward, creating an urge to push them further in life and providing a sense of empowerment. Most of the respondents also raised the topic of social status and prestige and talked about achieving a certain kind of level in a society by using luxury fashion brands. Also the meanings of self-esteem and self-enhancement were discussed. Thus, luxury fashion brands were acting as motivational drivers. The origin for motivation came either from social or personal goals.

> I think luxury goods give you a higher social standing among other people. This picture shows this. People want to be beautiful; they want to be a star. Everyone wants to be a star! (Source: Respondent F).

4.1.5 Connecting and Expressing the Self

Brands can be used to satisfy psychological needs, such as reinforcing and expressing the self (Escalas and Bettmann 2003). The most important function in moderating the relationship between one's self-image and one's image of the brand is self-congruity (Wiedmann et al. 2007). Respondents confirmed the impact of self-congruity on their luxury brand use, but they focused mainly on the outer part of the self. They talked less about the connections between the brands and their personal identity, but emphasized the congruency between the brands and their social self. It was also important for respondents to feel themselves unique. In contemporary consumer cultures, consumers usually acquire and display material possessions, such as brands, for the purpose of feeling differentiated from others (Chan et al. 2012).

> Chinese people get more and more money and they know more about luxury brands so there are more people who want to raise their social level among their peers by buying luxury brands and they can choose the one that contributes to their social identity (Source: Respondent A).

4.1.6 Seeking Connectedness to Others

In addition to being used to assert one's individuality and allowing one to differentiate him/herself from other people luxury fashion brands can also serve a social purpose by reflecting social ties and reinforcing the feeling of belonging (Escalas and Bettman 2003). Through the use of luxury fashion brands respondents felt that they were connected to other like-minded people, with whom they shared similar tastes and lifestyles. For the respondents, the feeling of being connected to others and the sense of belonging emerged as crucial factors. Respondents also stressed the role of reference groups in their buying behavior. These results are in line with Shukla and Purani (2012), who recognized that the collective mindset of Asian consumers reinforced their need to feel united.

> Luxury brands should keep in mind that consumers in this country are not yet so mature to have an independent insight, where you can make the choice based on the brand, instead, we need to have a king or queen that just controls the feeling of other consumers, like just follow me (Source: Respondent B).

4.1.7 Matter of Investment

One of the most common meanings attached to luxury fashion brands is the expensive price and consumers' willingness to pay a premium (Turunen 2015). Price played a positive role in determining respondents' perceptions about quality, but higher price was also considered to signal wealth, status and prestige. Thus, higher price suggesting higher quality or higher status may make some products or brands even more desirable and consumers more willing to pay the premium (Wiedmann et al. 2007). According to various studies, seeking prestige by acquiring higher-priced products is acceptable in many collectivist cultures, like in China (Shukla 2010; Shukla and Purani 2012). However, respondents considered luxury fashion brands as expensive and acknowledged the financial costs of these products.

4.1.8 Valuing Sustainability

While luxury goods have traditionally been associated with a lifestyle of materialism, hedonism, conspicuousness and extravagant consumption—quite the opposite of the concept of sustainability—a paradigm shift is currently taking place in the field of luxury consumption (Hennigs et al. 2013). Consumers are increasingly concerned about ecological and ethical issues, and they prefer products that reflect their own values. As Hennigs et al. (2013) suggest, ecological and sustainable values are not necessarily antithetical to luxury. The essence of luxury fashion brands is based on high quality, natural materials, craftsmanship, superior durability and timelessness. Respondents recognized the ecological aspects, such as the use of natural materials and superior durability of the products. Ethical meanings, such as craftsmanship versus mass-production, and the mindset against fast fashion, were also surfaced.

> The timing for luxury brands is really good now in China. We have just suffered from the haze for the past couple of months and everyone is talking about the change of environment. I think every family in Shanghai is concerned about this. Sustainability and responsibility are becoming more important for Chinese consumers (Source: Respondent B).

When the meaning orientations were examined in more detail, it was recognized that five of the meanings were similar to the findings of previous studies. The meanings of pursuing hedonistic pleasure; appreciating beauty, art and quality;

connecting and expressing the self; seeking connectedness to others; and matter of investment are widely identified in the contemporary literature (Vickers and Renand 2003; Vigneron and Johnson 2004; Wiedmann et al. 2007; Berthon et al. 2009; Christodoulides et al. 2009; Tynan et al. 2010; Shukla and Purani 2012). However, three of the meaning orientations that emerged from the data were new in the field: daydreaming and fantasy world, driving force in life and valuing sustainability. The reason these meanings have not been identified before might be connected to the method being used. Projective methods are able to reveal vivid and detailed meanings, some of which are deep and perhaps subconscious (Christensen and Olson 2002).

4.2 The Role of Socio-cultural Factors in the Construction of Brand Meanings for Luxury Fashion

Besides the dimensions of the luxury brand meanings, the theoretical framework included the reciprocal interaction among the three different elements that decisively affect the outcome of the brand meanings: the culture, the brand and the individual. The second research objective was fulfilled by elucidating the characteristics of Chinese consumers that might derive from the specific socio-cultural environment of the respondents.

First of all, the relatively short history of consumerism in China might explain the materialist values behind the meanings Chinese respondents gave to luxury fashion brands. According to Inglehart (1990), an individual places the greatest subjective value on those things that are in relatively short supply and that are affected by the conditions that prevailed during one's pre-adult years. Although Chinese showed clearer signs of materialist values, it is assumed that the rise of prosperity in the country will encourage the spread of postmaterialist values (like meanings of sustainability and self-actualization), especially among the younger generations.

Second, the evolutionary stage of the luxury market may affect to consumers' perceptions about luxury brands. In China, the luxury industry is still in its introductory phase. Consumers in China may belong to the first or second generation of their families to purchase brands rather than buying commodities with trade vouchers, as was common during the Cultural Revolution (Oswald 2012). The recent history of wars, colonization and communism has disrupted the Chinese history of luxury, which might explain why Chinese respondents found it difficult to relate themselves personally with luxury brands and reflected their relationship with luxury fashion brands more from the social point of view. The ways consumers negotiate meanings often stem from the economic and political histories and worldviews of the specific cultures.

Third, the confrontation of individualistic versus collectivist cultures might explain why Chinese respondents sought status and showed sensitivity to prestige

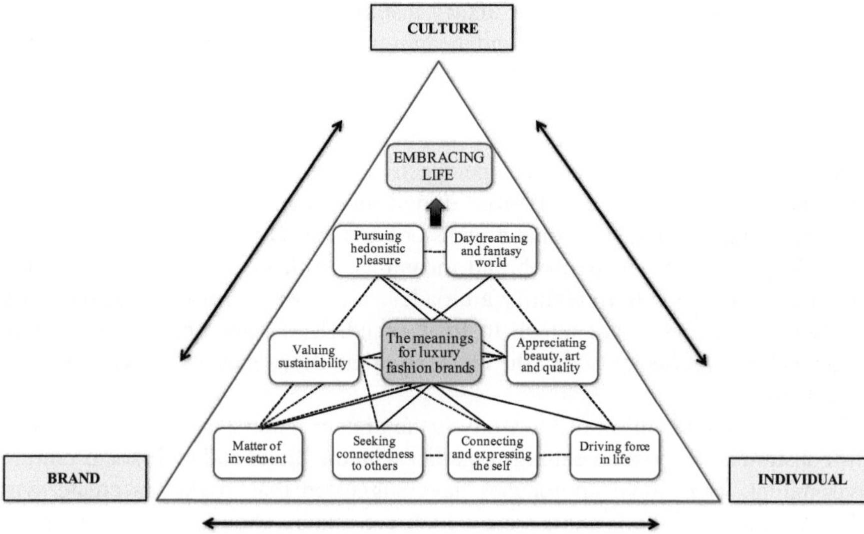

Fig. 4 The meanings for luxury fashion brands

and social recognition. Markus and Kitayama (1991) and Escalas and Bettman (2003) suggest that Easterners are characterized by the focus on the social, public self and social recognition while the individualist Westerners tend to focus more on the personal, private self. It has been claimed that the different conceptions of the self, and of the relationship between the self and others, are the most significant sources of differences among cultures (Solomon et al. 2013). However, there were also signs of individualist meanings, and it is widely assumed that Chinese culture is moving towards the Western one and the differences between individualist and collectivist behavior might diminish.

Figure 4 illustrates the re-evaluation of the theoretical framework created by the authors, where the brand meanings associated with luxury fashion brands are represented in the form of the consensus map rather than divided into the different dimensions of functionality, experientialism and symbolism. The meanings in the consensus map are influenced by the interaction among the culture, the brand and the individual, of which culture was studied with greater emphasis in this study.

5 Conclusions and Implications

All the three dimensions of luxury brands were identified, but it was further revealed how these dimensions occur in practice, through the eight meaning orientations. It was also recognized that the prevalence of materialist/post-materialist priorities, the evolutionary stage of the luxury market and the collectivist/individualist culture might explain how socio-cultural factors affect the brand meanings consumers construct for luxury fashion brands. Overall, it is suggested that the heterogeneous nature of brand meanings highlights the role of consumers in co-creating the meanings together with the brand and their socio-cultural environment.

The first implication of this study is that the heterogeneous nature of brand meanings is understood in a wider perspective than the earlier categorization of functional, symbolic and experiential dimensions suggests. The consensus map integrates cognitive and emotional dimensions and leads to a holistic understanding of the deeper drivers of luxury brand meanings. With the aggregated consensus map, marketers are able to identify a broader variety of potential brand meanings that their customers might attach to their brand. It is recommended that brand managers focus on one or two of the meaning orientations instead of trying to cover all of them.

The second implication of the study is the greater understanding of the process how consumers negotiate meanings together with the brand and their socio-cultural environment. Traditional approaches have suggested that marketers create symbolic meanings for the brands; from which consumers choose the ones that best correspond to their own self-concepts. This study highlights the role of consumers in the process of shaping meanings for brands. This is an especially important notion in the context of luxury fashion brands, where the dominant view has long suggested that consumers should not co-create luxury brands, since luxury brands need to stay ahead of their customers (e.g., Kapferer and Bastien 2012). This study extends the managerialist view by incorporating the consumer and identifying the co-construction of brand meanings.

The third implication of this study is the better understanding of the way in which social, economic and cultural forces lead consumers to construct different brand meanings in the global markets. As the previous research shows, considerable cross-national variations exist in the meanings consumers attach to luxury fashion brands. For example, the collectivist/individualist mindset of the consumers may strongly affect the other-/self-directed symbolic meanings. Besides the cultural factors, historical and political forces also have an impact on the market actors in contemporary consumer cultures, for example affecting the materialist/postmaterialist values of the consumers. It is suggested that marketers should develop global brand strategies that are sensitive to local differences and that take into consideration the social, historical, economic and cultural factors.

6 Limitations and Avenues for the Future Research

The limitations of this study create interesting possibilities for future research. This study concentrated only on China, when further comparative studies involving other countries and cultures would provide interesting insight into the subject. Moreover, the study focused on affluent, urban citizens, but examining the interpretations of luxury by Chinese consumers living in the big cities and in the countryside would increase the understanding of the socio-cultural nature of the brand meanings.

This study focused on socio-cultural constructs, not on the individual-level factors that obviously influence the creation of different brand meanings. By focusing on the psychological level in the meaning-making process, future research would gain fruitful insight about the personal drivers behind brand meanings. Furthermore, the third element of the meaning-making process, the brand, could be in focus of future studies, for example by exploring the brand meanings that the brand managers have created for the specific brand and how these meanings differ from those created by their customers.

However, apart from the methodological and contextual possibilities, the most interesting subject for future research is the concept of luxury for today's consumers. In societies where people have already adopted, or are starting to adopt the postmaterialist values, the interpretations of what is felt as luxurious are very different from those that have been dominating the economic, and marketing, view of the luxury concept. Signs of more experiential and more personal meanings can be recognized in this study, and these meanings are something that future consumers are increasingly interested in—and future researchers should be, too.

References

Arnould, E. J., & Thompson, C. J. (2005). Consumer culture theory (CCT): Twenty years of research. *Journal of Consumer Research, 31*(4), 868–882.

Astous, A., & Deschenes, J. (2005). Consuming in one's mind: An exploration. *Psychology and Marketing, 22*(1), 1–30.

Bain and Company. (2014). *Annual global luxury study 2014* [online]. Accessed June 27, 2015, from http://www.bain.com/about/press/press-releases/bain-and-companys-2014-annual-global-luxury-study.aspx

Batey, M. (2008). *Brand meaning*. New York: Routledge.

Bengtsson, A. (2002). *Consumers and mixed brands. On the polysemy of brand meaning*. Lund: Lund Business Press.

Berger, A. (2010). *The objects of affection: Semiotics and consumer culture*. New York: Palgrave MacMillan.

Berthon, P., Pitt, L., Parent, M., & Berthon, J.-P. (2009). Aesthetics and ephemerality: Observing and preserving the luxury brand. *California Management Review, 52*(1), 45–66.

Bian, X., & Veloutsou, C. (2007). Consumers' attitudes regarding non-deceptive counterfeit brands in the UK and China. *Journal of Brand Management, 14*(3), 211–222.

Brun, A., & Castelli, C. (2013). The nature of luxury: A consumer perspective. *International Journal of Retail and Distribution Management, 41*(11/12), 823–847.

Catchings-Castello, G. (2000). The ZMET alternative. *Marketing Research, 12*(2), 6–12.

Cayla, J., & Eckhardt, G. (2008). Asian brands and the shaping of a transnational imagined community. *Journal of Consumer Research, 35*(2), 216–230.

Chadha, R., & Husband, P. (2006). *The cult of the luxury brand: Inside Asia's love affair with luxury*. London: Nicholas Brealey International.

Chan, C., Berger, J., & van Boven, L. (2012). Identifiable but not identical: Combining social identity and uniqueness motives in choice. *Journal of Consumer Research, 39*(3), 561–573.

Christensen, G., & Olson, J. (2002). Mapping consumers' mental models with ZMET. *Psychology and Marketing, 19*(6), 477–502.

Christodoulides, G., Michaelidou, N., & Li, C. (2009). Measuring perceived brand luxury: An evaluation of the BLI scale. *Journal of Brand Management, 16*(5/6), 395–405.

Dubois, B., Czellar, S., & Laurent, G. (2005). Consumer segments based on attitudes toward luxury: Empirical evidence from twenty countries. *Marketing Letters, 16*(2), 115–128.

Escalas, J., & Bettman, J. (2003). You are what they eat: The influence of reference groups on consumers' connections to brands. *Journal of Consumer Psychology, 13*(3), 339–348.

Hansen, J., & Wänke, M. (2011). The abstractness of luxury. *Journal of Economic Psychology, 32* (5), 789–796.

Hennigs, N., Wiedmann, K.-P., Klarmann, C., & Behrens, S. (2013). Sustainability as part of the luxury essence: Delivering value through social and environmental excellence. *Journal of Corporate Citizenship, 52*(11), 25–35.

Hirschman, E., & Holbrook, M. (1982). Hedonic consumption: Emerging concepts, methods and propositions. *Journal of Marketing, 46*(3), 92–101.

Holt, D. (1997). Poststructuralist lifestyle analysis: Conceptualizing the social patterning of consumption in postmodernity. *Journal of Consumer Research, 23*(4), 326–350.

Inglehart, R. (1990). *Culture shift in advanced industrial Society*. Princeton, NJ: Princeton University Press.

Joy, A., & Li, E. (2012). Studying consumption behavior through multiple lenses: An overview of consumer culture theory. *Journal of Business Anthropology, 1*(1), 1–33.

Kapferer, J., & Bastien, V. (2012). *The luxury strategy: Break the rules of marketing to build luxury brands*. London: Kogan Page.

Li, G., Li, G., & Kambele, Z. (2012). Luxury fashion brand consumers in China: Perceived value, fashion lifestyle and willingness to pay. *Journal of Business Research, 65*(10), 1516–1522.

Ligas, M., & Cotte, J. (1999). The process of negotiating brand meaning: A symbolic interactionist perspective. *Advances in Consumer Research, 26*(1), 609–614.

Markus, H., & Kitayama, S. (1991). Culture and the self: Implications for cognition, emotion and motivation. *Psychological Review, 98*(2), 224–253.

McCracken, G. (1986). Culture and consumption: A theoretical account of the structure and movement of the cultural meaning of consumer goods. *Journal of Consumer Research, 13* (1), 71–84.

Mick, D., & Oswald, L. (2006). The semiotic paradigm on meaning in the marketplace. In R. Belk (Ed.), *Handbook of qualitative research methods in marketing* (pp. 31–45). Cheltenham: Edward Elgar.

Mulvey, M., & Kavalam, B. (2010). Mining deeper meaning in consumer decision maps. *Qualitative Market Research: An International Journal, 13*(4), 372–388.

Nueno, J., & Quelch, J. (1998). The mass marketing of luxury. *Business Horizons, 41*(6), 61–68.

Okonkwo, U. (2007). *Luxury fashion branding: Trends, tactics, techniques*. New York, NY: Palgrave MacMillan.

Oswald, L. (2012). *Marketing semiotics: Signs, strategies, and brand value*. Oxford: Oxford University Press.

Roper, S., Caruana, R., Medway, D., & Murphy, P. (2013). Constructing luxury brands: Exploring the role of consumer discourse. *European Journal of Marketing, 47*(3/4), 375–400.

Shukla, P. (2010). Status consumption in cross-national context. Socio-psychological, brand and situational antecedents. *International Marketing Review, 27*(1), 108–129.

Shukla, P., & Purani, K. (2012). Comparing the importance of luxury value perceptions in cross-national contexts. *Journal of Business Research, 65*(10), 1417–1424.

Silverstein, M., & Fiske, N. (2003). Luxury for the masses. *Harvard Business Review, 81*(4), 48–57.

Solomon, M., Bamossy, G., Askegaard, S., & Hogg, M. (2013). *Consumer behavior: A European perspective*. Harlow: Pearson Education Limited.

Thompson, C., & Haytko, D. (1997). Speaking of fashion: Consumers' uses of fashion discourses and the appropriation of countervailing cultural meanings. *Journal of Consumer Research, 24* (1), 15–42.

Turunen, L. (2015). *Consumers' experiences of luxury: Interpreting the luxuriousness of a brand.* Vaasa: Publications of University of Vaasa.

Turunen, L., & Laaksonen, P. (2011). Diffusing the boundaries between luxury and counterfeits. *Journal of Product and Brand Management, 20*(6), 468–474.

Tynan, C., McKechnie, S., & Chhuon, C. (2010). Co-creating value for luxury brands. *Journal of Business Research, 63*(11), 1156–1163.

Vickers, J., & Renand, F. (2003). The marketing of luxury goods: An exploratory study – Three conceptual dimensions. *The Marketing Review, 3*(4), 459–478.

Vigneron, F., & Johnson, L. (2004). Measuring perceptions of brand luxury. *Journal of Brand Management, 11*(6), 484–506.

Wiedmann, K., Hennigs, N., & Siebels, A. (2007). Measuring consumers' luxury value perception: A cross-cultural framework. *Academy of Marketing Science Review, 7*(3), 1–21.

Zaltman, G. (1997). Rethinking market research: Putting people back in. *Journal of Marketing Research, 34*(4), 424–437.

Environmental Decision Support Systems: A Literature Review

Faten F. Kharbat and Jehan A. Abo Sultan

Abstract A large amount of decision support systems for different management areas exist. Literature on decision systems supporting environmental management in particular is relatively limited. Given this evolving research field, the goal and purpose of this paper is to explore the scientific research in international scientific journals that focus on decision support systems for environmental management. In this paper, a brief review was conducted to recent publications in some of the respected journals and conferences. Published scientific research from 2010 to 2015 is reviewed based on the following: (i) what are the main components used in the decision support system, and (ii) how environmental support systems are integrating with other techniques and methods to optimize the needed solutions. The DSS tools and components play a great role in solving the complexity problem of the eco-system and in the environment. According to our review, researchers found that environmental problems have common characteristics. EDSS, also, has been used in different fields. A further critical analysis should be completed and gaps in the current literature are to be identified in the future to identify improvements for such systems and possible future directions.

Keywords Decision support systems • Environmental systems • EDSS • Information systems

F.F. Kharbat (✉)
MIS and Management Department, Al Ain University of Science and Technology, Abu Dhabi, UAE
e-mail: faten.kharbat@aau.ac.ae

J.A. Abo Sultan
MIS Department, Al Ain University of Science and Technology, Abu Dhabi, UAE
e-mail: 201410054@aau.ac.ae

M.H. Bilgin et al. (eds.), *Empirical Studies on Economics of Innovation, Public Economics and Management*, Eurasian Studies in Business and Economics 6,
DOI 10.1007/978-3-319-50164-2_12

1 Introduction

The environment consists of different dimensions such as economic, ecological, social, technical, cultural, physical, chemical and biological. The increasing pace of industrialization, development and population growth across the world negatively affects environmental quality in all aspects: plant, animal and human life, soil, water, and the climate (Al Janabi and Al Kaisi 2012; Poch et al. 2004). It is also believed that the economic performance is affected by environmental investment in companies (Nakamura 2011).

Decision makers are trying to challenge and confront all the environmental issues, but they are facing difficulties due to complexity while they are making interaction among their processes. The problem is either unknown or difficult to represent which will cause a degree of uncertainty (Sànchez-Marrè et al. 2008; Fedra 2000). Some of the sources of this uncertainty can be controlled by collecting additional data or having further investigation (Sànchez-Marrè et al. 2008). Another way to control uncertainty is to engage human mind into the system to avoid "chaotic behavior or self-organizing processes" (Sànchez-Marrè et al. 2008, p. 120). Many ecological theories have been applied in systems where humans were absent or considered as an external factor or harmful disruption (Poch et al. 2004).

It is important to realize that environmental problems are characterized by dynamics and interactions among other ecology factors. This will not allow an easy deviation between social and bio-geophysical phenomena (Poch et al. 2004; Sànchez-Marrè et al. 2008). According to the Sànchez-Marrè et al. (2008 p. 121), this interaction will develop "environmental issues belong to a set of critical domains where wrong management decisions may have disastrous social, economic and ecological consequences". Also, lack of information will lead to bad decisions and miss attraction among the environmental management process (Anzaldi et al. 2014). Therefore, it is impossible to advocate a single perspective of environmental factors using simple models; it is very difficult and ineffective to encompass all factors in a system when dealing with high level of complexity. The alternative is developing an environmental system to consider complex issues.

Any environmental system can be characterized by sophisticated, multiscale, spatial and time-based-dependent processes (Sànchez-Marrè et al. 2008). However, the environmental systems do not have the same level of complexity; they vary based on their degree of uncertainty and the risk associated with their decisions (Sànchez-Marrè et al. 2008; Poch et al. 2004).

According to Poch et al. (2004), the environment has three levels of complexity. Through the last few years, mathematical/statistical models, numerical algorithms and computer simulations have been used as suitable means to solve environmental management problems and provide useful information to decision-makers (Sànchez-Marrè et al. 2008). The scientists provide a wide set of scientific techniques to be applied to environmental management problems to gain good results and achieve better performance (Poch et al. 2004). But, most of these efforts were focused on problems of level (one) and level (two) of complexity. On the other hand, the complex environmental problems of level (three) have not been effectively addressed by the scientific community (Sànchez-Marrè et al. 2008). These environmental issues cannot be undertaken with traditional tools using mathematical modeling. To confront this complexity, new models are needed, which indicate that new intellectual challenges are rising up.

Through the previous decades new technology, new artificial intelligence tools were addressed to deal with more complex environmental problems which have directed to the development of what is called the Environmental Decision Support Systems (EDSSs) (Sànchez-Marrè et al. 2008). "The efforts to integrate new tools to deal with more complex systems have led to the development of the so-called Environmental Decision Support Systems (EDSSs)" (Poch et al. 2004, p. 860). EDSS has gained high opportunities as a tool to solve problems from the environment belonging to the second and third levels of complexity (Poch et al. 2004). It has been applied to variety of tasks in which they vary from "monitoring, data storage to prediction, decision analysis, control planning, remediation, management, and communication with society" (Poch et al. 2004, p. 860).

2 EDSS in a Nutshell

Decision Support System (DSS) is known as a computerized information systems that support decision-making activities (Kautish and Thapliyal 2013; Sharda et al. 2014) to support business and organizations (Jąderko and Białecka 2015) and assist decision-makers in differentiating between alternative actions by "applying knowledge about the decision domain to arrive at recommendations for the various options" (Poch et al. 2004, p. 860). According to Sharda et al. (2014), DSS is an interactive, flexible, and adaptable computer based information system, which is developed for enhancing the decision making process in the unstructured and semi-structured management problem. It utilizes data which provides an easy-to-use interface, and allows for the decision maker's own insights.

Environmental management has been adopted in DSS development since early 1980s (Reynolds and Hessburg 2014). EDSS has been generated to tackle the complexity of levels two and three. An EDSS [also called IEDSS (Sànchez-Marrè et al. 2008)] is an intelligent information system that supports decision making process in an "environmental domain" to improve the reliability and quality of those decisions (Poch et al. 2004).

EDSS is meant to be an efficient tool to find an optimal or sub-optimal solution for existence alternatives. Moreover, EDSS has been vital for decision making process in order to become more open and transparent. Open in terms of the factors that the system is depending on since the EDSS aims at tackling environmental problems from different dimensions at once. Transparency is the ability to play a key role in the interaction of humans and ecosystems (Sànchez-Marrè et al. 2008) especially after the efforts done by Reynolds and Hessburg (2014) to lay a theoretical and practical framework for applying DSSs to the more difficult goals of ecosystem management. The value of EDSS has increased due to the interference

Table 1 Example of the construction of one table

Application	Paper title	Summary	Reference
Waste management	GIS based environmental decision support system for municipal landfill site selection	This paper developed a user-friendly EDSS-MSWI for MSW management applicable under Indian socio-economic. It developed a policy framework to report the methodology and application of the EDSS-MSWI for municipal landfill site selection. The paper applied the proposed framework onto a case study from Varanasi city (India)	Ohri and Singh (2013)
	Decision support systems in waste management—a review of selected tools	This paper determined the location of landfills and assessed the technology collection or waste treatment and its disposal. It conducted analysis and evaluation of the possibility of disposing of sewage sludge in the process of energy recovery to choose the best solution	Jąderko and Białecka (2015)
	Decision support systems for environmental management: a case study on wastewater from agriculture	This paper developed three multi criteria methods (AHp, fuzzy, DRSA) in which GIS model was utilized for environment management. It applied the application in waste water from agriculture case study	Massei et al. (2014)
Water management	Climate change and decision support systems for water resource management	This paper investigated how the combination between some models, water management and climatic scenarios, simulation and using historical hydrological data can be useful in areas where the data is changing across the time. The proposed system allowed the stakeholder to evaluate easily the impact changes in each scenario	Pierleoni et al. (2014)
	Dynamic metabolism modeling as a decision-support tool for urban water utilities applied to the upstream of the water system in Oslo, Norway	This paper tested the impact of external factors on decision making process by selecting sustainability indicators to compare and test their changes. It also	Venkatesh et al. (2014)

(continued)

Table 1 (continued)

Application	Paper title	Summary	Reference
		focused on simulating the expected, planned and future imagined point from the current value for different scenarios of each intervention	
	Earth observation and DSS technical support tools for operational water management: User's feedback on MyWater project	This paper built a platform by joining three scientific research areas: earth observation (EO), catchment modeling and meteorology. It aimed to provide reliable information on water quantity, quality and usage for target water management by high rate of speed and performance	van Andel et al. (2015)
	Towards an enhanced knowledge-based decision support system (DSS) for integrated water resource management (IWRM)	This paper integrated various inference engines (RBR and CBR) with several water supply and distributions chain management. It focused on the implementation of a holistic perspective decisional process that combines human interaction with natural path This leads to (i) improve coordination among actors, (ii) foster behavioral change, (iii) reduce water and energy consumption, and (iv) optimize water accountability	Anzaldi et al. (2014)
	Deriving simple predictions from complex models to support environmental decision-making	The paper demonstrated how individual-based models of birds can be used along with their prey and habitats, to provide the evidence-base for coastal bird conservation and shellfishery management. It showed how such models can be used to identify threshold values for perturbations of food abundance that can impact negatively on bird populations. Also, it illustrated how environmental thresholds could be used more widely to inform management of species and habitats under environmental change	Stillman et al. (2016)

(continued)

Table 1 (continued)

Application	Paper title	Summary	Reference
	A decision support system for supplier selection and order allocation in stochastic, multi-stakeholder and multi-criteria environments	This paper proposed an integrated method for dealing with complex problems using a combined analytic hierarchy process, quality functions deployment (AHP-QFD). The algorithm approach selected best suppliers and allocate orders between them in the field of bioenergy industry	Scott et al. (2015)
	A decision support methodology for integrated urban water management in remote settlements	This paper developed methodology for wastewater technology selection based on sustainability principles which were applied to a remote settlement with failing sewerage systems. The methodology adopted a systems perspective, IUWM principles and tools such as LCC, LCA and MCA to integrate economic, environmental, social factors. The research increased the transparency in decision-making process	Tjandraatmadja et al. (2012)
	Using system dynamics for sustainable water resources management in Singapore	This paper aimed to build system dynamics (SD) as a decision support tool to help achieving sustainable water management in Singapore. A system dynamics model called Singapore Water was built to analyze the long-term impacts of various investment plans The paper focused on the need to build water infrastructures well in advance in order to meet Singapore's future water demand	Xi and Poh (2013)
	Application of a three-dimensional water quality model as a decision support tool for the management of land-use changes in the catchment of an oligotrophic lake	This paper developed a modeling, simulating and integrated assessment of all of the ecological, cultural, and socio-economic implications of irrigation. This developed model linked land-use change, changes in sediment and nutrient loads, and water quality effects in the downstream receiving environment	Trolle et al. (2014)

(continued)

Table 1 (continued)

Application	Paper title	Summary	Reference
Marine management	A decision-support tool to facilitate discussion of no-take boundaries for Marine Protected Areas during stakeholder consultation processes	This paper provided a method to identify which ecological boundary minimize spatial over lab and total area of highly vulnerable species and a dominant stressor It provided stakeholder groups, government agencies an objective decision support tools in order to gain great protection of vulnerable species at limited socio-economic cost	Stortini et al. (2015)
Green manufacturing	Green manufacturing supply chain design and operations decision support	This paper provided a platform for sharing knowledge base and highlighting the critical aspects of green manufacturing supply chain design and operations decision support The paper included 15 contributions presenting new and significant research in the relevant area. "Contributions present a novel green/sustainable manufacturing supply chain design and operations decision support approach, or a state-of-the-art method on Green/sustainable factors in supply chain design and operations."	Bhattacharya et al. (2015, p. 6340)
Agriculture management	Decision support system and monitoring of eco-agriculture based on web GIS in Shule Basin	This paper analyzed the impact of the integration between the irrigation management and the decision support system with consideration of improving the efficiency of irrigation management. It ensured the sustainable development of irrigation.	Zhang et al. (2012)
	Agricultural decision support systems facilitating co-learning: a case study on environmental impacts of sugarcane production	This paper developed framework that demonstrate the value of using DSS development/application as a co-learning process, on which it can increase the agriculture sustainability of	Thorburn et al. (2011, p. 325)

(continued)

Table 1 (continued)

Application	Paper title	Summary	Reference
		natural resources It utilized a DSS to explore opportunities for reducing environmental losses of nitrogen (N) from sugarcane farms and illustrated how the DSS has capabilities for "simulating N dynamics in sugarcane systems."	
Transportation	Decision making for transportation systems as a support for sustainable stewardship: freight transport process evaluation using the ETIENNE-Tool	This paper introduced a framework to determine the deficiency within existing instruments and tools used in evaluation logistic transportation process. It developed the so-called "ETIENNE-Tool" for environmental and/or economic evaluation of transport processes to supporting decision making and the sustainable stewardship of transportation in Enterprises	Guenther and Farkavcová (2010)
	Decision support for environmental-friendly vehicle relocations in free-floating car sharing systems: the case of Car2go	This study introduced an integrated decision support approach for cost and emission efficient vehicle relocation in FFCS based on real-world data from car2go. The proposed approach appeared to be effective and had a significant potential to reduce costs and related emissions	Schulte and Voß (2015)
Pollution	Decision support model for assessing aquifer pollution hazard and prioritizing groundwater resources management in the wet Pampa plain, Argentina	This paper applied methodological framework and implemented decision support system (Application of EMDS) that "allows decision makers to rank the state of each evaluated sub-water shed with respect to aquifer pollution hazard and support planning activities such as priority setting, alternative selection, and resource allocation." The system used logic model, analysis tools for communicating clearly and effectively with the general public who have a strong	Lima et al. (2012, p. 5126)

(continued)

Table 1 (continued)

Application	Paper title	Summary	Reference
		interest in the topic of aquifer pollution hazard and want to be involved in any proposed solution.	
	Decision support tool for soil sampling of heterogeneous pesticide (chlordecone) pollution	This paper addressed the problem of sampling polluted soils. It aimed to design a decision support tool and procedures to optimize soil sampling in order to have an easy and cost-effective enough to be carried out at regional scale, to representatively assess soil mean CLD content	Clostre et al. (2013)
	Decision support methods for the environmental assessment of contamination at mining sites	This paper reviewed and evaluated some of the decision support methods that have been developed and applied to mining contamination. It provided a 'holistic' approach to the complex problem by using the following tools: (1) landscape ecology, (2) industrial ecology, (3) landscape geochemistry, (4) - geo-environmental models, (5) environmental impact assessment, (6) environmental risk assessment, (7) material flow analysis and (8) life cycle assessment	Jordan and Abdaal (2013)

Source: *The authors' effort*

between management and DSS in each decision making process in which co-learning process can lead to great confront all complex challenges.

The construction of EDSS varies depending on the type of the environmental problem and the type of the information and knowledge needed to be acquired. EDSS has different areas of applications including: waste management (Jąderko and Białecka 2015; Massei et al. 2014; Ohri and Singh 2013), water management (Pierleoni et al. 2014; Venkatesh et al. 2014; van Andel et al. 2015; Anzaldi et al. 2014; Tjandraatmadja et al. 2012; Trolle et al. 2014), pollution (Jordan and Abdaal 2013; Lima et al. 2012; Clostre et al. 2013), marine protection (Stortini et al. 2015), agriculture management (Zhang et al. 2012; Thorburn et al. 2011), transportation management (Guenther and Farkavcová 2010; Schulte and Voß 2015) and green manufacturing (Bhattacharya et al. 2015). Table 1 demonstrates the different applications from 2010 until 2015.

3 EDSS Components

The components of the environmental DSS do not differ from regular DSS in general. However, there are some special tools used within the components of EDSS that may distinguish them (Sànchez-Marrè et al. 2008; Anzaldi et al. 2014; Jąderko and Białecka 2015; Bhattacharya et al. 2015; Reynolds and Hessburg 2014; Sugumaran et al. 2004). EDSS consists of the following main components:

- The Database: The main power source of EDSS in which the data is collected, enhanced and stored to present relevant and applicable data. The data can be collected from internal sources or external sources, static or dynamic, fixed or series, simple or complicated object oriented. For example, Pierleoni et al. (2014) used data in the climate management that can be highly variable in time.
- The Model(s): Models vary in complexity and type based on the problem in hand; some can be simple and can be created from scratch as Excel Sheet, others are complex and need specific technology to work properly; some of them are commercial products, others are expensive customized, or can be available online. Different models are the mean to integrate economic, environmental, and social factors to increase the transparency in decision-making (Tjandraatmadja et al. 2012).

Some systems use combined models for stronger integration based on the complexity of the environmental aspects. Models focus on analyzing data stored in databases by using different tools such as GIS functionalities, On-Line Analytical Processing (OLAP). Also, sustainability assessment methods to evaluate the sustainability of developed systems are used, such as Cost Benefit analysis (CBA), Life Cycle Costing (LCC), Life Cycle Assessment (LCA), Material flow (MCA), Exergy analysis, Microbial Risk Assessment (MRA), Multi Criteria Analysis (MCA) (Eslamian 2014; Schulte and Voß 2015).

For example, Clostre et al. (2013) used special model to design systematic sampling procedures as the only way to assess the pollutant such in the soil and agriculture which is easy and cost effective. Xi and Poh (2013) used System Dynamic (SD) models to help achieving sustainable environmental aspect, such as water management resources.

- The Knowledge Base: some complicated system need for the Experts to depend on their experience in knowing the reasons of the problem in order to solve it.
- User Interface: considered to be a crucial component since it is the basic mean of communication between the user and the internal components. User interface should be user friendly which can be a web page or software that is responsible for the interaction with the user.

4 EDSS Review from 2010 Until 2015

Many efforts have been generated by corporate, government, and private research to combine the Decision Support System (DSS) into environmental issues to support decision making while the complexity is raising with the urbanization of the countries. They manage the development processes on a sustainable basis by using different tools and analysis methods, the following research are examples on efforts to apply the EDSS in their environmental systems as shown below.

5 Conclusion

The environment management and environment planning management cannot stand alone in facing and solving the environment complexity issues related to ecosystem. It is shorten in the main important aspects of decision making process: having information and being able to choose from alternatives.

The DSS applications can be standalone system, multi- functional system and applied in various environmental fields to overcome the complexity issues facing the management and decision makers. There is no specific modeling of DSS application; it varies based on the environmental unstructured problem. In past decades many investments have been done on research and development to enhance and develop the DSS system. The frame work of the DSS cannot be standardized, but must include the main components of DSS: Database, Model, User Interface (standalone application or web based), and in some cases it contains knowledge base. However the model must be set as combination of multiple models on which can nurture all natural resources.

The DSS tools and components play a great role in solving the complexity problem of the eco-system and in the environment. In this paper, a brief review was conducted to recent publications in some of the respected journals and conferences. According to our review, researchers found that environmental problems are characterized by sophisticated, multi-scale, spatial and time-based-dependent processes, dynamics and interactions among other ecology factors on which will not allow an easy deviation between social and bio-geophysical phenomena. EDSS has been used in different fields: Waste Management, Water management resources, Environment pollution, Green management, Transportation, Earth observation, Supplier selection and Order allocation in stochastic, Multi-stakeholder and multi-criteria environments, Sustainable water resources management, Green manufacturing supply chain, Monitoring of Eco-Agriculture, and other fields as well. Most papers analyzed the impacts of the integration between the aspect management and the decision support systems with consideration of improving the efficiency of irrigation, environment, waste, water, earth, and soil and ecosystem management.

References

Al Janabi, S., & Al Kaisi, K. (2012). *Science and life*. Amman: Al Falah Publications.

Anzaldi, G., Rubion, E., Corchero, A., Sanfeliu, R., Domingo, X., Pijuan, J., & Tersa, F. (2014). Towards an enhanced knowledge-based decision support system (DSS) for integrated water resource management (IWRM). *Procedia Engineering, 89*, 1097–1104.

Bhattacharya, A., Dey, P., & Ho, W. (2015). Green manufacturing supply chain design and operations decision support. *International Journal of Production Research, 53*(21), 6339–6343.

Clostre, F., Lesueur-Jannoyer, M., Achard, R., Letourmy, P., Cabidoche, Y., & Cattan, P. (2013). Decision support tool for soil sampling of heterogeneous pesticide (chlordecone) pollution. *Environmental Science and Pollution Research, 21*(3), 1980–1992.

Eslamian, S. (Ed.). (2014). *Handbook of engineering hydrology*. Boca Raton, FL: CRC Press.

Fedra, K. (2000). Environmental information and decision support systems. *Informatik/ Informatique, 4*(2000), 14–20.

Guenther, E., & Farkavcová, V. (2010). Decision making for transportation systems as a support for sustainable stewardship. *Management Research Review, 33*(4), 317–339.

Jąderko, K., & Białecka, B. (2015). Decision support systems in waste management—A review of selected tools. *Systems Supporting Production Engineering: Review of Problems and Solutions, 1*(10), 32–41.

Jordan, G., & Abdaal, A. (2013). Decision support methods for the environmental assessment of contamination at mining sites. *Environmental Monitoring and Assessment, 185*(9), 7809–7832.

Kautish, S., & Thapliyal, M. P. (2013). Design of new architecture for model management systems using knowledge sharing concept. *International Journal of Computer Applications, 62*(11), 27–30.

Lima, M., Romanelli, A., & Massone, H. (2012). Decision support model for assessing aquifer pollution hazard and prioritizing groundwater resources management in the wet Pampa plain, Argentina. *Environmental Monitoring and Assessment, 185*(6), 5125–5139.

Massei, G., Rocchi, L., Paolotti, L., Greco, S., & Boggia, A. (2014). Decision support systems for environmental management: A case study on wastewater from agriculture. *Journal of Environmental Management, 146*, 491–504.

Nakamura, E. (2011). Does environmental investment really contribute to firm performance? An empirical analysis using Japanese firms. *Eurasian Business Review, 1*(2), 91–111.

Ohri, A., & Singh, P. (2013). GIS based environmental decision support system for municipal landfill site selection. *Management of Environmental Quality: An International Journal, 24*(5), 583–598.

Pierleoni, A., Camici, S., Brocca, L., Moramarco, T., & Casadei, S. (2014). Climate change and decision support systems for water resource management. *Procedia Engineering, 70*, 1324–1333.

Poch, M., Comas, J., Rodríguez-Roda, I., Sànchez-Marrè, M., & Cortés, U. (2004). Designing and building real environmental decision support systems. *Environmental Modelling and Software, 19*(9), 857–873.

Reynolds, K., & Hessburg, P. (2014). An overview of the ecosystem management decision-support system. In K. M. Reynolds, P. F. Hessburg & P. S. Bourgeron (Eds.), *Decision support for environmental management: Applications of the ecosystem management decision support system* (pp. 3–22). Heidelberg: Springer.

Sànchez-Marrè, M., Gibert, K., Sojda, R., Steyer, J., Struss, P., Rodríguez-Roda, I., et al. (2008). Intelligent environmental decision support systems. In A. J. Jakeman, A. A. Voinov, A. E. Rizzoli, & S. H. Chen (Eds.), *Environmental modelling, software and decision support: State of the art and new perspectives* (pp. 120–134). Amsterdam: Elsevier.

Schulte, F., & Voß, S. (2015). Decision support for environmental-friendly vehicle relocations in free-floating car sharing systems: The case of Car2go. *Procedia CIRP, 30*, 275–280.

Scott, J., Ho, W., Dey, P., & Talluri, S. (2015). A decision support system for supplier selection and order allocation in stochastic, multi-stakeholder and multi-criteria environments. *International Journal of Production Economics, 166*, 226–237.
Sharda, R., Delen, D., & Turban, E. (2014). *Business intelligence and analytics: Systems for decision support* (10th ed.). New York, NY: Pearson.
Stillman, R., Wood, K., & Goss-Custard, J. (2016). Deriving simple predictions from complex models to support environmental decision-making. *Ecological Modeling, 326*, 134–141.
Stortini, C., Shackell, N., & O'Dor, R. (2015). A decision-support tool to facilitate discussion of no-take boundaries for Marine protected areas during stakeholder consultation processes. *Journal for Nature Conservation, 23*, 45–52.
Sugumaran, R., Meyer, J., & Davis, J. (2004). A web-based environmental decision support system (WEDSS) for environmental planning and watershed management. *Journal of Geographical Systems, 6*, 1–16.
Thorburn, P., Jakku, E., Webster, A., & Everingham, Y. (2011). Agricultural decision support systems facilitating co-learning: A case study on environmental impacts of sugarcane production. *International Journal of Agricultural Sustainability, 9*(2), 322–333.
Tjandraatmadja, G., Sharma, A., Grant, T., & Pamminger, F. (2012). A decision support methodology for integrated urban water management in remote settlements. *Water Resour Manage, 27* (2), 433–449.
Trolle, D., Spigel, B., Hamilton, D., Norton, N., Sutherland, D., Plew, D., et al. (2014). Application of a three-dimensional water quality model as a decision support tool for the management of land-use changes in the catchment of an oligotrophic lake. *Environmental Management, 54*(3), 479–493.
van Andel, S., Stavrinos, E., van der Zwan, R., & Alexandridis, T. (2015). Earth observation and DSS technical support tools for operational water management: User's feedback on MyWater Project. *Agriculture and Agricultural Science Procedia, 4*, 232–241.
Venkatesh, G., Ugarelli, R., Sægrov, S., & Brattebø, H. (2014). Dynamic metabolism modeling as a decision-support tool for urban water utilities applied to the upstream of the water system in Oslo, Norway. *Procedia Engineering, 89*, 1374–1381.
Xi, X., & Poh, K. (2013). Using system dynamics for sustainable water resources management in Singapore. *Procedia Computer Science, 16*, 157–166.
Zhang, H., Yi, S., & Wu, Y. (2012). Decision support system and monitoring of eco-agriculture based on WebGIS in Shule Basin. *Energy Procedia, 4*, 382–386.

Are You Really Influencing Your Customers?: A Black-Friday Analysis

Camelia Delcea, Elsabeta Ioanas, and Ramona Paun

Abstract The concept of Black Friday appeared more than 50 years ago and is known as an American holiday retail and in time it has crossed the borders of US and was been widely adopted by other countries from all over the world. For this, the present paper aims to analyze some qualitative aspects related to the consumers' behavior and the Black Friday promotions, such as: what are the most purchased products, what are the most preferred brands, to whom are bought these products, what is the average budget, what is the allocated time, the post-sale consumer satisfaction, etc. Moreover, the paper uses a questionnaire for determining the impact that Black Friday has on the consumers' future opinion over the different brands and how the companies' advertisements and campaigns on online social net-works can change the consumers' behavior in this day. In addition, the grey systems theory, a newly developed theory in the field of artificial intelligence, was used in order to shape the relationship among the considered variables which are influencing the consumers' behavior on Black Friday.

Keywords Black Friday • Shopping influences • Grey systems theory • Consumer behavior

C. Delcea (✉)
Department of Informatics and Cybernetics, Bucharest University of Economic Studies, Bucharest, Romania
e-mail: camelia.delcea@csie.ase.ro

E. Ioanas
Department of Marketing, Bucharest University of Economic Studies, Bucharest, Romania
e-mail: elisabetaioana@gmail.com

R. Paun
Department of Business and Technology, Webster University, Bangkok, Thailand
e-mail: paunr@webster.th

M.H. Bilgin et al. (eds.), *Empirical Studies on Economics of Innovation, Public Economics and Management*, Eurasian Studies in Business and Economics 6,
DOI 10.1007/978-3-319-50164-2_13

1 Introduction

The concept of Black Friday appeared more than 50 years ago and is known as an American holiday retail and in time has crossed the borders of US and was adopted by other countries. This day is recognized for discounts and deals both online and in physical stores. Black Friday is immediately after Thanksgiving and has become a consumer tradition for shoppers to get the best deals of the year for the upcoming gift-giving holidays. Many deals are in physic store and are on a first-come-first-serve basis, which means customers line up hours prior to opening to secure a first place in line.

Another such event is known in US and Cyber Monday is known for substantial deals and offers in several product categories in the online environment. Cyber Monday encourages users to take advantage of the high discounts offered by major brands, free shipping and multitude of products. This way has become an awaited event by online users. This event is more known more in US and started to become available also in some countries from Europe.

The Black Friday event is awaited every year by people who want to buy electronics, cloths, gardening tools, cosmetics, or other stuff like books, CDs, PS4s, games or XBOX or even meds without prescription. Many people save many year round so that they can spend on this day and also document themselves about the products they want to buy, compare prices with specialized sites, follow products on social media and sometimes enter on the companies' sites to see the offers in advance.

Some companies try to get closer to their consumers by posting or announcing their offers, with a few days before the event, in social media, newspapers, special catalogues, tv or even posting on their site 24 h before the mid-night. Electronics chain stores in Romania also apply discounts to all products in stock, some of them reach to 70–80% discounts. Depending on the category the products have different discounts and promotions. Also the discounts are different to the same shops but one online and the other offline. The promotions are adjusted to the specified consumer target. For holiday's packages, but also for wedding items, spring and winter periods are more favorable.

The Romanian saying "to buy in winter sledge and in summer car" is exactly the model that must be applied when planning a vacation: book in spring-summer Christmas break and set your winter the vacation at sea because of the great offers given by travel agencies. Travel agencies can give up to 60% discounts on airfares and holiday packages bought by 6–8 months before. This year, the biggest online shops have organized the Black Friday event a week earlier so that the products to arrive to the consumer homes before the national day (1st December).

The other online shops followed the leader and started differently. Some started on midnight, others had the whole week of offers and discounts and others started in the morning. All of them had their offers announced on social media on their pages but also in promotional brochures and online ads. The excitement of the sales led in various times to technical issues like sites were blocked because of the high traffic of people or was loading really slowly and products were not updating properly.

Discounts in Romania have their law regulations so retailers can guide you to. Merchants have access to a 45-day period in which they can sell products at low prices but follow certain rules:

- Price reductions must be clearly signaled so there is no doubt about the final price;
- Indicated price should be the total cost of all services to be paid by the consumer;
- Price must be reduced below the reference price—the product is sold before applying the discount at the same selling space during the last 30 days.

The paper is organized as follows: the following section deals with an overview on the Black Friday event, by providing some insights about the products and the behavior adopted by the companies in advance to that of both in hiring employees and being active on the online social media environment; section three brings to the reader's attention the grey systems theory, an artificial intelligent theory that has proved to be well-used over the economic field, especially to the cases in which one is dealing with uncertainty; while section four presents a case study on the consumers' behavior on the Black Friday and how they are being influenced or not in making their buying decisions, the type of the products they are targeting, preferred brands, allocated budget, allocated time for this activity—some of these being shaped using the elements taken from the grey systems theory.

2 Black Friday Overview

Consumers are searching for the best deals on Black Friday and every new post on social media in an interested product may lead from excitement to sadness if the product does not meet the users' preferences. So, according to the deal news website, the retailers post in social media many new posts with advices and updates of offers or invite users to install applications for a better monitoring. Also, according to the same website, in this period there are a lot of ads and campaigns to certain products in order to attract consumers.

E-commerce has gained a great area in the last few years especially on events created by major online shops or ones taken from international markets. According to Adobe Digital Index (2015), e-commerce sales hit referred on the internet retailer website, the half-billion-dollar mark and were up 24% Thursday morning compared to the same period last year.

The consumer is very attentive to such events and retailers are receptive and besides Black Friday also organizes other events but with a smaller scale in other periods of the year. Black Friday period is synonymous with the period of big discounts, especially in electronics. Although the celebration is the day US Thanksgiving holiday succeed and, also opens the Christmas shopping season.

Brasel and Gips (2014, p. 3) consider that "as touchpads and touchscreens rapidly become the primary means of computer interaction, touch interfaces may generate implied endowment, and ownership of the interface may transfer to viewed objects.". In this context, the authors are showing that the shifting nature of interfaces is increasingly important in online consumer behavior. Also, Brasel and Gips (2014, p. 3) suggest that "over 8% of e-commerce website visits come from tablets, and the 2012 Black Friday weekend saw almost 20% of online sales from tablets and smartphones".

As expected, compared to non-shoppers, Black Friday shoppers reported higher levels of shopping motivations. Adventure and gratification shopping motives were related to Black Friday apparel shopping. In addition, Black Friday shoppers with more positive experiences reported more extensive shopping behaviors and reported shopping for products that were similar to those products that they shop for on a regular monthly basis.

Analyzing the motive characteristics and the experiences of the shoppers on the Black Friday, (Kwon and Brinthaupt 2012) are underlying the fact that in anticipation of this day, retailers will typically add employees, increase their inventories, prepare new promotions, and change store layouts. Therefore, these factors combine to create a unique shopping event, despite its popularity. Also, Kwon and Brinthaupt (2012) are emphasizing the fact that in this period there are a lot of suggestions and recommendations for online users about the delivery and promotions, with the expressed intent of each firm to attract the potential customers and convince them to buy the firm's goods or services, from which both firms and customers may take advantage. Same conclusions are also being confirmed by Cotfas et al. (2015), Cotfas and Roxin (2013), and Orzan et al. (2015).

Laroche et al. (2003) argue that there are not only promotion strategies influential on consumer perception but further research suggests that different types of promotions yield various consumer effects and consumers tend to be more influenced by the previous experience, expectation and internal stimuli. Also they are sensitive to flyers and advertised promotions, as was reflected in their purchases (Delcea et al. 2013; Walters and Jamil 2003). Consumers with the intent to do other types of shopping, such as for specific items or a major shopping trip for which they intended to purchase multiple items, were less sensitive to flyers and advertised promotions (Rehman 2016; Smeureanu et al. 2012; Walters and Jamil 2003).

According to Blanaru (2015), 50% of the online shops have a Facebook page and 46% of all of online shops the consumer can buy with a card, the rest of users pays on delivery or by banking transfer. Most of the online shops fill in the next categories: IT&C, Fashion, Home and gardening, beauty and health, gifts & jewelry and there are shops that enter in more than one category (Blanaru 2015).

The present paper aims to analyze some qualitative aspects related to the consumers' behavior and the Black Friday promotions, such as: what are the most purchased products, what are the most preferred brands, to whom are bought these products, what is the average budget, what is the allocated time, the post-sale consumer satisfaction, etc. Moreover, the paper uses a questionnaire for determining the impact that Black Friday has on the consumers' future opinion over the different brands and how the companies' advertisements and campaigns on online social networks can change the consumers' behavior in this day. For this, the grey systems theory is used for calculating the impact of the considered variables on consumers' behavior.

3 Grey Incidence Analysis

The grey systems theory (Liu and Forrest 2010) part of the artificial intelligent theory, has been highly used over the time in economics when dealing with uncertain and/or incomplete information, in bankruptcy prediction, decision making, efficient production, companies' diagnosis, multi-criteria analysis (Bradea 2014; Delcea 2015a, b). Furthermore, over the time, the artificial intelligence techniques have been successfully used in economic analysis from different areas of the economy, both private and public (Cotfas 2011; Cotfas et al. 2015; Diosteanu and Cotfas 2010).

From the grey systems theory, the grey incidence analysis is one of the most used techniques when dealing with the economic uncertainty (Delcea et al. 2016) the values for the degrees of the grey incidence are computed according to the considerations presented in the following. The results will take values within the (0, 1) interval and as the values obtained is reaching a higher value in this interval, the relationship among the considered variables is stronger.

3.1 The Absolute Degree of Grey Incidence

Assume that X_0 and X_j, j = 1 ... n, are two sequences of data with non-zero initial values and with the same length, with t = time period and n = variables (Liu and Forrest 2010):

$$X_0 = (x_{1,0}, x_{2,0}, x_{3,0}, \ldots, x_{t,0}) \tag{1}$$

$$X_j = (x_{1,j}, x_{2,j}, x_{3,j}, \ldots, x_{t,j}) \tag{2}$$

The images of zero-start points are:

$$X_j^0 = (x_{1,j} - x_{1,j}, x_{2,j} - x_{1,j}, \ldots, x_{t,j} - x_{1,j}) = \left(x_{1,j}^0, x_{2,j}^0, \ldots, x_{t,j}^o\right) \tag{3}$$

The absolute degree of grey incidence is given by:

$$\varepsilon_{0,j} = \frac{1 + |s_0| + |s_j|}{1 + |s_0| + |s_j| + |s_0 - s_j|} \tag{4}$$

where $|s_0|$ and $|s_j|$ are computed as follows:

$$|s_0| = \left| \sum_{k=2}^{t-1} x_{k,0}^0 + \frac{1}{2} x_{t,0}^0 \right| \tag{5}$$

$$|s_j| = \left| \sum_{k=2}^{t-1} x_{k,j}^0 + \frac{1}{2} x_{t,j}^0 \right| \tag{6}$$

3.2 The Relative Degree of Grey Incidence

Assume that X_0 and X_j, $j = 1 \ldots n$, are two sequences of data with non-zero initial values and with the same length, with t = time period and n = variables (Liu and Forrest 2010; Scarlat et al. 2010):

$$X_0 = (x_{1,0}, x_{2,0}, x_{3,0}, \ldots, x_{t,0}) \tag{7}$$

$$X_j = (x_{1,j}, x_{2,j}, x_{3,j}, \ldots, x_{t,j}) \tag{8}$$

The initial values images of X_0 and X_j are:

$$X_0' = (x_{1,0}', x_{2,0}', \ldots, x_{t,0}') = \left(\frac{x_{1,0}}{x_{1,0}}, \frac{x_{2,0}}{x_{1,0}}, \ldots, \frac{x_{t,0}}{x_{1,0}} \right) \tag{9}$$

$$X_j' = \left(x_{1,j}', x_{2,j}', \ldots, x_{t,j}' \right) = \left(\frac{x_{1,j}}{x_{1,j}}, \frac{x_{2,j}}{x_{1,j}}, \ldots, \frac{x_{t,j}}{x_{1,j}} \right) \tag{10}$$

The images of zero-start points calculated based on (9) and (10) for X_0 and X_j are:

$$X_0^{0'} = (x_{1,0}' - x_{1,0}', x_{2,0}' - x_{1,0}', \ldots, x_{t,0}' - x_{1,0}') = (x_{1,0}'^0, x_{2,0}'^0, \ldots, x_{t,0}'^0) \tag{11}$$

$$X_j^{0'} = \left(x_{1,j}' - x_{1,j}', x_{2,j}' - x_{1,j}', \ldots, x_{t,j}' - x_{1,j}' \right) = (x_{1,j}'^0, x_{2,j}'^0, \ldots, x_{t,j}'^0) \tag{12}$$

The relative degree of grey incidence is given by:

$$r_{0j} = \frac{1 + |s'_0| + |s'_j|}{1 + |s'_0| + |s'_j| + |s'_0 - s'_j|} \tag{13}$$

where $|s'_0|$ and $|s'_j|$ are computed as follows:

$$|s'_0| = \left| \sum_{k=2}^{t-1} x'^0_{k,0} + \frac{1}{2} x'^0_{t,0} \right| \tag{14}$$

$$|s'_j| = \left| \sum_{k=2}^{t-1} x'^0_{k,j} + \frac{1}{2} x'^0_{t,j} \right| \tag{15}$$

3.3 *The Synthetic Degree of Grey Incidence*

The synthetic degree of grey incidence is based on the absolute and relative degrees of grey incidence obtained earlier (Delcea et al. 2016; Liu and Forrest 2010; Maracine et al. 2013):

$$\rho_{0j} = \theta \varepsilon_{0j} + (1 - \theta) r_{0j}, \tag{16}$$

with $j = 2, \ldots, n$, $\theta \in [0, 1]$ and $0 < \rho_{0j} \leq 1$.

Having all these preliminaries, we can move now to the next section, where the grey incidence will be applied to the data gathered from the questionnaire used in the case study.

4 Case Study

In order to respond to the research questions posted in introduction, a questionnaire was applied in December 2014–January 2015. From the received answers, only 211 forms have complete answers and have been kept in analysis. As for the respondents of these 211 forms, they are persons with ages between 18 and 45 years old, with more than half of them having the age between 26 and 33 years old, the great majority of them having bachelor degree and a stable job. Some of the questions have been evaluated using a 5-points Likert scale and the most relevant received answers are presented and analyzed in the following. Another set of questions was asked to the respondents to indicate the answer by

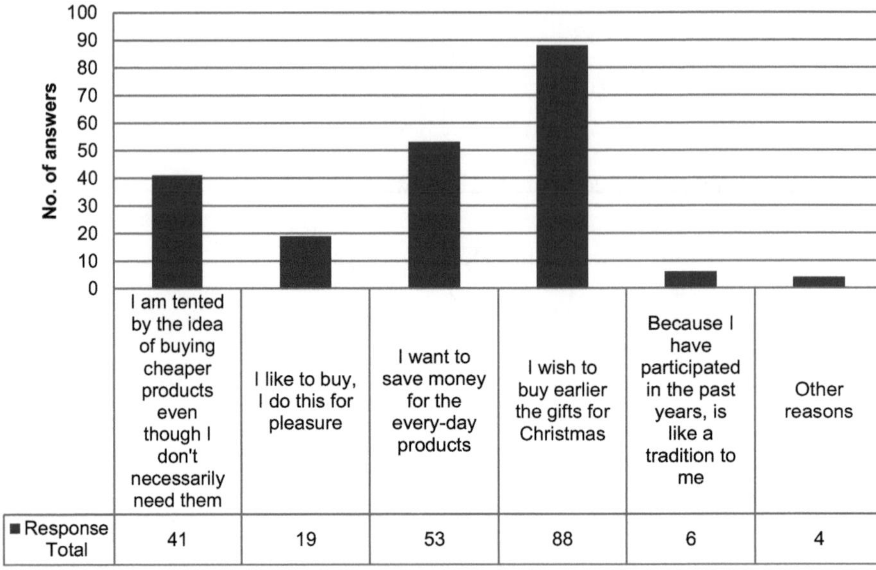

Fig. 1 The main triggers for buying on Black Friday

choosing among a series of possible answers or to write down their answer if it was not in the proposed list.

After checking that all the respondents have participated in at least one Black Friday event, they were asked "which was the main trigger when decided to make acquisitions during this event?" From Fig. 1 it can be seen that the main reason to participate at Black Friday was represented by the fact that the buyers were thinking to the up-coming Christmas which is not very far from the Black Friday, scoring 88 of the answers (almost 41.71% of the respondents). The second and the third place on the possible reasons why the consumers decided to buy on Black Friday are closely one to another regarding the number of received answers: 53 of the respondents admitting that they want to save money on the day-to-day products (representing 25.12% of the respondents), while another 41 have said that they are tempted by the idea of buying cheaper products even though they are not a necessity for them (19.43%). On the opposite, the smallest number of answers were including the fact that participating every year to Black Friday is a tradition (six answers, representing 2.84%) and only four of the answers were indicating personal reasons (1.9%).

As for the time spent in order to document and planning for this event, the answers from Fig. 2 have been received. It can be observed that more than half of the answers are spending between 3 and 6 h for this activity (54.98%), while the least part of them (5.69%) are allocating less than 1 h for this activity.

Another aspect taken into account when analyzing the consumers' behavior on this event is the information sources the buyers are using in order to help them make

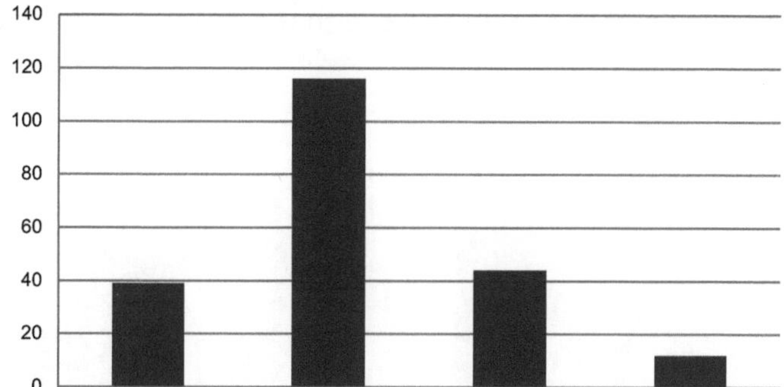

	More than 6 hours	3-6 hours	1-3 hours	Less than 1 hour
Response Total	39	116	44	12

Fig. 2 The time spent for documentation and planning on Black Friday

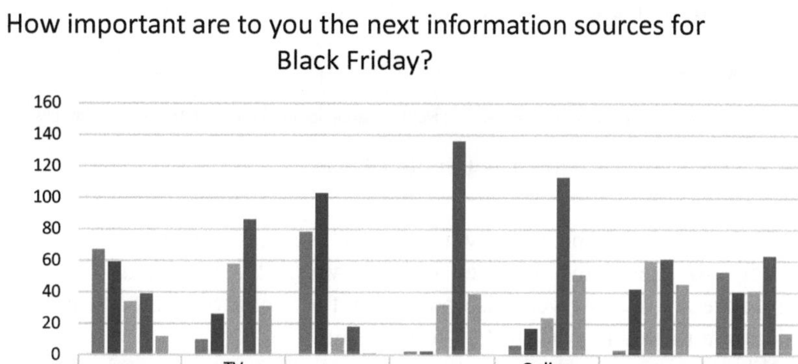

	Written press	TV commercials	Radio	Internet	Online social networks	Friends	E-mail/ newsletter
Very unimportant	67	10	78	2	6	3	53
Unimportant	59	26	103	2	17	42	40
Neutral	34	58	11	32	24	60	41
Important	39	86	18	136	113	61	63
Very important	12	31	1	39	51	45	14

Very unimportant ■ Unimportant ■ Neutral ■ Important ■ Very important

Fig. 3 Information sources used for Black Friday

their mind. As depicted in Fig. 3 the respondents were asked to indicate how important they consider to be a series of information sources, such as: written press, TV commercials, radio, internet, online social networks, friends, e-mail, and newsletter. For each of these sources, the respondents were able to indicate whether for them it is a very important, important, neutral, unimportant or very unimportant source. Online social networks (51 answers from the 193 answers received in the very important category, representing 26.42%) and Friends (with 45 answers,

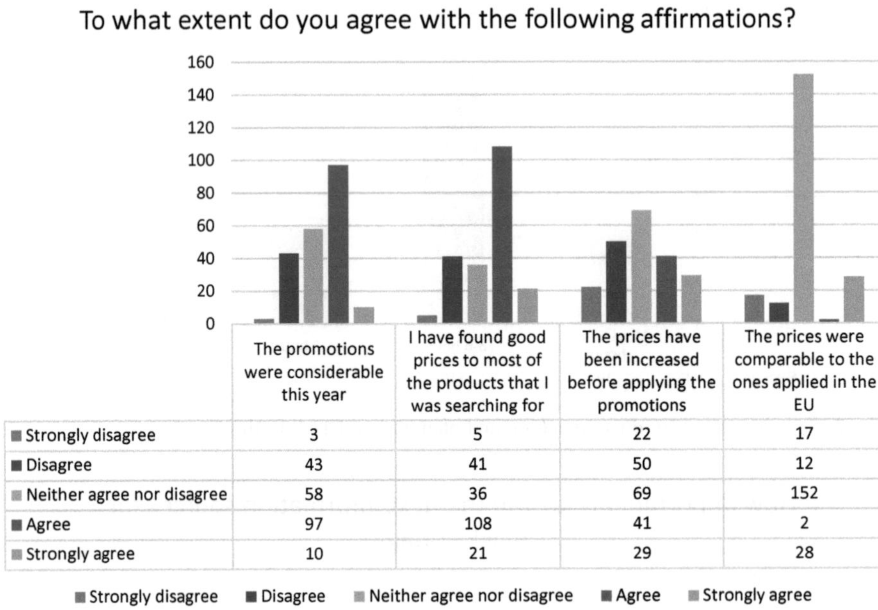

	The promotions were considerable this year	I have found good prices to most of the products that I was searching for	The prices have been increased before applying the promotions	The prices were comparable to the ones applied in the EU
Strongly disagree	3	5	22	17
Disagree	43	41	50	12
Neither agree nor disagree	58	36	69	152
Agree	97	108	41	2
Strongly agree	10	21	29	28

Fig. 4 Opinions on the prices payed on Black Friday

23.32%) were the most "very important" sources selected by the consumers. Closely to them, the internet (39 answers, 20.21%) and TV commercials (31 answers, 16.06%) were also pointed out as being very important when making a decision related to what to buy in that day.

When focusing on the important information sources, it can be seen that by far the Internet is leading this category, scoring 136 nominations from 516 answers (26.36% of the total answers given in the "important" category), followed by the Internet with 113 answers (21.90%). As for the "unimportant" and "very unimportant" options, Radio is evidencing by far (a total of 181 answers being received in both categories), followed by the Written press (with a total of 126 answers).

Regarding the prices for the goods and services commercialized in this period, the great majority of the respondents believe that they have found good prices on most of the products (108 answers with "agree" and 21 with "strongly agree") and that the promotions were considerable this year (97 "agree" and 10 "strongly agree"), as can be seen in Fig. 4.

As for the fact that the prices have been increased before applying the promotions, the opinions are almost equally divided: 72 respondents disagree and strongly disagree (34.12%), 69 have no opinion regarding this matter (32.70%), while 70 are agree and strongly agree (33.18%). The last question was trying to get the consumers' opinion on the local prices compared to the one practiced in the European Union (EU). It can be seen that the great majority of the respondents have no opinion about whether they are comparable (a number of 152 answers has been

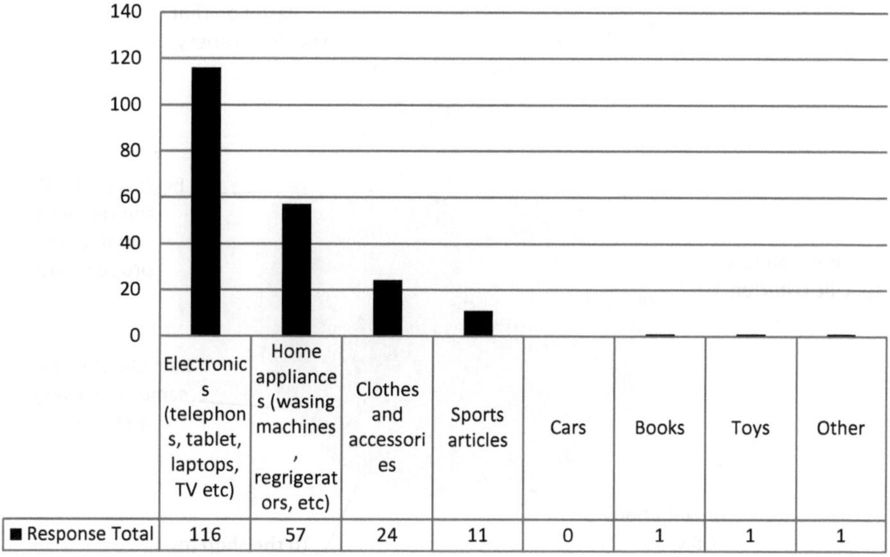

Fig. 5 The main categories of products bought on Black Friday

received, counting 72.04% from the total). This can be explained due to the fact that, in general, it is hard to buy online from the other countries in the EU as the companies from these countries are not shipping to Romania or they are shipping at very large shipping prices which make their products unattractive to the Romanian consumers.

From the received answers, the main categories of products bought on Black Friday have been highlighted (see Fig. 5). The electronics category was the most sought (116 answers, 54.98%), getting more than half of the answers, followed by home appliances (57 answers, 27.01%).

Surprisingly, 67 of the respondents are saying that they don't have a specific criterion when looking for a shop, while 53 are arguing that they use the online social networks recommendations when making a decision—Fig. 6. More, a number of 46 respondents believe that the main criterion is just the number of offered products and their prices. The destination of these products is presented in Fig. 7.

From Fig. 3 it could be seen that 105 respondents were considering the "Friends" opinion on certain products when buying on Black Friday and 164 were counting on the opinions expressed in the online social networks (OSN), but are they going to recommend the companies to their friends or to the general audience on online social networks? From the received answers—Fig. 8.—it can be concluded that only 67 of them (31.75%) are going to share their experience with both friends and audience, while 103 are saying that they can do that, but to a small extent (48.82%). 19.43% of them are sustaining that they do not consider recommending the companies neither their friends nor audience.

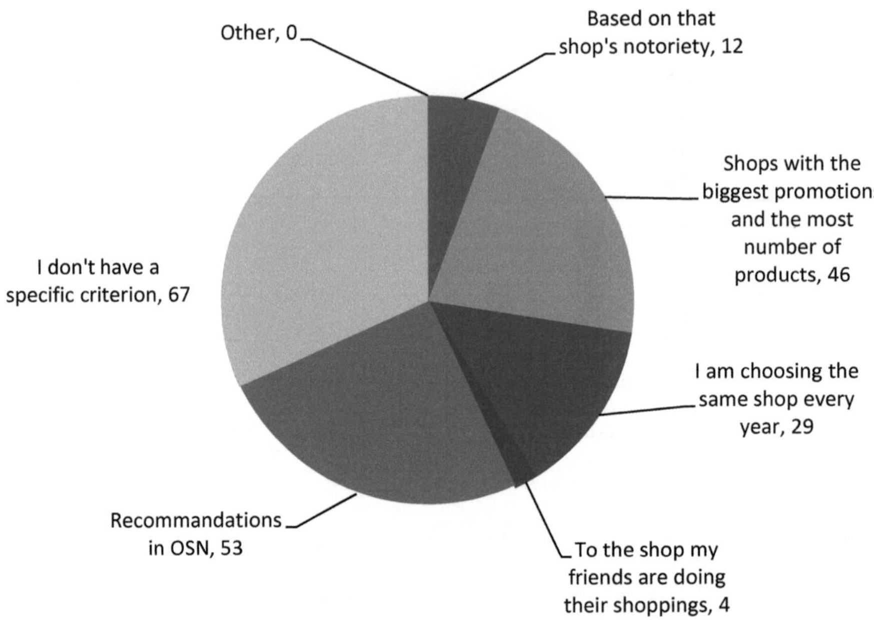

Fig. 6 The main criterion when choosing a shop

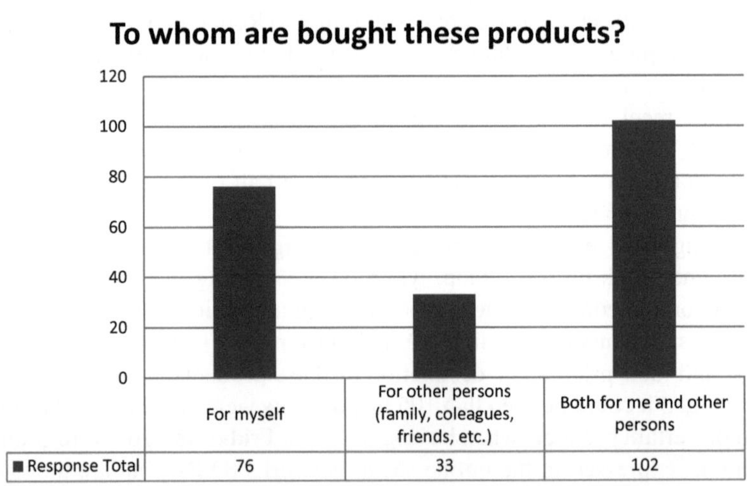

Fig. 7 The destination of the bought products

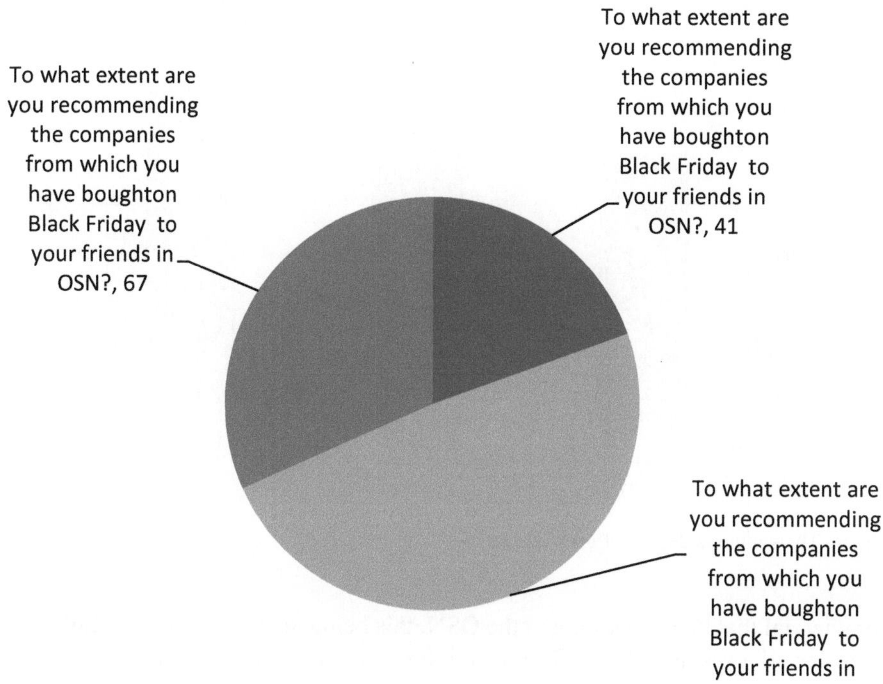

Fig. 8 After sale companies' recommendation to friends and online audience

5 Grey Incidence Analysis

In order to conduct the grey incidence analysis and to see which are the main triggers for a future buying decision related to a specific company, the respondents were asked to answer the following questions using a 5-points Likert scale:

Think on the first company that comes into your mind when speaking about Black Friday and relatively to it, please answer to the following:

- Have you considered buying a product/service from that company in the next Black Friday event? (DEC)
- How often have you seen commercials or advertisements from that company in the OSN? (V1)
- What is you friends' opinion on this company or brand? (V2)
- To what extent do you prefer the products of this company instead of similar products offered by other companies (similar both from quality, price, etc.)? (V3)

The grey incidence analysis, as presented in Sect. 3, has been applied on the received answers, conducting to the results presented in Fig. 9.

After applying the grey incidence analysis, it can be concluded that the smallest influence on the consumers' decisions on Black Friday is represented by the

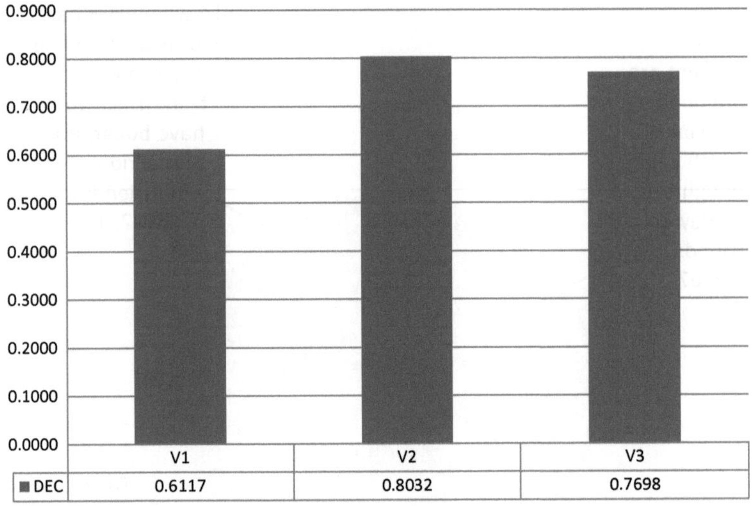

Fig. 9 The synthetic degree of grey incidence

commercial that they are seeing in the OSN, this being also due to the absence of an intensive advertising in OSN. The most influent indicator is their friends' opinions on OSN (V3), followed shortly by their personal attachment on a specific product or company. This result can be put in correspondence with the general answers presented above related to the destination of the bought products, the upcoming holydays and the fact that most of the products bought during the Black Friday are electronics. Therefore, at least for the companies that are producing this type of goods, they should try to improve their image by attracting on their side the most influential persons in OSN and by investing more time and effort in reaching a large number of audience in OSN before the Black Friday event trough intense advertising in social media.

6 Conclusion

After analyzing the answers received through the questionnaire, it can be concluded that the most of the respondents are taking into account the promotions offered by the Black Friday, buying in this day the most of the presents that they are going to offer for the Christmas. More, they are spending more than 3 h for documentation and planning for this event and they are recommending this shopping event to their friends via online social networks.

The main buying category are the electronic products and the calculated grey impact of their friends' opinion on this brand is very high for this event, being easily influenced in taking their decisions by the other friends' opinion and personal preference. Based on this, the recommendation can be that the firms should invest more on their advertising companies so they can get to the targeted customers and to their friends (Bradea et al. 2014).

Even though the study is made on persons belonging to a certain part of Europe, the authors believe that it can be extended to the other parts of the world, as the characteristics of this event are similar and its time placement is before the winter holydays. For future developments, we intend to study the consumers' behavior in relation with their personal characteristics, by adding a PANAS analysis (Eisingerich et al. 2015).

Acknowledgments The authors are acknowledging the support of Leverhulme Trust International Network research project "IN-2014-020". Also, they are thanking to the Webster University Thailand for its support and to the participants of the 18th EBES Conference on their constructive remarks.

References

Adobe Digital Index. 2015. *Holiday Spending Report*. [online] Accessed November 23, 2015, from http://landing.adobe.com/en/na/solutions/digital-index/246230-2015-holiday-shopping-infographic/

Blanaru, C., 2015. *GPeC study: Romanian e-commerces in 2015*. [online] Accessed November 23, 2015, from http://www.adhugger.net/2015/10/22/gpec-study-romanian-e-commerces-in-2015/

Bradea, I. A. (2014). Risks in hospitals. Assessment and management. *Romanian Economic Journal, 17*(54), 25–36.

Bradea, I. A., Delcea, C., Scarlat, E., & Boloş, M. (2014). KRIs in hospitals-network, correlations and influences. *Economic Computation and Economic Cybernetics Studies and Research, 48* (1), 81–94.

Brasel, S. A., & Gips, J. (2014). Tablets, touchscreens, and touchpads: How varying touch interfaces trigger psychological ownership and endowment. *Journal of Consumer Psychology, 24*(2), 226–233.

Cotfas, L.-A. (2011). Collaborative itinerary recommender systems. *Economy Informatics, 11*(1), 191–200.

Cotfas, L.-A., & Roxin, I. (2013). Adaptable alternate reality games platform. *Journal of Mobile, Embedded and Distributed Systems, 5*(4), 130–135.

Cotfas, L.-A., Delcea, C., Roxin, I., & Paun, R. (2015). Twitter ontology-driven sentiment analysis. In D. Barbucha, N. T. Nguyen, & J. Batubara (Eds.), *New trends in intelligent information and database systems* (pp. 131–139). Cham: Springer.

Delcea, C. (2015a). Grey systems theory in economics—Bibliometric analysis and applications' overview. *Grey Systems: Theory and Application, 5*(2), 244–262.

Delcea, C. (2015b). Grey systems theory in economics—A historical applications review. *Grey Systems: Theory and Application, 5*(2), 263–276.

Delcea, C., Bradea, I., & Scarlat, E. (2013). A computational grey based model for companies risk forecasting. *Journal of Grey System, 25*(3), 70–93.

Delcea, C., Cotfas, L.-A., Paun, R., Maracine, V., & Scarlat, E. (2016). A grey approach to online social networks analysis. In N. T. Nguyen & R. Kowalczyk (Eds.), *Transactions on computational collective intelligence XXII* (pp. 60–79). Berlin: Springer.

Diosteanu, A., & Cotfas, L.-A. (2010). Multi-agents and GIS framework for collaborative supply chain management applications. In R. Brad (Ed.), *2010 9th Roedunet International Conference (RoEduNet 2010)* (pp. 157–162). Piscataway, NJ: IEEE.

Eisingerich, A. B., Chun, H. H., Liu, Y., Jia, H. M., & Bell, S. J. (2015). Why recommend a brand face-to-face but not on Facebook? How word-of-mouth on online social sites differs from traditional word-of-mouth. *Journal of Consumer Psychology, 25*(1), 120–128.

Kwon, H. J., & Brinthaupt, T. M. (2012). Teaching the social aspects of clothing in an online course. *International Journal of Fashion Design, Technology and Education, 5*(2), 129–134.

Laroche, M., Bergeron, J., & Goutaland, C. (2003). How intangibility affects perceived risk: The moderating role of knowledge and involvement. *Journal of Services Marketing, 17*(2), 122–140.

Liu, S., & Forrest, J. Y.-L. (Eds.). (2010). *Advances in grey systems research.* Berlin: Springer Science & Business Media.

Maracine, V., Delcea, C., Bradea, I., Scarlat, E., & Cotfas, L. (2013). Banking sector risks identification via GRA. In S. Liu (Ed.), *Proceedings of 2013 I.E. International Conference on Grey systems and Intelligent Services* (pp. 11–15). Piscataway, NJ: IEEE.

Orzan, G., Delcea, C., Ioanas, E., Orzan, M.C., 2015. Buyers' decisions in online social networks environment. *Journal of Eastern Europe Research in Business & Economics.*

Rehman, N. U. (2016). Network alliances and firms' performance: A panel data analysis of Pakistani SMEs. *Eurasian Business Review, 6*(1), 37–52.

Scarlat, E., Delcea, C., & Mărăcine, V. (2010). Genetic-fuzzy-grey algorithms: A hybrid model for establishing companies' failure reasons. In M. El-Hawary (Ed.), *2010 I.E. International Conference on Systems Man and Cybernetics (SMC)* (pp. 955–962). Piscataway, NJ: IEEE.

Smeureanu, I., Ruxanda, G., Diosteanu, A., Delcea, C., & Cotfas, L. A. (2012). Intelligent agents and risk based model for supply chain management. *Technological and Economic Development of Economy, 18*(3), 452–469.

Walters, R. G., & Jamil, M. (2003). Exploring the relationships between shopping trip type, purchases of products on promotion, and shopping basket profit. *Journal of Business Research, 56*(1), 17–29.

Part IV
Growth & Development

Institutional Clusters and FDI Flows to the MENA Region

Wasseem Mina

Abstract The empirical literature on the institutions-FDI nexus has treated the influence of institutions individually despite the correlation among them. This is a conceptual shortcoming. To overcome this limitation, we cluster institutions using Principal Component Analysis (PCA). We apply PCA to ICRG institutions for 17 Middle East and North Africa countries during the period 1984–2011. Three institutional clusters have been extracted: stability and order, quality of public administration, and presence of democratic systems. Using feasible generalized least squares estimation methodology, estimates show that stability and order and the presence of a democratic system have a positive influence on FDI flows, while the quality of public administration has a surprisingly negative influence.

Keywords Institutions • Institutional clusters • FDI • MENA • Principal component analysis

1 Introduction

The influence of institutions on capital flows has been examined in the extant capital flows literature. Recent studies, such as Daude and Fratzscher (2008), Fratzscher (2012), and Papaioannou (2009), have examined the role of institutions and risk in attracting capital flows. In investigating the effect of global shocks on global portfolio investment flows, Fratzscher (2012) finds that it depends on the recipient country's quality of formal political institutions, country risk, and the strength of macroeconomic fundamentals and policies, a result which Daude and Fratzscher (2008) similarly obtain. They find that the quality of institutions matters most for portfolio investment and least for FDI. Papaioannou (2009) examines the role of institutions in driving capital flows and finds that imperfect legal and judicial institutions deter banking flows.

W. Mina (✉)
Department of Economics and Finance, United Arab Emirates University, Al Ain, UAE
e-mail: wmina@uaeu.ac.ae

M.H. Bilgin et al. (eds.), *Empirical Studies on Economics of Innovation, Public Economics and Management*, Eurasian Studies in Business and Economics 6,
DOI 10.1007/978-3-319-50164-2_14

In the empirical capital flows literature, institutions were treated individually and separately from each other. Such treatment implies that individual institutions are uncorrelated to one another, and ignores their possible clustering around a broader institutional function. This same point is emphasized by Leschke (2000) in the search of components of economic freedom and political liberty that influence prosperity.

In this paper, we use principal component analysis (PCA) to extract institutional components for 17 Middle East and North Africa (MENA) countries using ICRG's political risk indicators for the period 1984–2011. These countries include Algeria, Bahrain, Egypt, Iran, Iraq, Jordan, Kuwait, Lebanon, Libya, Morocco, Oman, Qatar, Saudi Arabia, Syria, Tunisia, UAE, and Yemen. We find that institutions can be grouped into three clusters or components, which may be interpreted as stability and order, quality of public administration, and the presence of democratic system. We then use these clusters to explain aggregate FDI flows to the region together with other FDI location determinants.

To account for panel heterogeneity and serial correlation, we adopt feasible generalized least squares (FGLS) estimation methodology. FGLS estimation results show that stability and order and the presence of democratic system have a positive influence on FDI flows, while the quality of public administration has a surprisingly negative influence.

The structure of the paper goes as follows: Sect. 2 empirically examines correlation among institutions for the sample MENA countries and identifies the main principal components. Section 3 specifies the empirical model, and the data sources. Section 4 discusses the empirical issues and estimation methodology, while Sect. 5 discusses briefly the empirical results. Section 6 concludes.

2 Institutional Correlation and Principal Component Identification in the MENA Region

We explore the institutional correlation for the MENA region using the International Country Risk Guide (ICRG) political risk indicators for 17 MENA countries over the period 1984–2011. These countries include Algeria, Bahrain, Egypt, Iran, Iraq, Jordan, Kuwait, Lebanon, Libya, Morocco, Oman, Qatar, Saudi Arabia, Syria, Tunisia, UAE, and Yemen.

The ICRG indicators include government stability, investment profile, internal and external conflicts, corruption, military and religion in politics, law and order, ethnic tensions, democratic accountability and bureaucracy quality. A higher score for each of these indicators reflects better performance.

Government stability measures the government power to undertake its announced economic and political programs and remain in office. This power depends on and is measured by government unity, legislative strength and the support of people. The maximum score is 12. Investment profile assesses risk factors, which affect investment in the country. Risk factors include the extent of contract expropriation, the degree to which investors repatriate earned profit and delays in government payments back to investors. The maximum score is 12. Internal conflict measures political violence and its impact on governance. The maximum score is 12. External conflict measures the risks of wars and cross-border conflicts to the incumbent government. The maximum score is 12. Corruption assesses the degree of corruption within the political system. The maximum score is 6. Military in politics assesses the degree of interference and involvement of the military establishment in politics. The maximum score is 6. Religion in politics measures the domination of a single religious group and its intent, attempts and/or success to replace civil laws by religious law and exclude other religions from the social and/or political process. The maximum score is 6. Law and order measures the degree of strength, independence, and unbiasedness of the legal system and people's observance of law. The maximum score is 6. Ethnic tensions measure the degree of racial, national, and linguistic tensions. The maximum score is 6. Democratic accountability measures the responsiveness of government to its people. The maximum score is 6. Bureaucracy quality assesses the strength to govern without severe changes in policy and/or interruptions in the provision of public services. The maximum score is 4.

Table 1 shows the correlation coefficients matrix for these institutions. Many institutions are strongly correlated to each other.[1] Internal conflict is strongly and moderately correlated to five institutions in total. It is strongly correlated to law and order, ethnic tensions, and external conflicts, and moderately correlated to religion and military in politics. Government stability is moderately correlated to three institutions: internal conflict, investment profile, and ethnic tensions. As the table shows, investment profile, external conflict, law and order, military and religion in politics, and bureaucracy quality are moderately or strongly correlated to two institutions each.

Instead of examining the influence of individual institutions on FDI flows, an approach which disregards correlation between the different institutions, we use principal component analysis (PCA) to reduce the number of dimensions into a smaller number of principal components.

As Norman and Streiner (2008) explain, the idea of PCA is to explain the variance among a number of variables or institutions in this paper in terms of orthogonal principal components. In doing so, PCA obtains a series of linear combinations of institutions, which define each component. The number of linear combinations or components is equal to the number of institutions examined.

Choosing among the extracted principal components, we use the Kaiser criterion, according to which principal components with eigenvalues exceeding 1 are selected. In interpreting the principal components, we will adopt the results of the orthogonal (Varimax) rotation method.

[1]Correlation is strong if the correlation coefficient is 0.7 and above, and moderate if it is 0.5 and less than 0.7.

Table 1 Institutions correlation coefficients matrix

	GS	IP	IC	EC	C	MP	RP	LO	ET	DA	BQ
GS	1										
IP	0.573	1									
IC	0.575	0.443	1								
EC	0.523	0.501	0.699	1							
C	−0.063	−0.06	0.159	0.16	1						
MP	0.295	0.42	0.543	0.4	0.286	1					
RP	0.409	0.286	0.582	0.445	0.06	0.25	1				
LO	0.499	0.527	0.767	0.587	0.146	0.592	0.471	1			
ET	0.513	0.478	0.748	0.602	0.143	0.438	0.389	0.684	1		
DA	−0.097	0.051	−0.013	0.11	0.051	0.03	−0.167	−0.086	0.111	1	
BQ	0.179	0.328	0.413	0.413	0.302	0.568	0.003	0.486	0.367	0.178	1

Notes: *IP* investment profile, *IC* internal conflict, *EC* external conflict, *C* corruption, *MP* military in politics, *RP* religion in politics, *LO* law and order, *ET* ethnic tensions, *DA* democratic accountability, *BQ* bureaucracy quality. For each variable, missing values are replaced with the variable mean

Table 2 Principal component analysis of institutions

Comp.	Initial eigenvalues		
	Total	% Variance	% Cumulative
1	4.92	44.71	44.71
2	1.5	13.67	58.38
3	1.09	9.9	68.28

Table 3 Principal component analysis

Comp.	1	2	3
	Non-rotated components		
IC	0.891	−0.085	−0.096
LO	0.863	−0.016	−0.114
ET	0.81	−0.007	0.102
EC	0.795	−0.009	0.112
GS	0.685	−0.4	0.178
MP	0.684	0.358	−0.159
IP	0.677	−0.141	0.367
RP	0.574	−0.447	−0.3
BQ	0.566	0.609	0.04
C	0.212	0.598	−0.553
DA	0.024	0.51	0.674
	Rotated components		
IC	0.827	0.321	−0.152
GS	0.794	−0.141	−0.107
ET	0.777	0.245	0.056
LO	0.777	0.372	−0.126
EC	0.766	0.232	0.063
IP	0.756	−0.047	0.198
RP	0.590	0.035	−0.521
C	−0.111	0.827	−0.108
BQ	0.356	0.654	0.37
MP	0.492	0.614	0.06
DA	0.036	0.039	0.844

Notes: *IP* investment profile, *IC* internal conflict, *EC* external conflict, *C* corruption, *MP* military in politics, *RP* religion in politics, *LO* law and order, *ET* ethnic tensions, *DA* democratic accountability, *BQ* bureaucracy quality

Table 2 shows the PCA for MENA institutions with eigenvalues exceeding 1. These components explain about 70% of the total variance in the data. The first component alone explains about 45% of the variance. The factor loadings of the first component, as shown in Table 3, show highest correlation (absolute value of about 0.6) with eight institutions: (1) internal conflict, (2) law and order, (3) ethnic tensions, (4) external conflicts, (5) government stability, (6) military in politics, (7) investment profile, and (8) religion in politics.

The second component explains about 14% of total variance with factor loadings that are correlated the highest with bureaucracy quality and corruption. The third component explains about 10% of total variance with factor loadings that are correlated the highest with democratic accountability.

To help interpret the results of PCA, we rotate the principal components using the orthogonal (Varimax) rotation method. The orthogonal rotation approach assumes no correlation among the components. Table 3 reports the rotated factors.

The Varimax method reports internal conflict, government stability, ethnic tensions, law and order, external conflicts, investment profile and religion in politics, displaying the highest factor loadings (of greater than or equal to 0.60). Corruption, bureaucracy quality, and military in politics have the highest factor loadings on the second component. The factor loadings of the third component show highest correlation for democratic accountability.

One may interpret the first component as stability and order. The second component may be interpreted as the quality of public administration. The third component may be interpreted as the presence of a democratic system. Guided by these results, we will introduce these three principal components into the empirical model.

3 Empirical Model and Data

The conceptual framework underlying the empirical model is Dunning's (1981) location advantage hypothesis. To engage in foreign investment abroad, the firm is attracted to the host country by the available location advantages. For example, the host economy may enjoy large domestic or regional market size and potential, developed infrastructure, openness to trade and capital flows, developed financial markets, friendly business environment, and quality domestic institutions. Accordingly, we express the empirical model as:

$$\begin{aligned} \mathrm{FDI}_{i,t} = \beta_0 + \beta_1 \mathrm{CLUSTER}_{i,t} + \beta_2 \mathrm{TRADE}_{i,t} + \beta_3 \mathrm{INFRASTRUCTURE}_{i,t} \\ + \beta_4 \mathrm{FINANCE}_{i,t} + \varepsilon_{i,t} \end{aligned} \quad (1)$$

where FDI is FDI inflows as a percentage of GDP, CLUSTER is institutional clusters extracted using PCA, TRADE is trade openness as measured by the sum of imports and exports as a percentage of GDP, INFRASTRUCTURE is the degree of infrastructure development as measured by the number of mobile cellular subscriptions per 100 people (in log form), FINANCE is the degree of financial system depth as measured by percentage of private sector credit to GDP.

Data on FDI are obtained from the UNCTADSTAT database. Data on TRADE, INFRASTRUCTURE, and FINANCE are obtained from the World Development Indicators. Data on CLUSTER are obtained from ICRG.

4 Empirical Issues and Estimation Methodology

In constructing the empirical model, we consider two main empirical issues. These are heterogeneity and serial correlation. MENA countries are diverse with respect to FDI inflows, trade openness, degree of economic development, and financial system depth. This is likely to generate heteroskedasticity in the error term. In presence of heteroskedasticity, coefficient estimates are consistent but inefficient. Standard errors of coefficients are biased and result in inference problems in presence of heteroskedasticity. To detect heteroskedasticity, we conduct a Wald test for panel heterogeneity.

Serial correlation is likely to arise in a long series of data. In this paper, we examine a period of 28 years (1984–2011). In presence of serial correlation, coefficient estimates are consistent though inefficient. The associated standard errors are also not unbiased. To detect the presence of autocorrelation, we conduct a test for autocorrelation as demonstrated by Wooldridge (2002).

5 Empirical Results

Panel heterogeneity test indicates rejection of the null hypothesis of homoskedasticity at the 1% level. Serial correlation test indicates rejection of the null hypothesis of no serial correlation at the 1% level. These results lend support to the use of FGLS estimation methodology.

Table 4 shows the estimation results. The Stability and Order cluster (CLUSTER1) exerts a statistically significant, positive influence on FDI flows at the 1% level. In other words, an improvement in the institutions forming this cluster, as a group, results in an increase in FDI flows to the MENA region. As mentioned in Sect. 2 above, these institutions comprise internal conflict, government stability, ethnic tensions, law and order, external conflicts, investment profile and religion in politics.

Similarly the Democratic System cluster (CLUSTER3) exerts a statistically significant, positive influence at the 5% level. In other words, an improvement in the institution forming this cluster, which is democratic accountability, results in an increase in FDI flows. This result is consistent with Jensen (2003) for a panel of more than 100 countries and with Asiedu and Lien (2011) for countries whose share of natural resources in total exports is below a critical value. For the MENA region, this result is consistent with Zouhaier and Karim (2012) who found a positive association between democracy and investment.

In contrast to the influence of these two clusters, the Quality of Public Administration (CLUSTER2) exerts a statistically significant, negative influence on FDI flows at the 1% level. Thus, an improvement in corruption, bureaucracy quality, and military in politics, as a group, reduces FDI flows to the MENA region. Although this negative result seems surprising, Helmy (2013) obtained a similar finding on

Table 4 Influence of institutional clusters on FDI flows

VARIABLES	Estimates	Robust SE
CLUSTER1	0.464[a]	−0.132
CLUSTER2	−0.367[a]	−0.1
CLUSTER3	0.216[b]	−0.091
TRADE	0.014[a]	−0.005
INFRASTRUCTURE	0.014[a]	−0.003
FINANCE	0.022[a]	−0.005
Constant	−0.374	−0.333
Obs.	382	
Wald test	236.26[a]	
Countries	17	

Notes: Robust standard errors in parentheses. CLUSTER1 refers to stability and order. CLUSTER2 refers to quality of public administration. CLUSTER3 refers to the presence of democratic systems

[a,b,c]Indicates significance at the 1%, 5%, and 10% levels, respectively

the relation between corruption and FDI in the MENA region. This negative relationship sheds light on the perception about the association between rent seeking and FDI flows.

The signs of the coefficients of the other explanatory variables are as positive as expected and are statistically significant at the 1% level. Trade openness, the degree of infrastructure development, and the depth of the financial system all have positive influence on FDI flows to the MENA region. An increase in each of these variables attracts more FDI flows to region. An increase in the sum of exports and imports (relative to GDP) and in the number of mobile cellular subscriptions per 100 people by one percentage point increases FDI flows by 0.01 percentage point of GDP, while an increase in the extended private sector credit (relative to GDP) by one percentage point increases FDI flows by 0.02 percentage point of GDP.

6 Concluding Remarks

In this paper, we have examined the influence of institutional clusters on FDI flows to a sample of 17 MENA region countries. Institutions have been clustered using PCA to account for the correlation between the different institutions, which have been largely overlooked in the institutions-FDI nexus literature. The included MENA countries are Algeria, Bahrain, Egypt, Iran, Iraq, Jordan, Kuwait, Lebanon, Libya, Morocco, Oman, Qatar, Saudi Arabia, Syria, Tunisia, UAE, and Yemen.

Results show that the groups of correlated institutions which serve the stability and order function and constitute the presence of a democratic system encourage FDI inflows to the region. We should note at this point that a democratic system can be more generally viewed as a government, which is responsive to people's needs and wants or their collective choice.

Results also show that the group of correlated institutions which relate to the quality of public administration, including corruption, surprisingly reduces FDI inflows. If the MENA countries target more FDI flows to overcome the finance and technology gaps, then they should fight corruption and enhance the quality of the bureaucracy. Controlling corruption pays off in terms of additional investment and economic growth.[2]

The positive relation between responsive or democratic governments and regional FDI flows constitutes an invitation to policy makers in the MENA region to take a deeper look at how can governments be more responsive to their own people without instigating much instability as the Arab Spring did. The mechanisms through which democracy encourages FDI flows to the MENA region need to be explored.

References

Asiedu, E., & Lien, D. (2011). Democracy, foreign direct investment and natural resources. *Journal of International Economics, 84*(1), 99–111.

d'Agostino, G., Dunne, J. P., & Pieroni, L. (2016a). Corruption and growth in Africa. *European Journal of Political Economy, 43*, 71–88.

d'Agostino, G., Dunne, J. P., & Pieroni, L. (2016b). Government spending, corruption and economic growth. *World Development, 84*, 190–205.

Daude, C., & Fratzscher, M. (2008). The pecking order of cross-border investment. *Journal of International Economics, 74*(1), 94–119.

Dunning, J. (1981). *International production and the multinational enterprise*. London: George Allen & Unwin.

Fratzscher, M. (2012). Capital flows, push versus pull factors and the global financial crisis. *Journal of International Economics, 88*(2), 341–356.

Helmy, H. E. (2013). The impact of corruption on FDI: Is MENA an exception? *International Review of Applied Economics, 27*(4), 491–514.

Jain, A. K. (2001). Corruption: A review. *Journal of Economic Surveys, 15*(1), 71–116.

Jensen, N. M. (2003). Democratic governance and multinational corporations: Political regimes and inflows of foreign direct investment. *International Organization, 57*(3), 587–616.

Leschke, M. (2000). Constitutional choice and prosperity: A factor analysis. *Constitutional Political Economy, 11*(3), 265–279.

Mauro, P. (1995). Corruption and growth. *Quarterly Journal of Economics, 110*(3), 681–712.

Méon, P.-G., & Sekkat, K. (2005). Does corruption grease or sand the wheels of growth? *Public Choice, 122*(1–2), 69–97.

Mo, P. H. (2001). Corruption and economic growth. *Journal of Comparative Economics, 29*(1), 66–79.

Norman, G. R., & Streiner, D. L. (2008). *Biostatistics: The bare essentials*. Shelton, CT: PMPH-USA.

[2]On the effect of corruption on the economy, see for example d'Agostino et al. (2016a, b), Jain (2001), Mauro (1995), Meon and Sekkat (2005), Mo (2001), and Tanzi (1998).

Papaioannou, E. (2009). What drives international financial flows? Politics, institutions and other determinants. *Journal of Development Economics, 88*(2), 269–281.

Tanzi, V. (1998). Corruption around the world: Causes, consequences, scope, and cures. *IMF Staff Papers, 45*(4), 559–594.

Wooldridge, J. M. (2002). *Econometric analysis of cross section and panel data*. Cambridge, MA: The MIT Press.

Zouhaier, H., & Karim, K. M. (2012). Democracy, investment and economic growth. *International Journal of Economics and Financial Issues, 2*(3), 233–240.

TFP and Possibility of Convergence in OECD Countries: The 2000–2012 Period

Aziz Kutlar, Ali Kabasakal, and Ahmet Gulmez

Abstract This study discusses efficiency, productivity, and the existence of convergence in 34 OECD countries between 2000 and 2012. Physical capital per worker and human capital per worker are used as inputs to determine total factor productivity while gross domestic product per worker is used as the output. Analysis of productivity by using the Malmquist Index indicates that productivity was positive but increased less than 1% at the end of the period. Panel regression estimation is used for standard deviations of convergence and to determine beta convergence. However, the convergence effect of Total Factor Productivity values could not be determined. Similar results are reported for Sigma convergence.

Keywords Panel data • Malmquist index • TFP • OECD countries • Convergence

1 Introduction

The Organization for Economic Co-operation and Development (OECD) was established in 1961 and has 34 members. The OECD budget is approximately $357 million. During the study period, total real GDP rose by 22%, reaching $39 trillion. Capital increased by 8%, reaching $7.8 trillion, while labor force increased 11%, reaching 610 million people within the same period. GDP growth was greater than capital and labor force growth. There was significant total factor productivity growth in OECD countries.

Growth dynamics of countries as well as convergence among those countries have been studied for a long time according to neoclassical growth theories in various studies. A series of studies indicate convergence among OECD countries. The majority of such studies use productivity per worker and total factor productivity in order to analyze convergence.

The economic productivity and convergence issue of OECD countries, the economic structures of which are partially similar to each other and that are

A. Kutlar • A. Kabasakal (✉) • A. Gulmez
Department of Economics, Sakarya University, Sakarya, Turkey
e-mail: akutlar@sakarya.edu.tr; kabasakal@sakarya.edu.tr; agulmez@sakarya.edu.tr

M.H. Bilgin et al. (eds.), *Empirical Studies on Economics of Innovation, Public Economics and Management*, Eurasian Studies in Business and Economics 6,
DOI 10.1007/978-3-319-50164-2_15

representative of relatively advanced economies, has been investigated by our study for the period between 2000 and 2012. In that regard, MI, which is interpreted by Caves et al. (1982), and the data envelopment analysis (DEA) method used by Charnes et al. (1978) are used for Total Factor Productivity (TFP). The description is used as inputs and outputs. Physical capital is used as input and is among some of the most important factors that affect technological development and productivity. Gross national product is used as output. All variables are divided into labor unit and necessary analyses are performed. Data sources are provided below. The whole variable value is calculated based on 2005 US dollars. A total of 34 OECD countries are included in the analysis. Although some of the countries were not OECD member during the entire given period, they are still included. Whether there are any differences between these countries will be observed during the analysis process.

The aim of this study is to analyze convergence in OECD countries over a reasonable period of time at the beginning of the new millennium. The period between 2000 and 2012 is chosen intentionally in order to examine the results of the financial crisis of 2009. The set of values in the study are obtained from OECD StatExtracts. Real physical capital per worker, real human capital per worker, and real GDP per worker are calculated based on 2005 US dollars.

The literature and methodology forms the first part of the study while MI analyses of TFP are given in the following chapter. The conclusion and assessment make up the last part of this study.

2 Literature

In recent years, there have been many studies that examine convergence and economic growth. Barro et al. (1991), Barro and Sala-i Martin (1992), and Färe et al. (2006) are the major contributors to the relevant literature. According to Krüger (2003), experiential growth investigations over the last 10 years have been pursued at least three different ways. First, the most immense strand of literature applies linear regressions to clarify the growth ratio of real GDP per capita by a great amount of different growth driving factors while at the same time struggling to anticipate the ratio of convergence of countries to their steady state positions. Second, some studies provide new anticipations of ratio of total factor productivity growth on an economy-wide scale as precautions of technological progress. The third basic approach of experiential growth searches for the dynamics of the entire distribution of real GDP per capita or per worker. The second significant issue forms the focus of interest of a range of studies that aim to find whether the economies of two such country groups converge with one other (Barro et al. 1991; Barro and Sala-i-Martin 1992; Mankiw et al. 1992).

In their study regarding growth and productivity in OECD countries, Dowrick and Nguyen (1989) analyzed the hypothesis that GDP levels and total factor productivity in OECD countries converged following the postwar period. Their findings suggest that convergence of income levels had been weak since 1973; however, they argue that income convergence is contingent upon sample selection and that TFP catch-up is the prevailing trend. In the study concerning the EU countries conducted by Färe et al. (2006), growth in productivity and the phenomenon of convergence was investigated during the period between 1965 and 1998. Efficiency and productivity of human and physical capital are examined as inputs. The existence of convergence among these countries is also investigated. Additionally, relevant countries are divided into sub-groups and the existence of a single "convergence club" is investigated.

Margaritis et al. (2007) conducted a similar study to that of Färe et al. (2006) and developed it further. In the productivity and convergence analysis of OECD countries between 1979 and 2002 by Margaritis et al. (2007), which is one of the most comprehensive studies concerning productivity and convergence among OECD countries, various tests are applied using the time series method as well as σ and β calculation techniques. Afterwards, the analysis is extended to 1960 by developing the field of series, confirming convergence for the OECD countries. In another study conducted among OECD countries by using the β convergence test by Maudos et al. (2000), labor productivity convergence was investigated. Following a range of analyses, the existence of convergence between labor productivity and the relevant countries is observed; however, the level of convergence was low.

In another study, in which a different methodology is used to analyze growth and convergence in OECD countries (Yörük and Zaim 2005), factor productivities measured using the Malmquist index (MI) and the Malmquist Luamberger index are examined. Lee (2009) also examines time series properties of long-run productivity convergence of 25 sample countries between 1975 and 2004 by performing panel unit-root procedure.

Chen and Yu (2014) included not only OECD countries but some other country categories as well in order to increase the number of countries in the study. They studied the total factor productivity of 99 countries. Their study examines the capital-using/labor-saving, capital-using/energy-saving, and energy using/labor-saving tendencies of the countries. Their findings suggest that most of the countries profit from advantages of technological innovation. Madsen (2007) examines the imports of technology and total productivity in OECD countries between 1870 and 2004. The study focuses on the transmission of knowledge through trading among the relevant countries over a period of 135 years. His findings prove that patent flows and information reflections among countries complicate convergence. Rivera-Batiz and Romer's (1991) study on the internal growth approach state that R&D information obtained as a result of trade between developed nations is reflected in such countries by means of a trade route and consequently affects TFP and increases productivity.

There are some studies that investigate convergence on an industrial basis. Shestalova's (2003) study examines the productivity of the manufacturing sectors of 11 OECD countries between 1970 and 1990; the findings of the study suggest that only the chemical industry showed strong convergence levels.

The relationship between technology transfer and convergence in developed and developing economies is a widely discussed topic as well. Given that sufficient technological transfers are not provided, it might be difficult for developing countries to catch up with developed economies. With respect to technological catch-up and capital deepening, it is essential to emphasize the thesis by Kumar and Russell (2002) that states that technological development is not detached. In other words, convergence leads to contrary divergence.

3 Methodology

Debreu (1951), Koopmans (1951), and Farrell (1957) are prominent scholars who apply the analysis of efficiency in economic literature and a great deal of research concerning efficiency measurement has been conducted following their work. Use of the frontier function has grown into a significant part of efficiency measurement.

3.1 Malmquist Index

MI is one of the indices investigating change in production (Malmquist 1953). Applied in the DEA of Caves et al. (1982), the index comprises of different functions which stand for multi-output and multi-input technologies that are based on input and output amounts. In short MI, which is defined as CCD with the names of these authors, is the indexing of amounts in terms of distance functions.

Linear programming methods of database studies (Charnes et al. 1978) could be used in productivity performance with regards to DEA. According to Cooper et al. (2011), the combination of the studies of Färe et al. (1992, 1994a, b), Farrell (1957), Charnes et al. (1978), and Caves et al. (1982) a DEA estimation method is presented for Malmquist productivity index.

According to Färe et al. (1994b) in S^t production technology, $t = 1 \ldots T$ for each period, output based MI, which indicates the productivity change, models the conversion of inputs $x^t \in R_+^N$ to outputs $y^t \in R_+^M$. It is described as $S^t = [(x^t, y^t) : x^t \; can\, produce\, y^t]$. Output distance function defined in "t" period (Färe 1988) is as follows:

$$D_o(x^t, y^t) = \inf[\theta : (x^t, y^t/\theta) \in S^t] \tag{1}$$

This function defines x^t inputs and maximum output y^t vector. This function is first-degree homogeneous and its value is ≤ 1. If the technology is over the frontier, $D_o(x^t, y^t) = 1$. According to Farrell (1957) this situation indicates technical change. A similar description could be made for t + 1 period as well.

Output-based CCD-type Malmquist productivity change index is the geometric mean of MI;

$$M_o\left(x^{t+1}, y^{t+1}, x^t, y^t\right) = \left[\frac{D_o^t\left(x^{t+1}, y^{y+1}\right)}{D_o^t\left(x^t, y^t\right)} \frac{D_o^{t+1}\left(x^{t+1}, y^{t+1}\right)}{D_o^{t+1}\left(x^t, y^t\right)}\right]^{0.5} \tag{2}$$

This index can be written in two different ways:

$$M_o\left(x^{t+1}, y^{t+1}, x^t, y^t\right) = \overbrace{\frac{D_o^{t+1}\left(x^{t+1}, y^{t+1}\right)}{D_o^t\left(x^t, y^t\right)}}^{EC} \overbrace{\left[\left(\frac{D_o^t\left(x^{t+1}, y^{y+1}\right)}{D_o^{t+1}\left(x^{t+1}, y^{t+1}\right)}\right)\left(\frac{D_o^t\left(x^t, y^t\right)}{D_o^{t+1}\left(x^t, y^t\right)}\right)\right]^{0.5}}^{TC} \tag{3}$$

The part of index outside the brace indicates proportional efficiency change between two periods, and the index inside the brace indicates technical change. This equation can be defined in two parts as follows:

$$Efficiency\,Change\,(EC) = \frac{D_o^{t+1}\left(x^{t+1}, y^{t+1}\right)}{D_o^t\left(x^t, y^t\right)} \tag{4}$$

$$Technical\,Change\,(TC) = \left[\left(\frac{D_o^t\left(x^{t+1}, y^{y+1}\right)}{D_o^{t+1}\left(x^{t+1}, y^{t+1}\right)}\right)\left(\frac{D_o^t\left(x^t, y^t\right)}{D_o^{t+1}\left(x^t, y^t\right)}\right)\right]^{0.5} \tag{5}$$

If there is a need to express it briefly, MI is defined as;

$$M_o^{t,t+1} = EC^{t,t+1}\,TC^{t,t+1} \tag{6}$$

In this study, for each t period, (here t = 2000, . . ., 2012), for each k = 1, . . ., K country (34 OECD countries including recently joined ones) two inputs and one output are used.

3.2 Convergence

The lack of convergence across countries is an unusual finding as it suggests that cross-country income equality tends to increase and that countries that are projected to be richer a few decades from now are the same countries that are rich today. This finding is not compatible with widely accepted neoclassical growth theories (Solow 1956; Swan 1956; Cass 1965; Koopmans 1965).

The idea behind the abovementioned conclusion is the following: the assumption of diminishing returns to capital implicit in the neoclassical production function predicts that the rate of return to capital is quite large when the stock of capital is small and vice versa. If countries only differ in terms of their initial levels of capital then, according to neoclassical growth model, which indicates cross-country beta-convergence, countries with little capital will be poor and will grow faster than rich countries.

This anticipation is not compatible with the endogenous growth model (Romer 1986). Such models depend on the existence of externalities, increasing returns, and the lack of inputs that cannot be accumulated. The fundamental point of such models is the lack of diminishing returns to capital, so these models do not exhibit similarities with the neoclassical model in terms of convergence.

When analyzing convergence, the studies by Barro et al. (1991), Mankiw et al. (1992), Barro and Sala-i-Martin (1995), and Sala-i-Martin (1996a) are usually referred to by economists. The concepts of β-convergence and σ-convergence are prevalent in classical economic growth literature.

If poor economies tend to grow faster than wealthy ones then there is β-convergence. In other words, a negative relationship between the growth rate of income per capita and the initial level of income suggests β-convergence in a cross-section of economies. That concept of convergence is usually mistaken for **σ**-convergence as the dispersion of real per capita income across groups of economies tends to fall over time. These two concepts examine conceptually different phenomena: **σ**-convergence studies the distribution of income over time and β-convergence studies the mobility of income within the same distribution. Despite the differences, these two convergences are related. Suppose that β-convergence holds for a group of regions i, where $i = 1 \ldots N$. In a given time period, which likely corresponds to annual data, the real per capita income for economy i can be approximated[1] by

$$\log(y_{it}) = \alpha + (1 - \beta)\log\left(y_{i,t-1}\right) + u_{it} \tag{7}$$

where α and β are constants, with $0 < \beta < 1$, and u_i is a disturbance term. The condition $\beta > 0$ suggests β-convergence since the annual growth rate $\log(y_{it}/y_{i,t-1})$ is inversely related to the $\log(y_{i,t-1})$. A higher coefficient β indicates a greater tendency for convergence. The disturbance term captures temporary shocks to the production function, the saving rate, and so on. We assume that u_{it} has a mean of zero, the same variance, $\boldsymbol{\sigma}_u^2$, for all economies, and is independent of time and different economies.

If β-convergence holds ($\beta > 0$), then $\boldsymbol{\sigma}_t^2$ monotonically approaches its steady-state value ($\boldsymbol{\sigma}^{2*}$). The key point is that $\boldsymbol{\sigma}_t^2$ can rise or decline towards the steady-state depending on whether the initial value of $\boldsymbol{\sigma}^2$ is above or below the steady-state.

[1]The value of β coefficient is calculated using Barro et al. (1991) and Barro and Sala-i-Martin's (1992) approach. $\frac{1}{T}\log\left(y_i/y_{i,t-T}\right) = x^* + \log\left(\widehat{y}^*{}_i/\widehat{y}_{i,t-T}\right)\left(1 - e^{-\beta T}\right)/T + u_{it}$

In this equation, i represents economy, t represents time, y_{it} represents output per capita, x^* represents the steady state grow rate per capita, $\widehat{y}_{it}$ is output per active labour, $\widehat{y}^*_{it}$ is steady–state output level per active labour, and T is the observation interval. Inspired by this equation, we have achieved some results by adding other variables to the panel regression.

above average in 1965 to below average by 1998. Ireland showed the most dramatic productivity improvements in the sample.

In Krüger's (2003) study, which included OECD countries as well, the universal effect of productivity deceleration is indicated by the comparison of the sub-periods 1960–1973 and 1973–1990. With regards to TFP after 1973, not only TPF but also labor productivity measures decline in the majority of country groups, apart from in Asia. In particular, the fact that the deceleration affects the technological progress ratios indicates that all parts of the frontier function at least stagnate after 1973. When it comes to the positive side, there exists remarkable efficiency development keeping up in all country groups following 1973; however, getting behind movements was extensive before. The low level increase, which is not even 1%, in the TFP in the OECD countries following 2000 coincides with the abovementioned study's findings.

Table 2 represents the annual efficiency changes of the relevant countries. From this dynamic analysis, it is seen that *tfpch* is above one for 5 years but below one for 7 years. In other words, TFP decreased for 7 years within the 13 year-period in comparison to the reference year. TFP increased by 10.8% in the period of 2008/2009. In fact, the technical change value for the same period reached the highest value of all with an increase of 14%. We can conclude that the rise of TFP results from Technical Change. When Technical Change is considered to be positive for only 3 years, it is found that the period of 2008/2009 navigates in remarkably high levels.

In the Table, *sech* navigates above one for 8 years. It can be understood that the most efficient of efficiency changes is *sech*. Furthermore, when the mean value is observed, it presents the highest growth of an average increase of 2.3%. In a study supporting the increase in TFP, Danquah et al. (2014) listed the variables increasing TFP for the OECD countries. According to this study, investment price, consumption share, trade openness, and the labor force are robustly correlated to TFP growth. In the study by Färe et al. (2006), labor and multi-factor productivity

Table 2 Changes in efficiency scores

Years	efch	techch	pech	sech	tfpch
2000/2001	0.900	1.120	1.033	0.872	1.008
2001/2002	1.063	0.958	1.005	1.057	1.018
2002/2003	1.048	0.946	0.992	1.056	0.992
2003/2004	0.994	0.991	0.999	0.995	0.985
2004/2005	1.011	0.962	0.983	1.029	0.973
2005/2006	1.031	0.945	1.006	1.025	0.975
2006/2007	1.067	0.918	1.017	1.049	0.979
2007/2008	1.046	0.970	0.995	1.051	1.014
2008/2009	0.968	1.145	1	0.968	1.108
2009/2010	1.136	0.903	0.996	1.141	1.025
2010/2011	0.955	1.028	0.968	0.987	0.981
2011/2012	0.985	1.012	0.979	1.005	0.996
mean	1.015	0.989	0.992	1.023	1.004

improved for most of the countries in their sample. Portugal showed dramatic improvements (largely due to capital deepening) until the 1990s, when it started a sharp decline.

Table 3 presents certain different results regarding the OECD countries. The percent change in real physical capital per worker (grpc) and mean percentage of change for 13 years are given in the table ($grpc_{13}$). Similarly, *grpk* indicates the percentage of change in real human capital per worker, and *ggdp* indicates the mean percentage of change of real GDP per worker. The digit 13, added to the values, indicates mean percentages of change over 13 years. The findings of the table indicate that 12 countries incurred losses of physical capital per worker and the others increased this ratio within 13 years. Spain, Portugal, and Greece, the latter of which has shown signs of serious economic constriction in recent years, incurred losses of physical capital. However, according to the table, some countries such as Iceland, Japan, and even Germany, England, and the Netherlands suffer from the same situation. At the same time, the increases of physical capital per worker are the highest in the countries like Poland, Hungary, the Czech and Slovak Republics, and Estonia among former Soviet Union countries. The increase in Estonia is particularly high. We can conclude that Scandinavian countries and Turkey are among the countries that increased their physical capital significantly. Estonia, Chile, and Turkey are the top three countries to have increased their physical capital per worker within the given period.

In the same table, different results are seen upon the examination of human capital. According to the data, it is understood that only four countries (Luxembourg, Canada, Israel, and Sweden) incurred losses of human capital per worker during the time period. Although this is a low ratio, it is noteworthy. The digit is negative only for Italy and Luxembourg when we examine *ggdp* among countries. The relevant data for Israel is below one (<1). A decrease exists in both *grpk* and *ggdp* for Luxemburg; it is a low level, however. As seen in Table 1, while mean TPF values of Luxembourg and Canada are below one, it does not show any changes in Israel.

Figure 1 indicates the growth (y) of three countries that increased their physical capital the most and those that lost their human capital. Growth rates of five countries in 2009, except for Israel, are negative as a common feature. However, the growth in 2001 is negative only for Israel and Turkey. In general, growth trends of the three countries incurring losses of human capital navigate below those of the other three countries. Low growth rates might have decreased the attraction to these countries.

4.2 Convergence

Convergence is the approximation of two economies in terms of growth. According to technological innovation theory, diffusion is one of the ways that innovation is transformative. Innovation in a developed nation can spread to developing nations.

Table 3 Changes in variables over the investigated period

Countries	grpc	grpk	ggdp	$grpc_{13}$	$grpk_{13}$	$ggdp_{13}$
Australia	54.61	73.03	12.90	4.20	5.62	0.99
Austria	−4.35	59.54	8.69	−0.33	4.58	0.67
Belgium	4.72	22.27	7.46	0.36	1.71	0.57
Canada	32.73	−4.23	6.18	2.52	−0.33	0.48
Czech Republic	23.81	119.30	36.02	1.83	9.18	2.77
Denmark	−0.59	27.50	4.97	−0.05	2.12	0.38
Estonia	84.47	435.35	47.22	6.50	33.49	3.63
Finland	8.19	20.77	13.76	0.63	1.60	1.06
France	6.43	14.43	7.42	0.49	1.11	0.57
Germany	−7.91	25.48	4.20	−0.61	1.96	0.32
Hungary	20.99	93.90	20.40	1.61	7.22	1.57
Ireland	−37.36	78.47	19.58	−2.87	6.04	1.51
Italy	−18.65	14.75	−5.74	−1.43	1.13	−0.44
Luxembourg	8.05	−19.68	−8.80	0.62	−1.51	−0.68
Netherlands	−11.60	18.84	6.65	−0.89	1.45	0.51
New Zealand	23.08	53.88	9.27	1.78	4.14	0.71
Norway	32.17	145.05	5.74	2.47	11.16	0.44
Poland	31.06	103.88	46.00	2.39	7.99	3.54
Portugal	−33.18	127.79	10.87	−2.55	9.83	0.84
Slovak Republic	42.32	100.39	57.75	3.26	7.72	4.44
Spain	−15.30	55.74	8.68	−1.18	4.29	0.67
Turkey	83.39	211.88	62.07	6.41	16.3	4.77
United Kingdom	−6.69	6.25	10.19	−0.51	0.48	0.78
United States	0.35	26.00	18.2	0.03	2.00	1.40
Sweden	25.49	−1.48	14.82	1.96	−0.11	1.14
Switzerland	−1.73	20.96	5.12	−0.13	1.61	0.39
Japan	−11.38	25.12	12.03	−0.88	1.93	0.93
Mexico	9.61	25.46	−0.01	0.74	1.96	0.00
Korea	17.12	158.65	36.26	1.32	12.20	2.79
Chile	88.28	24.26	21.00	6.79	1.87	1.62
Slovenia	12.76	135.52	23.74	0.98	10.42	1.83
Israel	0.86	−1.66	0.96	0.07	−0.13	0.07
Iceland	−32.65	17.99	19.34	−2.51	1.38	1.49
Greece	−24.97	35.41	14.21	−1.92	2.72	1.09

Thus, developing countries stimulate economic growth, which enables them to converge with developed economies (Abramovitz 1986).

Changes in the logarithm of real GDP per worker (dlgdp), TFP (tfpch), and efficiency (efch) variables are used in β-convergence tests. The values in the first row of Table 4 indicate that the F statistic is significant according to *dlgdp* estimation and the model is significant. On the other hand, the Durbin-Watson

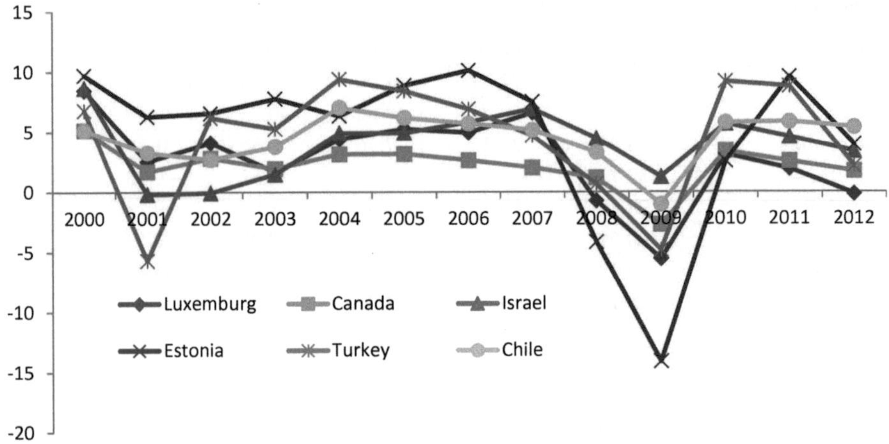

Fig. 1 Growth trends of the three best and three worst OECD countries

Table 4 Regressions for β-convergence

Variable	Coefficient	Std. Error	t-Statistic	Prob.
Dependent Variable[a]: dlgdp				
LGDP	−0.284258	0.044992	−6.318024	0.0000
C	3.240360	0.490573	6.605261	0.0000
R-squared	0.555045			
F-statistic	39.91743	Durbin-Watson stat		2.592135
Prob(F-statistic)	0.000000			
Dependent Variable: tfpch				
LGDP	0.007195	0.009040	0.795879	0.4320
C	0.925708	0.098570	9.391407	0.0000
R-squared	0.019410			
F-statistic	0.633424	Durbin-Watson stat		1.850105
Prob(F-statistic)	0.431967			
Dependent Variable: efch				
LGDP	0.005306	0.009153	0.579705	0.5662
C	0.957472	0.099796	9.594301	0.0000
R-squared	0.010393			
F-statistic	0.336058	Durbin-Watson stat		1.605166
Prob(F-statistic)	0.566173			

[a]# of observations is 34

value, which represents autocorrelation, is acceptable. The β-convergence value for *dlgdp* is significant with a significance level of 1%, which indicates convergence.

Nevertheless it is not possible to arrive at a similar conclusion for the dependent variables tfpch (in the second row) and efch (in the last row). β-convergence values

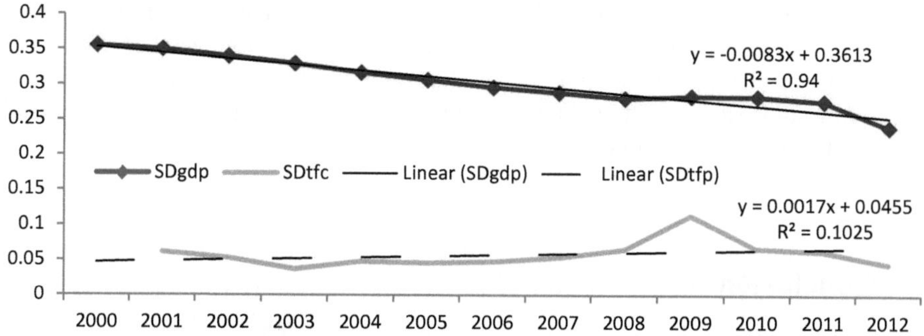

Fig. 2 Standard deviations of the GDP and TFP

in both estimations are not statistically insignificant and it is hard to say whether these variables cause convergence or divergence.

The following Fig. 2 provides enough information on σ-convergence. As stated before σ-convergence indicates income dispersion. However, β-convergence is a must for the relevant dispersion. Thus it is stated that the cross-section regression analysis above has β-convergence, yet the same result could not be achieved for TFP and EFC variables. The figure indicates that standard deviation of log GDP per worker (SDgdp) follows a negative pattern. The same dispersion can be seen in the regression equation and the inclination of the graphic. On the other hand, standard deviation of log TFP (SDtfp) value does not show similar tendencies. Even though it is not readily apparent, the curve deviates dramatically in 2009 and tends to decline following this period. Linear regression values present slightly positive parameter values.

It is useful to remember Kumar and Russell (2002), who suggest a different thesis regarding convergence. The authors criticized the empirical studies of convergence by stating that the technological progress was not unbiased in their study, and they emphasized that convergence was only found among developed countries in the production frontier on the world scale by using intensive capital-including technologies. That is out of the question for countries with lower incomes. Only developed nations benefit from technological innovations. The study analyzed 57 countries. As all the OECD countries do not benefit from the same technological innovations and they do not have similar income levels, we should not expect to find convergence in our study.

Sondermann (2014) obtained some results by using a time series in convergence analysis of Eurozone countries. In his study, he investigated the agriculture, service, and manufacturing sectors and their sub divisions and tested convergences in the relevant sectors. According to his results, convergence is observed in few sectors and no average convergence is observed. For example, while convergence is observed in agriculture, transportation, and nonmarket services between 1970 and 1998, no convergence is observed for total economies.

The findings of Färe et al. (2006) on convergence in OECD countries is that cross-section results support convergence in principle, although when they take advantage of the decomposition of productivity into technical change, capital deepening and catch-up, they find that technical change (especially input biased technical change) is a source of divergence.

5 Conclusion

In our study, productivity and convergence of the OECD countries between 2000 and 2012 are examined in 34 countries. The gross domestic product of Chile increased 4.5% over 13 years, ranking second among member countries. After ranking first among the member countries, Estonia experienced severe economic shrinkage in 2008 and 2009. Four countries with the lowest performance experienced fluctuations over 13 years and tended to exhibit stagnation towards the end of the study period. The average growth rate of OECD countries over 13 years is 1.87%, whereas the average growth rate of Denmark is below one. Switzerland is a striking example because the growth rate of the country is around 4% in the beginning of the study period but drops to 1.1% in the end.

TFP, which is calculated in geometric means, showed an increase of 4%. While TPF values of 22 countries increased in comparison to reference year, those of 12 countries decreased within the given period. A substantial part of the increase results from scale efficiency change (sech). Furthermore, it is observed that TFP is above one for 5 years, but below one for 7 years. In other words, TFP decreased for 7 years in comparison to the reference year over 13 years. In the period of 2008/2009, TFP increased by 10.8%. The technical change value for the same period reached the highest value of all with an increase of 14%. We can conclude that the high level of TFP results from Technical Change. In order to investigate the presence of convergence among the OECD countries, it is determined that standard deviations of TFP logarithmic values do not indicate regular decline. In addition, conditional β value is found to be above zero and significant in the panel regression analyses carried out using both TFP values and logarithmic values of GDP per worker. According to these results, no convergence occurs in the OECD countries in the model where capital per worker and human capital per worker are used as inputs.

Changes in logarithm of GDP per worker, TFP, and efficiency variables are used to test the β-convergence and σ-convergence in OECD countries. A cross-sectional regression analysis of *dlgdp* indicates that the β value is negative and significant. However, we could not arrive at a similar conclusion for *tfpch* and *efch* variables, the β values of which were not significant. We can conclude that these variables show divergence rather than convergence. The graphic illustration of σ-convergence shows that the standard deviation of the *dlgdp* variable tends to be downwards and negative in the study period.

At the same time, the graphic illustration of σ-convergence indicates that the standard deviations of *dlgdp* (SDgdp) variable in the study period tend to be downwards and negative. However, we cannot make similar observations for the standard deviations of logTFP (SDtfp). Total Factor Productivity does not seem to have any impact on σ-convergence or β-convergence.

The average annual growth rate of some OECD countries is around 4.5% while the relevant figure is reported to be 0.5% for Portugal and Greece. Such a difference is expected to have a negative impact on convergence. Likewise, the difference between top 10% and bottom 10% is 7% in 1980s, while the figure is almost 10% in 2012 which indicates an unequal distribution of income.

In general, Latin America and Eastern European countries, (including Turkey), which participated in OECD community later, have more efficient indications in comparison to other countries. A noteworthy detail is that human capital per worker loss occurs in countries such as Canada, Luxembourg, and Sweden, which have considerably highly-qualified labor and high incomes, and in Israel, where political unrest and fear of war is always on the agenda.

References

Abramovitz, M. (1986). Catching up, forging ahead, and falling behind. *Journal of Economic History, 46*(2), 385–406.

Barro, R. J., & Sala-i-Martin, X. (1992). Convergence. *Journal of Political Economy, 100*(2), 223–251.

Barro, R. J., & Sala-i-Martin, X. (1995). *Economic growth*. Cambridge, MA: MIT Press.

Barro, R. J., Sala-i-Martin, X., Blanchard, O. J., & Hall, R. E. (1991). Convergence across states and regions. *Brookings Papers on Economic Activity, 1991*(1), 107–182.

Cass, D. (1965). Optimum growth in an aggregative model of capital accumulation. *Review of Economic Studies, 32*, 233–240.

Caves, D. W., Christensen, L. R., & Diewert, W. E. (1982). The economic theory of index numbers and the measurement of input, output, and productivity. *Econometrica, 50*(6), 1393–1414.

Charnes, A., Cooper, W. W., & Rhodes, E. (1978). Measuring the efficiency of decision making units. *European Journal of Operational Research, 2*, 429–444.

Chen, P. C., & Yu, M. M. (2014). Total factor productivity growth and directions of technical change bias: Evidence from 99 OECD and non-OECD countries. *Annals of Operations Research, 214*(1), 143–165.

Cooper, W. W., Seiford, L. M., & Zhu, J. (Eds.). (2011). *Handbook on data envelopment analysis* (2nd ed.). New York: Springer.

Danquah, M., Enrique, M. B., & Bazoumana, O. (2014). TFP growth and its determinants: A model averaging approach. *Empirical Economics, 47*(1), 227–251.

Debreu, G. (1951). The coefficient of resource utilization. *Econometrica, 19*(3), 273–292.

Dowrick, S., & Nguyen, D. T. (1989). OECD comparative economic growth 1950-85: Catch-up and convergence. *The American Economic Review, 79*(5), 1010–1030.

Färe, R. (1988). *Fundamentals of production theory*. Heidelberg: Springer.

Färe, R., Grosskopf, S., Lindgren, B., & Roos, P. (1992). Productivity changes in Swedish pharmacies 1980–1989: A non-parametric Malmquist approach. *Journal of Productivity Analysis, 3*(1–2), 85–101.

Färe, R., Grosskopf, S., Lindgren, B., & Roos, P. (1994a). Productivity developments in Swedish hospitals: A Malmquist output index approach. In A. Charnes, W. W. Cooper, A. Y. Lewin, & L. M. Seiford (Eds.), *Data envelopment analysis: Theory, methodology and applications* (pp. 253–272). Norwell, MA: Springer.

Färe, R., Grosskopf, S., Norris, M., & Zhang, Z. (1994b). Productivity growth, technical progress, and efficiency change in industrialized countries. *The American Economic Review, 84*(1), 66–83.

Färe, R., Grosskopf, S., & Dimitri, M. (2006). Productivity growth and convergence in the European Union. *Journal of Productivity Analysis, 25*(1), 111–141.

Farrell, M. J. (1957). The measurement of productive efficiency. *Journal of the Royal Statistical Society, 120*(3), 253–281.

Koopmans, T. C. (1951). An analysis of production as an efficient combination of activities. In T. C. Koopmans (Ed.), *Activity analysis of production and allocation* (pp. 33–97). New York: Wiley.

Koopmans, T. C. (1965). *On the concept of optimal economic growth in The Econometric Approach to Development Planning*. Amsterdam: North Holland.

Krüger, J. J. (2003). The global trends of total factor productivity: Evidence from the non-parametric Malmquist index approach. *Oxford Economic Papers, 55*(2), 265–286.

Kumar, S., & Russell, R. R. (2002). Technological change, technological catch-up, and capital deepening: Relative contributions to growth and convergence. *The American Economic Review, 92*(3), 527–548.

Lee, J. (2009). Trade, FDI, and productivity convergence: A dynamic panel data approach in 25 countries. *Japan and the World Economy, 21*(3), 226–238.

Madsen, J. B. (2007). Technology spillover through trade and TFP convergence: 135 years of evidence for the OECD countries. *Journal of International Economics, 72*(2), 464–480.

Malmquist, S. (1953). Index numbers and indifference surfaces. *Trabajos de Estatistica, 4*, 209–242.

Mankiw, N. G., Romer, D., & Weil, D. N. (1992). A contribution to the empirics of economic growth. *Quarterly Journal of Economics, 107*(2), 407–437.

Margaritis, D., Färe, R., & Grosskopf, S. (2007). Productivity, convergence and policy: A study of OECD countries and industries. *Journal of Productivity Analysis, 28*(1-2), 87–105.

Maudos, J., Pastor, J. M., & Serrano, L. (2000). Convergence in OECD countries: Technical change, efficiency and productivity. *Applied Economics, 32*(6), 757–765.

Rivera-Batiz, L. A., & Romer, P. M. (1991). International trade with endogenous technological change. *European Economic Review, 35*(4), 971–1001.

Romer, P. M. (1986). Increasing returns and long run growth. *Journal of Political Economy, 94*(5), 1002–1037.

Sala-i-Martin, X. (1996a). Regional cohesion: Evidence and theories of regional growth and convergence. *European Economic Review, 40*(6), 1325–1352.

Sala-i-Martin, X. (1996b). The classical approach to convergence analysis. *The Economic Journal, 106*(437), 1019–1036.

Shestalova, V. (2003). Sequential Malmquist indices of productivity growth: An application to OECD industrial activities. *Journal of Productivity Analysis, 19*, 211–226.

Solow, R. M. (1956). A contribution to the theory of economic growth. *Journal of Economics, 70* (1), 65–94.

Sondermann, D. (2014). Productivity in the euro area: Any evidence of convergence? *Empirical Economics., 47*(3), 999–1027.

Swan, T. W. (1956). Economic growth and capital accumulation. *Economic Record, 32*(2), 334–361.

Yörük, B. K., & Zaim, O. (2005). Productivity growth in OECD countries: A comparison with Malmquist indices. *Journal of Comparative Economics, 33*(2), 401–420.

Estimating the Value of the Honolulu Rail Transit Project: A Semiparametric Analysis of Property Values on Oahu, HI

Peiyong Yu and Jason Levy

Abstract This study assesses the impact of proximity to the Honolulu Rail Transit (HRT) on the single-family and condo values on Oahu, Hawaii. The data includes more than 32,000 single family homes and 47,000 condos between 2006 and 2015. In this paper, when semiparametric model using too large bandwidth, the results are not as rigorous as the fixed effects model with 130 controlled groups. The results indicate that after the ground-breaking event for HRT, the island-wide single family housing prices increase by 4%, but the condo values decrease by 4%; there are very slight positive distance spillover effects for single family housing market: houses located one mile closer to the HRT areas, the housing prices increase by 0.6%, however, this slight positive impact is at the costs of local housing values: for homes located within a 0.5 mile radius of the future HRT line, their values drop by 7.1%, for homes located between a 0.5 and 1 mile radius of the future HRT line, their values drop by 4.1%, and for homes located between a 1 and 2 mile radius of the future HRT line, their values drop by 2.1%. These negative local effects disappear after the 2 mile radius distance.

Keywords Honolulu Rail Transit (HRT) • Fixed effects model • Property values • Semiparametric model

1 Introduction

Oahu's notorious traffic congestion, limited land mass, growing population and attempts to diversify the economy require innovative public transit solution to promote the state of Hawaii's plans for sustainable growth. The America's first fully driverless rail transit project is currently under construction in Oahu, Hawaii:

P. Yu
Department of Economics, University of Hawaii – West Oahu, Kapolei, HI, USA
e-mail: pyu@hawaii.edu

J. Levy (✉)
Department of Public Administration, University of Hawaii – West Oahu, Kapolei, HI, USA
e-mail: jlevy@hawaii.edu

M.H. Bilgin et al. (eds.), *Empirical Studies on Economics of Innovation, Public Economics and Management*, Eurasian Studies in Business and Economics 6,
DOI 10.1007/978-3-319-50164-2_16

Honolulu Rail Transit (HRT) project, also known as the Honolulu High-Capacity Transit Corridor Project. By 2030, nearly 70% of Oahu's population and more than 80% of the island's jobs will be located along the 20-mile rail corridor (HART 2015) with stops in downtown Honolulu, Waikiki beach, at three University of Hawaii system campuses, Aloha Stadium, the Honolulu International Airport and several shopping centers including Ala Moana. However, the project is controversial. Pro rail advocates argue that rail constitutes an essential component of Hawaii's sustainable future initiatives and transit-oriented, high density, mixed use development plans since rail transit is expected to provide convenient access to the Central Business District (CBD), employment locations, commercial centers, schools, parks, and other recreational opportunities. Supporters note that rail will reduce traffic congestion along the 20-mile corridor; connect major residential areas with primary job centers; alleviate substantial traffic issues affecting the state's most populous urban region; as well as provide a reliable transportation alternative for visitors and commuters in southern Oahu. For example, the rail could provide a convenient means to get to work, school or home as well as attend special events (including Aloha Stadium sporting events and concerts at the Blaisdell Center) without the hassles of parking and traffic. On the other hand, those against the HRT feel that an above-ground rail system is not cost-effective (the project already overbudget and behind schedule) and will exacerbate traffic congestion and pollution.

The controversy over the rail line was a key issue in local politics in the 2008 Honolulu elections and resulted in a city charter amendment which left the final decision to the citizens of Oahu. Construction on the HRT began on February 22, 2011 after the amendment passed with 53% of voters in favor. This paper examines whether homeowners are willing to pay a premium to be close to the future HRT line and whether or not the single family housing values and condo values change in proximity to the HRT. It is expected that any economic benefits which accrue from HRT should be capitalized into the price of nearby homes or condo values. Since the HRT is currently under construction—the initial section of the rail transit system, from Kapolei to Aloha Stadium, is slated to open in 2018; and the entire system, from Kapolei to Ala Moana Center, is set to be fully operational in 2019—the impact of the partially completed (and not yet operational) HRT on surrounding single-family housing prices and condo values are examined after the HRT ground breaking ceremony in 2011 and after the real start of the construction work in 2014.

While many studies have investigated the economic impacts of rail station proximity on property values, this is the first to examine the impact of rail in the U.S.-affiliated Pacific Island Jurisdictions (USAPI) and the Pacific island region. Data from 2006 to 2015 is used to analyze the impact of the HRT on single-family house prices and condo values in the Oahu housing market. Hedonic pricing models are often utilized to analyze differentiated goods such as houses and cars (Rosen 1974). The differentiated products include distinct characteristics, which add or subtract from the property's overall total price according to how buyers in the market value that amenity or disamenity. This paper incorporates residential value hedonics to determine the value of both access to HRT stations under construction and other neighborhood locations, such as schools, parks, wetlands, hospitals, bus stops, ocean, farmers' markets, supermarkets, surf sites, and fire stations. To address the missing variables bias, this paper uses the dereference-in-difference (DID) fixed effects model to compare with the semiparametric models. The 32,053 single-family housing data includes 130 well-defined neighborhoods, and the 47,581 condo data includes 132 well-defined neighborhoods. Thus, the fixed effects model can help control for unobserved heterogeneities when these heterogeneities are constant over time. These constants can be removed from the data through differencing processes. The results indicate that after the ground-breaking event (in February, 2011) for HRT, the island-wide single family housing prices increase by 4% overall, but the island-wide condo values decrease by 4% overall; there are very slight positive distance spillover effects for single family housing market: houses located one mile closer to the HRT areas after the ground-breaking event, the housing prices increase by 0.6%, however, this slight positive island-wide impact is at the costs of local housing values: for homes located within a 0.5 mile radius of the future HRT line, their values drop by 7.1%, for homes located between a 0.5 and 1 mile radius of the future HRT line, their values drop by 4.1%, and for homes located between a 1 and 2 mile radius of the future HRT line, their values drop by 2.1%. These negative local effects disappear after the 2 mile radius distance. The real construction event (in March, 2014) has no significant island-wide as well as the local impact on the single-family housing market. For the condo market, there is no significant distance spillover effect after the ground-breaking event. However, condos located between a 1 and 1.5 mile radius enjoy a 9.2% value appreciation and condos located between a 1.5 and 2 mile radius enjoy a 5.4% value appreciation. After the construction began, it has slight negative distance spillover effect: for condos located one mile closer to the future HRT line, their values drop by 0.6%.

The contribution of this study to the literature is studying the first driverless rail transit system in an island economy and using both semiparametric and fixed effects model to see its impact on property values in the angles of both the periods of breaking-ground event and the real construction start.

2 Literature Review

Studies examining the relationship between the presence of the rail and house transaction have shown three very different results which can be categorized as follows: no measurable effects of rail on property values (category 1); mixed impacts of rail on property values (category 2), and positive impacts of rail on property values (category 3). In the first category, Mohammad et al. (2013) find that rail investments over time impact neither the location nor the values of property within the city. Moreover, it is shown that including property characteristics and neighborhood types in the estimation model does not change property values significantly.

In the second category, Duncan (2011) uses a hedonic price model with interaction terms and finds that the premium value associated with rail proximity is conditional upon permissive zoning arrangements and ordinances, which has a negative influence on home prices except in the area immediately surrounding rail stations. Cervero (2004) uses a simple hedonic pricing model to show that the values of multiple land parcels in different rail corridors of San Diego County appreciate, while commercial properties in some other areas accrued small or even negative capitalization benefits. Chen et al. (1998) find that the impact of light rail will negatively or ambiguously impact property values due to nuisance effects such as noise and vibrations. Chatman et al. (2012) find that the net impact of the rail on the owner occupied housing market in Southern New Jersey is neutral to slightly negative, while lower-income census tracts and small houses appear to appreciate near the rail station. Hess and Almeida (2007) find that rail impacts on residential property values in Buffalo, New York are experienced unevenly across the rail system: the proximity effects are positive in high-income station areas but negative in low-income station areas.

For the third category, a Difference-In-Differences (DID) model shows that light rail transit in Charlotte, North Carolina provides a neighborhood impact of 4% for single-family properties and 11.3% for condominiums sold within 1 mile of the rail stations (Billings 2011). And that the opening of a new rail on the Montreal (Canada) South Shore generates a location premium for houses located in the stations' vicinity as opposed to houses that do not experience any improvement in accessibility to the line (Dubé et al. 2013). Mathur and Ferrell (2013) find that the average home sale price increases by 3.2% ($21,000) for every 50% reduction in the distance between the home and the rail transit in San Jose, California. They also find that housing prices within 1/8 mile of the rail were 18.5% higher than the prices more than 1/8 mile from the line during the post-construction period, 7.3% higher during the construction period and not statistically different in the pre-construction period.

3 Study Areas

The study area is the island of Oahu in the US state of Hawaii. The study area, the HRT and the geocoded single family houses and condos are shown in Fig. 1, created by ArcMap.

This figure is created using ArcMap 10.3.1. It shows the study area of Oahu, HI. The circle dots are geocoded house addresses, the triangle dots are geocoded condo addresses, and the solid line is the Honolulu Transit Line.

Due to the highly congested transportation corridor situated between Kapolei and UH Manoa and Waikiki, a 20-mile elevated rail line featuring 21 stations is under construction to provide high-capacity rapid transit to connect West Oahu with the Honolulu International Airport continuing through downtown Honolulu with a final stop at Ala Moana Center. The Honolulu Authority for Rapid

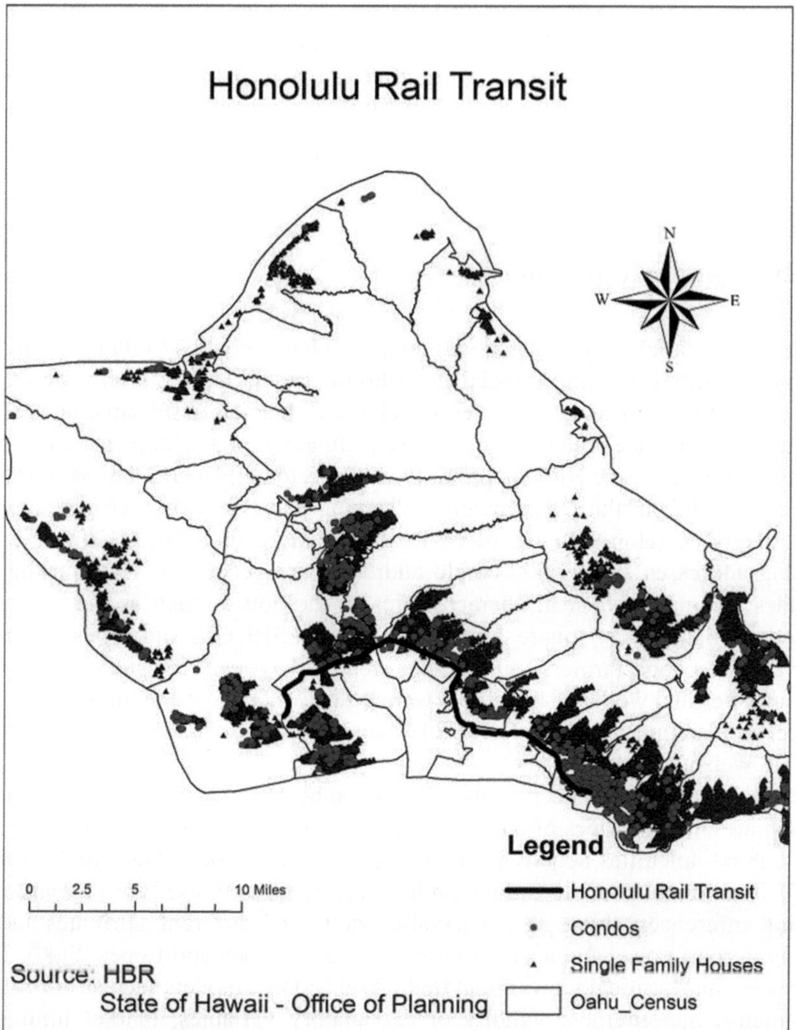

Fig. 1 Study area and Honolulu Rail Transit

Transportation (HART) unveiled its first rail column in East Kapolei in June 2012 and HART revealed that the funding of HRT comes from both local funding (0.5% surcharge on the General Excise and Use Tax paid by residents, businesses, and visitors on Oahu) and federal funding ($1.55 billion from the Federal Transit Administration). The 21 stations will pass through a 20-mile rail corridor that includes Waipahu, Pearl City, Waimalu, Aiea, and Halawa. Even though the ground-breaking event began on February 22, 2011, the real construction work started 3 years later in February, 2014. This paper investigates a number of key questions: does the ground-breaking event affect the housing market on Oahu? Does the real start of construction work affect the housing market on Oahu? And if the HRT indeed impacts property values, will the impacts occur locally or across the entire island?

4 Data and Methodology

There are 22 variables associated with housing characteristics (4 dummy variables of house qualities; 9 dummy variables of house views, and 4 dummy variables of car spaces) and 11 distance variables associated with amenities/disamenities. These distance variables are created using the 'near' function of ArcMap. The first step to assess the impact of the HRT on property values is to build a GIS database from the data collected from the Department of Planning and Permitting. Using sales data from the HBR (Honolulu Board of Realtors), more than 30,000 single family housing addresses and 47,000 condo addresses are geocoded. The housing data includes the major physical characteristics of the houses such as the number of bedrooms, bathrooms, square footage, age, etc. ESRI GIS shapefiles (including hospital, preschool, farmers' market, bus stop, park, ocean, fire station, supermarket, surf sites and wetland shapefiles) were downloaded from the State of Hawaii's Office of Planning website. The HRT shapefile is downloaded from the online ArcGIS website.

Hedonic analysis has been applied to data on heterogeneous goods in an attempt to estimate shadow prices of bundled characteristics such as housing attributes and public good amenities acquired through the housing market (Ohsfeldt and Smith 1985). Traditional hedonic estimation has been frequently used for the purpose of making inferences about non-observable values of different attributes like air quality, airport noise, and access to transportation (Espey and Lopez 2000). There have been many critical views about traditional hedonic models such as information asymmetry, measurement validity of explanatory variables, market limitations, multicollinearity and price changes. It is thus better to explore additional research designs or to use the hedonic price technique with application to other models. The hedonic pricing model is constructed based on three types of different house attributes: physical attributes, community attributes and attributes observed by the consumers but not econometricians (Bajari and Kahn 2005). These unobserved variables usually have some structural constraints associated with them and one can use these constraints to infer their values from the data (Chopra et al. 2007).

Assuming P is a vector of house prices associated with a vector of structure variables S and set of location variables N then it follows that their relationship can be represented by the following model:

$$\ln(P_i) = \beta_0 + \sum \beta_p S_{ip} + \sum \beta_q N_{iq} + \varepsilon_i \tag{1}$$

where $\ln(P_i)$ = natural logarithm of house sale price of property i; S_{ip} = physical attribute p of property i; N_{iq} = location variable q of property i; β_0, β_p, β_q = intercept and coefficients; ε_i = error. If the neighborhood feature affects house sale prices positively, the first-order relationship of house price with respect to the location variable is:

$$\partial \ln(P_i)/\partial N_{iq} < 0 \tag{2}$$

Nonparametric models offer significant advantages for hedonic price function estimation due to their functional form flexibility and spatially varying coefficients, which help to reduce spatial autocorrelation without imposing arbitrary contiguity matrices or distributional assumptions on the data (McMillen and Redfern 2010). The locally weighted regression (LWR), or *loess,* is a procedure for fitting a regression surface to data through multivariate smoothing: the dependent variable is smoothed as a function of the independent variables in a moving fashion analogous to how a moving average is computed for a time series (Cleveland and Devlin 1988). Detailed application of *loess* to the house price functions is in McMillen and Redfern (2010): let the target for the nonparametric estimator be a home with structural and locational characteristics given by the vector X. The LWR estimator is derived by minimizing the following equation with respect to α andβ:

$$\sum_{i=1}^{n} (\ln p_i - \alpha - \beta'(X_i - X))^2 K\left(\frac{X_i - X}{h}\right) \tag{3}$$

The kernel function K (z) determines the weight that each house sold as an observation in estimating the house price at target point X with $X_i - X$ defined as the distance between the target point and the ith neighboring house and h is a smoothing parameter called the bandwidth. As z increases, the weights decline. Though there are various types of kernel functions such as rectangular, triangular, bi-square, tri-cube or Gaussian, the choice of kernel weight function usually has little effect on the results. This study uses tri-cube kernel weighting function but h is more important since it determines how many observations receive positive weight when constructing the estimate and how rapidly the weights decline with distance. By replacing more weight on more distant observations, high values of h imply local regressions that produce more smoothing than do smaller bandwidths (McMillen and Redfern 2010). This helps the nonparametric part of the semiparametric model, which takes the form as:

$$\ln P_i = \beta S + m(N) + \varepsilon \tag{4}$$

where m() is the unknown smooth function with the location variables and it is estimated by a least square procedure. By including location variable whose structure is not known a priori, one may study the existence of nonlinearities.

5 Results and Discussion

The natural logarithms of single family house prices and condo prices are the dependent variables and a combination of structural and locational characteristics are the independent variables in our models. Table 1 records the parametric and semiparametric regression results for single family property values. The parametric model includes both the benchmark OLS model and DID fixed effects model. Due to the singular matrix problem when using small bandwidth for semiparametric model, this paper uses a 0.9 bandwidth for the last model. Larger bandwidth tends to over-smooth the data and produces the results that are close to the linear OLS models.

Even though the linear OLS model generates larger R-squared values, it is prone to the missing variable biases. The fixed effects model on the other hand, can get rid of the constant unobserved heterogeneities within the 130 groups in the single family housing data. For example, the linear OLS model indicates that houses located within a 1.5 and 2 mile radius of the future HRT line, the property values increase by 4.2%; this positive local impact might be affected by the missing

Table 1 Model results with dependent variable: LnsingleP (N = 32,053)

Variables	Coef.	Std. Err.	P > |t|	Coef.	Std. Err.	P > |t|	Coef.	Std. Err.	P > |t|
LnsingleP	Fixed effects model			Linear OLS model			Semiparametric		
HRT_t	0.040	0.013	**	0.017	0.017		0.018	0.016	
HRT	−0.013	0.008		0.012	0.002	***	−0.003	0.002	
DID_HRT	−0.006	0.001	***	−0.003	0.001	*	−0.003	0.001	*
HRT_0.5	−0.071	0.014	***	−0.054	0.017	**	−0.069	0.016	***
HRT_1	−0.041	0.010	***	−0.022	0.013		−0.023	0.012	
HRT_1.5	−0.021	0.010	*	0.033	0.012	**	0.033	0.012	**
HRT_2	−0.021	0.010	*	0.042	0.012	***	0.037	0.012	**
HRT_2.5	−0.014	0.009		0.016	0.011		0.010	0.010	
HRT_t1	0.012	0.013		0.020	0.017		0.008	0.017	
DID_HRT1	0.003	0.001		0.002	0.002		0.003	0.001	*
HRT1_0.5	0.015	0.019		0.003	0.024		0.006	0.023	
R squared	0.51			0.73					
# of groups	130								

Notes: *10% significance, ** 5% significance, ***1% significance variable such as the quality of the schools. The fixed effects model indicates that houses located within 1 1.5 and 2 mile radius of the future HRT line, the property values decrease by 2.1%. The semiparametric model generates very similar results as the OLS model due to its large bandwidth selection. So, this paper uses the results from the more rigorous fixed effects model.

The fixed effects model shows that after the ground-breaking event took place in 2011, the single family housing market values appreciate by 4% overall. Even though the year dummies are added in the regression taking account the annual trend, this island-wide positive impact is prone to the general positive housing market after the recent Great Recession. The HRT line produces slight positive distance spillover effect: houses located one mile closer to the line, their values appreciate by 0.6% after the ground-breaking event. However, this small positive overall effect is at the costs of local housing values: houses located with a 0.5 mile radius of the line, property values drop by 7.1%; houses located between a 0.5 and 1 mile radius of the line, property values drop by 4.1%; houses located between 1 and 2 mile radius of the line, property values drop by 2.1%; and this negative local effects disappear after the 2 mile radius distance. There is no significant effect after the construction started. In other words, the positive distance spillover effect disappeared during the construction period as well as the negative local effect. When the construction really started 3 years after the ground-breaking event overcoming many hurdles, it became a credible policy effect. People believe that the HRT line will eventually be finished and operating. This might explain the disappearing negative local effects. Figures 2 and 3 show the surface plots of the

Fig. 2 Surface Plot of single house price and distance variable across the years after ground-breaking event

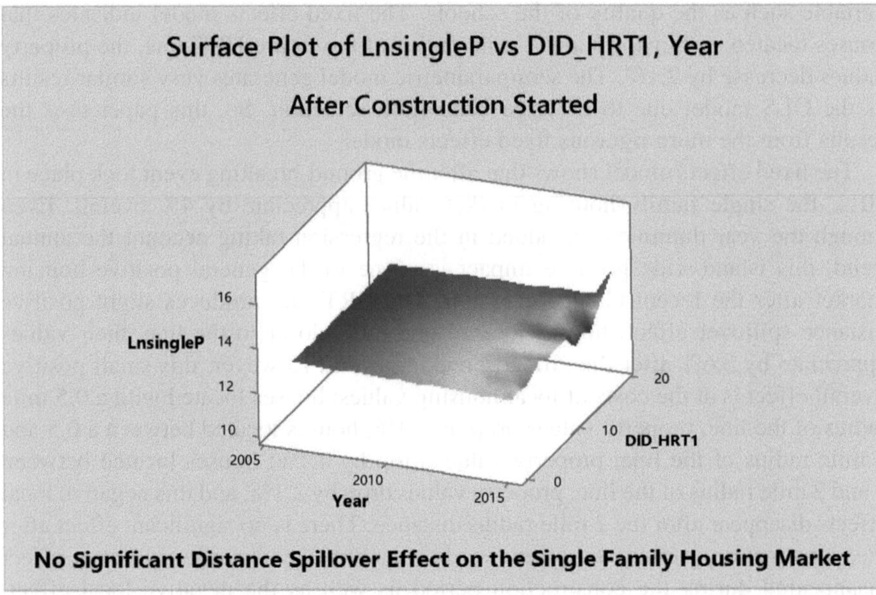

Fig. 3 Surface Plot of single house price and distance variable across the years after construction started

graphical relationship between the main distance variables '*DID_HRT*' and '*DID_HRT1*' and single family housing prices across the study periods.

For the condo market, Table 2 shows that the fixed effects model results reveal that after the construction started in 2014, the condo market values drop by 4% overall. This implies that even though the single-family housing market is getting better, the condo market is still at hot waters. Before the ground-breaking event, the planned HRT line already produces positive distance spillover effect: condos located one mile closer to the planned line, the property values increase by 7.1%, however, after the event, this significant positive effect becomes insignificant. And after the construction started, the line produces negative distance spillover effect: condos located one mile closer to the line, their values decrease by 0.6%. All these negative impacts are companied by some positive local effects: condos located between 1 and 1.5 mile radius of the line, their values increase by 9.2% and condos located between a 1.5 and 2 mile radius of the line, their values increase by 5.4%. There are no significant local effects after the construction event. Figures 4 and 5 show the surface plots of the graphical relationship between the main distance variables '*DID_HRT*' and '*DID_HRT1*' and condo prices across the study periods.

Table 2 Model results with dependent variable: LncondoP (N = 47,581)

Variables	Coef.	Std. Err.	P > |t|	Coef.	Std. Err.	P > |t|	Coef.	Std. Err.	P > |t|
LncondoP	Fixed effects model			Linear OLS model			Semiparametric		
HRT_t	−0.040	0.019	*	−0.008	0.020		−0.0003	0.021	
HRT	−0.071	0.010	***	−0.038	0.002	***	−0.055	0.003	***
DID_HRT	−0.003	0.002		−0.004	0.002	*	−0.007	0.002	***
HRT_0.5	0.024	0.015		−0.0001	0.015		−0.003	0.016	
HRT_1	0.005	0.014		−0.028	0.014	*	−0.057	0.015	***
HRT_1.5	0.092	0.014	***	0.053	0.012	***	0.030	0.015	*
HRT_2	0.054	0.014	***	0.032	0.014	*	0.003	0.015	
HRT_2.5	−0.027	0.018		0.070	0.018	***	0.092	0.019	***
HRT_t1	0.011	0.026		0.001	0.028		0.037	0.029	
DID_HRT1	0.006	0.003	*	0.007	0.003	*	0.003	0.003	
HRT1_0.5	0.022	0.025		0.030	0.027		−0.016	0.028	
R squared	0.61			0.70					
# of groups	132								

Notes: *10% significance, ** 5% significance, ***1% significance

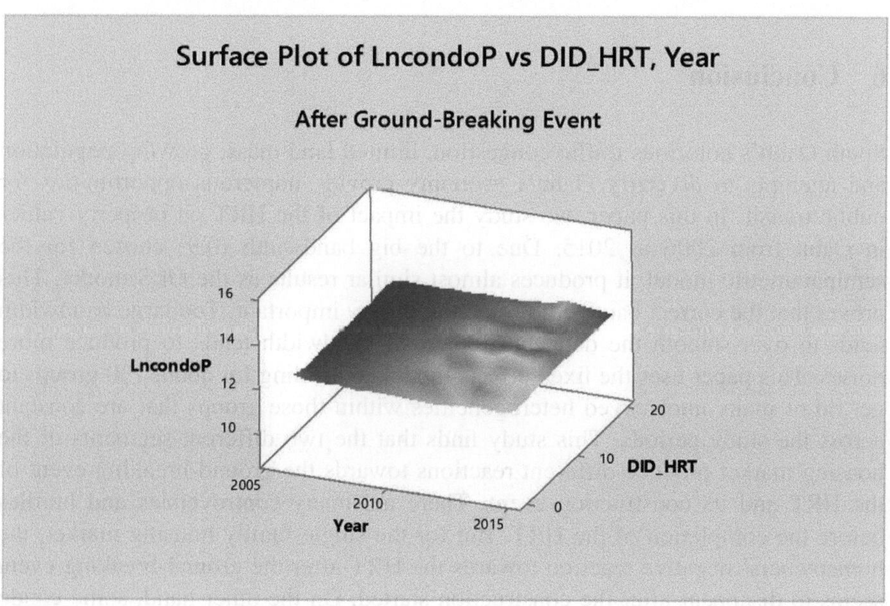

Fig. 4 Surface Plot of condo price and distance variable across the years after ground-breaking event

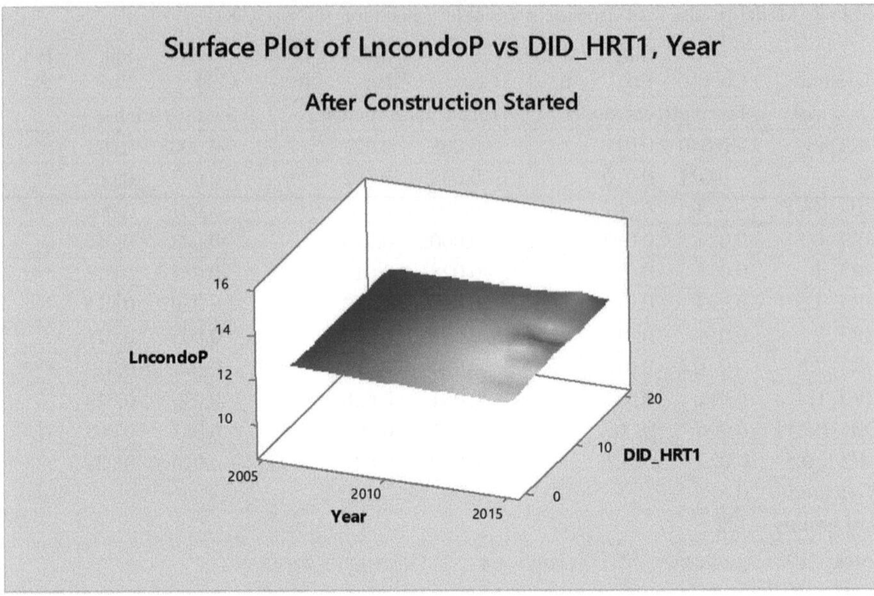

Fig. 5 Surface Plot of condo price and distance variable across the years after construction started

6 Conclusion

South Oahu's notorious traffic congestion, limited land mass, growing population and attempts to diversify Oahu's economy provide numerous opportunities for public transit. In this paper, we study the impact of the HRT on property values in Oahu from 2006 to 2015. Due to the big bandwidth (0.9) chosen for the semiparametric model, it produces almost similar results as the OLS model. This proves that the correct bandwidth selection is very important. Too large bandwidth tends to over-smooth the data, but too small bandwidth tends to produce more noises. This paper uses the fixed effects model controlling for about 130 groups to get rid of many unobserved heterogeneities within those groups that are constant across the study periods. This study finds that the two different segments of the housing market produce different reactions towards the ground-breaking event of the HRT and its construction event. There are many controversies and hurdles before the completion of the HRT. But for the single-family housing market, the homeowners' negative reaction towards the HRT after the ground-breaking event seems to disappear after the construction started. On the other hand, some condo owners' positive reaction towards the HRT after the ground-breaking event seems to disappear after the construction started. For future study, we need to do a survey to see the mentality changes between the single-family house owners and condo owners towards the two events.

References

Bajari, P., & Kahn, M. (2005). Estimating housing demand with application to explaining racial segregation in cities. *Journal of Business and Economics Statistics, 23*(1), 20–33.

Billings, S. (2011). Estimating the value of a new transit option. *Regional Science and Urban Economics, 41*(6), 525–536.

Cervero, R. (2004). Effects of light and commuter rail transit on land prices: Experiences in San Diego county. *Journal of the Transportation Research Forum, 43*(1), 121–138.

Chatman, D., Tulach, N., & Kim, K. (2012). Evaluating the economic impacts of light rail by measuring home appreciation: A first look at New Jersey's river line. *Urban Studies, 49*(3), 467–487.

Chen, H., Rufolo, A., & Dueker, K. J. (1998). Measuring the Impact of Light Rail Systems on Single-Family Home Values – a Hedonic Approach with Geographic Information System Application. *Land Use and Transportation Planning and Programming Applications, 1617*, 38–43.

Chopra, S., Trampy, T., Leahy, J., Caplin, A., & Lecun, Y. (2007). Discovering the hidden structure of house prices with a nonparametric latent manifold model. In *Proceedings of the 13th ACM SIGKDD International Conference on Knowledge Discovery and Data Mining* (pp. 173–182). New York: ACM.

Cleveland, W., & Devlin, S. (1988). Locally weighted regression: An approach to regression analysis by local fitting. *Journal of the American Statistical Association, 83*(403), 596–610.

Dubé, J., Thériault, M., & Des Rosiers, F. (2013). Commuter rail accessibility and house values: The case of the Montreal South Shore, Canada, 1992–2009. *Transportation Research Part A: Policy and Practice, 54*, 49–66.

Duncan, M. (2011). The synergistic influence of light rail stations and zoning on home prices. *Environment and Planning A, 43*(9), 2125–2142.

Espey, M., & Lopez, H. (2000). The impact of airport noise and proximity on residential property values. *Growth and Change, 31*(3), 408–419.

HART. (2015). *The rail facts—Honolulu Rail Transit*. [online] Accessed November 19, 2015, from http://www.honolulutransit.org/rail-facts.aspx

Hess, D., & Almeida, T. (2007). Impact of the proximity to light rail rapid transit on station-area property values in Buffalo, New York. *Urban Studies, 44*(5/6), 1041–1068.

Mathur, S., & Ferrell, C. (2013). Measuring the impact of sub-urban transit-oriented developments on single-family home values. *Transportation Research Part A: Policy and Practice, 47*, 42–55.

McMillen, D., & Redfern, C. (2010). Estimation and hypothesis testing for nonparametric hedonic house price functions. *Journal of Regional Science, 50*(3), 712–733.

Mohammad, S., Graham, D., Melo, P., & Anderson, R. (2013). A meta-analysis of the impact of rail projects on land and property values. *Transportation Research Part A: Policy and Practice, 50*, 158–170.

Ohsfeldt, L., & Smith, A. (1985). Estimating demand for heterogeneous goods. *The Review of Economics and Statistics, 67*(1), 165–171.

Rosen, S. (1974). Hedonic prices and implicit markets: Product differentiation in pure competition. *Journal of Political Economy, 82*(1), 34–55.

Part V
Public Economics

Solving the Cost Crisis in Healthcare: Can Poland Learn from the Kaplan and Porter's Model?

Monika Raulinajtys-Grzybek and Gertruda Krystyna Świderska

Abstract Recent publications by authors of Activity-Based Costing indicate that the cost analysis of the cycle of care is essential to reduce the growth in healthcare spending. Analysis of current situation in Poland reveals that the limit for the implementation of such solutions is the current organization of the Polish healthcare system. The aim of the article is to present the approach to calculating and controlling costs of health services used currently in Poland. This concept has been critically analyzed against the solution presented for the US health market. Analysis of primary and secondary sources describing organization of the Polish healthcare system has been conducted. Polish costing model is based on the Activity-Based Costing method. Contrary to the Kaplan and Porter's proposal, the cost calculation is conducted separately in each area of healthcare, currently mainly in relation to inpatient services. The comprehensive approach to the cost calculation of the cycle of care is not present, which results from a long-lasting division into autonomous sectors in healthcare.

Keywords Cost accounting • Activity-based costing • Value chain in healthcare • Healthcare in Poland

1 Introduction

In recent years, health expenditure in most OECD countries has been growing - both in nominal terms and in relation to Gross Domestic Product (OECD 2013). Some research proves that healthcare expenditure e.g. in the European Union is converging (Lau et al. 2014). The aging population, the development of modern and capital-intensive medical technology and increasing social expectations are among the basic reasons for the increase of expenditure (Walshe and Smith 2006; Jones and Mellett 2007; De Mello-Sampayo et al. 2013). Actions aimed at limiting the growth of spending should refer to optimization of the number of health services

M. Raulinajtys-Grzybek (✉) • G.K. Świderska
Faculty of Management Accounting, Warsaw School of Economics, Warsaw, Poland
e-mail: mrauli@sgh.waw.pl; gswide@sgh.waw.pl

M.H. Bilgin et al. (eds.), *Empirical Studies on Economics of Innovation, Public Economics and Management*, Eurasian Studies in Business and Economics 6,
DOI 10.1007/978-3-319-50164-2_17

and shift the burden of healthcare to outpatient sector, which generates lower costs than hospital sector.

An example of such steps was the introduction of diagnostic groups (Fetter et al. 1976) and pricing of health services (particularly in the inpatient sector, which historically absorbed the highest share of funds) based on their costs. Such action has been taken, among others, in Poland (Czach et al. 2011). The pricing object is every contact of the patient with the healthcare provider separately for each area of healthcare—inpatient care, outpatient care, rehabilitation etc.

Experiences of other European countries as well as American ones show that although these actions have led to changes in the expenditure structure and shifting the healthcare process on the outpatient care (OECD 2013; Averill et al. 1993; Duncan and Servais 1996). However, due to perceiving the healthcare process in a fragmentary way—as a sum of numerous independent services—the actions taken so far have only lead to optimization of single services and did not affect the whole treatment process.

The aim of the article is to analyze the possibility of applying a theoretical model invented by Kaplan and Porter (2011) for managing Polish healthcare and controlling its costs. The current organization of healthcare management in Poland, with a specific emphasis on a method of calculating and controlling costs of health services, has been presented based on the analysis of appropriate legal acts as well as secondary analysis of published sector analyses. The assumptions of the Kaplan and Porter's proposal have been presented based on their publication. The critical comparative analysis has been performed regarding the possibility of applying theoretical model in Polish conditions.

2 Healthcare Management Using Cost Information: Kaplan and Porter's Proposal

In 2011, Kaplan and Porter published an article "How to Solve the Cost Crisis in Healthcare" which presents best practices for healthcare management. Authors draw their conclusions based on practical experiences with several healthcare institutions as well as their previous experience and expertise. Kaplan is known as the co-author of the breakthrough concept of Activity-Based Costing (ABC) (Cooper and Kaplan 1988) and Time-Driven Activity Based Costing (TDABC) (Kaplan and Anderson 2004)—a modification of ABC allowing to assign costs accurately and relatively easily. Porter is the author of several publications on competition (Porter 1980) and value management—also in healthcare (Porter and Teisberg 2006; Porter 2009, 2010). In the latest article the authors analyzed the reasons for malfunctioning of healthcare and presented the method to solve the problem.

Developing the concept of diagnostic groups in the 60s and its implementation to the practice of healthcare financing for the first time in the U.S. in the 80s was aimed to build a model in which third party payers will reimburse for outcomes of treatment rather than for the procedures performed. In practice, modern DRG systems rather group cases based on treatment- or patient-specific factors—such as procedures performed, duration of stay, age, birth weight—than based on outcomes—reflected with health status achieved or retained, process of recovery or sustainability of health (Kobel et al. 2011). Research on the merits of supplementing the grouping systems with qualitative factors related to health condition of the patient was conducted in the Netherlands and confirmed the legitimacy of such movements, but it did not translate into changes in the local grouping system (Evers et al. 2002).

Kaplan and Porter pay attention to the fact that in addition to the lack of sufficient recognition of aspects related to the effects of treatment, too little emphasis is placed on proper analysis of the expenditure required to achieve these effects. The role of economic evaluation is widely described in the healthcare economics (Drummond et al. 2005; Folland et al. 2010) and includes the identification, measurement, valuation, and then comparison of the costs (inputs) and benefits (outcomes) of two or more alternative treatments or activities (WHO 2000). The most common methods include Cost-Effectiveness Analysis (CEA), Cost-Utility Analysis (CUA), and Cost-Benefit Analysis (CBA). All three assume comparing healthcare costs with outcomes expressed in natural units (CEA), quality adjusted life years (CUA), or monetary value (CBA). A common approach of all three methods is the payer-based approach to cost measurement. Costs are estimated based on the level of payer's expenditures. This perspective does not include the level of providers' costs related with a service.

In the U.S., costing model used by healthcare providers is a consequence of the model used for pricing of health services. In the area of inpatient services, Ratio of Cost to Charges (RCC) approach is used, which envisages allocating costs to services according to their prices. This model is obligatory for hospitals providing services under Medicare to prepare the annual cost report and often determines the costing model used for management. In the area of physician services, Relative Value Units (RVUs) are used, which are based on selective and idiosyncratic estimates of resources. Both approaches have long been subject to criticism (West et al. 1996; Baker 1998; Young 2007).

The problem with the optimization of a treatment process results from the fact that it is highly fragmented, and health services within a single treatment process are provided by a number of independent service providers. There are also few treatment standards, both at the level of a treatment process and at the level of a single procedure within a treatment. Patients with similar characteristics can pass a different path through the healthcare system, and in addition each of the services provided can vary in terms of resources used depending on the service provider.

The existing system of reimbursement present in most developed countries, in which the pricing unit is a single service provided to a patient—reported as a diagnostic group, procedure or number of days of stay—creates an incentive for transferring costs from one service provider to another or within payers. An example of such a cost-shifting was increased spending on outpatient care as a

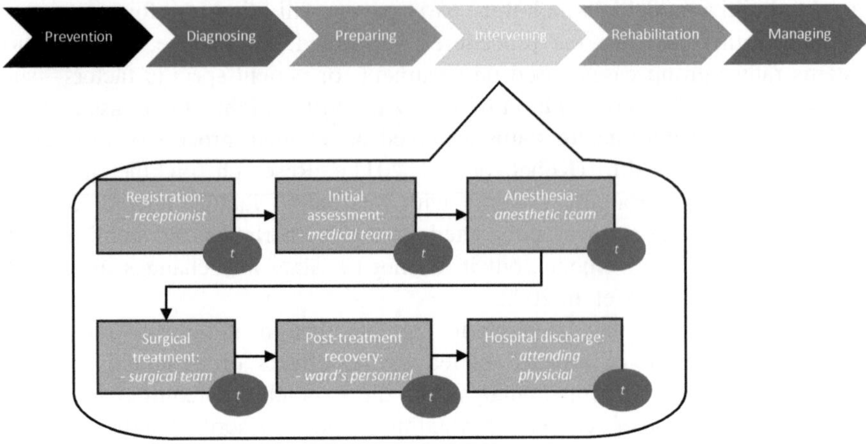

Fig. 1 Kaplan and Porter's proposal. **Source**: Own study based on Kaplan and Porter (2011)

result of the introduction of DRG-based pricing of inpatient services (Wilson et al. 2005; Kulesher and Wilder 2006).

The approach proposed by Kaplan and Porter counteracts both weaknesses associated with the healthcare management—the lack of adequate information about the cost of health services and lack of information to optimize treatment process. They propose application of TDABC to analyze the whole treatment process and cross-analysis of the costs of individual actions with the value they carry to the final outcome. Figure 1 shows a scheme of Kaplan and Porter's proposal.

Cost calculation applies to the entire treatment process (or a specified period of time in case of chronic diseases), and includes a path which patients pass during the treatment. The analysis also applies to all typical elements of the treatment process—prevention, diagnosing, preparing, intervening, rehabilitation and managing.

Each patient's contact with the healthcare provider is presented in form of actions taken. For every action in the treatment process the involvement of both capacity-supplying resources and consumable supplies is determined. The cost of each action is set by adding direct and indirect costs. Allocation of indirect costs is performed according to the amount of time each resource is involved in the action (e.g. the time of surgeon's work during the surgical procedure). The cost of the treatment process is the sum of the cost of all the supplies and the resources in all activities undertaken throughout it. Scenario approach based on the time equations allows for determination of multiple patient paths within a single treatment process.

The proposed solution, by providing a comprehensive analysis of the whole treatment process using TDABC enables value management and cost optimization. Its main advantages are:

- elimination of unnecessary process variations and processes that don't add value,
- improvement of resource capacity utilization,
- delivery of the right processes at the right locations,
- matching clinical skills to the process,
- speeding up cycle time,
- optimization over the full cycle of care.

3 Polish Experiences in the Use of Cost Information

After 1989 most healthcare institutions in Poland have been public and therefore costing models for healthcare have been regulated by law. Increasing level of managers' needs as well as more developed information systems were the main reasons for its redevelopment. In 2011 a solution based on Activity-Based Costing approach has been developed by Świderska's team in the Warsaw School of Economics in cooperation with the Polish Ministry of Health (Świderska 2011). The primary purpose was to develop a costing model useful for the management of a healthcare institution, including in particular decision-making and reporting inefficiencies. In 2015, a regulation came into force, making it the basis for cost-based pricing of health services. Figure 2 shows a scheme of the Polish costing model.

The calculation is based on microcosting approach, which assumes identification of numerous cost objects. Cost object is any object for which a cost is computed.

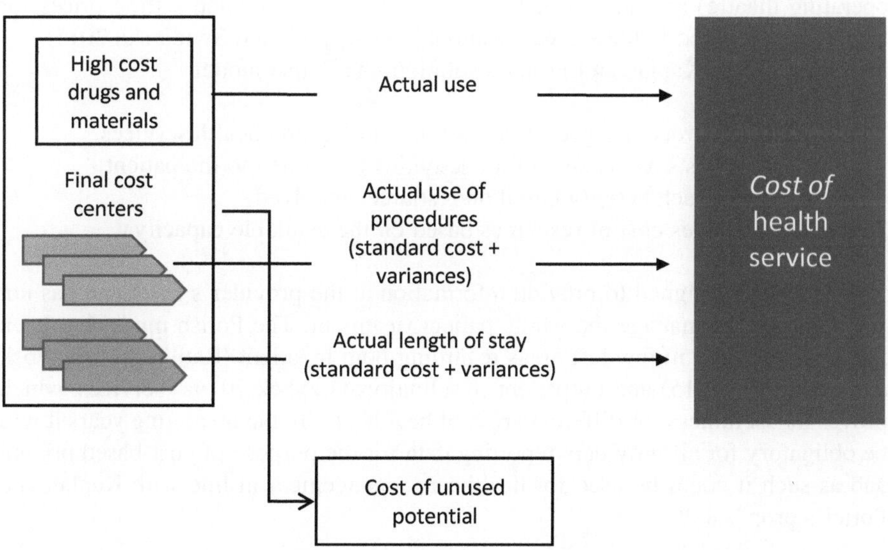

Fig. 2 Polish costing model. **Source:** Own work based on Ministry of Health (2015)

This approach ensures more accurate calculation, because every cost object can be individually assigned to a health service using suitable cost driver. Polish model is a combination of top-down and bottom-up approach. Top-down microcosting means that the average cost of each cost object is calculated (Chapko et al. 2009). For example, the cost of stay in a hospital ward is set per day of stay. Bottom-up approach assumes that the cost of each object is determined individually for each service based on real data (Wordsworth et al. 2005). For example, the cost of a surgical procedure for each patient will be determined based on the actual consumption of resources. Earlier research proves that such a combination is a good compromise between accuracy and labor-intensity of the calculation (Raulinajtys-Grzybek 2014b).

Typical cost objects are identified in every cost center and their standard cost is calculated. Cost of each patient contact is set according to data on the actual use of cost objects—such as procedures, hospitalization or other services provided. Cost of high-cost drugs and materials are assigned in real values, and for other cost objects a standard cost is determined (and then corrected using variances). Using standard cost approach differs the Polish model from Kaplan and Porter's proposal that was based on actual values. Previous research (Świderska 2011) showed that using standard times proved to be easier for data collection when information is not available from appropriate information systems (e.g. time tracking). The use of actual times may be implemented for most expensive procedures as part of the planning and control process.

A characteristic feature of this model is the determination of the cost of unused capacity which as a rule is not included in the cost of health service. The only exception from that rule is the costs of so called "standby". These are costs of unused capacity resulting from the constant readiness of specific areas (e.g. ICU or operating theatre) and should be taken into consideration when setting prices for healthcare provided in these areas (Raulinajtys-Grzybek and Świderska 2015).

Similarly like Kaplan and Porter's solution, the Polish model:

- is based on process approach to costing patients and health services,
- calculates costs as the sum of all activities performed to the patient,
- sets cost of each activity based on resources involved,
- and determines cost of resources based on the available capacity.

It has been designed to provide information at the provider's level and has not yet been used to manage the whole patient treatment. The Polish model has been implemented only in few test areas regarding both inpatient (Raulinajtys-Grzybek and Świderska 2015) and outpatient (Raulinajtys-Grzybek 2014a) services, which proves its usefulness for different areas of healthcare. In the upcoming years it will be obligatory for all providers reporting data for the purpose of cost-based pricing and as such it could be used for healthcare management in line with Kaplan and Porter's proposal.

4 Limitations on the Use of the Kaplan and Porter's Solution in Poland

The Kaplan and Porter's proposal assumes a holistic analysis of the entire treatment process involving a variety of providers—from primary care to long-term care. Its aim is to optimize the costs of the whole treatment of a specific disease. The implementation of this solution in Poland can be complicated due to a number of institutional arrangements.

The budget for healthcare in Poland is divided between the 16 regions where branches of the public payer (the National Health Fund) operate. Approximately 97% of Polish citizens are insured by the National Health Fund, which is financed with health insurance premiums. Each branch is financing the treatment of patients from their region within the available budget. There are separate sub-budgets for different areas of healthcare—e.g. outpatient, inpatient, or long-term treatment. Provision of services is carried out by healthcare providers, who concluded an agreement for certain services with the National Health Fund. Healthcare providers having a contract with a public payer can be either publicly owned (by central of local government) as well as privately owned (these are usually for-profit entities). The selection of service providers is based on an assessment of various criteria, including those related to price, quality and availability of services (Panteli and Sagan 2011).

Some of the problems associated with the healthcare management have been presented below, which hinder the implementation of a holistic approach to value-added analysis of the treatment process.

4.1 *Expenditure Optimization Within Subbudgets*

Management of public funds in Poland is carried out at a subbudget level in such a way as to ensure access to the greatest number of services of every type. Contracts with service providers are concluded to ensure the availability of particular types of services—e.g. inpatient care. So far the efforts of the public payer focused on signing agreements with the service providers guaranteeing the lowest level of costs and the implementation of more services within the same subbudget. There were some actions promoting the transfer of patients from inpatient to outpatient care but very limited—they included e.g. the organization of selected surgeries as one-day procedures, as well as the procedures fastening access to healthcare for cancer patients (Holecki and Romaniuk 2015). However, these actions were not accompanied by a detailed analysis of the cost of individual services subject to change.

4.2 Bottleneck in the Outpatient Care

Approximately 43% of all public funds are spent on the purchase of hospital services, and only less than 8% on the purchase of specialist outpatient services (National Health Fund 2016). This causes problems with the availability of outpatient services and long queues to specialists, lasting up to 6 months. Patients see the doctor late and often when the hospital treatment is necessary. This results in an increase in expenditure in the inpatient sector, which absorbs more and more public funds.

4.3 Shifting Costs Among Providers

The unit of payment for most types of care is the number of health services provided—for outpatient care they are measured by the number of procedures and for inpatient care by the number of cases grouped into diagnostic groups (DRG) or, in specific areas, by number of days of stay. Here are fixed prices set for each unit of payment—procedure, DRG, and day of stay. Primary healthcare and hospital emergency departments are paid a flat rate—respectively through capitation rates and a fixed budget. The profit of the provider is set as the difference between prices that are fixed (either at the service level or provider level) and costs. As a result of such a formula, providers take actions to minimize costs associated with the treatment and sometimes transfer the problematic cases to other providers. In areas paid per service they might also multiply the number of admissions of other low-cost patients. The consequence of such a behavior is health services that do not bring value to the patient and generate additional costs.

4.4 Lack of Treatment Standards

Despite numerous attempts, no standards have been developed so far in respect of the whole treatment process, and there are just few medical standards for individual services. The same disease can be treated using different methods, and patients can go different paths in the health system.

The implementation of a holistic approach for the management of the whole treatment process would require changes in the way of setting the budgets of the National Health Fund and shifting from subbudgets for areas of care into budgets for treating different health problems—for example, the treatment of heart diseases. Assessment of the entire treatment process would require analysis of large datasets on the services provided to patients to identify typical treatment paths. Such data is mostly already collected today by the public payer. Due to the features of the Polish healthcare system presented above, it would be necessary to provide a detailed verification of the data by the medical community. This would help to exclude services that do not bring added value, the implementation of which results from improper organization of healthcare, that occur due to the late initiation of treatment, and that are the result of multiplication of health services in order to generate additional revenue.

5 Conclusion

The costing model designed for Poland—like the Kaplan and Porter's solution—is based on the Activity-Based Costing concept. It assumes allocation of consumable supplies based on their use and the allocation of capacity-supplying resources based on time of their involvement in service. Separate calculation of costs for every patient helps identifying differences between them and allows for multiple patient paths. In contrast to the Kaplan and Porter's approach, the Polish model presented in the article uses information on the standard use of individual cost objects in each service and is not based on time equations.

The main area of improvement towards the Kaplan and Porter model is the implementation of a holistic approach towards treatment process. Analysis of the whole process including various services would require setting a different aim for the public payer. Instead of minimizing expenditure on different types of services it should concentrate on optimizing costs of treating specific health problems. Data on costs of different actions is necessary to analyze the area for improvement. The designed costing model can be adapted to different types of health services which forms a good starting point to begin the optimization process.

References

Averill, R. F., Goldfield, N. I., Wynn, M. E., McGuire, T. E., Mullin, R. L., Gregg, L. W., & Bender, J. A. (1993). Design of a prospective payment patient classification system for ambulatory care. *Healthcare Financial Review, 15*(1), 71–100.

Baker, J. J. (1998). *Activity-based costing and activity-based management for health care.* Gaithersburg, MD: An Aspen Publication.

Chapko, M. K., Liu, C. F., Perkins, M., Li, Y. F., Fortney, J. C., & Maciejewski, M. L. (2009). Equivalence of two healthcare costing methods: Bottom-up and top-down. *Health Economics, 18*(10), 1188–1201.

Cooper, R., & Kaplan, R. S. (1988). Measure costs right: Make the right decisions. *Harvard Business Review, 66*(5), 96–103.

Czach, K., Klonowska, K., Świderek, M., & Wiktorzak, K. (2011). Poland: The Jednorodne Grupy Pacjentów—Polish experiences with DRGs. In R. Busse, A. Geissler, W. Quentin, & M. Wiley (Eds.), *Diagnosis-related groups in Europe: Moving towards transparency, efficiency and quality in hospitals* (pp. 359–381). Maidenhead: McGraw-Hill/Open University Press.

De Mello-Sampayo, F., De Sousa Vale, S., & Camoes, F. (2013). Substitutability between drugs, innovation and growth in the pharmaceutical industry. In *10th EBES Conference Proceedings* (pp. 13–28).

Drummond, M. F., Sculper, M. J., Torrance, G. W., O'Brien, B. J., & Stoddart, G. L. (2005). *Methods for the economic evaluation of healthcare programs*. Oxford: Oxford University Press.

Duncan, D. G., & Servais, C. S. (1996). Preparing for the new outpatient reimbursement system. *Healthcare Financial Management, 50*(2), 42–49.

Evers, S., Voss, G., Nieman, F., Ament, A., Groot, T., Lodder, J., & Blaauw, G. (2002). Predicting the cost of hospital stay for stroke patients: The use of diagnosis related groups. *Health Policy, 61*(1), 21–42.

Fetter, R. B., Thompson, J. D., & Mills, R. E. (1976). A system for cost and reimbursement control in hospitals. *The Yale Journal of Biology and Medicine, 49*(2), 123–136.

Folland, S., Goodman, A. C., & Stano, M. (2010). *The economics of health and health care*. New York: Pearson Education.

Holecki, T., & Romaniuk, P. (2015). The oncological package: A new source of concern in Poland's health system. *Lancet Oncology, 16*(3), e104.

Jones, M. J., & Mellett, H. J. (2007). Determinants of changes in accounting practices: Accounting and the UK health service. *Critical Perspectives on Accounting, 18*, 91–121.

Kaplan, R. S., & Anderson, S. R. (2004). Time-driven activity-based costing. *Harvard Business Review, 82*(11), 131–138.

Kaplan, R. S., & Porter, M. E. (2011). How to solve the cost crisis in healthcare. *Harvard Business Review, 89*(9), 46–61.

Kobel, C., Thuilliez, J., Bellanger, M., & Pfeiffer, K. (2011). DRG systems and similar patient classification systems in Europe. In R. Busse, A. Geissler, W. Quentin, & M. Wiley (Eds.), *Diagnosis-related groups in Europe: Moving towards transparency, efficiency and quality in hospitals* (pp. 37–59). Maidenhead: McGraw-Hill/Open University Press.

Kulesher, R. R., & Wilder, M. G. (2006). Prospective payment and the provision of post-acute care: How the provisions of the Balanced Budget Act of 1997 altered utilization patterns for Medicare providers. *Journal of Healthcare Finance, 33*(1), 1–16.

Lau, C. K. M., Fung, K. W. T., & Pugalis, L. (2014). Is health care expenditure across Europe converging? Findings from the application of a nonlinear panel unit root test. *Eurasian Business Review, 4*(2), 137–156.

Ministry of Health. (2015). *Rozporządzenie Ministra Zdrowia w sprawie zaleceń dotyczących standardu rachunku kosztów u świadczeniodawców* [Regulation on costing standard for healthcare providers]. [online] Accessed March 7, 2016, from https://legislacja.rcl.gov.pl/projekt/268664

National Health Fund. (2016). *Annual budget for 2016*. [online] Accessed March 7, 2016, from http://www.nfz.gov.pl/download/gfx/nfz/pl/defaultaktualnosci/284/6356/1/projekt_planu_finansowego_na_2016_rok_zal_do_uchwaly_nr_10.pdf

OECD. (2013). *Health at a glance 2013: OECD indicators. OECD Publishing*. [online] Accessed March 7, 2016, from http://dx.doi.org/10.1787/health_glance-2013-en

Panteli D., & Sagan A. (Eds.). (2011). Poland: Health system review. Health systems in transition. *WHO Health Systems in Transition, 13*(8), 1–216. http://www.euro.who.int/__data/assets/pdf_file/0018/163053/e96443.pdf

Porter, M. E. (1980). *Competitive strategy: Techniques for analyzing industries and competitors*. New York: Free Press.

Porter, M. E. (2009). A strategy for healthcare reform: Towards a value-based system. *The New England Journal of Medicine, 361*, 109–112.

Porter, M. E. (2010). What is value in health care? *The New England Journal of Medicine, 363*, 2477–2481.

Porter, M. E., & Teisberg, E. O. (2006). *Redefining health care: Creating value-based competition on results*. Boston, MA: Harvard Business School Press.

Raulinajtys-Grzybek, M. (2014a). Учет затрат по видам деятельности для амбулаторной клиники [Activity-based costing for an ambulatory clinic]. *Экономика и современный менеджмент: теория и практика, 5*(37), 43–55.

Raulinajtys-Grzybek, M. (2014b). Cost accounting models used for price-setting of health services: An international review. *Health Policy, 118*(3), 341–353.

Raulinajtys-Grzybek, M., & Świderska, G. K. (2015). Payment by results vs. costs of 24-hour standby in hospitals: Evidence from Poland. *Argumenta Oeconomica, 2*(35), 85–104.

Świderska, G. K. (Ed.). (2011). *Rachunek kosztów w zakładach opieki zdrowotnej. Podręcznik* [Cost accounting in healthcare institutions]. Warszawa: Oficyna Wydawnicza SGH.

Walshe, K., & Smith, J. (Eds.). (2006). *Healthcare management*. Maidenhead: Open University Press.

West, T. D., Balas, E. A., & West, D. A. (1996). Contrasting RCC, RVU, and ABC for managed care decisions. A case study compares three widely used costing methods and finds one superior. *Healthcare Financial Management, 50*(8), 54–61.

WHO. (2000). *Economic evaluation.* [online] Accessed March 7, 2016, from http://whqlibdoc.who.int/hq/2000/WHO_MSD_MSB_00.2i.pdf

Wilson, S. F., Shorten, B., & Marks, R. M. (2005). Costing the ambulatory episode: Implications of total or partial substitution of hospital care. *Australian Health Review, 29*(3), 360–365.

Wordsworth, S., Ludbrook, A., Caskey, F., & Macleod, A. (2005). Collecting unit cost data in multicentre studies. Creating comparable methods. *The European Journal of Health Economics, 6*(1), 38–44.

Young, D. W. (2007). The folly of using RCCs and RVUs for intermediate product costing. *Healthcare Financial Management, 61*(4), 100–108.

The Efficiency of the Low Water Retention in the Area of Poland: Chosen Aspects

Zbigniew Piepiora, Marian Kachniarz, and Arkadiusz Babczuk

Abstract In 1997 and 2010, two great floods occurred in the area of Poland. In the year 2015, the area of Poland was affected by extreme temperature. In the time of global warming, the low water retention should play the significant role. Thus, the aim of this article is to verify the efficiency of the low water retention in Poland. The methodology consists of two parts: data collection and data analysis. The data were collected from two databases: the EM-DAT and the BDL-GUS. After the analysis, conclusions were drawn. The hypothesis of the article was verified negatively: the efficiency of the low water retention in Poland did not better after the great flood in the year 2010. The average cost of 1 m^3 capacity in the period 2003–2009 exceeded US$10 and in the period 2010–2014—US$21. In the case of man-made reservoirs, fish ponds and staging lakes, the situation is similar—the average costs increased.

Keywords Low water retention • Drought • Flood • Efficiency • Poland • Natural disaster • Financing

1 Introduction

In 1997 and 2010 two great floods occurred in the area of Poland. The most devastating inundation the Oder River basin recently happened in the year 1997. In the Vistula River basin, the great flood appeared in 2010. Five years later, the area of Poland was affected by extreme temperature, causing drought. Extreme temperatures, droughts and floods are examples of natural disasters (Abbott 2009;

Z. Piepiora (✉)
Department of Spatial Economy, Wroclaw University of Environmental and Life Sciences, Wroclaw, Poland
e-mail: zbigniew.piepiora@up.wroc.pl

M. Kachniarz
Department of Spatial Economy, Wroclaw University of Economics, Wroclaw, Poland
e-mail: marian.kachniarz@ue.wroc.pl

A. Babczuk
Department of Finance and Accounting, Wroclaw University of Economics, Wroclaw, Poland
e-mail: marian.kachniarz@ue.wroc.pl

M.H. Bilgin et al. (eds.), *Empirical Studies on Economics of Innovation, Public Economics and Management*, Eurasian Studies in Business and Economics 6,
DOI 10.1007/978-3-319-50164-2_18

Alexander 1993). The phenomena such as flood, drought and extreme temperatures can be defined, according to the Natural Disaster Act, as events connected with impacting of nature's forces. In the time of global warming, the significant role should play the low water retention (Piepiora 2012).

It is worth noting that the welfare impact of a disaster does not depend only on the physical characteristics of the event (Hallegatte 2016). Natural disasters also occur in a political space because the level of government preparedness and response determines the area of suffering incurred by the affected population (Cohen and Werker 2008). Because the data concerning the drought in the year 2015 are still being estimated, the aim of this article is to verify the hypothesis: the efficiency of the low water retention in Poland bettered after the great flood in the year 2010. The research question of the article is: whether the efficiency of the low water retention after 2010 is better than the one before 2010?

2 The Methodology

The methodology consists of two parts: data collection and data analysis. The data were collected from two databases: the EM-DAT and the BDL-GUS (GUS 2015).

The Emergency Events Database EM-DAT was established in 1988 by the Centre for Research on the Epidemiology of Disasters (CRED). It was created with the initial support of the WHO and the Belgian Government. The main goal of the EM-DAT database is to serve the purposes of humanitarian action at national and international levels. The Emergency Events Database EM-DAT contains essential core data on the occurrence and effects of over 18,000 mass disasters in the world from 1900 to present. The database is compiled from various sources, including UN agencies, non-governmental organizations, insurance companies, research institutes and press agencies (Guha-Sapir et al. 2016). The EMDAT data (Advanced Search for natural disasters in Poland) concerns the period 1919–2015 because Poland was re-recreated as the independent country on 11 November 1918 after the World War I and 123 years of partitions by Austria-Hungary, Germany and Russia (Dybkowska et al. 1994).

The BDL-GUS (Local Data Bank of the Central Statistical Office of Poland) is the largest in Poland and ordered set of information about the social, socio-economic, demographic state of the environment, describing provinces, counties and municipalities as agents of the system of social organization and administration of Poland. The BDL-GUS also describes regions and sub-regions constituting elements of the nomenclature of territorial units for statistical purposes (GUS 2015). The BDL-GUS data concerns the period 1998–2014 because only data for these years was available.

After collecting the data, the analysis in spreadsheet was conducted. The data was converted from CSV files and presented in tables and figures. In the case of GUS-BDL data, the currency was changed in the spreadsheet from Polish Zloty to US dollar using the exchange rate of the NBP website (NBP 2015). After the analysis, conclusions were drawn.

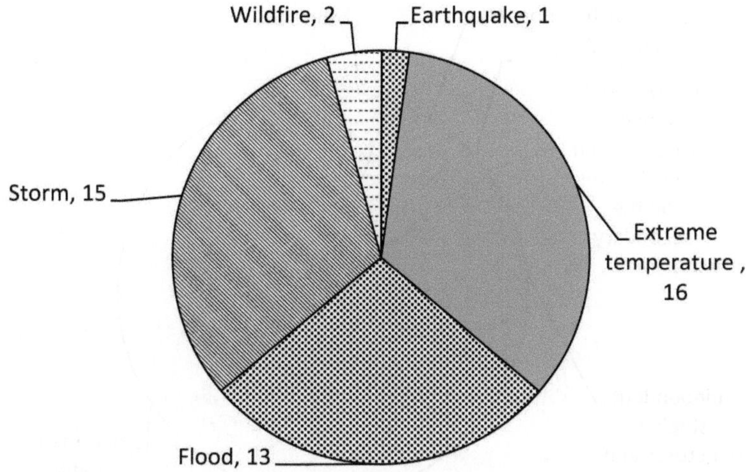

Fig. 1 The manifestation of the natural disasters in the area of Poland in the years 1919–2015. **Source**: Own study based on Guha-Sapir et al. (2016) and Piepiora et al. (2016)

3 The Examined Area

The Republic of Poland is located at the Baltic Sea in the Middle-East Europe. The south part of Poland has two mountain rages called the Sudetes (Sudety) and the Carpathian Mountains (Karpaty). The main rivers of the country are Oder (Odra) and Vistula (Wisła). The climate of the examined country is characterized as a transient of the mesothermal zone (Piepiora et al. 2015a, b).

The manifestation of the natural disasters and their effects in the area of Poland in the period 1919–2015 is presented in the Fig. 1. As we can see at the figure, extreme temperatures, storms and floods occurred most often in the examined area. Extreme temperatures, storms and floods are hydrometeorological disasters (Rodzik 2008; Somorowska 2009).

4 The Efficiency of the Low Water Retention in the Examined Area

Investing expenses for the low water retention—shares in Poland according to investing directions in the years 2003–2014 are presented in the Fig. 2. Investing expenses for man-made water reservoirs exceeded US$146 million. Total investing expenditures for the low water retention amounted to approximately US$215 million. As it can be seen in the Fig. 2, the main direction of investing was man-made water reservoirs (68%).

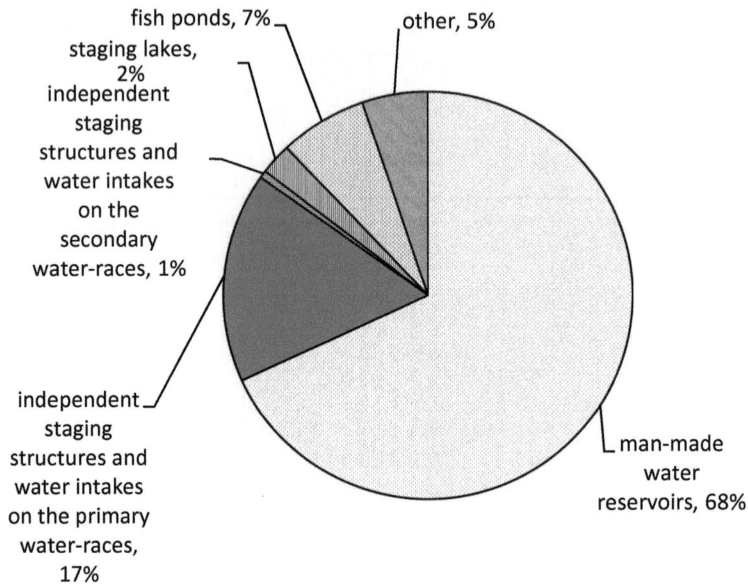

Fig. 2 Investing expenses for the low water retention—shares in Poland—directions of investing in the years 2003–2014 (in '000 US dollars indexed to the year 2014). **Source**: Own study based on GUS (2015) and NBP (2015)

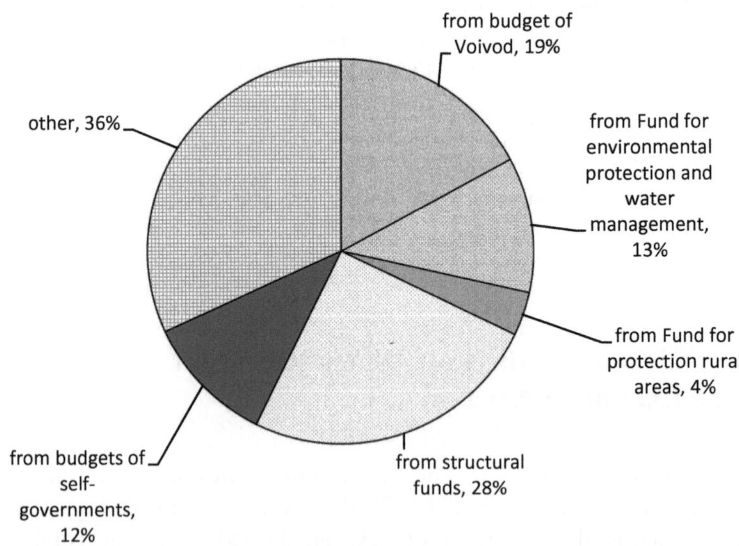

Fig. 3 Investing expenses for the low water retention—shares in Poland—directions of investing in the years 2003–2014 (in '000 US dollars indexed to the year 2014). **Source**: Own study based on GUS (2015) and NBP (2015)

Investing expenses for the low water retention—shares in Poland according to financing sources in the years 2003–2014 are presented in the Fig. 3. As it can be seen, expenses were financed mainly from structural funds of the European Union and from the other sources.

Investing expenses for the low water retention in Poland in the years 2003–2014 are presented in the Fig. 4. It is worth noting the increase in spending can be associated with the possibilities of funding from the EU after accession to the European Union (2000–2006 programming period, the de facto 2004–2006 and 2007–2013). Thus, the Fig. 3 confirms a link between increasing expenditures and the possibilities of absorption of the European Union' measures—a significant

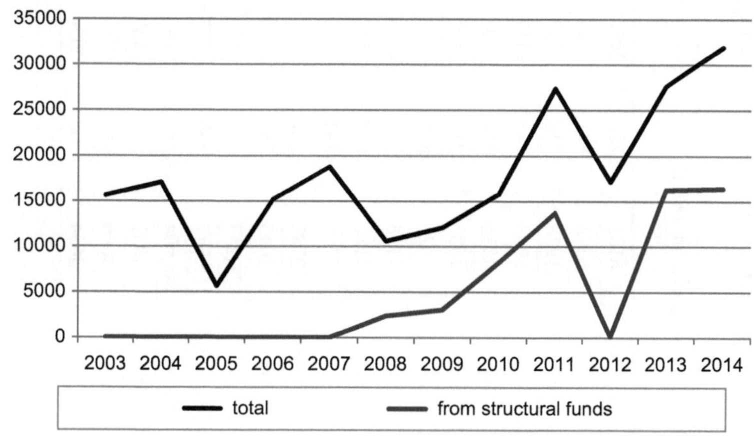

Fig. 4 Investing expenses for the low water retention in Poland in the years 2003–2014 (in '000 US dollars indexed to the year 2014). **Source**: Own study based on GUS (2015), NBP (2015), and Piepiora et al. (2015b)

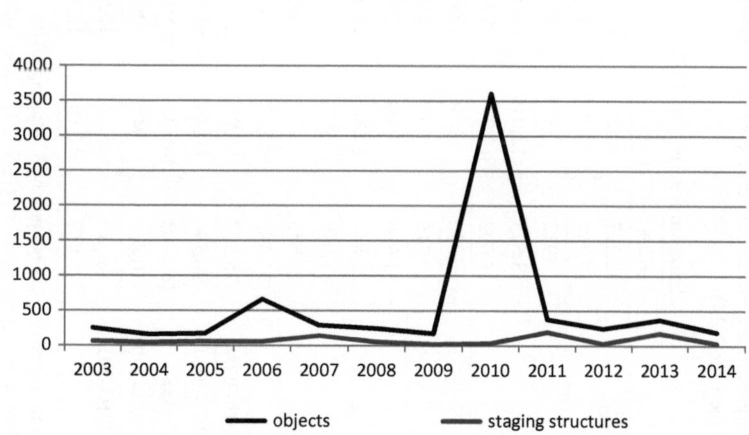

Fig. 5 Effects of investing in the low water retention—the range of objects in Poland in the years 2003–2014. **Source**: Own study on the basis of GUS (2015), NBP (2015), and Piepiora et al. (2015b)

Table 1 Expenditures, effects and efficiency of permanent assets serving the low water retention in Poland in the period 1998–2014 (in '000 US dollar indexed to the year 2014)

	Expenditures (in '000 US$)				Effects (capacity in '000 m^3)				Efficiency (exp./effects)			
years	1 + 2 + 3	1	2	3	1 + 2 + 3	1	2	3	Total	1	2	3
2003	12,297	10,291	1961	46	10,824	6185	1702	2937	1.14	1.66	1.15	0.02
2004	13,757	12,783	752	222	13,162	6348	841	5974	1.05	2.01	0.89	0.04
2005	4913	3875	970	68	4943	1928	1018	1997	0.99	2.01	0.95	0.03
2006	13,623	12,044	1349	231	9568	6068	1783	1717	1.42	1.98	0.76	0.13
2007	14,002	12,289	930	784	5940	4516	631	793	2.36	2.72	1.47	0.99
2008	7000	5646	1285	69	4751	1686	2910	155	1.47	3.35	0.44	0.44
2009	10,216	9025	1178	13	6204	1526	4678	0	1.65	5.92	0.25	N/A
2010	11,916	8440	1357	2119	7456	1126	1751	4579	1.60	7.50	0.77	0.46
2011	21,848	19,846	1300	701	6821	4188	1077	1556	3.20	4.74	1.21	0.45
2012	11,978	9997	1035	946	11,475	5206	1331	4938	1.04	1.92	0.78	0.19
2013	21,872	21,289	583	0	3285	2783	502	0	6.66	7.65	1.16	N/A
2014	22,982	20,797	2103	81	2633	2045	589	0	8.73	10.17	3.57	N/A
Total—2003–2009	75,807	65,952	8424	1432	55,391	28,257	13,562	13,573	10.08	19.66	5.92	0.11
Total—2010–2014	90,596	80,369	6379	3847	31,669	15,347	5249	11,073	21.23	31.98	7.50	0.35
Total—all years	166,403	146,321	14,803	5279	87,061	43,604	18,811	24,645	31.31	51.63	13.42	2.76
Average 2003–2009	10,830	9422	1203	205	7913	4037	1937	1939	1.44	2.81	0.85	0.28
Average 2010–2014	18,119	16,074	1276	769	6334	3069	1050	2215	4.25	6.40	1.50	0.37
Average	13,867	12,193	1234	440	7255	3634	1568	2054	2.61	4.30	1.12	0.31

1. Man-made reservoirs, 2. Fish ponds, 3. Staging lakes
Source: Own study on the basis of: GUS (2015) and NBP (2015)

increase until 2003, after a significant decline until 2005, then increase until 2007 (it is considered 1 year delay due to bureaucratic procedures—the means can be captured a year later, and then spend a year longer than the time of the designation of the programming period). A significant increase in expenditures in 2010 and 2011 is also visible. The highest level of expenses was noted a year after the great flood in 2010.

Effects of investing in the low water retention are presented in the Fig. 5. The range of objects in Poland in the years 2003–2014 amounted to 6750. Total increasing capacity in the examined period exceeded 87,061,000 m^3. The data presented in the Fig. 5 is corresponding with the data of previous figure.

Expenditures, effects and efficiency of permanent assets serving the low water retention in Poland in the period 2003–2014 are presented in the Table 1. The average cost of 1 m^3 capacity in the period 2003–2009 exceeded US$10 and in the period 2010–2014—US$21. In the case of man-made reservoirs, fish ponds and staging lakes, the situation is similar—the average costs increased.

5 Conclusion

After the analysis of the efficiency of the low water retention in the area of Poland, the following conclusions can be drawn. The range of objects in Poland in the years 2003–2014 amounted to 6750. Total increasing capacity in the examined period exceeded 87,061,000 m^3. The hypothesis from the beginning of the article was verified negatively: the efficiency of the low water retention in Poland did not better after the great flood in the year 2010. Thus, the answer for the research question of the article is that the efficiency of the low water retention after 2010 is not better than the one before 2010.

The average cost of 1 m^3 capacity in the period 2003–2009 exceeded US$10 and in the period 2010–2014—US$21. In the case of man-made reservoirs, fish ponds and staging lakes, the situation is similar—the average costs increased. The reason of decreasing efficiency of the low water retention in Poland can be connected with organizing by Poland the Euro 2012 tournament. According to authors, the preparation to this event could increase prices of materials in the building branch but verifying that need further research.

Acknowledgements It is worth to notice that the article is part of the research project 'Financing catastrophic damages' chaired by PhD Zbigniew Piepiora.

References

Abbott, P. L. (2009). *Natural disasters*. San Diego, CA: San Diego State University.
Alexander, D. (1993). *Natural disasters*. Berlin: Springer Science & Business Media.

Cohen, C., & Werker, E. D. (2008). The political economy of 'natural' disasters. *Journal of Conflict Resolution., 52*(6), 795–819.

Dybkowska, A., Żaryn, J., & Żaryn, M. (1994). *Polskie Dzieje. Od czasów najdawniejszych do współczesności* [Polish history. From ancient times to the present day]. Warszawa: PWN.

Guha-Sapir, D., Below, R., & Hoyois, P. (2016). *EM-DAT: International Disaster Database—www.emdat.be—Université Catholique de Louvain—Brussels—Belgium.* [online] Accessed February 17, 2016, from http://www.emdat.be

GUS. (2015). *Bank Danych Lokalnych* [Local Data Bank]. Accessed December 2, 2015, from http://www.stat.gov.pl/bdl/app/strona.html?p_name=indeks

Hallegatte, S. (2016). The indirect cost of natural disasters and an economic definition of macroeconomic resilience. *Public Finance and Macroeconomics* (Paper 3). [online]. Accessed August 29, 2016, from https://www.gfdrr.org/sites/gfdrr.org/files/documents/Public%20finance%20and%20macroeconomics,%20Paper%203.pdf

NBP. (2015). *Narodowy Bank Polski* [National Bank of Poland]. Accessed December 8, 2015, from http://www.nbp.pl/kursy/kursyc.html

Piepiora, Z. (2012). *Ekonomiczne aspekty lokalnej polityki przeciwdziałania skutkom katastrof naturalnych* [Economic aspects of the natural disasters policy on the local level]. Kowary: Zbigniew Piepiora.

Piepiora, Z., Kachniarz, M., & Babczuk, A. (2015a). Financing the counteraction of natural disasters' effects in lower Silesian Voivodeship. *Advances in Economics, Business and Management Research.* [online] Accessed December 8, 2015, from http://www.atlantis-press.com/php/pub.php?publication=icmemi-15&frame=http%3A//www.atlantis-press.com/php/paper-details.php%3Ffrom%3Dsession+results%26id%3D16211%26querystr%3Did%253D30

Piepiora, Z., Babczuk, A., & Kachniarz, M. (2015b). Preventing effects of natural disasters in Poland—Financial aspects. *International Journal on Recent and Innovation Trends in Computing and Communication, 3*(10), 6062–6066.

Piepiora, Z., Babczuk, A., & Kachniarz, M. (2016). Active natural disasters policy in Poland. *Proceedings of the 2016 International Conference on Intelligent Control and Computer Application in Advances in Computer Science Research, 30.* [online] Accessed May 30, 2016, from http://www.atlantis-press.com/php/pub.php?publication=icca-16

Rodzik, J. (2008). Wpływ deszczów ulewnych i roztopów na rozwój wąwozu lessowego [The impact of torrential rains and thaws on the development of the gully loess]. *Landform Analysis, 8*, 56–59.

Somorowska, U. (2009). Wzrost zagrożenia suszą hydrologiczną w różnych regionach geograficznych Polski w XX wieku [The increase in risk of hydrological drought in different Polish geographical regions in the twentieth century]. *Prace i Studia Geograficzne, 43*, 97–114.

The Management and Economics of a Life-Threatening Invasive Species in Hawaii

Jason Levy and Peiyong Yu

Abstract While many of Hawai'i's native terrestrial ecosystems have been heavily impacted by human activities, invasive species continue to pose one of the greatest threats to the health of Hawaii's native forests and watersheds. *Falcataria moluccana (F. moluccana)* removal and reforestation with native species can enhance watershed integrity, improve habitat for native species, and generate sustainable ecosystem services and forest products. Public cost-sharing and tax incentives are valuable strategies to encourage private landowners to invest in long-term *F. moluccana* management and reforestation. The characteristics of real estate properties affected by the highly invasive *F. moluccana* are examined in depth. Key sections of the Puna zone of Hawaii Island (Big Island) are graphically displayed and statistically analyzed based on property and land characteristics. The fraction of properties affected by *F. moluccana* receiving a homeowner exemption, the value of buildings and land on properties affected by *F. moluccana* and the number of property uses in each section (PITT codes for tax purposes) are provided.

Keywords Real estate economics • Hawaii • Invasive species • Property values

1 Introduction

The Hawaiian Islands, an archipelago of high islands rich in forest cover, with lush windward valleys, has an extremely diverse climate and unique biota. Accordingly, the US state of Hawaii provides a significant opportunity for the establishment of invasive alien species. While many of Hawai'i's native terrestrial ecosystems have been heavily impacted by human activities, invasive species continue to pose one of the greatest threats to the health of Hawaii's native forests and watersheds. When

J. Levy (✉)
Department of Public Administration, University of Hawaii – West Oahu, Kapolei, HI, USA
e-mail: jlevy@hawaii.edu

P. Yu
Department of Economics, University of Hawaii – West Oahu, Kapolei, HI, USA
e-mail: pyu@hawaii.edu

M.H. Bilgin et al. (eds.), *Empirical Studies on Economics of Innovation, Public Economics and Management*, Eurasian Studies in Business and Economics 6,
DOI 10.1007/978-3-319-50164-2_19

the first Polynesians arrived in Hawaii around the ninth century A.D., they inadvertently brought rats, geckos, and the first introduced weeds to the most isolated archipelago in the world. By the time of Captain James Cook's arrival to the islands of Hawaii 1778, much of the original lowland forest had been greatly altered by almost 1000 years of intensive agriculture and the impacts of introduced species such as weeds, feral animals, and alien insects.

Native to the southwest Pacific island of New Guinea, the archipelago of Indonesia, the Solomon Islands, and the Bismarck archipelago in Papua New Guinea (Wagner et al. 1999) this soft and fast-growing tree species (growth rates can exceed 15 feet per year and can reach over 100 feet high in 10 years) was introduced post-Cook to Hawaii from the Molucca archipelago (Indonesia) and hence is commonly known as the Moluccan *F. moluccana*. The tree is cultivated for timber and ornamental purposes throughout South and Southeast Asia. In 1917 botanist Joseph Rock first planted *Falcataria moluccana* (*F. moluccana*) in the Manoa valley on the island of Oahu, Hawaii, as an ornamental and reforestation tree, and to provide shade. By mid-century, thousands of *F. moluccana* seedlings were planted on Kauai, Oahu and the Island of Hawaii. Located in the legume family (Leguminosae), *F. moluccana* rapidly naturalizes in the natural lowland humid forests of Indian Ocean islands and Pacific islands (including American Samoa and the Hawaiian archipelago).

The species is highly invasive and reproduces prolifically in the archipelago of Hawaii for a number of reasons. The first issue involves growth rates: *F. moluccana* trees in Hawaii are the world's fastest growing tree species. They can grow as rapidly as an inch (2.5 cm) a day, reach reproductive maturity within 4 years and produce abundant seed. With a typical growth rate of 4.5 meters per year (Little and Skolmen 1989) and an average height of 108$\pm$ 13 feet (33 $\pm$ 4 m) individual trees rapidly and routinely reach heights exceeding 120 feet (36 m): trees can reach heights of more than 20 feet in their first year, 45 feet in their third year, and 60 feet by the end of their tenth year. (Asner et al. 2008). The canopy of a single *F. moluccana* tree can extend over a 50,000 square foot (one-half hectare) area while the broad umbrella-shaped canopies of multiple trees commonly coalesce to cover dozens or hundreds of acres (Hughes et al. 2011). The trees thrive best in moist soils and in poor, heavy clay environments from sea level to approximately 800 feet in elevation. The highest known elevation of *F. moluccana* in the State of Hawaii appears to occur in the Akatsuka Orchid community (Mountain View subdivision in the Puna district): they are also present at heights exceeding 1000 feet in Kaumana region of Hilo, Hawaii Island.

The second reason for the rapid naturalization of *F. moluccana* in Hawaii involves dispersal strategies. Designated as a highly invasive species in the Hawaii-Pacific Weed Risk Assessment, *F. moluccana* has become naturalized in many wet lowland areas where it spreads due to large numbers of wind-blown seeds. Contained within light seed pods, *F. moluccana* seeds are wind-dispersed over substantial distances (i.e. more than 600 feet), allowing the trees to spread rapidly over large areas. Once they land, seedpods lay dormant in the earth until ready to sprout. Hence, even when *F. moluccana* trees are physically removed there may still be a seed bank waiting to germinate. In other words, *F. moluccana* establishes easier (faster growth rates and seed production) than native tree species such as *Acacia koa* (Woodcock 2003) particularly in areas below 1000 feet (305 m) elevation with 80–150 inches (2032–3810 mm) annual rainfall. For instance, in the Rainbow Falls area of Hilo (Hawaii Island) the *F. moluccana* population grew from 10 acres to 35 acres in 15 years—a 253% increase. On the island of Hawaii they are found in every zone and more than one million board feet have been harvested on Hawaii Island alone (Little and Skolmen 1989).

The third reason that *F. moluccana* dominates the lowland humid forests of Hawaii is due to several unique characteristics and strategies which lead to aggressive growth in, and significant damage to, Hawaii's native terrestrial ecosystems. Most importantly, *F. moluccana can* ultimately suppress, displace or eliminate "nutrient-thrifty" native plants and trees from Hawaii's ecosystems which are specially adapted to grow in Hawaii's nitrogen poor soils including native 'ōhi'a lehua (*Metrosideros polymorpha*), *Acacia koa*, and lama trees (Asner et al. 2008). As prolific nitrogen (N_2) fixers, *F. moluccana* profoundly changes the soil composition of Hawaii's forests, pulling nitrogen from the air and adding nitrogen and phosphorus outputs to the soil and leaf litter. Fallen leaves also improve the soil characteristics for *F. moluccana*, helping it to rapidly invade the landscape. In the Puna district of Hawaii Island *F. moluccana* trees currently threaten the largest intact lowland wet forest in the entire Hawaiian archipelago (Hughes and Denslow 2005).

Hence, in nitrogen-rich soils Hawaii's native plants lose an important competitive advantage over *F. moluccana* (and other invading species) since the indigenous plants evolved for millennia in Hawaii's nitrogen-thrifty environment. By dramatically increasing nitrogen inputs, *F. moluccana* creates soil conditions that favor weeds and invaders such as Koster's curse (clidemia), miconia and strawberry guava trees. This can lead to significant environmental costs. For example, strawberry guava trees have formed impenetrable thickets on all six of Hawaii's largest isles, altering water production, providing a refuge for fruit flies and posing serious threats to Hawaii's endemic flora and fauna. In summary, *F. moluccana* creates a soil chemistry which disfavors indigenous plants by providing a hospitable environment for alien invasives.

2 The Properties of *F. moluccana*

F. moluccana is not only one of the most aggressive growing trees on earth but also a soft, highly brittle, breakage-prone tree: the tree's brittle branches and shallow roots easily break in wind or rain, then fall on homes, roads, and power lines. Hence, *F. moluccana* constitutes a growing and serious threat throughout the state of Hawaii and has imposed significant costs on society and the environment. Due to the hazards posed by *F. moluccana* to human health and critical infrastructure, natural areas, critical infrastructure, and the economy, the species should be aggressively controlled (and where possible eradicated) through community engagement, legislative action, private-public sector partnerships, citizen empowerment, education and training, and the creation of buffer zones in high-priority areas.

The primary focus of invasive species professionals deals with identifying and removing the most serious incipient invasions before an "*F. moluccana*-scale invasion" has developed: there is a very brief window of time after invasion in which a species can be quickly and cost-effectively eradicated. For *F. moluccana* this window has closed on most islands in the Hawaiian archipelago. With a presence dating back over 100 years, *F. moluccana* management is now primarily an issue of containment, and with a focus on controlling the spread of this naturalized, fast-growing invasive tree with thin, broad spreading crowns of large twice compound leaves (Little and Skolmen 1989). The proactive removal of *F. moluccana* costs significantly less than the combined direct and indirect costs of removal if and when trees land on critical infrastructure and population centers, causing damage, death or injury. For example, the Big Island Invasive Species Committee (BIISC) has demonstrated the effectiveness and necessity of an integrated and strategic approach to controlling the growth and spread of *F. moluccana*.

A complete eradication of *F. moluccana* is impossible so it is important that authorities in Hawaii prioritize policies, cooperation and funding for the long-term management of this highly invasive species. Key regions and roadways should also be targeted in a coordinated and systematic manner. For example, Senate Bill 2750, introduced by state Sen. Russell Ruderman (D-Puna) and its companion, House Bill 2516, introduced by state Rep. Nicole Lowen (D-Kailua-Kona), give priority to the removal of *F. moluccana* from right-of-ways (ROWs) in the Puna district of the Island of Hawaii: targeted areas include the two-mile stretch of Pahoa-Kapoho Road between Lava Tree State Park and Pahoa; isolated patches of *F. moluccana* trees between Kalapana and Pahoa; isolated patches of *F. moluccana* trees between Pahoa and Keaau; the hospital corridor, particularly the segment of Waianuenue Avenue from Komohana Street to Akolea Road; the segment of Akolea Road from Waianuenue Avenue to Kaumana Drive; Puainako Street from Highway 11 to Kaumana Drive. In addition to efforts by city, county, state and federal authorities, community based approaches are valuable such as the identification of areas where homes, utility lines or other structures are threatened.

Managing the *F. moluccana* problem requires increased cooperation and an integrated, well-coordinated approach, particularly around schools, critical infrastructure homes, playgrounds, and roadways. Like most invasive weeds *F. moluccana* ignores property boundaries and management jurisdictions, confounding the ability of any single entity to manage immediate hazards or halt its spread. Unique to *F. moluccana* is its massive height, which creates the urgent need for cross-jurisdictional cooperation. Integrated efforts of state, federal, county agencies and private entities in Hawaii are needed to prioritize projects and strategies for the management of *F. moluccana*, in order to establish a comprehensive plan to address high priority areas. It is important for the Governor of the State of Hawaii and the Hawaii State Legislature (through powers granted under Article III of the Constitution of Hawaii) mandate and fund *F. moluccana* mitigation policies, prevention systems and controls as high-priority issues and to coordinate their response with invasive species partners on a statewide level and across jurisdictional boundaries. The most cost-effective means of *F. moluccana* control is (local) prevention—stopping *F. moluccana* from invading new areas before they spread (the species is already endemic in many regions of the state). Federal, state, and country authorities should increase efforts to establish policies to protect Hawaii's unique environment from the further expansion of *F. moluccana.*

The Hawaii Invasive Species Council (HISC) is a key organization involved in holistic *F. moluccana* hazard mitigation and management in the state of Hawaii that involves an inter-departmental collaboration comprised of the Hawaii Department of Land and Natural Resources (DLNR), the Hawaii Department of Agriculture (DOA), the Hawaii Department of Health (DOH), the Hawaii Department of Transportation (DOT), the Hawaii Department of Business, Economic Development and Tourism (DBEDT), and the University of Hawaii (UH). HISC was established in 2003 for the objective of controlling and, where possible, eradicating destructive introduced species infestations throughout the state of Hawaii and for preventing the introduction of other, non-native species that may be potentially harmful. HISC fulfills this mandate by providing policy level direction, coordination, and planning among state departments, federal agencies, and international and local initiatives. Specifically, HISC issues resolutions, provides plans, and strategically disburses funds to enhance invasive species prevention, control, outreach, and research. Other possible sources of funding for *F. moluccana* management in Hawaii include a range of non-profit, public and private sector organizations. This includes the US government (through FEMA's hazard mitigation assistance, etc.) and the Hawaii State Legislature. Several pieces of legislation in Hawaii proposing funding specifically for *F. moluccana* have been introduced in the last few years to support comprehensive plans to address high priority areas.

Other possible sources of financial include allocations by city and county governments, the use of private monies, discretionary funds, and grants. For example, BIISC, a project of the University of Hawaii Pacific Cooperative Studies Unit, is using a combination of grant money, federal funds, and HISC funding to provide outreach, training and assistance on *F. moluccana* management to interested communities. Comprised of roughly 20 individuals, BIISC is tasked with addressing invasive species issues across Hawaii Island.

In 2014, a team of state, federal, county agencies and private entities met for more than 2 months to prioritize projects and develop a strategic approach to *F. moluccana* management. Community based solutions are also essential. For example, working in cooperation with the County of Hawaii and the State of Hawaii, the Nanawale Community Association Board of Directors made initial efforts on an *F. moluccana* management plan called *F. moluccana* Push 2008 that included surveying properties in the Puna subdivision to designate *F. moluccana* threat zones 1 through 5 (where Zone 1 indicates areas where homes or other structures are threatened while Zone 5 constitutes an *F. moluccana*-free zone, where no *F. moluccana*, including seedlings, are growing.) The *F. moluccana* Push 2008 goal was to establish Zone 5 throughout the subdivision.

3 The Invasion of Hawaii by *F. moluccana*

By the time of Captain James Cook's arrival in the Hawaiian Islands in 1778, much of the original lowland forest had been greatly altered by the Polynesians who cleared lowland forest (over nearly 1000 years of intensive agriculture) and introduced animals (especially rats) since arriving in the Island of Hawaii around the ninth century AD. Livestock brought by European and American settlers in the eighteenth and nineteenth centuries (pigs, goats, sheep and especially cattle) further denuded forests throughout the Hawaiian archipelago. By the mid-nineteenth century large-scale forest destruction above Honolulu, Oahu led to grave concerns about the city's water supply. Early foresters in the US Territorial Government of Hawai'i sought to reforest mauka (upland) forests, to restore damaged watersheds and to provide the necessary water requirements for the lowland agriculture demands and surrounding communities. This was particularly urgent in light of Hawai'i's extensive ranching and agricultural production of sugarcane, together with growing populations, and urbanization.

By the late nineteenth century, forest destruction above Honolulu, Oahu was so great it had all but stripped Nu'uanu Valley of its greenery, leading to grave concerns about the city's future water supply. Accordingly, from 1917 to Territorial Forestry (the Division of Forestry in the Territorial Government of Hawai'i) and the Hawaiian Sugar Planters' Association (an unincorporated, voluntary organization of sugarcane plantation owners) widely distributed *F. moluccana* (Woodcock 2003). By 1927, Territorial Forestry dispersed *F. moluccana* by aerial seeding. Territorial Forestry also planted millions of *F. moluccana* (and other invasive trees and seedlings) inside the dedicated State Forest Reserves (a public-private partnership to protect forested mauka lands) and supplied *F. moluccana* to ranchers, farmers and landowners for planting outside reserves, likely doubling total tree counts (Nelson and Forest 1965; Skolmen 1980; Woodcock 2003; Wagner et al. 1999). For example, nearly a thousand. *moluccana* were planted throughout the Keaouhana, Malama Ki and Nanawale Forest Reserves in the Puna district of Hawaii Island (Skolmen 1963; Nelson and Forest 1965). By mid-century, *F. moluccana* and hundreds of other exotic and native species of trees, grasses, ferns, and shrubs were planted across the Hawaiian Islands (Skolmen 1980; Woodcock 2003).

4 Case Study Area

The case study area is located in the Puna zone of Hawaii Island (Big Island) as shown in Fig. 1. The Puna zone is broken into nine sections.

The seven sections of Puna most affected by *F. moluccana* and the total number of real estate tax records (TMKs) in each section are provided in Table 1. It is shown that Pahoa (Sect. 5) has the highest number of TMKs (13,609) followed by

Fig. 1 Hawaii Island district map with mapped Puna District shaded

Kea'au (Sect. 6) at 11,845, and Mountain View (Sect. 8) at 5820 while Kurtistown (Sect. 7) has the least number of TMKs at 1646.

Among those properties affected by *F. moluccana*, the fraction of properties receiving a homeowner exemption is shown in Fig. 2. It is clear that Pahoa (Sect. 5) has the highest percentage of homeowner exemptions (exceeding 50%) followed by Kalapna (Sect. 2 at approximately 50%) while Kea'au (Sect. 6) has the lowest percentage at under 20%. Figure 3 highlights the median value of buildings and land on properties affected by *F. moluccana*. The number of property uses in each section (PITT codes for tax purposes) are shown in Fig. 4. Sample PITT categories include Residential, Agricultural and Commercial land uses. The Median land area (acres) of properties impacted by *F. moluccana* are provided in Fig. 5.

5 Threats to Human Health and Safety

Forestry experts have been warning government officials in Hawaii for years that fragile and unstable *F. moluccana* trees are a significant threat to the health and safety of communities and residents. *F. moluccana* quickly reach extreme heights

Table 1. Sections of Puna, Census Area and Total TMKs

County zone section	2	3	4	5	6	7	8
Census area	Kalapana	Leilani Estates	Nawale Estates	Pahoa	Kea'au	Kurtistown	Mountain View
Other towns and areas of interest	Kehena Kaimu Town Kaimu Beach (Black Sands)	Opihikao	Kapoho	Hawaiian Beaches Eden Rock Ainaloa	Orchidland Fern Forest Fern Acres Hawaiian Paradise Park		Glenwood
Total TMKs	3694	2968	5597	13,609	11,845	1646	5820

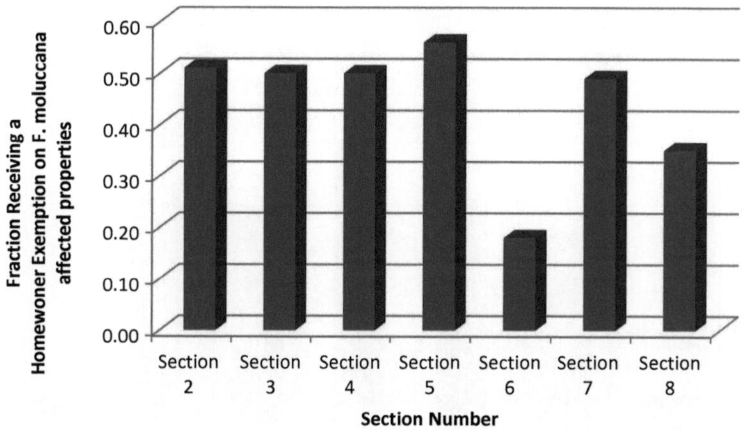

Fig. 2 Fraction of properties affected by *F. moluccana* receiving a homeowner exemption

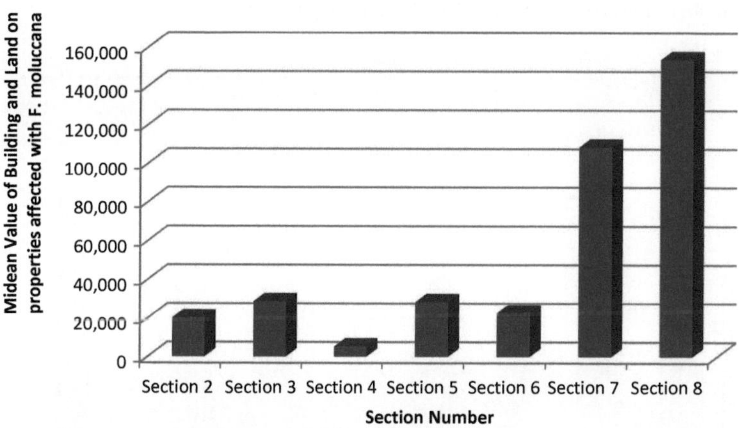

Fig. 3 Median Value of Buildings and Land on Properties affected by *F. moluccana*

despite their weak wood that breaks under even modest weather conditions, with age, or even spontaneously, leading to heavy branches snapping off and even whole trees toppling over in moderate to heavy winds. Due to a large canopy, weak structure, long limbs, brittle wood, and susceptibility to wood rot and insect infestations, *F. moluccana* are susceptible to sudden branch failure and limbs can drop unexpectedly at any time.

Because of their brittle wood and weak structure, large *F. moluccana* trees pose a hazard to nearby humans, property and critical infrastructure. Specifically, this large, hazardous, fast-growing and nitrogen fixing tree represents a predictable risk and any *F. moluccana* (regardless of current size) within 250 feet of infrastructure and individuals should be considered a roadside, urban forest and residential hazard of major significance. Routine weather incidents present a key threat to these

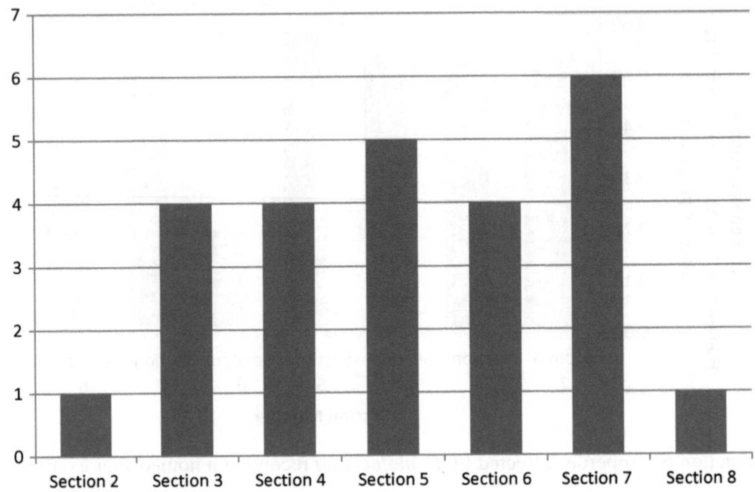

Fig. 4 Number of property uses (PITT codes for tax purposes)

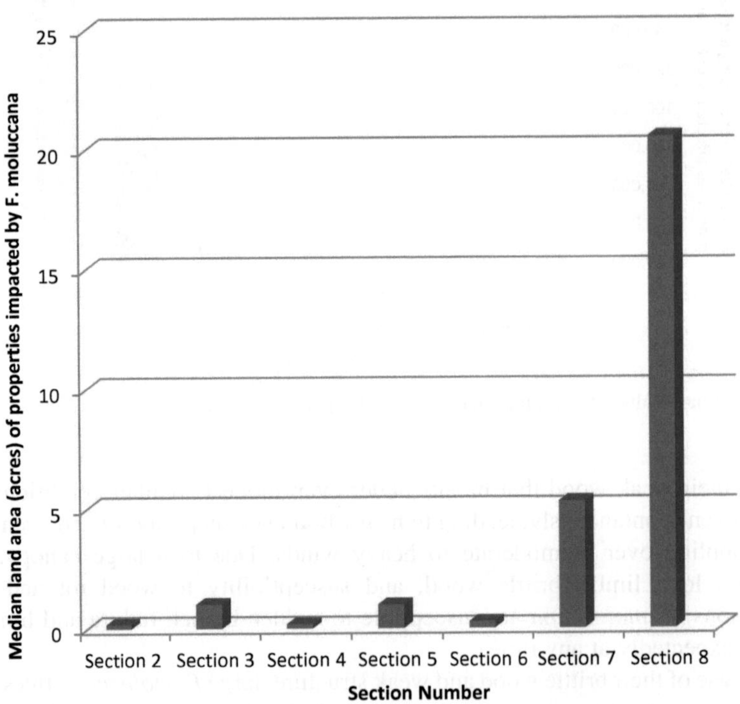

Fig. 5 Median land area (acres) of properties impacted by *F. moluccana*

massive, weak, and brittle trees: *F. moluccana* limbs commonly fall during minor weather events characterized by relatively light gusts (less than 35 mph) or heavy rain (in the absence of wind).

The broad but extremely shallow root system also contributes to tree toppling in unique soil conditions. For example, *F. moluccana* trees can be shallow-rooted when they grow in young lava soils on the Island of Hawaii, or where the soils are primarily infertile subsoils, such as along a road cut. In such cases, the entire tree may uproot resulting in catastrophic root plane failure.

High winds can cause the large branches easily snap. The large, broken limbs then drop onto whatever may be underneath, often from significant heights: trees can reach heights of more than 20 feet in their first year, 45 feet in their third year, and 60 feet by the end of their tenth year. Falling branches routinely cause costly damage to power lines, houses, and roads, fences, cars and powerlines. The trees are extremely unstable in strong wind and pose a predictable hazard to the public. This short-lived but rapidly growing tree routinely reaches heights near 110 feet and large branches have been recorded breaking and falling due to age or hidden weaknesses which are not visually observable (the wood is prone to rot and insect infestation). Specifically, the soft, weak wood of *F. moluccana* is prone to "sudden limb drop," where the branches will break off and plummet to the ground without any apparent disturbance and despite the lack of any visible defect in growth form or structural integrity.

There are several poignant recent examples of the threat posed by this highly invasive tree with top-heavy canopies. In 2007 an empty home on Molokai Road in the Nanawale subdivision (Puna district) suffered major structural damage when an *F. moluccana* tree on a neighboring property fell on the home and utility lines. In 2010, an *F. moluccana* tree fell onto a residential street in Puna (Hawaii Island), destroying power lines and fences in an area where children play. *F. moluccana* trees constitute a singular threat to residents, potentially affecting the most vulnerable members of society, including children playing outdoors in schoolyards or their own backyards. For example, on April 16, 2010, in a residential community of the Puna District on the Island of Hawaii, an *F. moluccana* tree exceeding 80 feet (25 m) fell across a residential street and landed in a family's backyard where young children often play, destroying utility poles, fences and transmission lines (Hughes et al. 2011). Even the most experienced loggers, arborists, and woodcutters are at risk. For example on January 6, 2016 an *F. moluccana* branch killed a Green Energy Hawaii employee while logging *F. moluccana* (Star-Advertiser Staff 2016). Green Energy Hawaii burns wood chips from *F. moluccana* (and other invasive species and locally grown trees) on state land at Kalepa, island of Kauai.

The risks are on the rise as the density and scale of the *F. moluccana* invasion increases. A combination of in-situ data (direct measurements recorded by different instruments in the forest, roadside mapping etc.) and remote sensing results (satellite mapping occurring over a large area) show the presence of *F. moluccana* in 5000 acres of the Puna district, with hundreds more acres in additional populations across the island of Hawaii, particularly in South Hilo and Kau districts. The largest stand of *F. moluccana* in the state of Hawaii is located at the Moloaa Forest Reserve on Kauai (more than 5 million board feet of sawtimber) and they are commonly seen along roadsides and in communities across the Hawaiian islands (Little and Skolmen 1989). On Oahu, they can also be found along the Pali and Likelike Highways.

Thousands of acres of hazardous, untreated *F. moluccana* stands continue to proliferate across the State of Hawaii in residential areas and across infrastructure corridors such as roads and power lines. Falling trees contribute to road closures, flooding, electrical outages, personal property damage and destroyed utility lines. In 2014, thousands of toppled *F. moluccana* caused widespread havoc and largescale damage during Hurricane Iselle in lower Puna (Hawaii Island). As the storm approached and made landfall on Hawaii Island fallen *F. moluccana* damaged homes, trapped residents in their neighborhoods by blocking roadways, and knocked out power for weeks in some locations.

6 Conclusions

F. moluccana constitutes a grave threat to native forests, already under pressure from a fungus causing Rapid Ohia Death: the large broad, canopy of *F. moluccana* blocks the sunlight and its shallow roots consume much of the available rainfall, which essentially starves native trees (such as ohia) to death. The nitrogen added by *F. moluccana* makes the soil more welcome to aggressive invasive understory weeds that are shade-tolerant and can survive in the *F. moluccana* understory. When *F. moluccana* is introduced, the added nitrogen improves conditions for species like Koster's curse (clidemia), strawberry guava, miconia and other invaders that can use that free fertilizer to displace native plants. These invaders take up all remaining resources, preventing native species from developing. Hence, *F. moluccana* impacts ecosystem services in Hawaii in profound ways and the potential damages to native forests, endangered-species habitat and water quantity must be carefully considered and weighed against *F. moluccana* control costs.

Management of *F. moluccana* is essential to restore Hawaii's ecosystems to their natural state and to protect water resources from these large, canopied umbrella trees since important native watershed forests are found on public and private agriculturally zoned lands on Hawai'i island. Accordingly in cooperation with ranchers, increased public and private efforts are needed to control *F. moluccana* and return agriculturally zoned state lands (currently leased for marginal pasture operations) to restored koa forests. *F. moluccana* removal and reforestation with native species can enhance watershed integrity, improve habitat for native species, and generate sustainable ecosystem services and forest products. Public cost-sharing and tax incentives are valuable strategies to encourage private landowners to invest in long-term *F. moluccana* management and reforestation. Federal and state laws should encourage a long-term commitment to *F. moluccana* control and promote the re-establishment of native habitats on private lands.

Acknowledgements *F. moluccana* GIS shapefiles for Puna (Hawaii Island) were provided by J. Gaertner as part of a 2016–2017 Hawaii Invasive Species Council (HISC) grant on Albizia Economics and Management. The HISC grant was awarded to the authors and other collaborators in the University of Hawaii and across the state of Hawaii.

References

Asner, G. P., Jones, M. O., Martin, R. E., Knapp, D. E., & Hughes, R. F. (2008). Remote sensing of native and invasive species in Hawaiian forests. *Remote Sensing of Environment, 112*(5), 1912–1926.

Hughes, R. F., & Denslow, J. S. (2005). Invasion by a N2-fixing tree alters function and structure in wet lowland forests of Hawaii. *Ecological Applications, 15*(5), 1615–1628.

Hughes, R. F., Johnson, M. T., & Uowolo, A. (2011). The invasive alien tree *F. moluccana*: Its impacts and management. In Y. Wu, T. Johnson, S. Sing, S. Raghu, G. Wheeler, P. Pratt, K. Warner, T. Center, J. Goolsby, & R. Reardon (Eds.), *Proceedings of the XIII International Symposium on Biological Control of Weeds* (pp. 218–223). Waikoloa, HI: Department of Agriculture, Forest Service, Forest Health Technology Enterprise Team, 2012–07.

Little, E. L., & Skolmen, R. G. (1989). *Common forest trees of Hawaii*. Washington, DC: US Department of Agriculture, Forest Service.

Nelson, R. E., & Forest, P. S. (1965). Record of forest plantings in Hawaii. *USDA Forest Service Resource Bulletin PSW-1*. Albany, CA: Pacific Southwest Research Station.

Skolmen, R. G. (1963). *Wood density and growth of some conifers introduced to Hawaii* (U.S. Forest Service Research Paper PSW-12) [online] Accessed March 10, 2016, from http://www.fs.fed.us/psw/publications/documents/psw_rp012/psw_rp012.pdf

Skolmen, R. G. (1980). *Plantings on the forest reserves of Hawaii, 1910–1960*. Honolulu, HI: Institute of Pacific Islands Forestry, Pacific Southwest Forest and Range Experiment Station, U.S. Forest Service.

Star-Advertiser Staff. (2016, January 8). Man killed in Kauai Albizia tree accident identified. *Star-Advertiser*. [online] Accessed July 10, 2016, from http://www.staradvertiser.com/breaking-news/man-killed-in-kauai-albizia-tree-accident-identified/

Wagner, W. L., Herbst, D. R., & Sohmer, S. H. (1999). *Manual of the flowering plants of Hawai'i* (Vol. Vols. 1 and 2, 2nd ed.). Honolulu: University of Hawai'i and Bishop Museum Press.

Woodcock, D. (2003). To restore the watersheds: Early twentieth-century tree planting in Hawai'i. *Annals of the Association of American Geographers, 93*(3), 624–635.

The Change of Structures or Institutions? Views on the Methods for the Elimination of Territorial Division Dysfunctions

Marian Kachniarz, Arkadiusz Babczuk, and Zbigniew Piepiora

Abstract The article pursues three research objectives. The first one refers to the presentation of theoretical arguments supporting units' consolidation and the review of global *ex post* experiences in achieving the expected results of such reforms. The second goal consists in presenting the authors' recommendations regarding the elimination of territorial division dysfunctions. The article draws attention to the fact that changing the rules of local authorities' functioning can bring more effective results. Despite inexplicit results of empirical analyses, consolidation still remains the leading trend of local government reforms. It is determined by political considerations, since it is easier to carry out a consolidation reform rather than take up laborious efforts in order to create institutional changes within units.

Keywords Local government • Consolidation • Reform • Administration structure

1 Introduction

Public sector reforms, carried out following the spirit of new public management (NPM), derive numerous inspirations from the experiences of private sector, where one of the methods for costs reduction is the achievement of economically optimal production scale. Therefore, the desire to reduce costs of the services provided in public sector (along with ensuring their general and equal accessibility) often

M. Kachniarz (✉)
Department of Spatial Economy, Wroclaw University of Economics, Wroclaw, Poland
e-mail: marian.kachniarz@up.wroc.pl

A. Babczuk
Department of Finance and Accounting, Wroclaw University of Economics, Wroclaw, Poland
e-mail: arkadiusz.babczuk@ue.wroc.pl

Z. Piepiora
Department of Spatial Economy, Wroclaw University of Environmental and Life Sciences, Wroclaw, Poland
e-mail: zbigniew.piepiora@up.wroc.pl

M.H. Bilgin et al. (eds.), *Empirical Studies on Economics of Innovation, Public Economics and Management*, Eurasian Studies in Business and Economics 6,
DOI 10.1007/978-3-319-50164-2_20

results in consolidation processes. These activities cover both, the units providing services and the entire administrative structures, remaining an institutional base of the public sector. Consolidation focused activities enhanced by the economies of scale (bigger is better) are primarily popular in this area. The method applied in implementing these reforms quite frequently does not take into account the specific nature of public sector, which is in practice translated into minor effects of such activities.

The objective of the below presented discussion is to analyze the substantive grounds, as well as to assess the consolidation effects referring to administrative structures. Due to the limited scope of Polish studies (both *ex-ante* and *ex-post*) it was attempted to refer mainly to international experiences and research results in the area under analysis.

The first part of the article describes theoretical aspects of both, supporters and opponents of consolidation processes. It was sought to demonstrate that in the course of a scientific discussion, none of the parties presented arguments considered sufficiently convincing. In the second part these observations were supplemented by practical aspects, supported by *ex-post* studies, which verify the effects of the conducted consolidation reforms. The particular focus was placed on the consolidation of administrative units and health care institutions.

The introduction of local government in Poland remains one of the most important reforms after the systemic transformation in 1989. It was a two-tier implementation—local municipalities were introduced in 1990, whereas in 1999 the subsequent two stages were completed—local districts and regions were established. In March 1990, Polish Parliament passed the Law on Local Government, following which local government was implemented in almost 2500 municipalities. The next stage of administrative reform was initiated on 1st January 1999. While the reform covering municipalities did not raise major political discussions, heated debates referred to the number, competencies and financial construction of the subsequent two stages. Ultimately, as the result of the reform 373 districts and 12 regions were established.

The perspective of almost 25 years of municipalities' functioning and 15 years of introducing districts and regions seems sufficient to present comments, conclusions and assessments referring to the functioning of local government units' system. Therefore, in the course of recent years, apart from multiple discussions and opinions, several important reports about the condition of Polish local government were prepared. This particular cumulation of observations about the improvement of local government units' system, also including the conception of changes in the country territorial division, was the main motive for addressing the hereby subject matter. The experiences collected during many years of local governments' functioning allow for diagnosing the dysfunctional mechanisms, which have not been solved successfully by minor legislative amendments. Simultaneously, the challenges to be faced by Poland, in the decades to come, require higher effectiveness of the local government sector functioning. Such problems cover e.g. absorptive capacity of the European Union funds or demographic pressure observed in some areas.

In 2013 several expert reports, defining the dysfunctions in Polish local government system and offering solutions to eliminate imperfections, were published: "The growing dysfunctions, fundamental dilemmas, necessary actions. The report about the condition of local government in Poland"—prepared by the team of authors under the leadership of Hausner (2013), "The assessment of local government situation"—prepared by the Ministry of Administration and Digitalization (2013) and the "Local government 3.0"—prepared by the Forum Od-nowa [Renovation Forum] (Dąmbska and Trzyna 2013).

One of the methods, recommended in the reports aimed at the elimination of some problems, is the consolidation of units. It even seems that such consolidation is perceived as the basic instrument for local government efficiency enhancement. Each of these reports, however, offers slightly different guidelines. Therefore, they are worth more extensive coverage.

The so-called Hausner's report (2003) refers to the country territorial division as the value in itself, which should not be subject to frequent and thorough transformations. It is because of the inertia in the attachment to the previously experienced structures ingrained in local communities. Hence, the proposals for changes are based on the system of encouragements and bonuses along with respect for units' autonomy. The report refers to the problem of justification for further functioning of the so-called rural peri-urban municipalities, which in the authors' opinion should be amalgamated with the urban ones by establishing new rural-urban structures. The situation is similar in case of smaller municipalities, which in view of the so-called economies of scope and economies of scale should consider the possibility of executing their tasks jointly with other units and ultimately arrive at adequate consolidation decisions. According to the authors some of the municipalities are too small to perform all their competencies properly.

Ministry of Administration and Digitalization (MAD) report (2013) takes its recommendations a bit further by postulating imposed consolidation mechanisms of rural peri-urban and urban municipalities and also the small ones which number of residents does not exceed 4000. It also assumes the verification of districts' network by an automatic amalgamation of townships with the neighboring land districts. It is also postulated to implement a new level—the so-called metropolitan district, which is supposed to manage certain selected tasks (communication, planning) within the functional zones of the largest agglomerations.

The report by Odnowa *[Renovation]* Forum (Dąmbska and Trzyna 2013) postulates the most far-reaching changes in the local government administration network. According to this report, the existence of such small units is no longer rational in the period of changing communication forms. Therefore, it assumes the consolidation of municipalities to the structures inhabited by at least 20,000 residents. The emergence of such big municipalities automatically eliminates the grounds for the functioning of districts—the report authors recommend this level liquidation. Large municipalities took over the tasks of districts in their area. It somewhat confirms the thesis that the area similar to the existing districts remains the basic spatial unit of public services. The majority of catchment zones in terms of services (public and commercial) are functioning in such system (rather than a municipal one), or in terms of economic aspects (trade, labor market).

2 Theoretical Determinants

All the above presented a priori consolidation proposals assume that reducing units' number and enlarging their size shall rationalize administration. Moreover, this guideline is quite commonly raised in all public debates referring to administration functioning (not only to local government one). The basic quoted argument refers to the above mentioned economies of scale, which assume that along with the increasing production scale (in this case the scale of public services provision) product unit cost is reduced (e.g. administration services) (Begg et al. 2003).

The trend for units' size enlargement started disseminating to various areas of public sector, along with the concept called New Public Management, aimed at public administration economization. The basic arguments voiced by consolidation supporters based on the belief that larger entities have larger possibilities to undertake the execution of more extensive scope of tasks. Thus, territorial consolidation enhances deeper decentralization. The effect of economies of scale is also present in case of many services rendered by entities (the most direct evidence refers to administration expenditure). As a result, performing some tasks in large units is cheaper. Since larger local governments can perform more functions, it can be expected that their residents' involvement in local policy shall be larger. In such perspective, territorial consolidation plays the role of local democracy promoter. The organization of public services, where the size of basic units is large, results in less extensive diversification of the development level and the size of budget revenues between the particular areas. It presents smaller needs for horizontal alignment, which is both expensive for the national budget and also politically controversial. Large entities stand the change of more efficient functioning in terms of economic planning. The systems covering large units are more effective in reducing the phenomenon of a benefiting region (the situation in which the locally provided services are taken advantage of by residents/taxpayers from other functional zones). In other words, consolidation supports the reduction of discrepancies between the functional zones and the spatial range of services rendered by particular entities (Swianiewicz 2009).

On the other hand, however, the doctrine of new institutionalism, which has been evolving since the beginning of 80s of the twentieth century, draws attention to the paradox of the contemporary world referring to globalization. The processes accompanying such unification, within which more boundaries become theoretically blurred, are coupled with an identity reaction in the form of locality renaissance, intensified search for the sense of place, or one's own small homeland (Kempny 2004). Chłopecki (2005) emphasizes that the civilization of space produces nomads who enjoy freedom, but are deprived of security resulting from belonging to a particular place. In accordance with the new institutionalism theory, liberal approach to consolidation reforms in public sector results from taking a one-sided view, which narrows down an objective image of an institution functioning. Meanwhile, human interactions remain the consequence of restrictions, principles, the rule of conduct and procedures invented by people themselves (North

1994). Such perspective allows for appreciating the role of informal limitations, which constitute the part of cultural heritage established by a given society, the system of ideas and ideologies. North (1990) draws attention to the fact that informal rules are characterized by a specific inertia which causes that the occurring transformation of formal rules (e.g. legislation or, in a broader perspective, economic system) does not result in expected effects.

Therefore, the reform of local government administration structures should take the above determinants into account. The size of areas covered by public services provision, including health care services, should be based on the naturally created catchment zones and the residents' identification with a particular functional unit. Contrary to the neoliberal theories, the advocates of localism claim that smaller units support the affirmation for democratic attitudes. The relations between residents (electorate) and politicians in such units remain closer and more straightforward. The level of confidence is higher, the flow of information is easier and as a result the provided public services reflect residents' preferences much better. The control of decision makers' functioning remains direct, which enhances their functioning rationality and reduces the possibility of uncontrolled administration expansion. The identification of decision makers, and also lower level personnel, with the services provision area is higher. Therefore, the responsibility for particular projects is identified with particular individuals—its blurring effect on the structure does not occur. As a result, the interest of local community in the unit functioning is larger and also the awareness of residents' impact on its functioning is higher (Swianiewicz 2009).

Summarizing the theoretical presentation of the problem, it is worth noticing that no unequivocal theoretical evidence, allowing to determine an optimal size of local functional zones, exists. The interdisciplinary nature of local administration study, and the diversified specificity of institutions which influence it, does not allow for making simple and universal syntheses in this subject matter.

Many economists claim that over-extensive fragmentation of structures results in higher transactional costs of the provided services. The consolidation of entities rendering these services should therefore result in the reduction of unit functioning costs and in their effectiveness enhancement (Kieżun 2004). Such approach is justified by an opinion that larger units are characterized by better allocation of financial, material and personnel resources. In the latter sense they have e.g. better access to highly qualified staff. To sum up, the discussed trend can be defined by the phrase "bigger is better". This conviction is so deep that it frequently takes the form of an undisputable paradigm.

3 *Ex-post* Research

At this point a question can be asked—since consolidation is supposed to result in substantive effects should not they be diagnosed in *ex post* assessments in the countries which have already implemented such reforms? Anglo-Saxon countries are most advanced in terms of local units' consolidation, i.e. the ones in which the ideas of Thatcherism and Reaganomics were most common. In Australia and New Zealand, this process was carried out at the beginning of the 90s of the last century. It resulted in the reduced number of local government units by almost 30%. Apart from an amalgamation of small units, the municipalities forming metropolitan groups were also joined. Similar reforms, however on a smaller scale, were carried out in Canada, Great Britain (in its English part), in USA, Denmark and Germany (mainly in Eastern Lands).

The period of at least 20-year history in the functioning of consolidated units offers grounds for conducting credible analyses. From over a decade, a few research teams from worldwide have studied the economies of scale resulting from local government consolidation reforms (Dollery et al. 2008; Dollery and Robotti 2008). What kind of picture emerges from the review of these studies? The conclusions are quite unexpected. In *ex post* studies, as opposed to what was assumed in *ex ante* models, positive effects of consolidation were rarely identified. They did not confirm the economies of scale (defined as a procedure unit cost) in the perspective of either entire units or particular specialties. Dollery and Crase (2004) conclude that there is no evidence for cheaper function of larger units, whereas the experiences of many countries in the concentration of services and amalgamation of units did not prove to be a miraculous remedy for cutting costs. Paradoxically, spending increased in the areas which, as a result of consolidation, were supposed to bring the highest savings.

American research is similar regarding its effect (Pineda 2005; Sancton 2000). They summarized several dozens of North American studies on the consolidation effects of public services. In the course of the recent 20 years, many such case studies were analyzed, covering consolidation problems in USA and Canada. They failed, however, to provide evidence supporting the significant economies of scale for the majority of municipal services. The conclusions resulting from these and other studies showed that paradoxically, costs of many services, following large municipal consolidations, have grown (Municipal Research and Services Center of Washington 2003).

The review of 25 research studies (in USA and Canada), conducted in the period of the last two decades, suggests that the fragmented and deconcentrated system of local governments is usually connected with lower expenditure and higher efficiency. The power of bureaucracy grows along with unit size. It is explicitly visible when the politicians originating from local elections successfully construct their bureaucratic empires that grow with the local government size (Galambos 1999).

Attention is drawn to an organization, management methods, institutional determinants and motivations—i.e. internal components' characteristics of particular units which have impact on their functioning costs. It usually happens that the reformers do not appreciate the role of transactional costs, which can have an increasing tendency in larger units and thus eliminate the potential economies of scale.

A review of international experiences from empirical studies of structural reforms is presented by Dollery and Robotti (2008) and Dollery and Grant

(2013). They offer two major findings. Dollery and Grant (2013) confirm that the effects of empirical studies bring about ambiguous results. Dollery and Robotti (2008) lead to a conclusion that in spite of numerous consolidation reforms, the scope of research over their effects presents an ongoing causative nature. Therefore, an urgent need occurs for performing complex empirical studies by applying rigorous modeling, along with other analytical techniques.

At the above presented background, the European research remains relatively poorly developed. *Ex ante* studies are the dominating ones, which clearly favor neoliberal conviction of the need for public sector reduction. They frequently miss to perceive the specific functional determinants underlying the functioning of local governments by equalizing them with private sector institutions. Few studies, which discuss this problem in greater detail, are the publications by Houlberg (2008) and Swianiewicz (2010a).

4 Polish Empirical Research

Among Polish studies on the economies of scale, the most popular reports were prepared by Swianiewicz and Łukomska (2015) covering expenditure on public administration. In spite of the reservations by the authors himself, the results of this ranking are often approached as the crucial evidence confirming the relatively lower functioning costs of larger local government units' functioning. This method, however, does not take the organizational structure of performed tasks into consideration, and thus they do not cover costs of tasks execution by the utility companies and their employees. Therefore, false conclusions are drawn that in case of a municipality, where all public services are provided by the municipal office, administration remains more expensive from the ones which separated their organizational units and companies.

An extensive analysis, conducted by the authors of the hereby article, offers an example of empirical research covering the discussed problem. It specifies efficiency and productivity indicators of administration, technical and social services in 26 Lower Silesian districts. Next the correlation between the synthetic results of these indicators and a unit size, defined as the number of residents, was investigated. The approach, contrary to unequivocal opinions, frequently voiced during public debates, about higher efficiency of large units (bigger is better) in the light of presented findings, remains untrue. The details are presented on Fig. 1. The correlation coefficient between efficiency and district size (measured by the number of its residents) amounts to −0.1209. Hence, this value illustrates an even slightly reverse correlation. However, having considered an extensive dispersion of the results, it can be adopted that no statistical correlation occurs between these two measured variables.

The comparison of productivity measures against district size brings about similar findings. In this case the correlation result is also insignificant, even though the value is positive—0.0691. This time the analysis of results illustrated on Fig. 2

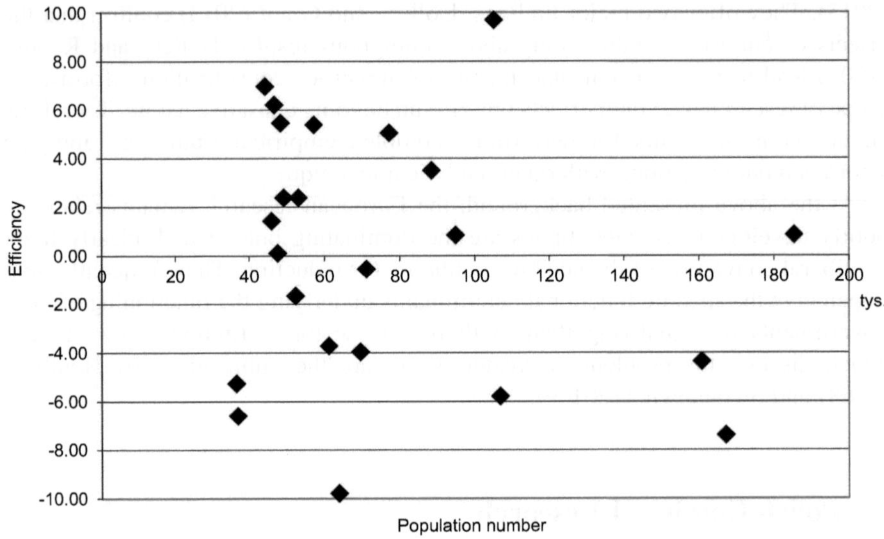

Fig. 1 Correlation between the size and efficiency of Lower Silesian districts

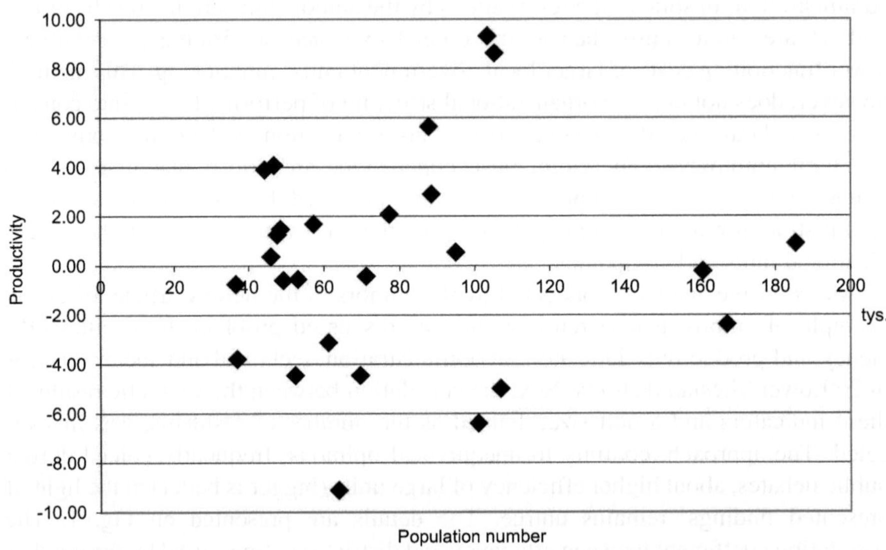

Fig. 2 Correlation between the size and productivity of Lower Silesian districts

also indicates high dispersion of values. It proves that the same size district groups cover both efficient units and the ones which achieve poor results in this matter. It is true for, on the one hand, small and, on the other, the largest districts. Hence, seeking any correlation in such circumstances is unfounded. In view of the above, the approach of higher efficiency of larger units is not true.

Therefore, if the results of the discussed correlations, as well as the research results conducted in other countries do not confirm the dependence between efficiency and local government unit size, why is this conviction so strongly emphasized in the course of public debate? Why do many representatives of organization and management science accept this statement a priori? The specificity of public sector causes that the theories which prove correct in the manufacturing sector cannot be fully applied in the domain of public administration, since it is subject to far more diversified determinants, defined as institutional standards.

Economies of scale can also be perceived from the perspective of cost structure presented in the operations of local government units. In the manufacturing sector economies of scale refer primarily to fixed costs—the higher their share in total costs the larger the expected economies of scale. Once this principle is transposed into the group of local governments under analysis, it should be adopted that the provision of the defined services' volume occurs along with a similar level of fixed costs. Meanwhile, however, the actual reality remains entirely different, which is confirmed by e.g. extensive differences in an employment rate. Local governments enjoy a considerable autonomy in influencing their budget management, which is translated into significant differences in their fixed costs level. Even a formal presentation of fixed costs proves their relatively low importance in the budget structure. They refer to expenditure provided for by the legislation in force, e.g. to the specific number of councilors, or hiring specialists meeting particular criteria. They do not exceed the level of 10% expenditure. Their remaining part is automatically arranged by each individual local government (Kachniarz 2012a).

The second problem is associated with determining at which point further unit development may result in diseconomies of scale. Such situation occurs when a unit size results in higher transactional costs. They are caused by e.g. multi-level management structure, tendencies for organizational sections and divisions, information flow problems, desire to collect resources as well as suppressing major objectives and principles in unit functioning. Perhaps the optimum below which diseconomies of scale occur is placed on a relatively low level and remains unnoticed by those who have always been seeking it within the largest units? In such circumstances the term large takes on a relative importance.

The third component, explaining the absence of unequivocal research results, can refer to the complex structure of services provided by local governments. The impact of economies of scale can be of various natures in particular areas. It may even result in negative couplings, i.e. economies of scale resulting from the provision of a given municipal service are eliminated by dis-effects in the service qualified in the group of social or administrative ones.

Even if it is assumed that a unit size should determine both efficiency and productivity, the absence of such correlation in the presented studies can also result from stronger influence of other factors. The discussed impact can be large enough to overcome entirely the possible advantages resulting from the economies of scale. Much stronger correlation occurred between the efficiency and quality of management. It allows for concluding that the more important elements influencing its efficiency, rather than unit size, can take the form of e.g. leadership type and municipal office organizational culture.

By the way, the empirical research results, which have already been mentioned in literature review, do not confirm the flagship argument expressed by the advocates of larger units who claim that their functioning remains more effective and efficient. In many cases, breaking the ties of direct public control and distancing administration from the local level resulted in relative expansion of structures, reduced efficiency and higher functioning costs. Kłodzki district represents the typical example corresponding to the above remarks, formed—as it has already been mentioned—from three districts functioning till 1975. The distance from local level operations results in the expansion of difficult to manage and expensive structures. As a result its efficiency is relatively low.

Social control also represents the crucial component—more direct in smaller units. Large structures are much more abstract for local communities, which translates into higher anonymity of their administration staff. Hence, all administration becomes less transparent for the local community. It also makes the direct supervision by managers more difficult preventing them from precise assessment of their actual functioning, as well as the grounds and directions indispensable for implementing transformations. The discussed experiences should serve as a warning before undertaking thoughtless changes in local administrative structures. They should be preceded by an interdisciplinary analysis, which takes into account the institutional determinants of a particular country or region. It is crucial to avoid extreme values, while investigating the discussed problems and focus on moderate solutions. Both, over-excessive consolidation and exaggerated territorial fragmentation can remain the source of problems (Swianiewicz 2010b).

5 Conclusions

The brief, out of necessity, literature review covering the effects of country territorial division reforms, illustrates that there is no unequivocal theoretical evidence allowing to determine the optimal size of local functional zones. The scientific interdisciplinary about local administration and the diversified specificity of the influencing institutions does not allow for making simple and universal syntheses in this subject matter. This fact itself should cool down the reformers' enthusiasm who believes that the economies of scale remain a practical mechanism which is always present in case of administrative units' enlargement.

This, however, does not mean that the country territorial division is rational by nature and its modification is unnecessary. It is especially true when the changing social, economic and technological environment has to be addressed. It is vital not to avoid implementing such changes based on the established dogmas, which in fact represent informal, empirically unverified knowledge. The activities which fail to account for complex interactions, binding the currently existing units, are also doomed to failure. So what, if breaking functional zones of many cities by granting them with a township status is criticized, since it is immediately followed by the postulate of their amalgamation with the surrounding land districts. From the perspective of functional zones integrity this postulate seems rational. One has to be aware, however, that other reasons are also vital, the effects of which can outweigh possible benefits resulting from integration, financial bonuses including. It has been very well verified practically by the example of Wałbrzych. Abandoning the township status proved to be absolutely wrong not only for the entire city, but also for the whole agglomeration (thus for the land district). It was not until the core agglomeration regained the township function when the new development incentives were initiated.[1] It is not surprising that local government can follow their rationale, since the divided system of two districts (a township and a land one) results in higher competencies and a greater inflow of the EU funds. Amalgamation into one entity can degrade such area in terms of both competencies and finance.

All the above presented arguments result in the fact that the proposal for local government units' consolidation, suggested in the discussed reports, do not constitute the guarantee for rational functioning. They can be regarded as guidelines for implementation no sooner than positive effects of these changes are certain. It should be strongly emphasized that the current form of these proposals does not guarantee such certainty, which does not stop some authors from manifesting strong attachment to their postulates. Their attitude is frequently based on the certainty about the effectiveness of their views, even though as it has been indicated in the previous sub-chapter that empirical studies rarely support such approach.

Many so-called "irrefutable arguments" are based on both financial and statistical data analyses. Supporting them by econometric methods is supposed to prove the objectivity of arguments. However, ignorance of the researched subject matter frequently results in erroneous conclusions. An incorrect assessment of administration functioning costs, based on budget reporting only, can serve as an example. It takes into account only a selected fragment of local governments' operations, which results in an opinion that smaller units spend relatively more on their maintenance. Such conclusion constitutes the axis for changes proposal in the report issued by the Ministry of Administration and Digitalization (2013). It is a serious methodological mistake—it does not account for the complicated structure underlying public tasks execution. The larger the local government, the more its tasks are executed through the separated budget entities, or institutions outside public finance sector. The expenditure of budget entities are presented in a different, than the above mentioned, division of budget classification, whereas in the latter case they can remain entirely outside the budget. The significance of conclusions based on such data is undermined by the research of costs, incurred by the authorities and administration, conducted by Wojciechowski (2014). He analyzed

[1] A competence based division regarding public roads is an example of such effects—townships integrate the management of all categories of roads, including national motorways, whereas in land districts it is divided into four management levels. Each of them can follow its own priorities, not necessarily coinciding with the city ones.

this group of costs in all regional capital cities in Poland, however, taking into account their, above mentioned, execution structure. It required, among others, to analyze balance sheets of all municipal companies. The results turned out to be far from the picture based exclusively on administrative expenditure in budget reporting. Moreover, the influence of a city size on the discussed effects was not confirmed. For example, an average resident of Cracow spends on city administration twice less than a resident of Warsaw. The respective amounts are: 63.5 € and as much as 118 €. In Opole these costs amounted to 89 €, whereas in Toruń only 49 €.

Therefore, instead of changes in local government structures, more attention should be paid to transformations within these institutions. It should, however, go beyond the strictly endogenous reasons, but also cover the external components (e.g. legislation) responsible for the relations inside units. As it turns out, this element is of much greater significance in influencing the general costs of local government system than structural imperfections. The financial weakness of districts does not depend on their small size (and this is how the problem is presented in public debate), but on the faulty system of their financing. Higher flexibility of local governments, in terms of organizational forms followed in tasks execution, can serve as a good example, or larger freedom in municipal agreements. Extensive changes should also be introduced in finance management. The current system of budget reporting is subject to central interests rather than local governments themselves (Kachniarz 2012b).

It is perfectly concluded by Regulski (2014), who states that: "The method of tasks execution has to be adjusted to a municipality size and other local conditions rather than vice versa. A shoe has to fit a foot rather than a foot fit a shoe". The same refers to the applied financial mechanisms, which are supposed to encourage for municipalities' amalgamation, whereas remaining gullible and missing actual mechanisms against amalgamation they are pathetic. The stability of administrative division represents the value in itself. It must not be violated if it is expected that local authorities are to think strategically about development. Administrative division has to result from the fact of recognizing municipalities as the communities of their residents. A community shall function well if its population is joined by common interests as well other functional, social and economic ties. When they are breached, neither a community nor a local government can exist (Cyrankiewicz 2014).

Following the ideas of new constitutionalism, the liberal approach to consolidation reforms in public sector results from a one-sided view narrowing down an objective picture of an institution functioning. Meanwhile, human interactions remain the consequence of restrictions, principles, the rule of conduct and procedures invented by people themselves (North 1994). Such perspective allows for appreciating the role of informal limitations, which constitute the part of cultural heritage established by a given society, the system of ideas and ideologies. North (1994) draws attention to the fact that informal rules are characterized by a specific inertia which causes that the occurring transformation of formal rules (e.g. legislation or, in a broader perspective, an economic system) does not result in expected effects. Therefore, the reform of local government administration structures should take the above determinants into account.

The disappointment following the implementation of New Public Management principles changed the perception of self-government units based on the model applied by private sector entities. They take into account much more diversified and complex reasons than consortiums. Sociological, legal, political or even ethical issues have the same impact on the nature of their functioning as economic determinants do.

Ignoring the complicated nature of these units can result in failing to achieve the assumed results by implementing the suggested changes. There is a real threat that rationalization measures will be addressed towards the incorrectly identified causes. Larger advantages can be achieved by internal institutional reforms—it is there where the majority of phenomena, reducing local government effectiveness, are located. Therefore, efforts should be invested in making current structures functioning more effective. As opposed to that, the effect of the economies of scale, accompanying structural changes, usually remains overrated.

The consolidation of two dysfunctional units shall enhance rather than reduce these dysfunctions. Their nature does not result from the scale of particular units, but from internal determinants. First the methods for improving the internal situation of such units should be investigated and only later obtaining the economies of scale effect should possibly be considered. Such effect may be achieved not necessarily by the consolidation itself. Good results are accomplished by the cooperation of local governments in the conditions of freedom in the process of formal structures formation. In Poland, current legislative provisions do not facilitate such cooperation (Kachniarz and Przybyła 2012).

In spite of the above presented evidence, it is hard to penetrate the well-established paradigm, following which consolidation remains the remedy for multiple problems. So, where does the alluring nature of such solution originate from? It is decided by political issues. From such perspective, it is much easier to implement a consolidation reform and emphasize one's involvement in introducing spectacular changes, rather than laboriously create institutional changes within units. Spectacular political actions miss the economic effects of changes.

References

Begg, D., Fisher, S., & Dornbush, R. (2003). *Mikroekonomia* [Microeconomics]. Warsaw: PWE Publishers.

Chłopecki, J. (2005). Tożsamości społeczne w globalnym świecie [Social identities in the global world]. In K. Bondyra, M. S. Szczepański, & P. Śliwa (Eds.), *Państwo, samorząd i społecznoś ci lokalne* [State, local government and local communities] (pp. 51–71). Poznań: Higher School of Banking Press.

Cyrankiewicz, M. (2014, April 7). Duże nie oznacza tańsze [Large does not mean cheaper]. *Rzeczpospolita*, p. 4.

Dąmbska, A., & Trzyna, S. (2013). *Samorząd 3.0* [Local government 3.0]. Warszawa: Forum Od-nowa [Renovation Forum].

Dollery, B., & Crase, L. (2004). Is bigger local government better? An evaluation of the economic case for Australian municipal amalgamation programs. *University of New England Working Paper Series in Economics, 4*, 1–27.

Dollery, B., & Grant, B. (2013). Symposium on amalgamation and financial sustainability in local government. *Public Finance & Management, 13*, 142–147.

Dollery, B., & Robotti, L. (Eds.). (2008). *The theory and practice of local government reform*. Cheltenham: Edward Elgar Publishing.

Dollery, B., Garcea, J., & LeSage, E. C. (2008). *Local government reform: A comparative analysis of advanced Anglo-American countries*. Cheltenham: Edward Elgar Publishing.

Galambos, E. C. (1999). *Sandy springs: A case study on centralization of local government*. Atlanta, GA: Georgia Public Policy Foundation.

Hausner, J. (Ed.). (2013). *Narastające dysfunkcje, zasadnicze dylematy, konieczne działania. Raport o stanie samorządności terytorialnej w Polsce* [Growing dysfunctions, fundamental dilemmas, necessary actions. The report on the condition of local government in Poland]. Cracow: Małopolska School of Public Administration.

Houlberg, K. (2008). *Municipal size, economy and democracy, consolidation or fragmentation? Lessons learned from territorial consolidation reforms—The European experience*. Warsaw: Warsaw University Press.

Kachniarz, M. (2012a). *Efektywność usług publicznych. Teoria i praktyka* [The efficiency of public services. Theory and practice]. Wrocław: Wrocław University of Economics Press.

Kachniarz, M. (2012b). Koncepcja systemu oceny efektywności samorządu lokalnego [The system concept of local government efficiency assessment]. *Research Studies of Wrocław University of Economics, 264*, 150–161.

Kachniarz, M., & Przybyła, Z. (2012). Instytucjonalne formy współpracy samorządów terytorialnych na przykładzie jeleniogórskiego zespołu miejskiego [Institutional forms of local governments' cooperation based on the example of Jelenia Góra conurbation]. *Research Studies of Wrocław University of Economics, 243*, 249–263.

Kempny, M. (2004). Tradycje lokalne jako podstawa kapitału społecznego. Co tradycja może znaczyć dla społeczności lokalnej w dobie globalizacji? [Local traditions as the basis of social capital. What is the significance of tradition for local community in the times of globalization]. In J. Kurczewska (Ed.), *Oblicza lokalności. Tradycja i współczesność* [Faces of locality. Tradition and present] (pp. 148–163). Warsaw: The Institute of Philosophy and Sociology Publishers Polish Academy of Science.

Kieżun, W. (2004). Struktury i kierunki zarządzania państwem [Structures and directions of the state management]. In W. Kieżun, J. Kubin (Ed.), *Dobre Państwo* [The good state] (pp. 35–77). Warsaw: Kozminski University Press.

Ministry of Administration and Digitalization. (2013). *Ocena sytuacji samorządów lokalnych* [The assessment of local governments' situation]. Warsaw: The Ministry of Administration and Digitalization.

Municipal Research and Services Center of Washington. (2003). *Is municipal consolidation the answer? Is bigger always better?* Washington, DC: Municipal Research and Services Center of Washington.

North, D. C. (1990). *Structure and change in economic history*. New York: Norton.

North, D. C. (1994). *Institutions, institutional change and economic performance*. Cambridge: Cambridge University Press.

Pineda, C. (2005). *City county consolidation and diseconomies of scale: Summary of selected literature*. Harvard, IL: Ash Institute for Democratic Governance and Innovation.

Regulski, J. (2014, January 8). Nie dopasowuje się nogi do buta [Not fit a foot to a shoe]. *Rzeczpospolita*, p. 1.

Sancton, A. (2000). *Merger mania*. Montreal, QC: McGill-Queens University Press.

Swianiewicz, P. (2009). Reformy konsolidacji terytorialnej—Teoria i praktyka krajów Europy Środkowo-Wschodniej [Territorial consolidation reforms—Theory and practice of Central and eastern European countries]. *Samorząd Terytorialny [Local Government], 4*, 5–22.

Swianiewicz, P. (2010a). Czy rozmiar ma znaczenie? Zróżnicowanie opinii mieszkańców o funkcjonowaniu samorządów lokalnych w zależności od wielkości gminy [Is size important? Diversification of residents' opinions about the functioning of local governments depending on a municipal size]. *Samorząd Terytorialny [Local Government], 4*, 5–16.

Swianiewicz, P. (2010b). If territorial fragmentation is a problem, is amalgamation a solution? East European perspective. *Local Government Studies, 2*(36), 183–203.

Swianiewicz, P., & Łukomska, J. (2015). *Oszczędny urząd* [Economical office]. [pdf] Warsaw: Wspólnota. Accessed April 20, 2016, from http://www.wspolnota.org.pl/fileadmin/pliki/Andrzej_Gniadkowski/Ranking_oszczedny_urzad.pdf

Wojciechowski, M. (2014). *Koszt władzy w polskim samorządzie terytorialnym* [The cost of authority in Polish local government]. Warsaw: Difin.

The Effect of Employment Status on Life Satisfaction in Europe

Mehmet Fatih Aysan and Ummugulsum Aysan

Abstract There has been a growing interest in the concept of happiness in economics, psychology, and sociology. The effect of employment status on life satisfaction has been of particular interest in the empirical research of economics. A substantial body of literature shows that unemployment is associated with lower levels of happiness conceptualized as life satisfaction. This paper investigates life satisfaction levels in three dimensions of life—social and demographic characteristics, social inequality, and employment—using the third wave of the European Quality of Life Survey (EQLS) conducted in 2011. Multiple regression results are consistent with that of previous literature. Even when the financial situation and other individual characteristics are held constant, unemployment reduces people's life satisfaction. The final model shows that the impact of social exclusion, deprivation, and financial differences on life satisfaction proves to be higher than the impacts of education level, marital status, age, and employment status. Hence, welfare state policies affecting social inequalities and labor market have significant effects on life satisfaction.

Keywords Life satisfaction • Happiness • Employment • Social policy • Europe

1 Introduction

Over the centuries thinkers have reflected on happiness and a good life. Nevertheless, due to lack of consensus on the definition of happiness and data sets, thinkers have not been able to check their assumption about the determinants of happiness and good life. Therefore, thinkers' understanding of what defines life satisfaction has remained theoretical. Empirical studies introduced by social scientists,

M.F. Aysan (✉)
Department of Sociology, Istanbul Sehir University, Istanbul, Turkey
e-mail: mfaysan@sehir.edu.tr

U. Aysan
Department of Social Services, Istanbul University, Istanbul, Turkey
e-mail: ummugulsum.aysan@istanbul.edu.tr

M.H. Bilgin et al. (eds.), *Empirical Studies on Economics of Innovation, Public Economics and Management*, Eurasian Studies in Business and Economics 6,
DOI 10.1007/978-3-319-50164-2_21

particularly psychologists and economists, have brought innovative approaches to comprehend the factors which affect life satisfaction, especially since the 1990s (Veenhoven 1991; Easterlin 1995, 2001; Christopher 1999).

The concept life satisfaction frequently denotes chances and capabilities for a good life, such as high education level, health status, income level, leisure, social relationship, and employment status. Efforts to create a better society after World War II started with attacking the long term social problems: namely unemployment, poverty, social security, and literacy Galbraith (1998) asserts three large goals important for the life satisfaction of individuals: government investment in public education, the poverty mitigation, and the growth of the new occupations that consists of white collar workers such as doctors, engineers, and teachers. In order to evaluate the welfare state programs and social development, new concepts were introduced, such as happiness, wellbeing, and quality of life since the 1950s. This new era of knowledge started to attract more researchers in the coming decades. Hence life satisfaction became a chief topic in this new part of study. Another central research area extensively studied for decades is the cause and consequences of employment status (Amine and Dos Santos 2013; Constant and Zimmermann 2014; van Stel et al. 2014; Charfeddine and Mrabet 2015; Mitra and Jha 2015).

In this study, various factors affecting life satisfaction will be analyzed. A vital determinant among these factors is the welfare state that mitigates inequalities and unemployment. The research questions, hence, are what set of the country characteristics best predict life satisfaction levels among European individuals? How do social policies affect life satisfaction across countries? How does the life satisfaction level change in accordance with the unemployment status?

This paper will first start with a brief discussion of the life satisfaction and related concepts will be briefly discussed. Second, the relationship between employment and life satisfaction will be analyzed. Third, data and method will be given. Fourth, multiple regression results will be analyzed. In light of the findings, the importance of social policies mitigating social inequality and deprivation will be discussed.

2 Life Satisfaction and Employment

The term life satisfaction denotes quality of life, well-being, and enjoyment. Quality of life mostly denotes chances for a good life, such as having a good education and career, working in a prestigious job. According to Sen (2001), an individual's capability to live a good life is determined in terms of the set of valuable beings and doings such as being in good health or having good relationships with others. Sen's approach was one of the first challenges to narrowly economic thinking in explaining human development, happiness, and quality of life with economic factors. Since the early 1990s, his approach has been employed widely in the context of human development by the United Nations Development Programme (UNDP). He claims that poverty must be understood as deprivation in the capability to live a good life, and development can be understood as capability expansion (Sen 2001).

In the literature, life satisfaction and happiness have been generally used interchangeably. In sociology, subjective indicators (life satisfaction and happiness) are used to supplement traditional objective indicators (income, health, and education). Life satisfaction and happiness have been utilized as a chief subjective indicator of social performance since the 1970s (Andrews and Withey 1976). In addition to sociologists, economists started to analyze the subjective indicators especially since the 2000s (e.g., Frey and Stutzer 2010). While some are interested in latent variables such as empathy, self-worth, goal autonomy, discrimination and etc. (e.g., Anand et al. 2011), others focused on concrete factors such as employment status, income, education, and health status (Diener and Suh 1997; Di Tella et al. 2001; Frey and Stutzer 2010). The contemporary literature has shown that the effects of personal characteristics and economic variables on the level of happiness are quite strong. Among these studies, the effects of employment status on life satisfaction have been heavily discussed (Veenhoven 2015).

Frey and Stutzer (2010) argue that being unemployed has a strong negative impact on life satisfaction and happiness when other factors are controlled. Among the active population, one of the most detrimental experiences is the lack of employment opportunity. Many studies have proved the devastating economic and psychological impacts of unemployment on one's life satisfaction (Kossek and Ozeki 1998; Lucas et al. 2004; Anand et al. 2011).

Di Tella et al. (2001) study how the unemployment rate, the inflation rate, and the unemployment influence the level of happiness based on Euro-Barometer Survey Series. They claim that when other factors are controlled for, unemployed people are less happy than employed people. Clark and Oswald (1994) use the UK micro data, and found that unemployment significantly reduces people's happiness. Pittau et al. (2010) examined the role of economic factors on life satisfaction in the regional level. They found that income has a strong effect in poor regions than in rich regions. After having controlled individual characteristics and interaction effects, regional differences in life satisfaction are significant, confirming that regional dimension is very important in one's life satisfaction. More importantly, even after having controlled income variable, being unemployed is negatively associated with life satisfaction (Pittau et al. 2010).

3 Data and Method

In the literature, the effects of unemployment on life satisfaction or happiness have been used as a dependent variable. In this article, the effects of social and economic factors on satisfaction are examined in three dimensions of life—social and demographic characteristics, social inequality, and employment—using the European Quality of Life Survey (EQLS). These three domains are among the most central determinants affecting one's life satisfaction. The EQLS records many aspects of the quality of life in Europe between 2011 and 2012. It includes social, economic, and environmental determinants along with well-being and the quality of European societies. This survey is the third wave of quality of life surveys started in 2003. Through these longitudinal surveys, Eurofound has developed a unified methodological approach and quality assurance system not only for the European Union but also for other countries in the region. This survey covers 43,636 people from the 27 EU Member States plus seven candidate countries (Croatia, Iceland, Kosovo, the Former Yugoslav Republic of Macedonia, Montenegro, Serbia, and Turkey), in total of 34 countries.

The sample size for each country ranges from 1001 to 3055, while the seven EU countries with the largest population, making up altogether 75% of the EU population, had a higher sample size so as to help to advance the accuracy of estimates at the national and European level. Survey interviews were conducted face to face in respondents' houses. The target population were all residents of the 34 European countries aged 18 and older (for details, see Eurofound 2013).

Respondents' answers to the dependent variable life satisfaction questions are coded on a 10-point scale ranging from 1 for "very dissatisfied" to 10 for "very satisfied." The reason for using life satisfaction variable to understand the good life or well-being of individuals is that subjective measures such as life satisfaction and meaning of life have been heavily used and considered as reliable measures by international studies and guidelines.

There are three sets of independent variables used in the multiple regression analysis. The first set of variables can be considered as control variables including age, education level, marital status, gender, place of residence, and health status. The second set of variables consists of social inequality variables namely, self-perceived financial situation (Could you please evaluate your financial situation in comparison to most people in your country?), social exclusion index, and deprivation index (number of items household cannot afford). Social exclusion can be defined as negative experience particularly about being left out or looked down upon. It captures recognition of one's activities, the sense of connectedness, and a sense of barriers to participation in broader society due to one's social position (Eurofound 2013: 81). The third item is employment status. Employment status may have significant impact on life satisfaction when other individual characteristics are held constant. Employment status and other categorical variables are recoded as dummy. Four dummies (unemployed, retired, disabled student and other, and homemakers) were created for employment status variable.

4 Results

4.1 Descriptive Results

Before examining the multivariate results of life satisfaction scores, some descriptive results on various variables can be insightful. Table 1 shows the average life satisfaction scores by selected variables. Overall, education level, health status

Table 1 Average life satisfaction scores by selected variables

	Min	Max	Mean	S.D.
Age				
18–24	1	10	7.34***	1.98
25–34	1	10	7.17***	2.03
35–49	1	10	6.93***	2.19
50–64	1	10	6.88***	2.23
65+	1	10	7.10***	2.28
Education				
No education	1	10	6.50***	2.51
Primary	1	10	6.66***	2.43
Lower secondary education	1	10	6.78***	2.34
Upper secondary	1	10	6.95***	2.15
Post-secondary	1	10	7.13***	2.23
Tertiary education (first level)	1	10	7.51***	1.81
Tertiary education (advanced level)	1	10	7.74***	1.61
Marital status				
Married or living with partner	1	10	7.22***	2.12
Divorced	1	10	6.58***	2.25
Widowed	1	10	6.67***	2.37
Unmarried	1	10	7.00***	2.08
Gender				
Male	1	10	7.05***	2.16
Female	1	10	7.02***	2.18
Place of residence				
Rural	1	10	7.00***	2.20
Urban	1	10	7.07***	2.14
Health status				
Very low	1	10	4.74***	2.69
Low	1	10	5.75***	2.34
Medium	1	10	6.66***	2.2
High	1	10	7.27***	1.93
Very high	1	10	7.68***	2.00
Financial situation				
Much worse	1	10	4.86***	2.61
Somewhat worse	1	10	6.04***	2.32
Neither worse nor better	1	10	7.15***	1.98
Somewhat better	1	10	7.77***	1.75
Much better	1	10	8.20***	1.80
Employment status				
Employed	1	10	7.27***	1.95
Unemployed	1	10	5.87***	2.50
Retired	1	10	7.02***	2.27
Homemaker	1	10	6.89***	2.34
Disabled, student, and other	1	10	7.04***	2.17

Note: *p < 0.5, **p < 0.01, ***p < 0.001 (t-test and ANOVA)

level, and financial situation increases or become better, the life satisfaction also increases.

All age groups reported a higher life satisfaction compared to the 50–64 age group, reinforcing the U-shaped relationship between age and happiness (Blanchflower and Oswald 2007). Life satisfaction scores of young people aged 18–24 is 7.34 on average, while it is 7.17 for 25–34 age group, 6.93 for 35–49 age group, and 6.88 for 50–64 age group. Life satisfaction level is higher for the old people aged 65 and over with 7.1 compared to adults. Education is one of the most important determinants of life satisfaction. The higher the education level is, the higher the life satisfaction score. While the score of uneducated people was 6.5, it was 7.7 for those people who have advanced tertiary education degree in 2012. Marital status also has an impact on life satisfaction. People who are married or living with a partner had 7.22 life satisfaction score, while divorced or separated had 6.58 and unmarried had 7.0 in 2012. There were small life satisfaction differences with regard to gender and place of residence. Health status is an important factor of life satisfaction score. People who had very low health status were scored 4.74, while very healthy people scored 7.68 on their life satisfaction score on average. Descriptive results of Table 1 display that financial situation is crucial on life satisfaction. While people who evaluate their financial situation worse in comparison to most people in their country had only 4.86 life satisfaction score on average, while it was 8.2 for those evaluated their financial situation better in comparison to most people. Last, employment status can give us insight about life satisfaction. Employed people had much higher life satisfaction scores with 7.27 on average compared to unemployed people with 5.87 on average.

As a precursor step towards the final analysis, bivariate correlation coefficients between and within (the numerical) independent and dependent variables are presented in Table 2. All of the correlations presented here are significant ($p < 0.01$). In addition, Table 2 does not report any correlation coefficient equal

Table 2 Correlations between dependent and independent variables

	1	2	3	4	5	6	7
1. Age	1						
2. Education	−0.22***	1					
3. Health status	−0.42***	0.24***	1				
4. Social exclusion index	−0.01***	−0.15***	−0.20***	1			
5. Financial situation	−0.05***	0.24***	0.23***	−0.28***	1		
6. Deprivation index	0.08***	−0.27***	−0.29***	0.38***	−0.48***	1	
7. Life satisfaction	−0.04***	0.13***	0.29***	−0.41***	0.34***	−0.41***	1

Note: *$p < 0.5$, **$p < 0.01$, ***$p < 0.001$ (2-tailed)

to or greater than 0.7, which would otherwise suggest the presence of a problem of multi-collinearity.

Table 2 confirms previous research which found that more educated and wealthier people are more likely to have higher life satisfaction levels compared to those with lower education and income levels (Easterlin 2001; Diener and Diener 2009). There is a negative correlation between life satisfaction level and the following variables; age, social exclusion index, and deprivation index. Combating financial problems and social exclusion is mainly the responsibility of welfare states and can explain the life satisfaction variances among individuals as well as societies. Last, employment status can be considered as the third dimension explaining life satisfaction variations. As mentioned above, employment can explain the variation in life satisfaction, since unemployment or fear of unemployment reduces people's life satisfaction and happiness.

4.2 *Results of Multiple Regression Analysis*

In multiple regression analysis, we can estimate the net effect by controlling for any other factors. Table 3 shows three different models predicting the life satisfaction scores in Europe. When controlling for age, gender, health status, marital status, and education, gender has no significant effect on life satisfaction. Therefore, gender was not included in the models.

Variables included in the first model explained around 10% of variation ($R^2 = 0.097$) in the distribution of life satisfaction variable. The intrusion of social exclusion index, financial situation, and deprivation index variables brought an additional 19% of explanatory power ($R^2 = 0.282$). Introduction of employment status variables in the third model also brought an extra statistically significant explanatory power of 0.7%. The final model and variables in the regression explains almost 29% ($R^2 = 0.289$) of variation in life satisfaction in Europe.

In the final model, social exclusion index variable, with a standardized Beta of −0.26 ($p < 0.001$), emerged as the strongest predictor of life satisfaction contrary to the assumption presented above. As social exclusion score increases, life satisfaction decreases significantly and substantially. One level increase in social exclusion index is associated with 0.65-point decline in the predicted life satisfaction level. The second strongest predictor of life satisfaction is the deprivation index variable (Beta = −0.20), which also negatively affects life satisfaction. One level increase deprivation index is associated with 0.24-point decline in the predicted life satisfaction level. The third strongest predictor is health status with standardized Beta coefficient of 0.17. Parallel with the previous literature, health status appeared to be a strong predictor of life satisfaction. In line with the descriptive results, we can see that health status has an important effect on life satisfaction. One-unit increase in health status may lead to 0.37-point increase in life satisfaction scores on average.

Respondents' perception of the financial situation in their country also exerts a stronger effect (Beta = 0.13). The higher the perception of financial situation, the

Table 3 Linear regressions of life satisfaction levels in 34 European countries in 2011

	Model 1		Model 2		Model 3	
	Coeff.	Beta	Coeff.	Beta	Coeff.	Beta
Constant	3.59***	0.08	6.65***	0.09	6.65***	0.09
Age	0.17***	0.10	0.06***	0.03	−0.01	−0.01
Education	0.13***	0.08	−0.05***	−0.03	−0.03***	−0.02
Marital status (married ref.)						
Divorced	−0.52***	−0.07	−0.27***	−0.04	−0.24***	−0.03
Widowed	−0.19***	−0.03	−0.10***	−0.01	−0.20***	−0.03
Single	−0.21***	−0.04	−0.15***	−0.03	−0.19***	−0.04
Health status	0.67***	0.30	0.35***	0.16	0.37***	0.17
Rural (urban ref.)	0.01	0.00	0.00	0.00	−0.01	0.00
Social exclusion index			−0.67***	−0.26	−0.65***	−0.26
Financial situation			0.34***	0.14	0.32***	0.13
Deprivation index			−0.24***	−0.21	−0.24***	−0.20
Employment status (employed ref)						−0.05
Unemployed					−0.36***	0.03
Retired					0.18***	0.07
Homemaker					0.36***	0.03
Disabled, student and other					0.24***	0.04
R square	0.097***		0.282***		0.289***	
R square change			0.185***		0.007***	

Note: *$p < 0.5$, **$p < 0.01$, ***$p < 0.001$

higher the life satisfaction is. Those people who evaluate their financial situation better in comparison to most people in their country have higher life satisfaction scores. One-unit increase in financial situation score leads to 0.32-point increase on average in life satisfaction scores after controlling for the other variables in the model.

Even though employment status variables can only explain 0.7% of variance in the life satisfaction level, employment status is still important to understand life satisfaction levels in Europe. Employed people are predicted to have, on average, 0.36-point more life satisfaction scores than the unemployed. Nevertheless, controlling for all other variables, the retirees are predicted to have 0.36-point more and homemakers are predicted to have 0.24-point more life satisfaction scores compared to employed people.

In the final model, significant coefficient values show interesting results explaining the effect of various determinants on life satisfaction levels. One level increase in education degree leads to an average of 0.03 decline in life satisfaction scores. People who are married or living with a partner are predicted to have, on average, 0.24-point more life satisfaction scores than divorced or separated people, 0.20-point more life satisfaction scores than widowed, and 0.19-point more life satisfaction scores than unmarried people.

Even though age appeared to be a statistically significant predictor of life satisfaction in the first and second models, its impact was explained out in the final model which added employment status variables. That is to say, age does not have a significant effect on life satisfaction when employment status is taken into consideration. Place of residence (rural versus urban) does not yield any significant explanatory power in any of the three models. Everything else being equal, individuals living in rural and urban areas have similar levels of life satisfaction. The final model shows that the impact of social exclusion, deprivation, and financial differences on life satisfaction proves to be higher than the impacts of age, education level, marital status, and employment status. Hence, social policies affecting social inequality across countries matter. In the next part, the impact of welfare state policies on life satisfaction will be discussed.

5 Life Satisfaction Levels Across Welfare States

The extent that unemployment causes unhappiness depends on individual, social, and institutional circumstances. According to some researchers, some factors which are affected by positional differences of individuals such as employment, education, and income have little relationship with life satisfaction in European societies (Veenhoven 2015). Poverty reduction or social inclusion is mainly the responsibility of national governments. Large social welfare policy differences among these countries are apparent. The impact of welfare states and their various social policies on well-being of citizens are crucial. As Di Tella et al. (2003) claim, countries with more generous benefit systems are happier than those countries, which have rudimentary and remnant social policies.

The importance of social policies and institutional differences on life satisfaction necessitates considering welfare state variations across Europe. Esping-Andersen (1990) constructed the threefold welfare state regime classification (namely the Liberal, the Social Democratic, and the Corporatist) to explain cross-national variations influenced by the role of the state, the market, and the family in the management of social risks. Later, some researchers included Southern European, Eastern European, Antipodean, East Asian, and Latin American welfare states to the welfare state typology.

The Liberal welfare regime (such as in Ireland and the UK) is well-known through the power of the market in the management of social risks, modest public transfers, and means-tested social assistance. The Social Democratic welfare regime (such as Denmark, Finland, and Sweden) emphasizes the role of the state with de-commodification and de-familization policies for its citizens' social well-being, rather than the market or the family. This welfare regime promotes a high social equality where all people are incorporated under universal social provisions. The Continental European welfare regime (such as in Austria, France, and Germany) has a conservative welfare tradition heavily influenced by the institutionalization of rights attached to social class rather than social citizenship. The Southern

European welfare regime (such as in Greece, Italy, Spain, and Turkey) is based on strong familialism, a residual form of public support and social assistance, patronage, and clientelism. The Eastern European welfare states (such as in Bulgaria, Hungary, and Romania) mostly have the social welfare contract based on communist system. It consists highly subsidized prices on food and housing, guaranteed employment, and universal health care and education. These welfare states, however, have experienced a rapid privatization and removal of already enjoyed social rights.

All of these welfare states, which evolved through different historical and institutional paths, have very diverse labor market policies and life satisfaction levels. In both the 2003 and 2011 EQLS, Europeans gave quite a positive life satisfaction score with about 7.0 on average. In 2011, life satisfaction average of selected European countries remained stable, with a slight decrease to 7.0. Table 4 shows the changes in life satisfaction scores for each of the 34 countries in Europe. Some countries which had lower life satisfaction scores in 2003 increased their average life satisfaction scores, while the average life satisfaction score declined in some countries, particularly in Continental Europe and Southern Europe, during this period. Bulgaria, Lithuania, and Turkey experienced the highest life satisfaction increase, while average life satisfaction declined in Greece, Ireland and Germany. Nevertheless, Social Democratic countries (Denmark, Finland, Iceland, and Sweden) which have strong welfare provisions get the highest life satisfaction

Table 4 Life satisfaction across Europe in 2003 and 2011

	2003	2011		2003	2011
Austria	7.8	7.8	Lithuania	5.4	6.7
Belgium	7.5	7.4	Luxembourg	7.7	7.8
Bulgaria	4.5	5.5	Macedonia	–	6.7
Croatia	–	6.8	Malta	7.3	7.2
Cyprus	7.2	7.2	Montenegro	–	6.9
Czech Republic	6.6	6.4	Netherlands	7.5	7.7
Denmark	8.5	8.4	Poland	6.2	7.1
Estonia	5.9	6.3	Portugal	6.0	6.8
Finland	8.1	8.1	Romania	6.1	6.7
France	6.9	7.2	Serbia	–	6.3
Germany	7.4	7.2	Slovakia	5.7	6.4
Greece	6.7	6.2	Slovenia	7.0	7.0
Hungary	5.9	5.8	Spain	7.5	7.5
Iceland	–	8.3	Sweden	7.8	8.0
Ireland	7.7	7.4	Turkey	5.6	6.6
Italy	7.2	6.9	UK	7.4	7.3
Kosovo	–	6.2	EU 25/EU 34	7.1	7.0
Latvia	5.6	6.2			

Source: Eurofound (2013)

scores in Europe, while many Eastern and Southern European welfare states have lower life satisfaction scores.

There are also significant variations in terms of employment and active labour market policies across Europe. Active labor policies are the state regulations to improve the access of unemployed people to the labor market and the functioning of the labor market in general (Powell and Barrientos 2004). According to Gallie and Paugam (2000), welfare regimes can be classified on the basis of criteria of coverage, level of compensation and expenditure on active labor market policies. The authors claim that expenditure on active labor market policies can be barely seen in the Southern European and the Liberal countries, while these policies are very widespread in the Social Democratic welfare states, particularly in Denmark and Sweden. Having universal welfare provisions, which mitigates social exclusion and inequality, as well as strong active labor market policies, Social Democratic countries prove that providing new employment opportunities and direct welfare state supports hand in hand.

6 Conclusion

This paper empirically analyzes what determines the life satisfaction level with particular focus on employment status, using the individual data obtained from the third wave of the EQLS. Multiple regression results are consistent with that of previous literature. Even with the same financial situation, those who are currently employed are more satisfied in their life than those who are unemployed. Nevertheless, employment status can only explain 0.7% of the variance in the life satisfaction level. The main finding from the empirical analysis is that while unemployment reduces people's life satisfaction, the most important determinant of life satisfaction is social inequality (social exclusion, and deprivation, and financial situation) along with health status. Social Democratic welfare states, which have strong and universal welfare provisions and good active labor policies, have the highest life satisfaction scores among 34 European countries. The Southern European welfare states which are considered as "late comer" welfare states due to their rudimentary welfare provisions and Eastern European welfare states experiencing the rapid liberalization process after the cold war have relatively lower life satisfaction scores compared to rest of the Europe. In light of aforementioned variations across Europe it can be concluded that social policies do matter.

Acknowledgments This research was supported by a Marie Curie FP7 Integration Grant (Project no: 618792) within the 7th European Union Framework Programme. The authors thank to editors, anonymous referees, Dr. Zubeyir Nisanci, David Albachten, and Suada Aga for their valuable comments and contributions.

References

Amine, S., & Dos Santos, P. L. (2013). Technological choices and labor market participation: Negative income tax. *Eurasian Economic Review, 3*(2), 98–113.

Anand, P., Krishnakumar, J., & Tran, N. B. (2011). Measuring welfare: Latent variable models for happiness and capabilities in the presence of unobservable heterogeneity. *Journal of Public Economics, 95*(3), 205–215.

Andrews, F. M., & Withey, S. B. (1976). *Social indicators of well-being: Americans' perceptions of life quality*. New York, NY: Plenum Press.

Blanchflower, D. G., & Oswald, A. J. (2007). *Is well-being U-shaped over the life cycle?* (IZA Discussion Papers, No. 3075).

Charfeddine, L., & Mrabet, Z. (2015). Trade liberalization and relative employment: Further evidence from Tunisia. *Eurasian Business Review, 5*(1), 173–202.

Christopher, J. C. (1999). Situating psychological well-being: Exploring the cultural roots of its theory and research. *Journal of Counseling and Development, 77*(2), 141–152.

Clark, A. E., & Oswald, A. J. (1994). Unhappiness and unemployment. *Economic Journal, 104* (424), 648–659.

Constant, A. F., & Zimmermann, K. F. (2014). Self-employment against employment or unemployment: Markov transitions across the business cycle. *Eurasian Business Review, 4*(1), 51–87.

Di Tella, R., MacCulloch, R. J., & Oswald, A. J. (2001). Preferences over inflation and unemployment: Evidence from surveys of happiness. *The American Economic Review, 91*(1), 335–341.

Di Tella, R., MacCulloch, R. J., & Oswald, A. J. (2003). The macroeconomics of happiness. *Review of Economics and Statistics, 85*(4), 809–827.

Diener, E., & Diener, M. (2009). Cross-cultural correlates of life satisfaction and self-esteem. In E. Diener (Ed.), *Culture and well-being. The collected works of Ed Diener* (pp. 71–91). Dordrecht: Springer Netherlands.

Diener, E., & Suh, E. (1997). Measuring quality of life: Economic, social, and subjective indicators. *Social Indicators Research, 40*(1), 189–216.

Easterlin, R. A. (1995). Will raising the incomes of all increase the happiness of all? *Journal of Economic Behavior and Organization, 27*(1), 35–47.

Easterlin, R. A. (2001). Income and happiness: Towards a unified theory. *The Economic Journal, 111*(473), 465–484.

Esping-Andersen, G. (1990). *The three worlds of welfare capitalism*. Cambridge: Polity Press.

Eurofound. (2013). *Third European quality of life survey—Quality of life in Europe: Trends 2003–2012*. Luxembourg: Publications Office of the European Union.

Frey, B. S., & Stutzer, A. (2010). *Happiness and economics: How the economy and institutions affect human well-being*. Princeton, NJ: Princeton University Press.

Galbraith, J. K. (1998). *The affluent society*. Boston, MA: Houghton Mifflin Harcourt.

Gallie, D., & Paugam, S. (Eds.). (2000). *Welfare regimes and the experience of unemployment in Europe*. New York, NY: Oxford University Press.

Kossek, E. E., & Ozeki, C. (1998). Work-family conflict, policies, and the job-life satisfaction relationship: A review and directions for organizational behavior-human resources research. *Journal of Applied Psychology, 83*(2), 139–149.

Lucas, R. E., Clark, A. E., Georgellis, Y., & Diener, E. (2004). Unemployment alters the set point for life satisfaction. *Psychological Science, 15*(1), 8–13.

Mitra, A., & Jha, A. K. (2015). Innovation and employment: A firm level study of Indian industries. *Eurasian Business Review, 5*(1), 45–71.

Pittau, M. G., Zelli, R., & Gelman, A. (2010). Economic disparities and life satisfaction in European regions. *Social Indicators Research, 96*(2), 339–361.

Powell, M., & Barrientos, A. (2004). Welfare regimes and the welfare mix. *European Journal of Political Research, 43*(1), 83–105.

Sen, A. (2001). *Development as freedom*. New York, NY: Oxford University Press.

van Stel, A., Wennekers, S., & Scholman, G. (2014). Solo self-employed versus employer entrepreneurs: Determinants and macro-economic effects in OECD countries. *Eurasian Business Review, 4*(1), 107–136.

Veenhoven, R. (1991). Is happiness relative? *Social Indicators Research, 24*(1), 1–34.

Veenhoven, R. (2015). Overall satisfaction with life: Subjective approaches. In W. Glatzer, L. Camfield, V. Moller & M. Rojas (Eds.), *Global handbook of quality of life. Exploration of well-being of nations and continents*. Dordrecht: Springer Netherlands.

Promoting Green Urbanism and Disaster Resilience in the Anthropocene: From Invasive to Community in Kakaako, Oahu

Jason Levy, Joey Valenti, and Peiyong Yu

Abstract As the most isolated land mass on earth, the Island of Hawaii has become heavily dependent on imports in the current era of globalization. This paper addresses major challenges facing the island chain of Hawaii including the current housing crisis and the disaster risks posed by climate change and invasive trees. This study assesses the viability of using scavenged albizia to promote green urbanism and disaster resilience in Hawaii. Kaka'ako, a commercial and retail district of Honolulu (situated along the southern shores of the island of O'ahu, Hawaii) is used as a case study. Local and practical solutions including green urbanism and technologic innovations such as Computer Numerical Control (CNC) are emphasized. This paper emphasizes local employment and University of Hawaii based technology, thereby minimizing the use of builders from outside the state. Innovative design strategies are herein proposed to overcome this dependency on imports and help the state of Hawaii to achieve long-term resilience and sustainability. Advances in ecological economics and multiple criteria decision analysis yield the following outcomes for the three decision alternatives: Status Quo/Disposal (0.14), Biofuel (0.39) and Manufacturing (0.37).

Keywords Cost benefit analysis • Disaster resilience • Green urbanism • Multi-criteria analysis

J. Levy (✉)
Department of Public Administration, University of Hawaii – West Oahu, Kapolei, HI, USA
e-mail: jlevy@hawaii.edu

J. Valenti
Department of Architecture, University of Hawaii at Manoa, Honolulu, HI, USA
e-mail: jvalenti@hawaii.edu

P. Yu
Department of Economics, University of Hawaii – West Oahu, Kapolei, HI, USA
e-mail: pyu@hawaii.edu

M.H. Bilgin et al. (eds.), *Empirical Studies on Economics of Innovation, Public Economics and Management*, Eurasian Studies in Business and Economics 6,
DOI 10.1007/978-3-319-50164-2_22

1 Introduction

Hawaii has set ambitious sustainability goals. For example, the 2050 Hawaii Sustainability Plan has the capacity to set the standard for other US states as communities seek to promote clean energy, smart economies, societal resilience, ecological quality and sustainable livelihoods. In the 1970s, the State of Hawai'i was a leader in long-range strategic planning. Conceived in the mid-1970s the visionary Hawai'i State Plan was among the first planning documents in the US that provided visionary and holistic policies for the economic, social and environmental future of an entire state.

Energy is a key sustainability challenge in the state of Hawaii: there are only two crude oil refineries (both located in the port of Honolulu on Oahu). Hawaii's electricity generators and its synthetic gas supplier are seeking economic alternatives to refined petroleum products, and the state is exploring options to maintain needed product supplies if one or both Honolulu refineries should shut down. With its limited natural gas supply and distribution network, Hawaii has the lowest overall natural gas consumption in the nation and the lowest per capita consumption. Coal is shipped in by ocean freighter (usually from Indonesia) to Hawaii's single operating coal-fired electricity generating a plant, a 180-MW facility on Oahu. In 2014, for the first time, net generation from petroleum slipped below 70%, and renewable sources including wind, biomass, and geothermal generator now supply 13% of the state's electricity from utility-scale generators

Currently, Hawaii produces about 21% of its electricity from renewable energy and depends upon imported fossil fuel. However, in 2015, Hawaii became the first state in the nation to adopt a 100% renewable energy portfolio standard: the clean energy initiative directs the state's utilities to generate 100% of their electricity from renewable sources by 2045. In other words, in 30 years, Hawaii should meet its goal of energy independence: all of its energy needs are expected to be met by renewable energy (and not fossil fuels). Due to the high cost of electricity in Hawaii adopting the goal of a 100% renewable energy portfolio standard by 2045 it is expected that this will not only improve environmental quality but also likely reduce the cost of electricity for residents and businesses.

Achieving the 100% renewable energy portfolio standard by 2045 involves a two pronged strategy. The first involves conservation by establishing energy efficient building codes and promoting energy efficient lifestyles. The second emphasizes modernizing the power grid, establishing alternative fuels, wisely harnessing renewable energy (from solar, wind, ocean, geothermal, hydroelectric, and biomass resources) and reducing the use of fossil fuels. For example, a significant step towards energy independence was taken when the Hawaii Public Utilities Commission approved the development of a $41 million solar farm on Kaua'i, which will provide 6% of the island's energy needs each day.

In April 2016, the Hawaiian Electric Co. (HECO) asked the State of Hawaii's Public Utilities Commission (PUC) for approval to build a $340 million (US dollar) smart-grid system: the HECO Smart Grid Foundation Project (a partnership with the Blue Planet Foundation, a clean energy organization) includes a wireless communication network, smart meters and enhanced technology. Modernizing the existing electric grid for HECO's 455,000 customers would make the system more automated and energy-efficient, allow more renewable energy sources to feed into the system, particularly rooftop solar. With more than 12% of Hawaii's homeowners installing solar panels the safety and reliability of the existing grid could be threatened as older substations were not designed for power to flow from customers to the substations. The smart grid project is also expected to improve reliability by enhancing HECO's ability to detect power outages and fix them, thereby restoring power more quickly. The proposed system would provide customers with personal electricity usage information on their computers and mobile devices to give them more control over their energy use and costs. If approved by the PUC, HECO would begin to install the smart-grid project in 2017 on Oahu and in 2018 on Hawaii Island and in Maui County. The smart grid program would cost HECO's customers on average $747 US dollars each. The Kauai Island Utility Cooperative began its smart-meter program in 2013 at a cost of $333 US dollars for each of its 33,000 members.

The future of sustainability in Hawaii rests in hands of business leaders, decision makers, government officials and local communities that are willing to engage in the planning process, promote a green economy, demand regulatory action, and embrace stewardship. Specifically, understanding the preferences and values of all affected parties interested in promoting a low carbon economy can help economists, decision makers and climate change professionals to understand the key administrative, management, and public policy issues associated with decarbonizing Hawaii's economy. The foundation of the 2050 Hawaii Sustainability Plan defines three key criteria of sustainability in the spirit of the Brundtland Report: respecting the state's island communities; striking a balance between economic, social, and environmental goals; and meeting the needs of the current generation without compromising the ability of future generations to meet their own needs. Key Hawaiian values include Auamo Kuleana (collective transformation through individual excellence), ʻIke ʻĀina (knowledge learned from connection to land) and Aloha ʻĀina (love and commitment to land). The 2050 Hawaii Sustainability Plan has designated the following five primary goals:

- "Living sustainably is part of our daily practice in Hawaii.
- Our diversified and globally competitive economy enables us to meaningfully live, work and play in Hawaii.
- Our natural resources are responsibly and respectfully used, replenished and preserved for future generations.
- Our community is strong, healthy, vibrant and nurturing, providing safety nets for those in need.
- Our Kanaka Maoli and island cultures and values are thriving and perpetuated." (Force 2008)

Achieving the five primary goals of the 2050 Hawaii Sustainability Plan and promoting a low carbon economy in Hawaii will require transformative actions including the development of advanced soft computing models to capture the complexity and uncertainty of modernity. The proposed approaches in this paper will help to promote the use of renewable materials on an unprecedented scale, to generate a deep public and private sector awareness of Hawaii's sustainability initiatives, and to promote smart and green economic development in the local context.

A growing number of pioneering bankers, insurers and institutional investors and policy makers continue to discuss ground rules for the low carbon economy, the role for investors, and climate change policy solutions. There are now a new array of policy tools for global business leaders and governments to draw upon ranging from placing "green financing" on balance sheets to measuring the carbon footprints for institutional investors to helping companies set up strategies for managing climate and environmental risks in their investment portfolios. Efforts to achieve a very low carbon economy represent one of the most significant global policy measures ever dedicated to a transnational challenge. As the most isolated land mass on earth, the Island of Hawaii has become heavily dependent on imports in the current era of globalization. This has created a more vulnerable and brittle economy. Innovative design strategies are herein proposed to overcome this dependency on imports and help the state of Hawaii to achieve long-term resilience and sustainability.

In previous years, significant revitalization funds have been allocated to key tourist regions of Honolulu long-including Waikiki and Ala Moana. On the Western outskirts of Honolulu, between the downtown city center and the airport, tactical urbanism is beginning to revive the urban fabric formerly scarred with industrial warehouses and undeveloped land plots, although empty parking lots and fenced plots of land remain abandoned and unused. However, the Kapalama and Kalihi regions remain predominantly gritty, industrial regions with large areas of underused urban areas. While TOD proposals associated with HRT propose revitalization solutions that should help these lower-income communities (home to many Pacific Island immigrant families) the ultimate location of the controversial rail project is uncertain.

Valenti (2016) explores the use of small-scale design, intelligent systems and sustainable design to promote more sustainable human communities. In a similar vein, this paper promotes green urbanism, an interdisciplinary collaboration of landscape architects, engineers, urban planners, ecologists, transportation planners, urban designers, systems engineers, psychologists, sociologists, economists and other specialists who seek create livable places, communities and lifestyles to not only reduce waste but also develop more sustainable patterns of industrial production and resource consumption (Beatley 2000; Karlenzig et al. 2007; Lehmann 2010). We seek to rescale urbanism and green design by creating a new nexus among invasive species management, local building resources and digitally fabricated transient structures in order to promote smart and sustainable growth.

The post-industrial built environment assumes that environmental and societal change is gradual, predictable and manageable. This is incompatible with the large scale and significant environmental impacts that are associated with rapid and transformative change in the Anthropocene under conditions of global climate variability and change. Accordingly, in the post-carbon era it is essential for society to promote climate adaptation and resilience of the built environment which is focused on adaptation and flexibility. We propose innovative design strategies aimed at "rescaling urbanism" (Valenti 2016), promoting digitally fabricated transient structures and creating an efficient approach for sustainable construction using local, renewable materials that embraces new, global technologies in digital fabrication. Built on the paradigm of Valenti (2016) our building paradigm emphasizes sustainable, transient and process-based structures and challenges the current *modus operandi* of Hawaii's building industry.

2 A Niche Market for Engineered Wood

To compliment Hawaii's stringent environmental mandates and sustainability goals, it is essential to promote a vernacular architecture that evolves to capture the environmental, socio-cultural, technological, economic, and historical context of its surroundings. We propose an innovative green urbanism paradigm based on community needs, the availability of vernacular and renewable construction materials, advances in wood engineering and closed-loop systems which reflect local values and traditions. In particular, Valenti (2016) proposes the use of the highly invasive Albizia tree as a source of lumber for use in digitally fabricated transient structures including temporary housing and disaster shelters. By reconceptualizing this life-threatening invasive pest as a valuable, sustainable building material, we propose a potentially viable solution to not only removing hazardous invasive species but also addressing Hawaii's housing deficit, post-disaster shelter needs.

The albizia wood is engineered through a cross lamination process (which adds strength, stability, longevity, and even fire resistance) in order to meet precise design specifications which are tested to meet national or international standards. To ensure termite resistance, a safe and efficient method will be used to treat the albizia wood before use as a building material (as is necessary for most types of wood). This paper emphasizes local employment and University of Hawaii based technology, thereby minimizing the use of builders from outside the state (i.e., outsourcing building). The architectural design and construction processes are fully integrated to enhance efficiency. Specifically, using scavenged local Albizia as the raw material, the building structure is digitally fabricated using Computer Numerical Control (CNC) routing in which the key functions (turning the spindle and coolants on and off, etc.) and motions of a machine tool (including input parameters such as depth of cut) are controlled by means of a prepared program leading to higher accuracy in manufacturing, shorter production times, greater manufacturing flexibility, simpler fixturing, contour machining (2–5-axis machining) and reduced human error. These significant advantages often outweigh the higher cost, the need for constant maintenance, and the requirement of skilled part programmer.

The resulting engineered wood (also known as composite wood or manufactured board) is then integrated with a novel digital fabrication technology for CNC in order to mill the building components into a "kit-of-parts" architecture/construction system (a subset of pre-fabrication)—also known as a Modular, Extensible, Scalable and Reconfigurable (MESR) system in the engineering community. This allows for not only assembly and disassembly flexibility (systems can be assembled and taken apart in a variety of ways like a child's toy) but also manufacturing efficiency. Kit-of-parts structures, systems and subsystems are upgraded with enhanced technologies (modularity), additional unit components can be added during later development phases (extensibility), the coupling or decoupling of components can accommodate new design requirements (scalability) while components can be easily moved to between locations and systems perform similar functions (reconfigurability). In particular, the engineered Albizia wood and individual parts are systematically organized into assemblies of uniform components, based on design criteria such as size, shape, grammar or increments (assemblies are typically sized for convenience according to handling or shipping constraints). Given the many steps in the tree to structure process, a prototype model has been developed to understand the challenges and to support an overall cost benefit analysis. Engineered wood is a resource-light material that supports rapid on-site construction. By merging the use of CNC routing with engineered albizia wood the entire building process is streamlined, enabling the fabrication of a sustainably sourced, high-precision, and easy to assemble building components. This process has been shown to significantly lessen project scope, cost, and construction time.

Hawaii is home to a number of non-native, invasive tree species which can provide a potential niche market for local, low-impact, and renewable building materials. While the highly invasive albizia is perceived to have little or no value in Hawaii due to its low density and average strength, the application of wood engineering has the potential to transform albizia into a higher-quality building material, similar to how hybrid poplar and ponderosa pine have recently proven successful for value added wood products like cross laminated timber (CLT). Accordingly, albizia could offer a valuable local wood-engineered material. It is proposed that innovation in design and sustainable building practices with Albizia wood (a local renewable material) can improve environmental and socio-economic well-being in cities.

This paper examines the use of this sustainable building material to create low-tech, digitally fabricated transient structures in a faster, cheaper and lighter manner than with traditional construction. The fabricated structures will be used to address the housing crisis and provide transient disaster shelters in Hawaii. If wild, scavenged albizia is proven to be a viable engineered wood product, it could help to address sustainability issues both locally and globally. Locally, it would open a new market for a high quality, low cost and renewable building material and reduce the demand for imported construction materials. Transforming this invasive pest into a valuable product for community-building can potentially provide local jobs, save lives from hazardous albizia and protect the environment. In short, we examine the potential of transforming this problematic species into a lucrative, local solution.

3 Using Locally Sourced Materials: From Invasive to Community

Hawaii's construction industry typically imports and outsources building material, from structure to finishes. However, communities across Hawaii want to increase the use of locally sourced building materials in order to be less reliant on imports and consume more sustainable products. This requires carefully considering the type of materials locally available and how far a building product must travel between its points of origin, the manufacturing site. Given Hawaii's limited natural resources and geographic isolation (the most isolated population center in the world), the local sourcing of building materials provides a number of benefits to the Hawaii economy. Using local sourced materials creates a greener supply chain by reducing transportation fuel related to produce transport, thereby creating a smaller carbon footprint for the materials and lessening a product's environmental impact.

Our proposed building approach provides a viable alternative to dependence on overseas products by eliminating nearly all traditional off-island building materials and by designing with a simple material palette. Albizia wood, being the primary material, will be used in the design process for building all components. Through wood engineering, digital fabrication and an intelligent design, it is proposed that Albizia will constitute the main structural material. Additionally, it can be used for interior finishes, flooring, furnishing, doors and louvers. Using scavenged or discarded albizia as a widely-available, locally sourced material will provide a new market for local building materials. The state of Hawaii has invested considerable funds in removing this hazardous tree. Using removed albizia as a supply material for disaster relief units and transitional housing is expected to yield a synergistic effect, where three major statewide goals could be addressed through one initiative.

Intact, diverse native forests constitute an essential natural resource, providing the air we breathe, the clean water we drink and the ecosystem services and resources we need to live. Forests also moderate the global climate and store 283 billion tons of carbon in their biomass. Covering 30% of the global land area forests support the livelihoods of more than 1.5 billion people (including indigenous communities), providing food, clothing and shelter for humans. Storing much of the planet's genetic material, forests shelter wildlife and maintain natural communities: they are home to many of the world's species and 70% of terrestrial flora and fauna. Forests are also essential in protecting watersheds and maintaining the quality of fisheries, etc.

There is an urgent need to reverse unsustainable wood harvesting, building design and construction practices to protect this vital environmental legacy. The quality of wood resources around the world is in decline and <5% of original US forest cover remains. The devastation of native forests (particularly the clearcutting of old-growth forests), deteriorating lumber quality, and rising wood prices are major concerns for not only the public but also environmentalists, elected officials and the building industry. The pulp and paper industry must do more to ensure sustainable levels of wood consumption in the US: when counting trees forest industry officials often fail to make a distinction between undisturbed native forests and monocrop (single-species) tree farms as well as the difference between older trees (with high quality heartwood which is more resistant to attack by insects and decay organisms) and young trees (where all of the wood in the stem is sapwood). Sustainable harvesting and building practices can only be achieved by promoting transformative change throughout the design and construction process. There are a number of strategies to sustain forest biodiversity and conserve wood resources: redesign, reuse, recycling, replacement, and reduction.

4 Homelessness in Hawaii

With more than 4900 currently homeless in Hawaii, problem of cleanliness and homelessness on city, county and state lands is one of the most challenging and critical contemporary social issues facing the State of Hawaii. Business leaders are concerned that the large, visible homeless population may significantly threaten Hawaii's tourist based economy: the homeless are often found panhandling or aimlessly carrying large piles of personal possessions (clothes, tents, etc.). Specifically, Hawaii has the highest rate of homelessness per capita among the 50 states, with an estimated 465 homeless individuals per 100,000 (Governor's Office of Hawaii 2015). As of January 2016, there were 2173 "unsheltered homeless" in Hawaii: individuals and families whose primary nighttime sleeping accommodation involves a public or private place that is not designed for human beings, including doorways, beaches, parks, automobiles, streets (even traffic medians). The homeless often suffer from mental health issues and/or substance abuse problems and typically lack a safety net to support them: of the 2173 unsheltered homeless, more than a quarter (631 individuals) suffer from severe mental illness while approximately the same number (623 individuals) have chronic substance abuse issues. (City and County of Honolulu 2016).

The alarming increase in unsheltered individuals and families over the past 2 years is particularly significant on O'ahu. Homeless encampments exist in Honoulu's central neighborhoods from Kakaako to Kapalama. Pacific Islanders make up a vast majority of the homeless population in these areas. This problem has become more acute in light of affordability issues and the increasing migration of individuals to Hawaii from other Pacific Islands (e.g., the Federated States of Micronesia (FSM), the Marshall Islands, and Palau) to Hawaii (in particular the city of Honolulu) under the Compact of Free Association which allows these Pacific islanders the right to work and move freely to the rest of the U.S. with legal non-immigrant status. Many of these migrants have moved to Hawaii in search of better work prospects, improved quality of life and enhanced benefits. Others may be fleeing climate-related threats to their native countries. For example, saltwater intrusion and other impacts of sea level rise are also pressuring Pacific Island communities off their land and many soon become climate refugees, thereby exacerbating the need to relocate from their home countries. In addition to Hawaii, citizens of Pacific Islands have also moved en masse to other US-affiliated Pacific islands including Guam, American Samoa, and the Commonwealth of the Northern Marianas Islands.

On October, 2015, Hawaii's Governor David Ige declared a state of emergency dealing with homelessness. The "Emergency Proclamation" enables the state government to expedite plans to help chronically homeless families and individuals (Governor's Office of Hawaii 2015). The released state funds ($1.3 million dollars) serve an additional one thousand homeless residents by providing increased funding for homeless services and programs that and to help homeless families and individuals quickly move to transitional or permanent housing, including the construction of a temporary housing facility (with a sunset date). In response to this "state of emergency", there was a coordinated effort aimed at removing homeless people that were formerly found in visible pockets of Honolulu: the City and County of Honolulu passed a battery of laws that effectively criminalize homelessness (similar to legislation passed in other US jurisdictions such as Orlando, Florida and Santa Cruz, California); the city's social work teams assisted homeless to relocate into shelters; the business and tourism sector covered the cost of a return flight for homeless arriving from the US mainland that were willing to depart (Nagourney 2016). However, frustrated by the recent prolonged encampment of homeless people in a traffic median in Waikiki (which ended in August, 2016), residents, elected officials (city councilmen, state representatives, etc.) and business leaders continue to highlight a perceived lack of leadership and insufficient communication among coordinating government, nonprofits and other entities to deal with the issues of homelessness and hygiene in Hawaii. There is a perception that unless there is high profile event (such as the hosting of an Asia-Pacific Economic Cooperation conference or the filming 'Hawaii Five-0') decisive action is not taken.

5 Disaster Risk in Hawaii

Despite laudable global efforts built upon proven and demonstrated Greenhouse Gas (GHG) mitigation and adaptation measures, the global response to the climate change challenge appears to be falling short: A large body of climate science has shown that to keep the global average temperature from rising further than 2 °C, emissions must peak soon and then fall steeply. Without significant reductions in the global emissions of GHGs, humans and ecosystems may face catastrophic, pervasive and long-lasting impacts (perhaps even irreversible change), including species extinction, widespread desertification, sea level rise and an increase in extreme weather events. A sustainable future requires communities, policy makers and leaders around the world to demand a faster transition to a low carbon energy future.

Global sea level is rising, with the highest rates in the world recorded in the tropical Pacific Ocean where many low-lying carbonate reef-lined atoll islands are located. These atoll islands are particularly vulnerable for a number of reasons: many of them have maximum elevations <4 m above present sea level; there is limited land and water available for human survival; and ecosystems are vulnerable to inundation from sea-level rise. The combined effect of storm-induced wave-driven flooding and sea level rise on island atolls in the Pacific is likely to be more intense and severe than previous estimates of inundation. Accordingly, Pacific island communities are especially vulnerable to a warming and more energetic climate system: they are faced not only with serious climate vulnerabilities at three tiers—exposure, sensitivity, and adaptive capacity—but also with a unique set of environmental and cultural issues pertinent to managing the unexpected and cascading impacts of sea level rise, coastal inundation and other human-caused climate-related disasters that cross policy domains, geographic, political, and sectoral boundaries. In the Pacific Ocean region, meltwater is expected to constitute a long term threat of sea-level rise (in the second half of the twenty-first century), with thermal expansion of the upper ocean posing the greatest immediate challenge. In the relatively near term, the impacts of global sea level rise are expected to contribute to the increased frequency of extreme water levels at the shoreline of Pacific Island nations.

Low-lying areas of the Hawaiian archipelago, particularly the low-lying airport, the industrial area (Mapunapuna) and the capital city (Honolulu) will continue to face severe sea level inundation challenges. It is predicted that Hawaii and other Pacific islands will be among the world's most impacted regions. The citizens of many Pacific island states do not have the luxury of retreating inland from the coast, and may face involuntary relocation. For example, in the Pacific nation of Tuvalu, a ring of nine Polynesian islands, several thousand people have already left for other nations because of rising seas and the displacement of communities from low-lying areas. Hazards associated with sea-level rise combine to create unique social vulnerabilities in the Pacific island region which lead to increased disaster risk, such as catastrophic inundation. Fresh water resources are under threat on many Pacific islands as the result of both climate-change, overuse and contamination while environmental resources in these tropical regions are ecologically sensitive and valuable, and similarly threatened by pollution and climate change.

While emergency and hurricane shelters exist throughout Oahu, a major disaster could quickly overwhelm available capacity. Accordingly, after a disaster, short-term shelter and long-term housing would likely be inadequate. We propose the use of digitally fabricated transient structures—built using local Albizia trees—in order to promote resilient, adaptive and responsive housing that is capable of coping with unpredictable natural disaster events in the post-disaster landscape.

Set atop a volcanic hotspot in the Pacific Ocean, the archipelago of Hawaii is vulnerable to a range of natural disasters including tsunamis, hurricanes, and flooding. While there may be a range of lead-time for these threats other hazards, such as earthquakes may occur unexpectedly and without warning. The island of Oahu (the "Gathering Place") contains more than 70% of the population of the US state of Hawaii, Honolulu International Airport, the state capital (Honolulu), the main deepwater marine port for the State of Hawai'i and the majority of its critical infrastructure.

Fortunately, Hawaii has educational programs emergency preparedness and disaster preparedness organizations that take a comprehensive, integrated and all-hazards approach to emergency management. Specifically, University of Hawaii West O'ahu (UHWO) offers a bachelor of public administration degree with a concentration in disaster preparedness and emergency management (DPEM), and a certificate in disaster preparedness and emergency management. All courses meet the national standards as established by the U.S. Department of Homeland Security (DHS) and the Federal Emergency Management Agency (FEMA) Higher Education Project. Through its courses and integrated programs, FEMA's Emergency Management Institute (EMI) serves as the national focal point for the development and delivery of emergency management training to enhance the capabilities of State, local, and Tribal government officials; volunteer organizations; FEMA's disaster workforce; other Federal agencies; and the public and private sectors to minimize the impact of disasters and emergencies on the American public. FEMA's curricula are structured to meet the needs of this diverse audience with an emphasis on separate organizations working together in all-hazards emergencies to save lives and protect property. Particular emphasis is placed on governing doctrine such as the National Response Framework, National Incident Management System, and the National Preparedness Guidelines.

Since its inception, the number of students in the DPEM Certificate has grown steadily and more than doubled from the 19 in 2003 to 43 in 2009, and grew to 65 in 2012 with 187 graduates so far. DPEM students have the opportunity to participate in a practicum. There are dozens of Hawaii based disaster related government agencies that employ DPEM graduates and current students. This includes the US Department of Homeland Security, Hawai'i State Department of Defense, Civil Defense Division, Department of Emergency Management of the City and County of Honolulu, PACOM, Camp Smith, University of Hawai'i System Civil Defense, FEMA, Hazard Mitigation, Pacific Area Office, Pacific Tsunami Warning Center. The UHWO Campus-Community Emergency Response Team (C-CERT) Program educates people about disaster preparedness for hazards that may impact their area and trains them in basic disaster response skills, such as fire safety, light search and rescue, team organization, and disaster medical operations. The National Domestic Preparedness Training Center or NDPTC at the University of Hawaii are working with FEMA and other external partners to offer training courses and to improve the strategic framework for Hawaii's disaster preparedness.

6 Case Study: Improving Underutilized Urban Space in Kakaako

Located east of downtown Honolulu, revitalization projects for Kakaako have transformed parts of an urban landscape that was formerly characterized by gritty body shops, run-down streets, industrial warehouses and dark streets (similar to the more industrial regions on the western edge of the greater Honolulu area) into a popular urban hot spot. Large developers have helped to renew and popularize parts Kakaako by recruiting local artisans, graffiti artists, and designers to brighten the dark alleys and renovate the once run-down streets, thereby creating a vibrant and trendy art district with a fresh brand and colorful charm. While this urban transformation has offered tangible value to parts of Kakaako (the entire neighborhood previously was similar to current industrial regions on the western edge of the greater Honolulu area) other outlying districts of Kakaako await growth, change and renewal. Moreover, Kakaako's redevelopment is more consistent with traditional top-down, profit-driven, large-scale development projects than the values of community-driven, small-scale tactical urbanism.

Removing albizia trees can be costly. For example, in late 2014 the University of Hawaii at Manoa began a half-year project remove 23 mature albizia from the Lyon Arboretum in Manoa Valley. Completed in 2015, the University had no plans but dispose of the massive timber logs on site to recycle nutrients and minimize inconvenience to local residents (although upon request, one of the trees was donated to the authors). Across the archipelago of Hawaii, it is a common occurrence for albizia to be removed and disposed without viable options for reuse due to a lack of perceived uses. The main two uses of albizia in the world involves livestock feed and peeling for multiplex boards (recently by a company in Malaysia) peeling. None of them have appeared feasible in Hawaii.

Albizia can be used for biofuel. Green Energy Team (GET) LLC has developed an efficient closed loop biomass system on Lihue, Kauai, using only local renewable material (primarily albizia and eucalyptus) and all local employees. According to Lebbe (2016), the GET resource manager of the biomass power plant (responsible for the propagation, planting, harvesting, and acquisition of the plant's biomass resources), albizia should be eradicated from the Hawaiian islands due to negative environmental impacts on both local native or non-invasive introduced species (both flora and fauna) and economic costs (costs associated with removal and storm damage), using a well-managed harvesting strategy in collaboration with a biomass plant. Based on experience with the Hawaiian Mahogany, Inc. (HMI) and GET plantations (both on Kauai) harvesting becomes more difficult and expensive with mixed plantations and non invasive Eucalyptus plantations grow better without albizia (provided soil and fertilization is managed properly). Accordingly, GET is replacing extensive areas of albizia plantations on Kauai with Eucalyptus species using an inventive solution which involves removing albizia during the initial "4–5 years" of operation (personal communication). He suggests starting a program to minimize removal costs whereby the general public, contractors, large landowners and the state of Hawaii can stage albizia (and other invasive trees for pickup by the GET biomass plant).

A unique group Multi-criteria analysis (MCA) approach for tactical urban decision making for sustainability under uncertainty has been developed that is modified from Levy and Taji (2007) and integrates with the Analytic Network Process (Saaty 1989). The proposed approach assumes that N decision makers, DM_k ($k = 1, \ldots, N$), evaluate m alternatives, A_j ($j = 1, \ldots, m$), under n criteria, C_i ($i = 1, \ldots, n$). The group MCA yields the following weights: Social factors (0.47), Environmental factors (0.19) and Economic factors (0.34) and overall scores for the Status Quo/Disposal (0.14), Biofuel (0.39) and Manufacturing (0.37) alternatives.

7 Conclusions

Hawaii has urgent needs to increase social, economic and environmental sustainability. In particular, this paper addresses two challenges facing the island chain of Hawaii: the current housing crisis and the disaster risks posed by climate change. This paper argues for local and practical solutions that use technologic innovations such as Computer Numerical Control (CNC) to improve sustainability, thereby improving social and environmental outcomes in Hawaii. As the most isolated land mass on earth, the Island of Hawaii has become heavily dependent on imports in the current era of globalization. This has created a more vulnerable and brittle economy. Innovative design strategies are herein proposed to overcome this dependency on imports and help the state of Hawaii to achieve long-term resilience and sustainability. This study assesses the viability of using scavenged albizia to promote tactical urbanism in Hawaii.

Scientists are only beginning to understand the significance of the human footprint in altering the Earth's landscapes, oceans, the atmosphere, cryosphere, and ecosystems. However it is known that human activities are having a profound impact on the functioning of global systems (including long-term global geologic processes); human-induced change is occurring at such an alarming rate that it will soon exceed even the greatest forces of Nature. A growing body of research suggests that the *Anthropocene* constitutes a functionally and stratigraphically distinct epoch from the Holocene (Waters et al. 2016). In other words, for the first time, advanced human society may be witnessing a new epoch—and one arising from the consequences of their own actions and behavior. According to the International Union of Geological Sciences (IUGS), we live in the *Holocene* epoch, which began 12,000–11,500 years ago at the close of the Paleolithic Ice Age (as Earth entered a warming trend, the glaciers of the late Paleolithic retreated). While the *Holocene* nominally continues through today, a growing body of evidence now suggests that there are climatic, biological and geochemical signatures of human activity that distinguish a new human-dominated time period—the "*Anthropocene*", the name of a proposed geological epoch that may soon enter the official Geologic Time Scale. This term is derived from *anthropo*, for 'man,' and *cene*, for 'new', the time period in which humans have a profound impact on Earth's geology and ecosystems. Based on atmospheric evidence, the *Anthropocene* may have begun around the beginning of the nineteenth century with the onset of large-scale industrialization which contributed to an enormous expansion in the use of fossil fuels (Steffen et al. 2007) and began to dramatically alter the planet, perhaps permanently. Specifically, the impacts of human activities on the earth since the Industrial Revolution include habitat loss, mass extinctions, species invasions, ocean acidification and spreading oceanic 'dead zones' as well as changes in erosion and sediment transport associated with anthropogenic processes, including colonisation, deforestation, urbanisation and global warming. The term *Anthropocene* has become a widely used buzzword in the global change research community since being popularized in 2000 by the atmospheric chemist and Nobel Laureate Paul Crutzen who argues that large-scale human influences on the atmosphere have contributed to a new geological epoch for the Earth's lithosphere. Use of the *Anthropocene* concept has picked up velocity in the popular press and become increasingly cachet in elite scientific circles and the academic community. For example, the Elsevier and Sage publishers recently launched new academic journals entitled *Anthropocene* and *The Anthropocene Review* respectively while a Google scholar search of the term highlights more than 2000 scholarly papers using the term in the first half of 2016 alone. To address this issue head-on a scientific working group of the International Union of Geological Sciences (IUGS), the Subcommission on Quaternary Stratigraphy (a constituent body of the International Commission on Stratigraphy), is expected to make a formal decision shortly on whether the *Holocene* has ended and the *Anthropocene* has begun.

Humans have become a dominant geophysical force producing previously unimaginable impacts on the Earth, from global climate-change to the destruction of native ecosystems. As the scale and pace of human interactions with Earth systems have intensified in recent decades, it is essential to consider best practices to promote sustainability, economic vitality, and socio-ecological resilience in the *Anthropocene*. It is proposed that the *Anthropocene* can inspire new understandings of politics, temporality, spatiality, ethics, values, and responsibility. To make this new paradigm of sustainability a reality, it is important to consider wide-ranging interpretations, explorations, and solutions on this theme.

References

Beatley, T. (2000). *Green urbanism: Learning from European cities*. Washington, DC: Island Press.

City and County of Honolulu. (2016). *Mayor's office of housing* [online]. Accessed March 10, 2016, from http://www.honolulu.gov/housing/ohou-who.html

Force, S. T. (2008). *Hawai'i 2050 sustainability plan*. Honolulu, HI: State of Hawai'i.

Governor's Office of Hawaii. (2015). *Governor's office new release: Governor Ige Signs emergency proclamation to address homelessness statewide* [online]. Accessed October 16, 2015, from http://governor.hawaii.gov/newsroom/governors-office-news-release-governor-ige-signs-emergency-proclamation-to-address-homelessness-statewide/

Karlenzig, W., Marquardt, F., White, P., Yaseen, P., & Young, R. (Eds.). (2007). *How green is your city, the SustainLane US city rankings*. Gabriola Island, BC: New Society Publishers.

Lebbe, G. (2016). *Meeting with green energy team resource manager* [e-mail] (Personal communication, 10 April 2016).

Lehmann, S. (2010). *The principles of green urbanism: Transforming the city for sustainability*. Oxford: Routledge.

Levy, J. K., & Taji, K. (2007). Group decision support for hazards planning and emergency management: A group analytic network process (GANP) approach. *Mathematical and Computer Modelling, 46*(7–8), 906–917.

Nagourney, A. (2016, June 3). Aloha and welcome to paradise. Unless you're homeless. *New York Times* [online]. Accessed June 8, 2016, from http://www.nytimes.com/2016/06/04/us/hawaii-homeless-criminal-law-sitting-ban.html

Saaty, T. (1989). Group decision making and the AHP. In B. L. Golden, E. A. Wasil & P. T. Harker (Eds.), *The analytic hierarchy process* (pp 59–67). Berlin: Springer.

Steffen, W., Crutzen, P. J., & McNeill, J. R. (2007). The Anthropocene: Are humans now overwhelming the great forces of nature? *AMBIO: A Journal of the Human Environment, 36* (8), 614–621.

Valenti, J. J. (2016). *[Re]Scaling urbanism: Fostering low-tech, digitally fabricated, and transient structures through innovation in local renewable material*. D.Arch Thesis, University of Hawaii at Manoa, Honolulu, HI.

Waters, C. N., Zalasiewicz, J., Summerhayes, C., Barnosky, A. D., Poirier, C., Gałuszka, A., & Jeandel, C. (2016). The Anthropocene is functionally and stratigraphically distinct from the holocene. *Science, 351*(6269), aad2622.

Econometric Estimation of the Quality and the Efficiency of Social Services for Children Deprived of Parental Care

Toshko Petrov and Plamena Markova

Abstract The study aims at developing and testing a methodology suitable for practical application, allowing to carry out a socio-economic assessment of the quality and efficiency of the provision of social services for children deprived of parental care by means of use of a combination of econometric and sociological methods. The study's subject is to establish a criteria system containing 185 indicators based on held series studies. The subjects of the study are several focus groups involving experts and users of services (children and families) in northeastern Bulgaria. The study methodology involves a sociological survey of various types of social services in the mentioned region, and the application of econometric methods—DEA and regression analysis. The survey has resulted in a developed methodology and performed assessment of the quality and efficiency of social services provided to the said target groups in northeastern Bulgaria. Formulated are conclusions about the comparative effectiveness of different types of social services and recommendations are outlined concerning the priorities for future social policy in the field of development of social services for children deprived of parental care.

Keywords Adoptive foster care • Institutional care for children • Alternative social services for children • Efficiency of social services • Regression analysis

1 Introduction

One of the most important strategic directions of the social policy of Bulgaria is developing of a social services system for children, provided in a family or similar-to-a- family environment. In accordance with the European standards for social policy, this type of services is indeed an alternative to the institutional care for children and the successful implementation of the policy of deinstitutionalization

T. Petrov • P. Markova (✉)
Department of Social and Legal Sciences, Technical University, Varna, Bulgaria
e-mail: thpetrov@tu-varna.bg; plamena454@gmail.com

M.H. Bilgin et al. (eds.), *Empirical Studies on Economics of Innovation, Public Economics and Management*, Eurasian Studies in Business and Economics 6,
DOI 10.1007/978-3-319-50164-2_23

depends to a large extent on the development, accessibility and quality of such services.

The problems of the institutional childcare, which have being identified long ago, and the need of synchronization of the social policy of Bulgaria with the same policy of the EU led to formulation of the policy of deinstitutionalization of this care. Regardless that the number of the children raised in specialized institutions in Bulgaria has significantly decreased in recent years, it is still quite big. Based on data from the Reports "Children, raised in specialized institutions" of the State Agency for Child Protection as of December, 2015 (State Agency for Child Protection 2015b) the total number of children raised in institutions, was 2107. In 2001 their number was 12,609, which means that in a 14-year period the number of children, raised in institutions, has decreased down about six times.

The widest exit from the institutions for the children from the Homes for Medical and Social Care for Children is placement in adoptive families. As from the beginning of the deinstitutionalization, the widest exit for the children from the Homes for Children, deprived from parental care, has always been returning to their biological families. In 2013, the number of the children placed in foster families "catches up" the returning to biological families (Ministry of Health 2011).

A new exit is provided in 2013 for the children from the Homes for Children with Disabilities in the form of a residential service in the community—every third child, removed from the institutions, goes to a Center for Family-type Accommodation. However, the share of the transfer "from home to home" remains big (23% are directed to other specialized institution). All this led to increasing the number of the children, using residence-type social services. As of 31.12.2013, the total number of the children, using social services in the community, including residence-type service is 9752 (Agency for Social Assistance 2014) and as of the end of 2014—10,639 (Agency for Social Assistance 2015).

In Bulgaria, within the period 2008–2012, the relative share of children, deprived from parental care, who are placed in specialized institutions has significantly decreased, compared to the total number of children in the country. Figure 1 shows data on the relative share of children, placed in the major institutions for childcare, compared to the total number of the same-age children in the country. As the data in the diagram of Fig. 1 shows, in 2004 the relative share of the children, raised in Homes for Medical and Social Cares was 0.86% from the total number of children of age under 3, but in 2012, this share dropped to 0.46%. Total for the country in 2004 the percentage of children, placed in institutions, made up 0.89% of all children of age under 18, and in 2012 this percentage was already 0.49.

The policy of deinstitutionalization, implemented by several Bulgarian governments since 2001 till now has been focused mainly on developing alternative childcare services, provided in a family of or similar-to-a-family environment. The aim of this policy is that such services completely replace institutional care for children. In pursuance of this policy, an alternative to the institutional care system of social services has been created within a few years that comprise shelters, centers for family-type accommodation, protected or transitional housings, crisis centers, centers for public support, units "Mother and Baby", etc. The foster care

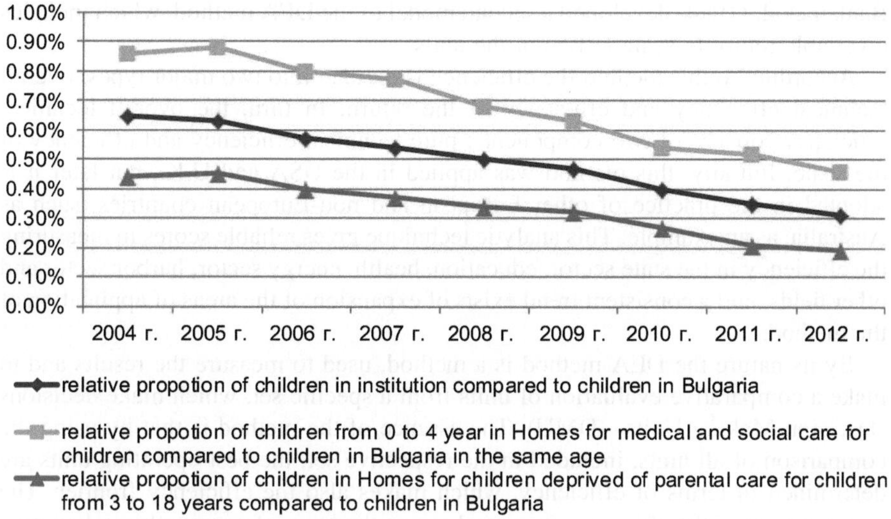

Fig. 1 Relative share of children, placed in specialized institutions in Bulgaria (2004–2012). Source: National Statistical Institute (2016), State Agency for Child Protection (2013), State Agency for Child Protection (2015a)

has also been developed as a social service, providing real family environment to children at risk. Many children have been accommodated in families of relatives and friends or foster families, which care for them until providing opportunities to them for reintegration in their biological families or to be adopted (Ministry of Labor and Social Policy 2015).

Irrespective of the positive results, stated herein, the task to estimate the efficiency of this section of the social policy remains very important. This is due to the circumstance that large amount of public funds are allocated in this field and the society needs to be sure that they are spent effectively, of the one hand, and on the other hand, at what price the respective results are achieved. This way, if it turns out that some issues relating to the objectives and contents of the social policy exist, the respective corrective actions will be formulated and undertaken within the framework of the abovementioned task.

2 Statement of the Study

We will carry out the analysis of the efficiency of the developed system of provision of social services to children, deprived from parental care by the DEA method (Data Envelopment Analysis). Initially this method was created by Charnes et al. (1978) and is deemed to be a sensitive method of calculation of the technical efficiency. The abovementioned authors developed a version of the method, known as CRS model, which ignores the impact of the scale-size (a constant) on the units. Later,

Banker et al. (1984) developed a second model of the DEA method, which includes a variable return to scale (VRS) of the units.

According to this method the efficiency is divided into two major types: overall technical efficiency and efficiency of the return. In turn, the overall technical efficiency consists of two components: pure technical efficiency and efficiency of the scale. Initially, this method was applied in the USA and U.K., but later it is adopted in the practice of other European and non-European countries, such as Australia, as an example. This analytic technique gives reliable scores in measuring the efficiency in the state sector, education, health, energy sector, harbor sector and other fields, and a consistent trend exists of expansion of the areas of application of the method.

By its nature the DEA method is a method, used to measure the results and to make a comparative evaluation of units from a specific set, which make decisions (Decision Making Units—DMU). The essence of the method is that by using the comparison of all units, included in the respective set, the best operating units are determined in terms of efficiency, which makes also the efficiency frontier. The measurement of the efficiency is carried out on the basis of comparable calculation of the input flow to the respective unit (expenses incurred for raw materials, staff, etc.) and the output flow from the unit (finished goods, provided services, etc.).

Higher is the efficiency of that unit, which produces more at constant value of expenses, or that unit, which incurs lower expenses at constant value of the production. The efficiency is estimated by the relation between the weighted sum of the input flow (the sum of input resources, each weighted by the respective relative weight, reflecting its place in the total volume) and the weighted sum of the output flow (the sum of output products (services) by their prices, weighted with relative weight, reflecting the place of each of them in the total volume).

Thus formulated task is limited to solving an optimization problem from the linear programming, where unknowns are the weights of the input-output data. There are two ways to solve this problem. By using the first one, the estimation of the efficiency is obtained by maximizing the numerator of the ratio (1) by assuming that the denominator is a constant (it is assumed that its value is 1). This means that we use the model, oriented to the output product, marked as CCR-O (output oriented DEA model). By the second way the estimation is obtained by minimizing the denominator of the ratio (1), assuming that the numerator is a constant with value of 1. In this case, we use the model oriented to the input product, marked as CCR-I (input oriented DEA model). The obtained value of the efficiency varies within the limits of the interval [0; 1], which means that the maximal result of efficiency is 1, and the maximal result of inefficiency is 0.

DEA is a method, by which the results are measured and it gives opportunity for evaluation of the relative efficiency of single units from a specific set, which make decisions autonomously—DMU (Banker 1996).

This method is applied by comparison of all units in this set, determining the best operating units, which make the efficiency frontier. In this sense, the relative efficiency represents the ratio of the input and output data, weighted by specific weights.

$$\text{Efficiency} = \frac{\text{Weighted sum of the output results}}{\text{Weighted sum of the input resources}} \tag{1}$$

For the needs of our study we use an input-oriented DEA model, where the formula of the relative efficiency of social services will be modified, as follows:

$$Ej = \frac{\text{Weighted sum of the Effect of using the respective social service}}{\text{Sum total of the costs for creation and implementation of the respective social service}} \tag{2}$$

The most significant issue of the evaluation of the efficiency of the social services is, without a doubt, the acceptance of some objective assessment of the value of the effect of using the respective social service. Because it is about of an effect, which has not only an economic but also a social aspect, it has to measure several different by its nature values. In all cases this effect has to reflect the level of meeting the customer needs, because this is a service, designated to meet the specific needs of the people, who it is designed for, which is impossible to be met by any other way. In this sense, it performs the function of providing an opportunity to the people, which are its users (customers) to have a life, close to the full life. This circumstance is extremely important for the children, deprived from parental care, because according to the Bulgarian legislation, many of the social services, designated for children, are provided not only to meet specific needs, but they also represent a protection measure. These services are provided to children, who have been in a situation, which gives rise to considerable risks for their life, security, physical and psychological health, opportunities for normal growing up and risk to find themselves in a deviance or crime environment.

In this context, the social services for children, especially for children, deprived from parental care, represent a key factor of vital importance for their further development and differ significantly from all other services, which have been used according to their customers' preferences.

The said effect has to reflect the level of quality of the respective service. Notwithstanding the existing differences in terms of the indicators of the quality of social services, they must comply with specific requirements, representing their nature.

The first group of requirements is related to the professional qualification and skills of the specialists, providing the service. Unlike other services in general, the social services are mainly provided by teams of highly qualified specialists with specific professional and qualification skills. Without such team of specialists, it is impossible to create and implement the respective social service. The more complex and complicated the service is, more and various specialists are needed for its creation and provision to the customer. In addition to this objective criterion, the quality of the respective social service depends on the organization of the activities of overall service of the customers and provision of the respective social service.

The abovementioned organization includes the performance, coordination and harmonization of all activities of provision of the social service from the respective service provider to the customers and clients. The material conditions, where the social service is being provided, the existence of the necessary buildings and premises, equipped with the respective main and auxiliary equipment, are also an important indicator of the quality of the respective social service.

2.1 Research Methodology

Taking into account all these circumstances, in order to be able to calculate the value of the nominator in formula (2), a research methodology has been developed, which includes a consecutive implementation of the following steps:

Conducting researches/focus-groups, a content-analysis, an interview, questionnaires/amongst three target groups, related with several selected typical social services for children, deprived from parental care, provided in the community and by specialized institutions, situated on the territory of North-eastern Bulgaria.

2.2 Researched Social Services for Children

The following social services have been studied: Center for Family-type Accommodation—this represents a complex of social services, provided in close-to-a-family environment to a limited number of children (not exceeding 15); Center for Public Support—this represents a complex of social services, related to prevention of abandonment, violence and dropping from school of children, deinstitutionalization and reintegration of children, training aimed at acquiring skills for independent life and social integration of children from institutions, consulting and support to families at risk, assessment and training of future foster and adoptive parents, consulting and support of children with anti-social behavior; Home for children, deprived from parental care—this represents a specialized institution, providing social services for bringing up and education of children aged from 3 to 18 or until completion of secondary school, but not older than 20 years. Transitional housing—This is a form of social service, where the young people lead independent way of life, supported by professionals, aimed at preparation for their removal from the specialized institution. Foster care—The foster care is defined as bringing up and education in family environment of a child, accommodated in a family of relatives or friends or in a foster family.

In the abovementioned region seven centers for family-type accommodation, one transitional housing, two centers for public support, one home for children, deprived from parental care, forty foster families, two teams, working with the foster families and 25 officers from the Child Protection Departments have been studied. Approximately 200 children are users of these services.

The target groups, subject of the study of the abovementioned social services, were: users of the service—children, who are using or have used the service and their biological parents and/or adoptive parents; specialists, participating directly in the creation and provision of the respective social service and taking care for the children, who are users of the service or are placed in the respective social institution; experts, participating in the implementation of the policy of management and development of the social services on the territory of the respective municipality—specialists from the related Directorates of Social Assistance and municipal directorates for social activities and social policy, specialists from the Child Protection Departments, operating in the respective municipalities; other experts—officers from the Regional Directorates of Social Assistance, accredited organizations of international adoption and tutors from higher education institutions.

2.3 Defined Criteria for Quality of Social Services for Children

After the research conducted in the abovementioned groups, all of them defined criteria, which, in their opinion, are necessary in order to provide high-quality social services. The research ended when repeatability of the stated criteria occurred. The said criteria have been processed and a questionnaire has been developed, by which the same groups had to assess the importance of each criterion. A rating scale from 1 to 6 has been used for evaluation of the importance of each criterion.

The questionnaire consists of three sections: (I) Criteria, relating to the quality and skills of the social workers; (II) Criteria, relating to the organization of the working process; (III) Criteria, relating to meeting the children's needs.

Table 1 contains the first section of the questionnaire, referring to the professional qualities of the specialists, carrying out directly activities of provision of the respective social service. In his section the respondents assess the team, providing the performance of all activities by using 28 indicators describing the provision of the respective social service, grouped into several strands: availability of professional qualification and professional experience relevant for the provision of the service; availability of necessary specific knowledge for work with the users and customers of the social services; availability of personal qualities relevant for the provision of the service; availability of emotional attachment to the work and to the children; and interactions with other parties in the process of provision of the service.

Table 1 Questionnaire, Section I: indicators for evaluation of the qualities of the specialists, participating in the provision of the respective social service

№	I. Criteria, relating to the quality and skills of the specialists	Rating scale					
1	Availability of professional qualification, obtained at higher education institution	1	2	3	4	5	6
2	Availability of experience in the qualification area	1	2	3	4	5	6
3	Availability of experience in the field—work with children deprived from parental care	1	2	3	4	5	6
4	The qualities, skills, knowledge and experience of the specialist correspond to the job requirements	1	2	3	4	5	6
5	Availability of expanded competences in the fields, relating to the work with children, deprived from parental care	1	2	3	4	5	6
6	Being aware of the customers' needs	1	2	3	4	5	6
7	Knowledge of the nature of the work—statutory framework, contingent, methods of work	1	2	3	4	5	6
8	Knowledge of own responsibilities	1	2	3	4	5	6
9	Knowledge of the functions of the other institutions and providers	1	2	3	4	5	6
10	Desire to work with children deprived from parental care	1	2	3	4	5	6
11	Awareness of the needs of the children deprived from parental care	1	2	3	4	5	6
12	Awareness of the needs of every child, who the specialist works with	1	2	3	4	5	6
13	Proper treatment and respect to the customer's needs	1	2	3	4	5	6
14	Readiness to respond at any time to the child's (customer's) needs	1	2	3	4	5	6
15	Skills to communicate with the child (customer) and predispose the child to share its problem	1	2	3	4	5	6
16	Interest to the children and their problems	1	2	3	4	5	6
17	Attention and concentration on the child	1	2	3	4	5	6
18	Positive attitude to the children deprived from parental care and their parents	1	2	3	4	5	6
19	Feelings of love toward the children	1	2	3	4	5	6
20	Having a vocation for the job	1	2	3	4	5	6
21	Flexibility	1	2	3	4	5	6
22	Ability to communicate with the customers (for example: Is the specialist able to create contact)	1	2	3	4	5	6
23	Ability to interact with his colleagues	1	2	3	4	5	6
24	Skills for teamwork	1	2	3	4	5	6
25	Clean criminal record (never been convicted)	1	2	3	4	5	6
26	Mentally healthy person	1	2	3	4	5	6
27	Aspiration for development and improvement	1	2	3	4	5	6
28	Enrollment in trainings, courses and other forms for qualification improvement and knowledge expansion	1	2	3	4	5	6

3 Theoretical Model

3.1 *Use the DEA Method or Linear Regression Model*

According to Cooper et al. (2011), the DEA method may be supplemented or replaced by a linear regression analysis. Such analysis will create an opportunity to be used for solving the DEA model. By its nature, the multiple regression model represents a statistic method for study of the relationship between two and more events provided that such relationship is of a non-determinable/correlative/type.

The broad expression of the multiple /multi-factor/ regression model is, as follows (Saykova et al. 2002):

$$Y = f\,(x1, x2, \ldots\ldots\ldots\ldots\ldots\ldots\ldots..x_m, e) \tag{3}$$

where,

Y—a dependent variable;

x_i—independent variables (i = 1, 2, ……….., m);

e—a random component in the model.

According to the form of the relationship between the dependable and undependable variables, the multiple regression models are linear and non-linear. In our study we use the lineal model. The analytical expression of a linear multiple regression model, is, as follows:

$$Y = \beta_0 + \beta_1 x_1 + \beta_2 x_2 + \ldots\ldots\ldots\ldots + \beta_m x_m + e \tag{4}$$

or

$$Y = \beta_0 + \sum_{i=1}^{m} \beta_i\, x_i + e \tag{5}$$

where,

Y—a dependent variable;

x_i—independent variables (factors), affecting the dependable variable (i = 1, 2, ….m) ;

e—a random component in the model;

β_i—parameters (coefficients) of the multiple model (i = 1, 2, ……...., m);

β_0—an constant term of the model.

The formulation of the problem is limited to finding the values of на β_i in the regression equation, where we assume that Eq. (3) constitutes a detailed description of the complex relationship between the independent and dependent variables. The coefficients β_i (regression coefficients) show the changes that will occur in the corollary (consequence) Y at unit of change of the factors x_i. Therefore, based on this model, upon each concrete change of x_i, we will be able to calculate within a specific confidence interval the exact forecast for the respective value of Y.

3.2 Regression Coefficients from Section I of the Questionnaire

Such regression model has been developed on the basis of the data from the processed questionnaires concerning their first section, by which we assess the quality of the social service (Table 1). A regression equation of type (3) is created, where the sum of the ratings of the respondents on each indicator, included in the first section of the questionnaire, is assumed as a dependent variable Y, and the values of the ratings on each indicator of the respective group represent the independent variables x_i. The regression coefficients in each of the mentioned regression equations represent the relative value of the change, occurring in Y_B as a result of a unit of change of the independent variables.

The calculation of the regression coefficients in the created regression equations is made by means of the standardized program package for processing of statistic information IBM SPSS Version 22. The data about the calculated regression coefficients from the equation, created on the basis of the data from the first section of the questionnaire—Indicators for evaluation of the qualities of the specialists, participating in the provision of the respective social service, is stated in Table 2.

The values of the unit Significance level calculated for each of the estimated coefficients (β_i) are less than the level of the statistical error $\alpha = 0.05$, which means that they can be accepted as statistically significant. As a statistically insignificant can only be accepted the value of the constant term in the model β_0 (constant), where the value of the unit t,Sign.t = 0.926 is greater than the level of the statistical error $\alpha = 0.05$. The values of the regression coefficients β_i are within the interval from 0.892 to 1.116, with the exception of the constant, which is an indicator for strong (>0.7) and positive relationship and effect of the factors on the dependent variable—the increase, and respectively, the decrease of the value of the independent variable lead to increasing, or decreasing, respectively, of the dependent variable. For each regression coefficient its respective standardized value Beta is calculated. The strongest effect has the factor, whose value Beta is the greatest. So, in our case, the factor No 23 (Skills for teamwork) has the strongest effect on the evaluation, related to the qualities of the specialists, providing the respective social service.

3.3 Indicators for Evaluation of the Organization of the Activities of Provision of a Social Service for Children

Table 3 contains the second section of the questionnaire, relating to the organization of the activities, included in the provision of the social service. In this section the respondents assess the overall organization of all activities, which are carried out by the team of specialists for the provision of the respective service on the basis of

Table 2 Value of the regression coefficients (β) from Section I of the questionnaire

Model		Unstandardized coefficients		Standardized coefficients		
		B	Std. error	Beta	T	Sig.
1	(Constant)	0.016	0.175		0.093	0.926
	VAR00001	0.937	0.034	0.056	27.526	0.000
	VAR00002	1.060	0.057	0.059	18.691	0.000
	VAR00003	0.943	0.046	0.053	20.547	0.000
	VAR00004	1.040	0.045	0.053	23.094	0.000
	VAR00005	0.991	0.055	0.049	18.173	0.000
	VAR00006	1.019	0.067	0.047	15.279	0.000
	VAR00007	0.919	0.063	0.039	14.484	0.000
	VAR00008	1.030	0.083	0.041	12.466	0.000
	VAR00009	1.073	0.043	0.046	25.130	0.000
	VAR00010	1.002	0.055	0.047	18.318	0.000
	VAR00011	0.919	0.079	0.039	11.694	0.000
	VAR00012	0.996	0.052	0.046	19.242	0.000
	VAR00013	1.116	0.055	0.051	20.314	0.000
	VAR00014	0.921	0.045	0.042	20.398	0.000
	VAR00015	0.920	0.069	0.038	13.331	0.000
	VAR00016	1.012	0.059	0.045	17.091	0.000
	VAR00017	1.007	0.040	0.048	25.244	0.000
	VAR00018	1.074	0.077	0.050	14.019	0.000
	VAR00019	0.892	0.056	0.041	15.883	0.000
	VAR00020	0.898	0.063	0.039	14.301	0.000
	VAR00021	1.406	0.051	0.063	27.582	0.000
	VAR00022	0.920	0.064	0.040	14.385	0.000
	VAR00023	0.973	0.067	0.042	14.438	0.000
	VAR00024	0.955	0.029	0.058	32.773	0.000
	VAR00025	1.028	0.046	0.049	22.234	0.000
	VAR00026	0.913	0.064	0.042	14.241	0.000
	VAR00027	1.062	0.059	0.046	17.884	0.000
	VAR00028	0.967	0.043	0.048	22.533	0.000

Note: The definitions of VAR00001–VAR00028 are given in Table 1

30 indicators, describing various aspects of the service—availability of a team of specialists, drawing up a quality assessment of the child's needs, coordination between the different specialists and information exchange between them, drawing up an optimal number of documents, obtaining feedback from the users of the service or their parents, and exercising different forms of control.

Table 3 Questionnaire, Section II: indicators for evaluation of the organization of the activities of provision of a social service

№	II. Criteria, related to the organization of the working process	Rating scale					
1	Personnel selection criteria are used for the service	1	2	3	4	5	6
2	Clear personal selection criteria are used for the service	1	2	3	4	5	6
3	The criteria for employee selection correspond to the functions, which the employee has to perform	1	2	3	4	5	6
4	The functions of the employees correspond to the needs of the users	1	2	3	4	5	6
5	The number of the children, who every specialist works with, is in line with his own abilities to work and meet the needs of his customers	1	2	3	4	5	6
6	The number of the documents, which the specialist writes, corresponds to the needs of work and does not put limits on the time, which the specialist needs to perform a direct social work	1	2	3	4	5	6
7	The service and its capacity are in accordance with the needs of the community/the municipality, the region	1	2	3	4	5	6
8	The provider provides all services, stated in the methodology	1	2	3	4	5	6
9	The service serves those customers, who need it, without selecting them by its own criteria	1	2	3	4	5	6
10	The services correspond to the customers' needs	1	2	3	4	5	6
11	The service is provided to every customer in accordance with his individual needs	1	2	3	4	5	6
12	The service supports the customer in accordance with his specific features	1	2	3	4	5	6
13	Upon planning its activity, the service takes into consideration the age of the children and the interactions between children from different age groups	1	2	3	4	5	6
14	The service is flexible	1	2	3	4	5	6
15	The length of provision of the service corresponds to the customer's needs	1	2	3	4	5	6
16	The service provides supporting external services, which meet those needs, which the service is not able to meet itself	1	2	3	4	5	6
17	The service provides the customer with the necessary team of specialists	1	2	3	4	5	6
18	The service carries out its duties, as stipulated in the regulatory framework	1	2	3	4	5	6
19	The service includes the user in the process of making decisions concerning the user	1	2	3	4	5	6
20	The service provides assistance to the other participants in the working process on the respective case	1	2	3	4	5	6
21	The service provides true/reliable information regarding the state of the user to the other participants in the working process	1	2	3	4	5	6
22	The service assumes its own responsibility for the work on the respective case	1	2	3	4	5	6
23	The service informs the other participants in the process regarding its actions and the results from such actions	1	2	3	4	5	6
24	Supervision is ensured for the customers and the caring personnel	1	2	3	4	5	6
25	Volunteers are included in the organization of work	1	2	3	4	5	6

(continued)

Table 3 (continued)

№	II. Criteria, related to the organization of the working process	Rating scale					
26	The service is able to participate in the distribution of the means of subsistence	1	2	3	4	5	6
27	The service disposes with sufficient funds for implementation of its activity	1	2	3	4	5	6
28	The working hours of the service are scheduled for the convenience of the users	1	2	3	4	5	6
29	The remuneration of the employees depends on the results of their work	1	2	3	4	5	6
30	There is an adequate form of control of the work	1	2	3	4	5	6

3.4 *Questionnaire for Abilities of the Social Services for Children to Meet the Needs of the Customer*

The third section of the questionnaire refers to the abilities of the social service to meet the needs of the respective customer, i.e., the children, who it is provided to. By using 127 indicators the respondents assess the following components of the environment, where the service is provided:

- Abilities to meet the physiological/domestic needs of the child—providing food according to the age and health state of the child, providing an adequate medical and dental service, providing the necessary premises and spaces for the child, good location and necessary utilities, etc.;
- Abilities to meet the needs of security—a safe environment is ensured for the children; clear rules and limitations are adopted; it is clear who makes the major decisions and what are the consequences of such decisions; control and specific forms of self-control are being exercised; a specific sustainability of the environment is ensured; preparing the child for the forthcoming changes, etc.;
- Abilities to meet the needs of the children of love and attachment—this means creation of relations of attachment between the children and due cares for them; children to feel that they are accepted in the environment in which they live; an adequate for the child's mind and sensibility behavior of the caring specialist (hugging, calming down, providing support, encouraging); maintaining contacts with close people, who are important for the child; respect to the child's origin, history and family, etc.
- Abilities to meet the needs of positive assessment—this group of indicators refer mainly to encouraging the positive perception of the child of itself. It includes indicators such as positive treatment to the child's successes, support in case of failure, no discrimination, etc.;
- Abilities to meet the needs of self-update—developing the cognitive abilities of the children and becoming acquainted with the environment; finding the answers on the questions, which the child asks itself; providing opportunities and support to the children to overcome the difficulties and impediments; encouraging the development of individual skills and talents of the children; providing

opportunities and support for the psychological development of the children; developing abilities to lead an independent life; the social environment has a positive influence on the emotional state of the children and helps them to overcome anxieties, stress, fear, traumas from the past, behavioral problems and other negative states, etc.

- Abilities to meet the cognitive needs of the children—the main indicators here are: becoming acquainted with the environment; development of skills for overcoming the difficulties single-handedly; providing additional services when necessary.
- Abilities for development of skills—the main indicators here are: development of skills for self-help, development of household skills, development of ability of spatial orientation/especially for disabled children etc.
- Abilities for having positive influence on the emotional state of the children—the main indicators here are: the caring personnel has to observe the emotional state of the children, to notice and undertake suitable steps if it is deteriorated; supporting the children to overcome current traumatic events; provision of suitable services to children, who have been victims of violence, and children, who are affected by the institutional care, etc.
- Abilities for social integration—this means providing opportunities to the children to become acquainted with various aspects of the social life, abilities for interaction with other people and children; the children have to understand the measures, applied on them and what happens with them and what to expect; preparation of the environment for admission of the children; receiving feedback regarding the integration of the children in specific environment (kindergarten, school, other social structures), etc.
- Abilities for support of the biological family of the children—the main indicators here are: presentation of the service, provided to the children, to their parents, a free access of the parents to information, identification of the parents' problems and difficulties, providing help and support to the parents.

Similar to the first section of the questionnaire, a multiple regression model is drawn up with the same parameters, as stated hereinabove. A regression equation of type (3) is created, where the sum of the ratings of the respondents on all indicators, included in the respective section of the questionnaire, is assumed as a dependent variable Y, and the values of the ratings of each indicator from the respective group are assumed as independent variables x_i. The regression coefficients in each of the mentioned regression equations represent the relative value of the change, which occurs in Y as a result of unit of change of the independent variables. The calculation of the regression coefficients in the created regression equations is performed by means of the standardized program package for procession of statistical information SPSS.

4 Conclusion

After calculating the values of the regression coefficients for each of the three sections of the questionnaire by groups of indicators, included in each group, a standardized value of the regression coefficient for each section is calculated. This could be performed by using an arithmetic mean of the calculated regression coefficients. It is rounded up to the nearest hundred for the respective group of indicators. Hence, the standardized value of the regression coefficients from Table 2 is 1.01. After that the calculation procedure is implemented in the following sequence:

For each section of the questionnaire and for all indicators, the most common rating, i.e., the rating that predominated in the answers of the respondents, is calculated by using the "mode" method. This rating is multiplied by the standardized value of the regression coefficient, obtained in the abovementioned way. Then, the resulted ratings under the three sections are summed up.

For each social service the questionnaires of each of the target groups, subject of the study, as stated in part 2 of the report, i.e., children-users of the service, and in cases where appropriate, their biological or foster parents, also the specialists, participating directly in the creation and provision of the respective social service and taking care for the children, and the users of the service or placed in the respective social institution, and experts, participating in the implementation of the policy of management and development of the social services system on the territory of the respective municipality, are processed. The ratings obtained under the three sections are summed up and this way, a generalized assessment of the quality of the respective service is obtained, which may be used as a global tool for measurement of the effect of the use of the social service in the formula (2) for calculating the efficiency.

The generalized assessment under the preceding paragraph according to formula (2) is divided by the total amount of the costs for the creation and provision of the respective social service for 1 year, calculated on the basis of the data reported for the preceding period. Hence, the value calculated by using this manner, represents "a coefficient of relative efficiency of the respective social service".

The coefficients of the relative efficiency of the respective services can be compared and analyzed for the needs of management of this sector, or can also be used for the purposes of various scientific researches.

References

Agency for Social Assistance. (2014, March). *Report on performance of the activity of the Agency for Social Assistance for 2013*. Sofia [pdf]. Accessed March 10, 2016, from http://www.asp.government.bg/ASP_Files/APP/GODISHEN%20OTCHET%20ASP%20-%202013-.pdf

Agency for Social Assistance. (2015, March). *Report on performance of the activity of the Agency for Social Assistance for 2014*. Sofia [pdf]. Accessed March 10, 2016, from http://www.asp.government.bg/ASP_Files/APP/GODISHEN_OTCHET_ASP_2014.pdf

Banker, R. (1996). Hypothesis tests using data envelopment analysis. *Journal of Productivity Analysis, 7*(2), 139–159.

Banker, R., Charnes, A., & Cooper, W. W. (1984). Some models for estimating technical and scale inefficiencies in data envelopment analysis. *Management Science, 30*, 1078–1092.

Charnes, A., Cooper, W., & Rhodes, E. (1978). Measuring the efficiency of decision making units. *European Journal of Operational Research, 12*(6), 429–444.

Cooper, W., Seiford, L. M., & Zhu, J. (2011). Data envelopment analysis: History, models, and interpretations. In W. Cooper, L. M. Seiford & J. Zhu (eds). *Handbook on Data envelopment analysis*, 2nd ed. New York, NY:Springer US. pp. 1–39.

Ministry of Health. (2011). *Rules on structure and activity of the Homes for medical and social care for children*. Published in State Gazette № 49 of 16.06.2000, amended published in State Gazette № 53 of 12.07.2011.

Ministry of Labor and Social Policy. (2015). Rules on application of the Social Assistance Act, adopted by Decree of Council of Ministers № 5.11.1998. Published in State Gazette № 133 of 11.11.1998, effective as from 01.11.1998, amended published in State Gazette № 63 of 18.08.2015.

National Statistical Institute. (2016). *Population by statistical regions, age, place of residence and sex as of 31.12.2015* [online]. Accessed March 10, 2016, from http://www.nsi.bg/sites/default/files/files/data/timeseries/Pop_6.1.2_Pop_DR.xls

Saykova, I., Stoykova-Kanalieva, A., & Saykova, S. V. (2002). Statistichesko izsledvane na zavisimosti [Statistical survey of addictions]. *Universitetsko Izdatelstvo "Stopanstvo", 1*, 79–111.

State Agency for Child Protection. (2013). *Report on the implementation of the "National program for child protection for 2012"*. Sofia.

State Agency for Child Protection. (2015a). *Children raised in specialized institutions in comparative perspective 2001–2009*. Sofia [online]. Accessed March 10, 2016, from sacp.government.bg/media/filer_public/.../spetsializirani-institutsii-za-detsa-2009.doc

State Agency for Child Protection. (2015b, December 15). *Children, raised in specialized institutions*. Sofia [online]. Accessed March 10, 2016, from http://sacp.government.bg/bg/statistika/

MIX
Papier aus verantwortungsvollen Quellen
Paper from responsible sources
FSC® C105338

If you have any concerns about our products,
you can contact us on
ProductSafety@springernature.com

In case Publisher is established outside the EU,
the EU authorized representative is:
Springer Nature Customer Service Center GmbH
Europaplatz 3, 69115 Heidelberg, Germany

Printed by Libri Plureos GmbH
in Hamburg, Germany